Guilford–
testing

Also by SILVANO ARIETI

Interpretation of Schizophrenia (1955)
Second Edition, Completely Revised and Expanded (1974)

*The Intrapsychic Self: Feeling, Cognition and
Creativity in Health and Mental Illness* (1967)

The Will To Be Human (1972)

American Handbook of Psychiatry (1959 and 1966)
EDITOR-IN-CHIEF
Second Edition, Revised and Expanded (1974 and 1975)

The World Biennial of Psychiatry and Psychotherapy (1970 and 1973)
EDITOR

New Dimensions in Psychiatry: A World View (1975)
CO-EDITOR WITH GERARD CHRZANOWSKI

Love Can Be Found (1977)
WITH JAMES ARIETI

*On Schizophrenia, Phobias, Depression, Psychotherapy,
and the Farther Shores of Psychiatry:
Selected Papers of Silvano Arieti, M.D.* (1978)

Severe and Mild Depression (1978)
WITH JULES BEMPORAD

Understanding and Helping the Schizophrenic (1979)

The Parnas (1979)

Creativity

The Peacock King, Tokyo National Museum; Kodansha, Ltd.

CREATIVITY

The Magic Synthesis

SILVANO ARIETI

Basic Books, Inc., Publishers   *New York*

Library of Congress Cataloging in Publication Data

Arieti, Silvano.
    Creativity: the magic synthesis.

    Bibliography: p. 415
    Includes index.
    1. Creative ability. I. Title.
BF408.A64   153.3'5   75–36374
ISBN: 0–465–01443–7 (cloth)
ISBN: 0–465–01442–9 (paper)

To the memory of my friend Ludwig Von Bertalanffy, who conceived broad systems of ideas, and of my grammar school teacher Luisa Orvieto, from whom I learned simple, pristine, and clear views of the world.

The two nourishments of the mind that these teachers represent find their place, one in the intellect, the other close to the heart, and at times mingle, fuse, and bring forth innovation.

Acknowledgments

The author gratefully acknowledges permission from the following sources to reprint the material indicated below.

Figures 6–1, 6–2, 11–1, 11–2, 11–3, 11–4—Basic Books, Inc., Publishers, New York.
Figures 9–1 and 9–2—Alfred Kröner Verlag.
Figure 9–3—UPI
Figure 9–4—The Metropolitan Museum of Art
Figure 9–8—Michael Holford Photo Library
Figure 9–9—Roger Wood, London
Figure 9–15—Tokyo National Museum; Kodansha, Ltd.
Figure 9–17—The Museum of Modern Art, New York. Mrs. Simon Guggenheim Fund.
Figure 9–20—Escher Foundation, Haags Gemeentemuseum, The Hague.

Extract from *Joseph Karo, Lawyer and Mystic* R. J. W. Werblowsky, © 1962 Oxford University Press, by permission of the Clarendon Press, Oxford.

Extract from *Guiding Creative Talent*, E. Paul Torrance, © 1962 Prentice-Hall, Inc., Englewood Cliffs, N.J.

Extract from *Essays*, by Henry Slonimsky (Quadrangle Books, 1967), reprinted by permission of Hebrew Union College.

"Canticle of All Created Things," St. Francis of Assisi, *Penguin Book of Italian Verse*. Edited and Translated by George Kay, © 1958 by George Kay.

Preface

WHETHER it is considered from the viewpoint of its effects on society, or as one of the expressions of the human spirit, creativity stands out as an activity to be studied, cherished, cultivated.

Creativity can be studied in many ways, all rewarding in various degrees. New dimensions are always found and added to the ones already known. Those who are interested only in a behavioristic or experimental approach will not find what they want in this book. My own interest in creativity follows different avenues of inquiry and understanding, and it has had a long history. It goes back to the preparation of an article on wit and the comic, published in 1950, in which I advanced my first ideas on the subject. My interest and my studies have grown in many directions in these intervening years. As a matter of fact, I consider this book the natural outcome of all my previous works.

My work started at a clinical level, with my observations on and therapeutic dealings with the seriously mentally ill as well as with creative people. My research also extended to cognition in general, in both intrapsychic and interpersonal perspectives. When I later studied creative products in various fields, such as wit, poetry, art, and science, I was able to recognize specific cognitive mechanisms of the creative process that I had already encountered in my clinical approach and cognitive research.

Finally, I have tried to integrate my findings in social, psychostructural, and general systems contexts, and I have advanced suggestions about the promotion of creativity at individual and social levels. I am fully conscious that some of these suggestions are preliminary and tentative. Much remains to be done in this area, both in the educational system and in respect to the later life of the individual.

This book grew out of my work presented earlier in the final section of *The Intrapsychic Self*, but that material has been greatly expanded in this volume and integrated with other approaches.

I wish to thank my friends Mr. Mortimer Cass, who prepared the section on music for Chapter 9, and Mr. Marcel Meth, who did the statistical work for Chapter 14.

SILVANO ARIETI

Contents

(xi)

Contents

PART THREE

The Creative Product

Contents

Contents

Contents

PART ONE

An Introductory Approach to Creativity

Chapter 1
The Creative Process

Introductory Remarks

> O somma luce, che tanto ti levi
> dai concetti mortali, alla mia mente
> ripresta un poco di quel che parevi
>
> e fa la lingua mia tanto possente
> ch'una favilla sol della tua gloria
> possa lasciare alla futura gente . . . .

* * * *

> O light supreme, who so far dost uplift
> thee over mortal thoughts, lend again to
> my mind a little of what thou didst seem
>
> and give my tongue such power that it may
> leave a single sparkle of thy glory to
> future men . . . .

THIS INVOCATION is made by Dante in the last canto of *The Divine Comedy* when he is about to attempt the most arduous of his efforts, the description of the presence of God. He asks God to help him; he wants to borrow from Him sufficient power to leave a spark of the divine glory to men to come. That power which transformed a vision into one of the highest human achievements and enabled Dante to transmit that spark to every subsequent generation is the creative process itself.

Creativity, a prerogative of man, can be seen as the humble human counterpart of God's creation. Whereas theologians and religious people in general believe that God's creation comes *ex nihilo*, from spatial and temporal nothingness, human creativity uses what is already existing and available and changes it in unpredictable ways.

Although there is a fundamental difference between the subhuman animal, with its limited number of responses, and the symbol-making human being, man, too, tends to act and relate in fixed ways. Whether his method of coping with any situation occurs immediately after the stimulus or whether it follows a complicated set of symbols and choices, man tends to use the repertory of activities provided by his usual psychological faculties or by ways that have become the common style of his culture. If his activities are mediated by cognitive processes, they generally follow what has been called Aristotelian or ordinary logical thinking, or, in Freudian psychoanalysis, the *secondary process*.

But the creative process goes beyond the usual means of dealing with the environment or with oneself. It brings about what is considered—by some people, at least, and perhaps by all—a desirable enlargement of human experience. People like B. F. Skinner (1971) have characterized man as being molded, conditioned, programmed by the environment in rigid, almost inescapable ways. Skinner should be appreciated for having shown the extent to which man can be affected in this manner; but I think that, contrary to Skinner's position, we must stress man's ability to escape this fate (Arieti 1972). Creativity is one of the major means by which the human being liberates himself from the fetters not only of his conditioned responses, but also of his usual choices. However, creativity is not simply originality and unlimited freedom. There is much more to it than that. Creativity also imposes restrictions. While it uses methods other than those of ordinary thinking, it must not be in disagreement with ordinary thinking—or rather, it must be something that, sooner or later, ordinary thinking will understand, accept, and appreciate. Otherwise the result would be bizarre, not creative.

A creative work cannot be considered in itself only; it must also be considered in reference to man. It establishes an additional bond between the world and human existence. The new bond varies in accordance with the different fields of creativity. The creative work may make us laugh, when we are confronted with something new which is witty and comical; may offer us aesthetic pleasure, when we are in the presence of works of art; may give us a feeling of transcendence, as in the fields of philosophy and religion; or may provide the qualities of usefulness, understanding, and predictability, as scientific innovations do. In the following chapters we shall see how difficult it is in some cases to understand the nature of this desirable experience and how large its scope is, ranging from the physiological to the spiritual, from the most practical to the most theoretical.

Creative work thus may be seen to have a dual role: at the same time as it enlarges the universe by adding or uncovering new dimensions, it also enriches and expands man, who will be able to experience these new dimensions inwardly. It is committed not just to the visible but, in many cases, to the invisible as well. Indeed, it is the perennial (and almost always unverbalized) premise of creativity, to show that the tangible, visible, and audible universe is infinitesimal in comparison to the one that awaits discovery through exploration of the external world and of the human psyche. A new painting, poem, scientific achievement, or philosophical understanding increases the number of islands of the visible in the ocean of the unknown. These new islands eventually form those thick archipelagos that are man's various cultures. Thus any creative product has to be considered from two points of view: that is, as a unity, in itself; and as part of a culture, either a specific culture or the general cultural patrimony of mankind. We might add a few more words on this matter of unity—of a creative work being something differentiated from what existed before it. That is, until the state of unity is achieved, it is difficult to conceive the new work as a creative product. And some products of creativity are themselves difficult to delimit or delineate: for instance, philosophical or religious systems. It is also true that some works are susceptible of different divisions: for instance, we may consider Dante's *Divine Comedy* as a single creative product; or we may consider the subsidiary parts of that great poem as creative unities in themselves. Whatever is self-consistent from a given point of view is a unity, but it may be also part of a larger whole as seen in another perspective.

The bond established between man and the creative product requires different and at times even antithetical attitudes in the various fields of creativity. For instance, in the making and appreciat-

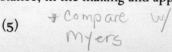

ing of a work of art, the individual retains a high degree of subjectivity. In scientific pursuits, on the other hand, he tries to disanthropomorphize his object of inquiry, to understand it fully without interferences caused by perception, preconception, or prejudice. And whereas the person who is about to listen to or to invent a joke is ready to accept and laugh at the littleness of the human condition, the person who wants to introduce or feel a religious, artistic, or philosophical experience eagerly expects enlightenment or uplift. But much more about this later.

Another important general characteristic of the creative process must be mentioned. The creative process is a way of fulfilling the longing or search for a new object or state of experience or existence that is not easily found or attained. This longing and search is often observed not only during the creative process but also in the creative product itself. Especially in aesthetic creativity, the work often represents not only the new object but also this longing, this indefinite search, this sustained and yet never completed effort, which has a conscious and an unconscious motivation.

Spontaneity and Originality Versus Creativity

IT IS IMPORTANT to distinguish between spontaneity, originality, and creativity. Man's spontaneity and originality manifest themselves in a flow of images, feelings, and ideas. In the present context, "spontaneity" means a certain range of possibilities immediately available to a person's psyche because of that person's intrinsic qualities and past and present experiences. These possibilities, however, do not tend to remain spontaneous. Learning, as well as the formulations of aims and goals, tends to eliminate what proves to be useless from the repertory of the mental flow. That is, spontaneous variabilities are probably ultimately based on the fact that groupings of synaptic or dendritic connections of the nerve cells (or the molecular substratum of such groupings) have a margin of inherent instability. The connections between dendritic endings (or bonds between atoms) form arrangements that are likely to have a large number of alternatives.

Learning and education, by predisposing the individual to use the same neuronal patterns, provide the individual with new groupings, but at the same time they limit the instability and spontaneity.

Freudian psychoanalysis has recognized the importance of spontaneity and has tried to recapture it in therapy through free association. The patient, lying on the couch, allows his ideas to emerge spontaneously, without any voluntary inhibition or editing, and must communicate them to the analyst. The aim of the technique is to remove conscious control and to allow images, feelings, and ideas to come freely into consciousness. From this free flow emerge patterns that will disclose the conflicts and then the personality of the patient. But in fact, this apparent spontaneity is largely based on present and especially on past realistic contingencies. What seems to be due to chance is totally or to a large extent the result of special combinations of biological circumstances and antecedent life experiences. These circumstances represent millions of separate events; and since they are never duplicated in their number, sequence, strength, and other characteristics, their combination is enough to explain the uniqueness or originality of the individual. When spontaneous ideas occur repeatedly or in cycles or special sequences, the analyst helps the patient recognize patterns in them. The patterns existed before; but without the intervention of the analyst, the patient would not have discovered them or at least would have discovered them only with great difficulty. [spontaneity]

If the average person does little or nothing with these free images and ideas—if he only experiences them, or even tries to put them into action with no or very few modifications—he cannot be considered creative. The characteristic of uniqueness or originality in a sequence of mental events or in certain forms of behavior is not enough to qualify them as creative products.

Original thinking should also not simply be identified with *divergent* thinking, a type of thinking that Guilford (1957a, b, 1959) has described. Divergent thinking rejects old solutions and strikes out in some new directions. For instance—in an example of divergent thinking given by Guilford (1959)—if a person is asked to give a number of words that mean about the same as "low," and he replies, "depressed," "cheap," "degraded," these responses are not the usual ones; but they satisfy the requirements. However, it is evident that divergent thinking is not free (although it may have different degrees of originality), because it aims at a solution. Original thinking is a broader category that includes both divergent and completely spontaneous thinking. The qualities of uniqueness, originality, and divergence are frequently recognized in the thinking of mentally ill persons, especially schizophrenics. These patients use unusual expressions in their speech; they give uncommon answers to common questions, and their behavior appears bizarre. However, their unusualness is very often associated with a quality of bizarreness and is almost always a far cry from creativity (Arieti, 1967, 1974).

A person may lose originality and retain spontaneity. This generally occurs to most people in the process of growing up and becoming educated. The young child loses his own individual, private ways and acquires those offered by society. Many of the private, unusual, very subjective experiences that the baby undergoes do not have names, or the child does not know these names and therefore he forgets them. (Schachtel explains childhood amnesia in this way [1959].) Later the child accepts the verbal clichés offered by his social environment and learns to use these clichés profusely. They may occur to him spontaneously, but of course not originally, unless he recombines them in unusual ways. The use of verbal clichés implies the adoption of usual ways of thinking. Thus in the process of socialization the child loses his primordial nonderivative originality, which he cannot recapture because it consisted of nameless experiences that he cannot remember. To become original again, he must use different ways, and the new forms of originality will be at least partially derivative.

Some researchers have studied originality in normal people. Maltzman (1960) has felt that originality is easier to study because it is not burdened by the problem of social evaluation, as creativity is. Originality presents itself as it is, without consideration for social judgment or the need to fulfill a social need or change society. There is no doubt that these considerations are accurate. But we must remember that in such cases we are studying the much simpler phenomenon of originality, not that of creativity. Moreover, originality, too, can be influenced. Following the lead from Lasswell (1954), who suggested that a "warmly indulgent relation" between innovator and recognizer would increase originality, Deutler and Machler (1964) tested originality in undergraduate students. They indeed found that such social and personal determinants as a climate of indulgence, safety, friendliness, cooperation, permissiveness, and so on, increased the originality of the students. This kind of social climate suggests to the individual that he does not need to be on guard. He does not need to eliminate what is likely to be unaccepted by the environment.

The difference between originality and creativity becomes particularly evident when we consider dreams. When we dream, the vigilance of the environment is removed; we are alone with our inner self. What is even more important is that we can place few or no restraints on the floating content of the dream. Dreams occur spontaneously and are always original. When we dream, we lose control of our actions, and as characters of our own dreams we do many original things. Even when dreams repeat certain themes, they present something new in each instance. Unexpected connections occur. Some combinations of scenes and events do not seem to have taken place ever before in nature or in the dreams of other people. On rare occasions dreams have been reported as conducive to the direct acquisition of insights, or even to the formulation of inventive procedures that generally occur in waking life, when the mind has access to the secondary process.

For instance, Sinnot (1959) reports that the Nobel Prize winner, Otto Loewi, saw the proof of the chemical mediation of nerve impulses in a dream. On awakening he could not remember the dream, but fortunately it was repeated the following night. And Antonio Ludovico Muratori, a scholar of the eighteenth century, reported that on the night of December 30, 1743, he had a dream in which he composed the following Latin verse, a pentameter, that ordinarily would require complex use of metric technique if composed in waking life: *Et quam multa queas, fac quoque multa velis.* ("If you can do much, you must will much." That is, you must equate your will and wish to your ability to actualize them.)

Some dreams should not be considered as just a reflection of the dreamer's state of psychological pathology or of his health, but rather as psychological attempts to solve conflicts.

In spite of all these characteristics, dreams cannot be considered products of creativity. With a few exceptions, they are of value only to the dreamer himself. They are private experiences that cannot be fully or correctly reproduced. They consist mostly of primitive mechanisms that are not sufficiently integrated with conceptual processes, so that they cannot be shared or communicated in the original form. When they are told to others, and even more, when they are interpreted, they are expressed with the usual words and with the ways of thinking of the waking mind. But then they are no longer dreams; they are translations of dreams.

Creativity must be distinguished not only from originality but also from those feelings, experienced by many people, of being surprised and affected by the new and being receptive to new ways. Although these feelings are prerequisites for creativity, they do not constitute its specific essence, according to the definition given at the beginning of the chapter.

Ordinary Versus Great Creativity

THERE HAS BEEN a tendency lately, especially among authors who are engaged in stimulating creativity in a large number of people and students in particular, to stress the point that creativity is not an attribute of great men exclusively but of every human being. Creativity does not depend on inherited talent or on environment or upbringing; it is the function of the ego of every human being (Matussek, 1974). We can affirm without hesitation that this statement is in fact valid—provided we refer to a different level of creativity: not to the creativity of a Shakespeare or a Newton, but to that of the ordinary fellow when he departs a little from the usual ways by modifying old things and improving them.

From a social point of view this ordinary creativity is extremely important. It gives a feeling of satisfaction and may eliminate a sense of frustration, thus providing one with a basic positive attitude about oneself and the work of one's life. As psychiatrists know, even this ordinary creativity is unattainable for many people. Neurosis exacts a heavy toll from many persons. Too many of them are so busy protecting themselves from insecurities of neurotic or social origin that they have no energy left for self-expansion and growth, especially in the field of innovation.

However, stressing the importance of ordinary creativity, which is one or two steps ahead of originality, should not make us neglect the study of great creativity, to which it is related. If it is true that ordinary creativity uplifts man's morale and dispels or decreases neuroses, great creativity is responsible for humanity's great achievements and social progress.

The present-day reluctance to study genius and great creativity is a temporary social phenomenon, based on pseudo-egalitarian premises. It affects a segment of the population that has also, with much more justification, developed a dislike for the hero (a person once much revered). The hero—an individual who has sacrificed, let us say, his life for his homeland or for the triumph of an idea—today is recognized as being (more frequently than previously suspected) a person programed or brainwashed by hypocritical propaganda that was generally put into motion by the vested interests of privileged classes or by people in political power. Had the "heroes" of the past lived in times or environments where certain dogmas, slogans, or ideologies could have been freely discussed, they would not have succumbed to the mystique of heroism. Nor would the masses have been influenced by the mystique of hero-worshiping. Today the skepticism toward heroes in some circles has been expanded to include all people "suspected" of greatness. As a matter of fact, this attitude reinforces a specific academic trend that (as we shall see in Chapter 13) attributes the changes made in history and society not to the deeds of great men, but to the evolution of the masses or to the overall cultural environment, of which "the great men" would be the representatives or necessary products.

However, the students of creativity know that this present outlook is in error. There is no valid parallelism between the one set of facts—ideology, heroes, hero-worshiping—and the other set—environment, creative men, admiration for such people as Dante, Galileo, Shakespeare, Newton. Even if we cannot hope that more than a handful in each century will reach the heights these men did, the study of creativity at such a level may have a great impact. Not only is it important in itself, as an inquiry into one of the most salient attributes of mankind; not only will it make us understand and better appreciate the innovations bestowed upon us; but also, hopefully, some traits of the creative style of life will rub off on us, no matter whether our own creativity be great, moderate, ordinary, or little.

From Primary to Tertiary Process

A SHARP DISTINCTION must be made between the creative process and the creative product. In contrast to what could be said about the creative product, the creative process is shorn of newness and sublimity; to a considerable extent it consists of ancient, obsolete, and primitive mental mechanisms generally relegated to those recesses of the psyche that are under the domain of what Freud called the primary process.

The *primary process*, for Freud, is a way in which the psyche functions, especially the unconscious part of the psyche. It prevails in dreams and some mental illnesses, especially psychoses. The primary process operates quite differently from the secondary process, which is the way of functioning of the mind when it is awake and uses common logic. Primary process mechanisms reappear in the creative process also, in strange, intricate combinations with secondary process mechanisms and in syntheses that, although unpredictable, are nevertheless susceptible of psychological interpretation. It is from appropriate matching with secondary process mechanisms that these primitive forms of cognition, generally confined to abnormal conditions or to unconscious processes, become innovating powers (Arieti, 1950, 1964, 1966, 1967). I have proposed the expression *tertiary process* to designate this special combination of primary and secondary process mechanisms (Arieti, 1964, 1966, 1967). For accuracy's sake, I must point out that in a certain number of creative processes the matching is not necessarily between primary and secondary process mechanisms, but between faulty or archaic and normal mechanisms, all of which belong to the secondary process. For these combinations, too, I have used the name tertiary process.

In making the distinction between primary and secondary process and in stressing the role of symbolism in general, the reader will soon recognize how much I owe to Freud and, also, how much I differ from him. The concept of the tertiary process does not exist in Freudian theory. Freud has the great merit of having stressed the importance of the psychic reality as something to be distinguished from the reality of the external world. But he insisted that the two realities must remain distinguished, lest psychic reality be used as an *escape* from external reality. Psychiatry has followed Freud's footsteps, especially in connection with therapy. However, when we deal with the problem of creativity, a different prospect is desirable. The tertiary process, with specific mechanisms and forms, blends the two worlds of mind and matter, and, in many cases, the rational with the irrational. Instead of rejecting the primitive (or whatever is archaic, obsolete, or off the beaten path), the creative mind integrates it with normal logical processes in what seems a "magic" synthesis from which the new, the unexpected, and the desirable emerge.

Although Freud started a very fruitful inquiry into the mechanisms and forms of the primary process, he became interested in them only as abnormal phenomena or as carriers of unconscious motivations. In other words, he was not particularly interested in them as structures, except for the description of the phenomena of displacement and condensation given in Chapter 7 of his book *The Interpretation of Dreams* (1901).

The present book deals with the unfolding of the creative process and the emergence of the creative product, as well as with the relationships between society and creativity and the cultivation of creativity.

In Part Two I shall illustrate the various components of the creative process that belong to both primary and secondary processes.

In Part Three I shall try to differentiate the specific modes by which the psychological mechanisms match and the magic synthesis occurs in the various fields of creativity. These fields are many, but only a few important ones will be taken into consideration, namely, wit and the comic; aesthetics, with particular emphasis on poetry and painting; religion and mysticism; and finally, science, philosophy, and general systems theory.

Part Four will deal with the relationship between creativity and the sociocultural environment, Part Five with the cultivation of creativity. Part Six will advance a view of creativity as a system, after taking into account various frames of reference, ranging from general biology to neurology.

Before undertaking these studies I shall review in Chapter 2 the major theories of creativity; and I shall make a critical evaluation of the problem of motivation, which plays a large role in some of these theoretical frameworks.

Chapter 2
The Major Theories of Creativity: A Critical Review

THEORIES OF CREATIVITY are specific or general. The specific theories are supposed to be valid only for particular fields. The general—the ones examined in this chapter—aim at individualizing the common mechanisms that occur in every process of creativity. I shall discuss: first, the major theories conceived within a framework of general psychology; second, the psychoanalytic theories; and third, the problem of motivation in relation to some of these theories. We shall then be able to draw some conclusions about the present status of theory in the field of creativity.

General Psychological Theories

MANY INVESTIGATORS have tried to understand the creative process by dividing it into different phases and analyzing each phase. The physiologist Helmholtz and the mathematician Poincaré were the first to follow this approach. Since their methods relate particularly to the field of science, we shall examine them in Chapter 11.

A theory that has been applied to every field of creativity and imitated many times with minor variations is the one advanced by Joseph Wallas (1926), who believed that the creative process consists of four stages: preparation, incubation, illumination, and verification. These words are in common use and clearly represent what the author meant. Preparation is the phase during which the creative person does all the preliminary work. He thinks in a sort of free way, he collects, he searches, listens to suggestions, lets his mind wander. The stage of incubation is inferred from the fact that a certain period of time, ranging from a few minutes to months or years, elapses between the period of preparation and that of illumination. We must thus assume that after the stage of external preparation, the collected material is not just stored in the creative person's mind, lying there in a state of passivity. Presumably, in ways unknown to us or of which we have little or no consciousness, the accumulated material undergoes an internal elaboration and organization. The illumination occurs when the creative person sees the solution to his problem. It is at times a sudden intuition, or a clear insight, or a feeling—something between a "hunch" and a "solution" and at other times the result of a sustained effort. In any case it has to pass the stage of verification in order to be definitely accepted by the critical evaluation of the innovator.

Many authors have accepted these four stages described by Wallas and have maintained the original terminology or have somewhat modified or amplified it. Catharine Patrick (1935, 1937, 1938), in her numerous studies on poets, artists, and scientists, confirmed the existence of Wallas's stages.

Joseph Rossman (1931), who examined the creative process in 710 inventors by means of a questionnaire, expanded Wallas's four stages to seven steps:

1. Observation of a need or difficulty
2. Analysis of the need
3. A survey of all available information
4. A formulation of all objective solutions
5. A critical analysis of these solutions for their advantages and disadvantages
6. The birth of the new idea—the invention
7. Experimentation to test out the most promising solution, and the

selection and perfection of the final embodiment by some or all of the previous steps (p. 57).

Osborn (1953), too, divided the creative process into seven stages, although he used a terminology somewhat different from that of Rossman:

1. Orientation: pointing up the problem
2. Preparation: gathering pertinent data
3. Analysis: breaking down the relevant material
4. Ideation: piling up alternatives by way of ideas
5. Incubation: "letting up," to invite illumination
6. Synthesis: putting the pieces together
7. Evaluation: judging the resulting ideas.

Taylor (1959) retains Wallas's four stages but also believes that creativity exists at five different levels: (1) expressive creativity, or independent expression, without reference to the quality of the product; (2) productive creativity, when the individual gains mastery over some section of the environment and produces an object; (3) inventive creativity, which requires the new use of old parts; (4) innovative creativity, when new ideas or principles are developed; and (5) emergent creativity, which requires the "ability to absorb the experiences which are commonly provided and from this produce something that is quite different."

Recently Morris Stein (1967, 1974) has advanced a theory in which the creative process is divided and examined in three stages (or processes): the stage of hypothesis formation, the stage of hypothesis testing, and the stage of communication of results. Preparation, or education, precedes these stages. These stages are generally separate but may overlap, with one being more salient than the other.

In his many investigations of creativity, Guilford follows a different procedure. He aims at isolating the essential features of creativity, after having advanced several hypotheses about the essence of these creative abilities. Although more attention will be paid to his work in Chapter 14, it is appropriate here to mention some of his basic concepts. Creativity as a cognitive function is to be distinguished from intelligence; it is not a unitary or uniform function but is to be accounted for in terms of a large number of factors, or primary mental abilities. The intellect can be divided into memory and thinking. In creativity it is thinking that counts. In its turn, thinking can be divided into cognition, production, and evaluation. Again production is the most important in creativity, but production can manifest itself in convergent and divergent thinking. For Guilford (1950, 1957a, b, 1959) it is in divergent thinking that we find the most important ingredients of creativity. Divergent thinking, to which we have already referred in Chapter 1, is a form of thinking that does not follow the beaten path of conformity or convention but proceeds toward unusual solutions. The three most important characteristics of divergent thinking are flexibility, originality, and fluency; or the ability to produce, rapidly, a succession of ideas that meet some requirements.

Proceeding along completely different lines, Wertheimer interpreted "productive thinking" in accordance with the tenets of the Gestalt school (1945). According to him, the creative process moves from a structurally unstable or unsatisfactory situation (S_1) to a situation (S_2) that offers a solution. In the passage from S_1 to S_2 a gap is filled; a better gestalt is formed. Wertheimer says that grouping, organization, and structuralization exists in all productive thinking. For him, the dividing of wholes into subwholes and the seeing of subwholes together (without losing track of the whole figure) are important steps in creative thinking. Wertheimer also describes another mechanism of the creative process, in which some features of S_2 are envisioned to start with by the creative person. From these few features the creative person must recapture the whole S_2. According to Wertheimer, the process starts as a search not for just any relation that would connect the elements, but "for the nature of their intrinsic interdependence." The entire process of creativity, for Wertheimer, is "one consistent line of thinking."

Although not a psychologist, Arthur Koestler, a writer of fiction and of nonfiction books of general interest, expanded his psychological theory of creativity in *The Act of Creation*, (1964), which includes concepts already expressed in his previous book *Insight and Outlook* (1949). Koestler's fundamental concept is that of *bisociation*. Bisociation, which according to him underlies every creative process, is "any mental occurrence simultaneously associated with two habitually incompatible contexts."

The interpretations of the creative process as postulated by Wallas, Rossman, Osborn, Taylor, Guilford, Stein, and Wertheimer all seem acceptable and good beginnings in a pioneering effort to understand this intricate subject. But we must also ask ourselves the question, "How far do they take us beyond what common sense indicates?" Certainly it is plausible to view the creative process as going through the stages of preparation, incubation, inspiration, and verification, but it is also so for the solution of any problem. Any process unfolds in time; and during its process of unfolding, we can distinguish different phases. It must be understood, however, that in several cases more than one phase may occur simultaneously, or the same phase may be repeated several times.

W. Edgar Vinacke (1952), who is particularly critical of the theories that assume the creative process always unfolds in a given sequence of stages, reminds us that in some types of creative work, and especially in fine art, there is a series of illuminations, which begins in the first draft or sketch of the work and ends with the completion of the work. He also states that incubation does not occur at a particular stage rather sharply differentiated from previous and subsequent stages, but that it operates to varying degrees throughout the creative process. Referring to studies of literature carried out by other authors, Vinacke concludes that poems and plays do not emerge suddenly or completely, but that they are gradually developed through the process of many incubations and illuminations.

Although Vinacke is correct, especially for complex works that can be divided into parts—that are creative works in themselves—the recognition of distinct phases may be maintained, with the proviso that in pure form they exist only as abstractions, an overlapping or repetition of phases always existing to varying degrees. However, we cannot be satisfied with distinguishing and labeling phases. We must understand what goes on internally and intimately in each phase. We must also distinguish what is specific to the creative process, from what is common to all mental efforts aiming at finding solutions of some sort. To be specific, in Wallas's interpretation it is the third stage, (illumination) which is basic for the creative process; the other three (preparation, incubation, and verification) are not. In Rossman's theory the sixth (the birth of the new idea) is the fundamental one, and in Osborn's theory it is also the sixth (the new synthesis). Rossman's and Osborn's sixth stage corresponds to Wallas's third. Of Wallas's four stages, the first (preparation—requiring study of the subject, collection of data, and so forth) and the last (verification through other examples, models, mathematical proofs, and so forth) are in the realm of consciousness and easy to understand. It is in regard to the stages of incubation and especially illumination that our knowledge and understanding leave much to be desired.

As far as incubation is concerned, it is a well-known fact—even in simple learning—that a process of consolidation is necessary. For instance, students know that they cannot well retain what they have studied and learned just before taking a test, for instance, in the early morning hours immediately preceding the examination. They must "sleep on" the material. It could be that the material to be committed to memory must reverberate in the neuronal circuits, completely outside of consciousness, in order to make lasting connections.

The crux of the problem is to understand how Wallas's first two stages bring about illumination and how Rossman's and Osborn's first five stages bring about the sixth. But the authors of these theories do not even begin to search how this happens. In their terms, it "just happens." We must also stress what Vinacke's criticisms, too, have implied: namely, that Wallas's theory, and those derived from it, are applicable to the creative process in the field of *science*, in particular. In literature and art, verification must be replaced by evaluation and improvement of different sorts, or by repetition of the stage of illumination.

aesthetic judgment

We must make similar remarks about Guilford's theoretical framework. Certainly divergent (or original) thinking, fluency, and flexibility are characteristics easily accepted in our understanding of the act of creativity. It is almost within the grasp of common sense to recognize that these are important for creativity; but it would be even more important to find out how, from being precursors of creativity, they bring about the creative process itself. We must nevertheless appreciate Guilford for several of his contributions, and especially for devising special testing procedures to subject psychological factors to statistical analysis.

Wertheimer is one of the authors who has tried to enter more deeply into the structure of the creative process. In my opinion Wertheimer's concepts are correct—but only in reference to some general aspects of creativity; they do not attack the core of the problem. His concepts have the merit of raising pertinent questions, but they do not provide the answers. If we accept his theoretical framework, we still must look for the mechanisms that fill what he calls "the gaps." How does one move from a structurally unstable situation (S_1)

to a situation (S_2) that offers a solution? Or how does one move from a few aspects of S_2 to the whole S_2? These questions again involve Wallas's stage of illumination, or Rossman's and Osborn's sixth stage. Wertheimer also ignores the difference between creativity and ordinary logical solutions of problems. He does not clarify or stress the occurrence of unusual mental processes.

As to Koestler's theory, I must remark that this author has gone far beyond the reach of common sense. He is correct in asserting that in many innovations we find a mental construct that usually appears in two habitually incompatible contexts. But Koestler does not explain how such two habitually incompatible contexts are united in the creative work. He does not seem to recognize that some contexts use forms and mechanisms that belong to the primary process.

At this point we must draw the conclusion that, with the possible exceptions of Wertheimer and Koestler, the psychological approaches mentioned so far—commendable as they are as pioneering approaches—have only scratched the surface of a complicated psychological phenomenon. Such concepts as illumination, divergency, fluency, and so forth, do not take us very far. Either they are terms that indicate an impression made by a subject on an examiner, or they refer to end-products at a conscious level, the outcome of many previous conscious or preconscious mechanisms or subvariables. These terms correspond to what, in psychiatry, is called *manifest symptomatology*. That is when one patient is described as suffering from phobias, or another patient as having hallucinations and delusions, we are referring only to symptoms or to constellations of symptoms to which we may give clinical names. For instance, we could say that a patient is phobic, another one a schizophrenic. A good psychiatrist wants to go further. As much as he can, he must try to understand the mechanism that brought about the symptom, the meaning of the content of the symptom, and why the symptom has assumed that particular form.

Similarly, the manifest approach cannot lead us very far in interpreting the creative process. However, it should be noted here that, as we shall see in later chapters, the manifest approach, in spite of its limitations, may be used with positive effects in promoting creativity, at least until deeper methods are devised. The excellent works of Torrance and others have demonstrated that the manifest approach may be helpful. In Parts Four and Five of this book I, too, shall return to this manifest approach. When they are studied in connection with interpersonal and social factors, these manifest characteristics form clusters of knowledge at a psycho-sociological level that can be useful. They may help us to establish a socio-interpersonal educational climate that can go a long way. We must realize at all times that every theory must start from knowledge, as a given sociological fact (Reichenbach 1938). In other words, any knowledge accrues from what has been built up by previous generations of thinkers, and it generally starts with description.

If we study the creative process and the creative product, we must realize that:

1. There are differences between the knowledge given as a sociological fact and the cognitive structures of creativity and of the creative product.

2. As we already mentioned in Chapter 1, there are differences between the creative product (which may be a very logical and integrated entity) and creativity as a psychological process.

3. Between external sociological factors and certain forms of behavior, connections can be found that can be of heuristic value in promoting creativity (see Chapters 13 and 14).

It is my conviction that to make deeper inroads into understanding the creative process we must use other methods: namely, the methods of deep psychology. Psychoanalysis is one of the methodologies generally linked with the term "deep psychology," but not the only one. In the next two sections we shall see that psychoanalysis, too, although it succeeds in clarifying some important aspects of the creative process, has not penetrated the essence of creativity itself.

Psychoanalytic Theories

WITHOUT fully realizing it, Freud was responsible for a breakthrough that led to a better understanding of the formal psychological mechanisms of the creative process (see Chapter 6). Nevertheless, Freud did not study these formal mechanisms. He intended to contribute to the study of creativity by reaffirming the importance of unconscious processes, especially of unconscious motivation.

An Introductory Approach to Creativity

As a whole Freud, although he contradicted himself many times on this subject, saw a great similarity between neurosis and creativity: they both originate in conflicts which spring from more fundamental biological drives. In other words, they are attempts to solve conflicts that originate in the powerful human instincts.

The concept of sublimation or diversion of sexual energy from the original aim plays an important role in Freud's concept of creativity. Thus, when sexual energy is not spent in the proper sexual activity, it is displaced and invested in pursuits, like the creative, which do not seem to be related to sex. The creative person is a frustrated individual who cannot find fulfillment in sexual gratification or other aspects of life and who therefore attempts to find it in creativity. In contrast to Freud's view, however, the biographies of many gifted people who also had a rich sexual life seem to contradict such assumptions.

The role of sexuality in creativity is prominent in other ways, according to Freud. He believed that the creative person's desire to know the unknown could be traced back to that curiosity about sexual matters which begins with the third year of life. According to Freud, the child's curiosity and frustrated inquiring have three outlets. The first is repression, which (as religious and educational institutions require) is quite "energetic." The second outcome occurs when sexual investigation is not totally repressed but is coped with by thought processes or by compulsive defenses. This transformation occurs when the intellectual development is sufficiently strong. In the third outcome, which is "the most rare and most perfect type," sexual curiosity is sublimated into that inquisitive attitude which leads to creativity. Freud compared literary work to daydreaming. Only unsatisfied people have fantasies or daydreams; happy people don't. "Unsatisfied wishes are the driving power behind fantasies; every separate fantasy contains the fulfillment of a wish, and improves an unsatisfactory reality" (Freud 1908).

Just as the child finds wish-fulfillment an improvement over reality, in play and games in which he generally impersonates the role of an important adult (leader, general, parent, and so forth), the adult creates a work of art in which he can satisfy his daydream wishes. However, people are often ashamed or embarrassed of their daydreams, just as they are of the drives that give rise to their nocturnal dreams. In nocturnal dreams, still according to Freud, the censorship diminishes the shame by making the manifest aspect of the dream very different from its meaning. In creative works, daydreams are also disguised. "The essential *ars poetica* lies in the technique by which our feeling of repulsion is overcome . . . The writer softens the egotistical character of the day-dream by changes and disguises, and he bribes us by the offer of a purely formal, that is, aesthetic, pleasure in the presentation of his fantasies" (Freud 1908).

According to Freud, childhood experiences are very important in accounting for the creative product. Personal experiences explain the peculiar characteristics of the creative work. For instance, in one of Leonardo da Vinci's famous paintings, the Virgin Mary and Saint Anne both appear with the infant Jesus—in contrast to the usual representation of the Holy Family in Italian paintings. This characteristic is not due to chance. Leonardo had the unconscious need to reproduce a childhood experience: He was raised by two mothers: his real biological mother, a peasant woman; and his father's legal wife, in whose home he grew up. According to Freud, Leonardo's conflicts over his homosexuality also explain some of his creative activities.

Today it is difficult to accept Freud's theory of creativity. What he wrote in his "Autobiographic Study" about psychoanalysis and creativity has to be taken very seriously: "[Psychoanalysis] . . . can do nothing towards elucidating the nature of the artistic gift, nor can it explain the means by which the artist works—artistic technique."

It is apparent that Freud was almost exclusively concerned with the importance and relevance of motivation in creativity and not with the essence of creativity itself. Motivation, conscious or unconscious, is indeed very important, but it is difficult to accept the idea that the whole phenomenon of creativity can be reduced to a motivational mechanism. Practically all human behavior is motivated, but only a small part of it can be called creative. There is no reason why we cannot assume that, in some cases, creative attempts are made for the purpose of correcting an unsatisfying reality. But is reality unsatisfying only because of sexual frustration and neurosis? Is the creative person's discontent only a disguise for lack of sexual gratification? What about his discontent about other aspects of the human predicament? The crucial problem is to determine why and how a few gifted men and women are able to transform their motivations and the effects of their early or late personal experiences into creative productivity. As important as it may be to discover why certain people had the need to create, it is even more important to find out how this need is transformed into a spiritual vision or epoch-making discovery.

Moreover, as Freud himself recognized, it is particularly in the mediocre work of art that the personal, conflict-born motivation is very important—for instance, in second- or third-rate paintings, plays, and psychological novels, which openly reveal the neurotic idiosyncrasies of the author. These works often remain at a primarily clinical level, hardly entering the aesthetic field. The neurosis of the creative person may be recognized as an important motivational factor and also as an important part of the content of a creative work. In these cases the neurosis is bypassed by the creative process itself, and what is important is not the neurosis but what has followed from it.

Within the theoretical framework of the Freudian school, Ernst Kris was perhaps the most prominent author who did not study creativity exclusively from the point of view of unconscious motivation. To Kris must be given the credit for having stressed the importance of the primary process in the formal mechanisms of creativity (Kris 1952). He considered the use of the primary process in creativity as "a regression in the service of the ego." In my opinion the use of the primary process is not necessarily to be viewed as a manifestation of regression but as an emerging accessibility or availability, which is connected with regression only occasionally. However, this difference between my view and that of Kris may be secondary and semantic in nature, based on a difference in our use of the word regression.

My main difficulty in accepting Kris's formulations concerns the way he tries to explain how this "service of the ego" takes place. To me, it is not enough to say that such mechanisms as displacement and condensation occur or are made congruous with ego function; we must understand how this congruity is carried out. Kris remains to a large extent in the energetic–libidinal framework of Freudian theory. He gives importance to the system preconscious rather than the unconscious in creativity, that is, to what is not present in consciousness but may more or less easily become conscious. He states that the preconscious process becomes subject to free or mobile energy that comes from the id and is drawn into the primary process. On the other hand, "The reverse (unconscious material becomes preconscious) occurs when id derivations are cathected [that is, invested] with ego energy and become part of preconscious mental processes . . ." (1950).

Still in the framework of orthodox Freudian theory, Lawrence

Kubie (1958) adds support to Kris's idea that creativity is a product of the preconscious and not of the unconscious, as had been assumed by many psychoanalysts. Conscious mental activity may hinder the creative process by the rigid use of symbolic functions. The unconscious may hinder it with an even more rigid anchorage in unreality. Thus, both Kris and Kubie realized that they could not remain in the original Freudian frame of reference and deal only with energy. In the attempt to deal with the symbolic forms that are indispensable in the creative process, they had to go beyond the most primitive areas of the psyche and consider at least the preconscious.

Another important author, working within the framework of Freudian theory, is Phyllis Greenacre. In an article that has had much impact (1957), Greenacre suggested that the ego of the future artist is capable of dissociating itself from real objects and thus developing a "love affair with the world." According to Greenacre, the potentially gifted infant may possess a much greater than average sensitivity to sensory stimulation, and this in turn may be responsible for an intensification and widening of experience. As a hypothetical example, Greenacre conceived that "the potentially gifted infant would react to the mother's breast with an intensity of the impression of warmth, smell, moisture, the feel of the texture of the skin and the vision of the roundness of form" in a much more intense way than the less gifted. As part of this intense reaction, the gifted child would experience "a greater vibration and need for harmonizing the inner object relationships . . . and the world of sensory impingement." From this situation derives the love affair with the world that brings about creativity.

Philip Weissman, also working within the Freudian frame of reference, was much inspired by Greenacre. But what was an example for Greenacre became, for Weissman, a regular event in potentially gifted people. Thus he believed that the future artist, as an infant, had the ability to hallucinate the mother's breast independently of oral needs. According to him the unusual capacities of the artist "may be retraced to the infancy and childhood of the artist wherein we may find that he is driven by the nature of his artistic endowment to preserve (or immortalize) his hallucinated response to the mother's breast independent of his need gratifications" (1968).

One major concept of Weissman is the "dissociative function of the ego" that he substitutes for Kris's concept of regression in the service of the ego. With the aid of this dissociative function, the creative person "may partially decathect the external object (mother's breast) and hypercathect his imaginative perception of it. He may then further elaborate and synthesize these self-created perceptions as anlagen or precursors of creative activity which must then await full maturation and development of his ego and his talent for true creative expression." In simple words, according to Weissman, the child who will become a creative person has the ability to diverge the energy originally invested in primitive personal objects and to invest it again in creative work. Or in still different words, the creative person is able to dissociate his early personal life from what will be the creative work, although this work derives from that same early personal life. Erikson (1968) has described how George Bernard Shaw's and William James's relations with their parents brought about a creative confusion and influenced their creative careers. Erikson's analysis is insightful on how these two creative persons developed their own identity and only tangentially touches on their creativity.

Jung, too, made a significant contribution to the study of creativity, especially in reference to the aesthetic process. Philipson has written an interesting book, *Outline of a Jungian Aesthetics* (Philipson, 1963), which will be my guideline in these brief comments on Jung's contributions. Jung believed that the creative process, at least when it pertains to art, occurs in two modes: the psychological and the visionary. In the psychological mode the content of the creative product is drawn from the realm of human consciousness. Although the vast realm of human experience—in its relation to such things as love, family, environment, society, crime, human destiny in general—usually appears in the content of the work of art, this mode of creativity "nowhere transcends the bounds of psychological intelligibility." Everything in it "belongs to the realm of the understandable." The psychological mode submits the material to a direct, conscious, and purposeful aim.

The visionary is the mode that concerns Jung more deeply. In this second mode, the content does not originate in the lessons of life but from timeless depth, from what Jung calls "the collective unconscious." The collective unconscious is the depository of the archetypes—primordial experiences that have repeatedly occurred in the course of generations. The archetypes may surpass man's understanding. They may be many-sided, demonic, and grotesque.

In the visionary mode the creative person is at the mercy of the re-emerging content. He is, according to Jung, in a passive situation.

"The work brings with it its own form, what he [the author] would add to it is declined; what he does not wish to admit is forced upon him." In the visionary mode the creative person is more conscious of an "alien" will or intention beyond his comprehension. Especially in the visionary mode, the emerging product of creativity is an *autonomous complex* which, like a neurotic complex, is a detached portion of the psyche that leads an independent life. Its psychic energy has been withdrawn from conscious control.

The creative process thus consists of an *unconscious animation of the archetype*. The primordial image, connected with the archetype, compensates for the insufficiency and one-sidedness of the creative person's experience of life, or even of the spirit of the historical time in which the creative person lives. In other words, the great work of art transcends life experiences, personal factors, and the historical period in which its producer happens to live. By reawakening the wealth of experiences dominant in the collective unconscious, the creative process confers on the work of art a universal significance. The artist's lack of adaptation to his environment becomes his real advantage: it facilitates the re-emergence of the archetypes; it induces him to enter into a mystical participation with the ancient sources.

It is easy to recognize that Jung's concept of the collective unconscious colors his whole theory of creativity, just as the concept of libido colored Freud's. Jung was definitely right in pointing out that the great work of art cannot be seen only as the result of personal life experiences, dependent on the usual cognitive mechanisms. However, Jung also believed that what goes beyond personal experience originates in the collective unconscious. Thus, in some ways, the collective unconscious occupies the role in Jungian theory that the primary process has in the Freudian system. Although in one of his writings he denies that the archetype is determined in regard to its content (1959), in most of his work Jung conveys the impression that he believes this is so. He finds in the archetype "an invariable nucleus of meaning."

In spite of their appealing quality, we may recognize in Jung's concepts a unilateralness that does not do justice to the creative process. Jung saw the greatness of the creative work in the reactivation of the archetype. The creative product could be compared to an old treasure that is exhumed. The unpredictable newness of the work of art, although an important inherent characteristic of any work of creativity, was not accounted for.

As an example from the neo-Freudian schools, I shall take Ernest

G. Schachtel's contribution into consideration. Schachtel recognizes that the creative person is not embedded in the clichés provided by society, but is subject to new experiences. Contrary to Freud and Jung, Schachtel does not give importance to cognitive modes that preceded the experiences of the creative person, such as those implied in the concepts of primary process and the collective unconscious. Nor does he see the creative process as an instinct discharge function. The creative person's new ways are the result of being *open to the world*.

The concept of the German philosopher Max Scheler (1928), that man as a spiritual and creative being is no longer subject to primitive drives but is "open to the world," may have influenced Schachtel. We must agree with Schachtel that openness to the world is an important attitude, but we must add that it is not sufficient for creativity. According to Schachtel, "The main *motivation* at the root of creative experience is man's need to relate to the world around him" (the italics are Schachtel's). Schachtel writes that "The quality of the encounter that leads to creative experience consists primarily in the openness during the encounter and in the repeated and varied approaches to the object, in the free and open play of attention, thought, feeling, perception" (Schachtel, 1959). Schachtel accurately describes some general attitudes of the creative person, but does not account for the newness of the creative work, or for the inner forces or mechanisms which substitute new and significant forms for society's worn-out clichés. While Schachtel gives much consideration to the encounter of the creative person with the world, he neglects the inner processes that give a creative form to such encounter.

Motivation and Creativity

AS STATED in the previous section, motivation, although necessary, is not the specific ingredient of creativity. And yet most writings of psychoanalysts continue to deal with the problem of creativity almost exclusively from the viewpoint of motivation and sublimation. In his 1972 book a noted psychoanalyst, Anthony Storr, investigates the motivation of creativity, which he calls "the dynamics of creation." Storr reviews the Freudian theories at length and, to a much less extent, the Jungian. He correctly concludes that the essence of creative process has not been clarified by the psychoanalytic inquiries about motivation.

Lest I am misunderstood, I wish to state again my firm convicton that psychology, psychoanalysis, and psychiatry can make major contributions to the field of creativity, as I shall try to demonstrate in this book. These contributions, however, do not need to deal with motivation. As I have already said, motivation is a phenomenon pertaining to every human activity. Present contributions, however, need deal only with those mental processes that intervene between motivation and the completion of the creative product. By no means do I imply that motivation has to be neglected. A motivation to create also exists, and I shall devote the rest of this section to it.

We have already seen that in Freud's theory some events play a significant role in motivating creativity. According to Freud, the creative person experiences a need to represent his conflict or his ungratified wishes by artwork. However, it is evident that early in life a large number of people experience conflicts and frustrations, similar, for instance, to those of Leonardo da Vinci. Yet Leonardos are extremely rare.

Early experiences can play a determining role in stimulating and directing the individual toward a certain kind of activity. The child who grows up in an environment that lacks stability and consistency may become an inventor in the field of mathematics, where he searches for and finds a feeling of certainty for some aspects of the world. The child who feels falsely accused may become a promoter of innovations that guarantee civil liberties. Another child may feel that only if he becomes a great man will he deserve and obtain his mother's love. However, in my experience, a different kind of relation with the mother is a more frequent antecedent of creativity: that is, the love of a good mother, accompanied by the faith that the child will be a worthwhile and creative individual. The child introjects; he learns to share mother's feeling; he accepts her prophecy. Now he must prove that his mother is right. The image of the trusting mother will sustain him throughout his life—in moments of doubts, tribulations, and impulses to withdraw from the pains of the innovating search. Freud himself is an example of this type. As he wrote to Ernest Jones, he felt that his mother's love and faith were a valuable support during his creative struggles.

Again, we could repeat that although the maternal influence is of great importance and in some cases necessary, it is hardly a sufficient causative factor. Too many are the mothers who nourish similar feelings for their children; too few are the children who respond to such feelings by becoming creative. As a matter of fact, this maternal influence leads oftener to competition with real or symbolic siblings than to creativity.

Later, in adolescence, other motivational forces develop at higher levels of cognition. These forces reinforce the creative person's original primitive motivational trends. A few adolescents start to think that their own personal growth will continue if they reach beyond the limits of what seems to them a restrained and small reality. The creative adolescent becomes aware of the vast discrepancy between the human condition and the ideals that his cognitive faculties permit him to envision. Also, a state of aloneness, or a detached or introverted personality, may not permit the young and gifted individual to savor life as much as he would like and may instead predispose him to crave for something that he does not have or see: an object that does not exist in his psychological reality. It is by searching for this object that he will continue to grow and give an acceptable meaning to his life. Although he obviously cannot express himself in these words, he recognizes in himself the reality described by the eighteenth-century philosopher Vico: *finitum, quod tendit ad infinitum,* or "a finitude which tends toward infinity." This realization, possible only because the young person has now a repertory of high concepts and can think in an abstract way, reactivates old feelings and longings which in early childhood were based partially or totally on archaic and primary process mechanisms. For instance, the child once had feelings of omnipotence, as described by Silverberg (1952). He thought he could do or obtain anything that he wished. His accomplishments and gratifications would equate with his desires. But in the process of growing up, he had to give up such feelings. These feelings, however, remained dormant inside of him, and eventually a creative urge has rekindled them, at times as early as in the first years of adolescence.

Another motivation of the creative person may stem from the fact that he is endowed with a very active or intense imagination on account of biological or other and as yet undetermined reasons. Whereas the average person very early in life learns to check his own imagination and to pay more attention to the requirements of reality than to his inner experiences, the creative person follows a different course. He feels himself to be in a state of turmoil, restlessness, deprivation, emptiness, and unbearable frustration unless he expresses his inner life in one or another creative way. As a matter of fact, we must acknowledge that this search for the new object—an external work that will substitute for the inner fantasy or unrest—is the most common and most powerful motivation, reckoned on its own, even if behind it are other hidden, and more primitive motivations. We must also acknowledge that in each instance that can be subjected to personal psychological inquiry, we find not one single motivation but a mixture of several of motivations, some of them conscious and some unconscious, with one perhaps prevailing.

When the urge for creative aspirations starts to be felt, nobody knows what the result will be. It is not necessarily a rewarding achievement. It may end in frustration, in disappointment, or in anger at society, one's family, or a few people. It may end in resignation and acceptance of the limitations of human existence, or in escapes of various sorts. It may even lead to mental illness. It will also lead to creativity, if a possibility exists of combining primary and secondary processes in a constructive way.

Because of my familiarity with their writings, I find it useful to examine as examples of creative motivation the two major Italian poets, Dante and Petrarch. Lest I be misunderstood, I want to stress that the following remarks do not aim at explaining the central part of the creative process of these two poets, but rather at showing how unjustified it is to seek the cause of their greatness in motivations of various sorts (personal or environmental) or in psychological disorders. The works of these two poets may be viewed to a considerable extent as the creative expression of a search for a special object—a type of love that at first has the characteristic of ordinary love but that later becomes mystical and transcendental. This concept of love was a prevalent one between the second half of the twelfth century and the first half of the thirteenth, an era still influenced by the chivalry-troubadour culture and permeated by an all-embracing religiosity. Love seems to be realizable on earth, and yet it always escapes the pursuer. A longing for it, possibly based on the reactivation of infantile wishes and strivings, becomes connected with (and therefore transformed by) the most ideal concepts. The medieval Christian concept that nothing noble and beautiful to the spirit and therefore really worthwhile can be realized on earth, becomes part of the conception of a love that is not attainable.

Dante's love for Beatrice has many archaic, obsessive, and schizophrenic-like elements (see Chapter 8). The poet met Beatrice Portinari three times in his whole life. No intimacy, no prolonged interpersonal contacts, not even an exchange of views seems to have occurred between the two. And yet it is on these puny segments of historical reality, rather than on his prolonged contacts with his wife and the mother of his children, the earthy Gemma Donati, that he has based his two great works *La Vita Nuova* and *The Divine Comedy*. These momentary and casual street encounters must indeed have been passionate personal experiences, but the memory of them through the years, together with Dante's creative process, transformed them and gave them unpredictable power.

At the same time that Beatrice remained a real person in her physical essence, she became the symbol of love and goodness. As many critics have pointed out, Dante often speaks of her as he would speak of God; at times, perhaps without realizing it, he identifies her with Christ. He calls her the daughter of God. The historical events of his casual encounters with her become surrounded by an atmosphere of mysticism, where the number 9 assumes a magic flavor. Dante had an obsessive–compulsive attitude toward this number. He lets us know that he was 9 years old when he met Beatrice for the first time and that it was 9 years later when he met her again, at 9 o'clock. This obsessional attitude toward the number 9 recurs frequently throughout his writings. In three visions that foretell Beatrice's death, the number 9 appears in one way or another.

The first part of *La Vita Nuova* is mainly the expression of a presentiment and expectation of Beatrice's death. But Dante does not even bother to give a descriptive account of the actual occurrence of her death. Her death makes her more alive in his artistic reality. She becomes the image of love and goodness, and finally the guide who will accompany him up to his encounter with God.

Petrarch's love for Laura is also unusual. Laura was a married woman who lived in southern France, between Avignon and Vaucluse.* Her actual encounters with the poet were very few and, in the eyes of the world, inconsequential. There is no indication whatsoever that Laura requited the feelings of the poet. Reading Petrarch's writ-

---

* It may be a matter of curiosity to know that Laura belonged to the family de Sade, from which the famous Marquis later descended (Bishop 1963).

ings, one could even imagine that he was not too distant from that form of paranoia called erotomania. He idealized this woman, but not to the degree that Dante idealized Beatrice. Laura remained fundamentally a terrestrial creature, although endowed with unusual qualities; for instance, that of beautifying whatever she touched—trees, water, grass, and so forth. Her death is described in detail by Petrarch in one of the best pieces of Italian poetry: even death looked beautiful when, like a soft snowfall, it descended over Laura's lovely face.

This account of Dante and Petrarch is not intended to give the impression that the two poets were suffering from psychosis. On the contrary, they both possessed unusual mental lucidity and were in full control of "secondary-process" thinking. In addition to presumed ungratified infantile wishes that we cannot retrace, they had a conscious motivation: expansion of their own self through the search for an ideal—a complex of feeling and concepts that they called love. This search, promoted by flimsy external events, drew its sustenance from the poets' personal encounters with a conceptual world of both external (or cultural) and internal origin. The searching itself created the object that was searched for. The two poets succeeded in finding the ideal love, but only as an aesthetic entity. The high value of this aesthetic entity is not explained by their motivations or by the psychological problems that they might have had. As an incidental remark, we can add that it is a very remote possibility that the aesthetic object which they created prevented the formation of delusional, psychotic thinking. It is more likely, however, that in the spirit of medieval mysticism and of scriptural acculturation, the poetical allegory tended to assume the validity of historical truth (Singleton 1954). Beatrice and Laura existed for those two poets as they had imagined the women to be. The poetical visions were as pregnant with truth for the poets as the revelatory experience was for the men who knew God.

Concluding Remarks

ALL OF THE METHODS used to study creativity have been rewarding to various degrees, and some of them still seem very promising. On the other hand, it is true that no major breakthrough has occurred as a consequence of any of the mentioned methods. We could make the same assessment, however, for practically every subject studied by psychology. Even the psychoanalytic approach, which delves below the surface and into the depths of the unconscious, has had a very limited impact because most of its inquiries have dealt with motivation, a phenomenon not specific to creativity.

In my opinion, a new form of "deep psychology" has to be added to our research repertory: a deep psychology that deals with structures, and with the underlying general principles on which these structures are based. I have found it very useful to apply to the field of creativity the psychostructural approach that I have applied to psychiatry. This approach was developed independently and along different lines from the structuralism of Levi-Strauss. It was first described in my study of schizophrenia (1948), nine years in advance of Chomsky's application of structuralism to other fields of inquiry. It was first applied to creativity in my work on wit and the comic (1950). I have later expanded my research in other areas, as reported in several other works (1955, 1956, 1961, 1962, 1964, 1965, 1966, 1974).

The structural approach does not aim at a description or at a mere classification, as do the descriptive and taxonomic approaches, but at an understanding of the mechanisms of the involved psychological functions. Although this approach studies elements, it also studies the particular patterns, the total structures, and the stable systems that they form. In other words, it varies between focusing on the structure, as a stable element, and on the process itself, which implies movement and a state of becoming. As we shall see in Chapter 18, when structuralism deals with general principles, it becomes difficult to distinguish from general system theory.

But even the psychostructural and the general system theories leave many aspects of the problem untouched; namely, those related to the specific characteristics of the sociocultural climate that favors creativity and the specific modalities of the cultivation of creativity. In other words, a psychostructural approach will help us greatly to elucidate the creative process and the creative product; but for the study of the personality of the creative person, as well as of the environments favoring creativity, or of the cultivation of creativity, we must resort to other methodologies.

PART TWO

The Psychological Components of Creativity

Chapter 3
Imagery

Contingencies and Symbols

THERE ARE two kinds of prerequisites for the unfolding of the creative process. One kind may be designated as *contingencies*, a category that includes everything external to the creative person. A human being cannot originate new things out of nothing. He must be exposed to an environment that gives him cultural opportunities and stimulates him in various ways, and he must have at his disposal some physical material such as a pen, a pencil, paper, a compass, a brush, a stone, a canvas, some object for scientific study, and so forth. Obviously realistic contingencies are necessary not just for creativity but for every form of life. We shall not discuss them here.

The second kind is much more specific. It refers to the psychological life of the individual, to anything that can be included under the category of *imagination* and *amorphous cognition*.

Imagination is a difficult concept to define. First of all, we must stress that it should not be confused with *images* or *imagery*. Imagery is only one type of imagination; it is the process of producing and experiencing images. Imagination is the capacity of the mind to produce or reproduce several symbolic functions while in a state of consciousness, of awakeness, without any deliberate effort to organize these functions. In other words, first of all, dreams are arbitrarily excluded. Secondly, whatever is unconscious is excluded, including such things as so-called unconscious images. What is left are conscious images, ideas, sequences of words, sentences, and feelings, just as they occur. Imagination is related to what is called "free association" in psychoanalysis. However, free association refers predominantly to what is expressed in words, whereas imagination can assume nonverbal forms. Imagination excludes all that which cannot assume or has not yet assumed a form, verbal or nonverbal. (A part of what is excluded is amorphous cognition, which will be studied in Chapter 4.) And in itself imagination, of course, is only a prerequisite for or a precursor of creativity. Subsequent elaborations of imaginations are necessary for creativity.

In our definition of imagination we used the word "symbolic." The *symbol* is a very important concept. The characteristic of being symbolic is the main feature that distinguishes some human psychological functions from those of other animals, and is at the basis of creativity. Other animals, too, exhibit cognitive processes, including such functions as learning, memory, intelligence. They learn to respond in special ways to stimuli and to generalize their responses to all stimuli that belong in given categories. Their responses depend entirely on their perceptions, on what is immediately given. They do not have to resort to their imagination and to elaborations thereof, except perhaps in rudimentary forms. In the conditioned reflex, too, an animal responds to the immediately given. For instance, in the Pavlov experiment, a dog learned to respond to a buzz as he would respond to the sight of food. He learned that food would arrive after the buzz, so that he began to salivate and was already prepared for food at the sound of the buzz. That is, the buzz had become a *sign* of incoming food. But a sign is not yet a symbol. It is true that it stands for something else (such as the buzz standing for food), but it stands for something that is about to be present and/or may be already a part of the present total situation. For instance, a cloud may be a sign of an incoming storm, of which it is a part; a certain rash on the skin may be a sign of chicken pox, of which disease it is a part, a condition.

Men, too, use signs; but they also use symbols. A symbol is a representative of something else, even when that "something else" is completely absent. In ordinary life, the most common symbol is the word. For instance, our friend Rosemarie may not be with us; as a matter of fact, she may be visiting Australia. But when we say the word "Rosemarie," we all know that we are speaking about that particular friend. The word stands for that person; it is a symbol of her. Symbols are also generally used in association. If I say "the beautiful panorama," the person who hears me has a definite knowledge of what the sound "beautiful" stands for and what the sound "panorama" stands for. In ordinary language, however, we select words and put them in special orders for special purposes, whereas when we resort only to our imagination, we allow words to occur freely as in free association.

The creative process differs from the ordinary functions of the mind insofar as it uses many kinds of symbols. It also uses the symbols in different contexts or proportions, so that these new, different contexts and proportions themselves become symbols of things never before symbolized or else symbolized previously in different ways. Some of these symbolic processes are primitive and belong to what Freud called the primary process. Others are high-level symbols and belong to what Freud called the secondary process. This chapter is devoted mainly to the study of the image, which is the most primitive form of symbolic function.

Perception

BEFORE DISCUSSING the image, however, we must devote a few pages to perception, which is not a symbolic function. Why isn't it? Because it reproduces what is present here and now. I see a rose in my garden. I smell it, I touch it, I pick it up, I hear the little sound of its breaking stem, and its thorns prick me. Within a few seconds I have visual, olfactory, tactile, thermal, kinesthetic, auditory, and pain perceptions. The rose is a *given;* I do not use my imagination to acknowledge its presence, although of course I can do a great deal with all those perceptions. What I undergo is a simple process, not a symbolic one.

Physiologists and psychologists, however, remind us that what to us seems a simple phenomenon, such as the perception of a rose, is not so simple after all. And they are right. Many studies on perception have been written, enough of them to fill several libraries; we shall not attempt even to summarize them. Hebb (1949) has incisively written that the simplicity and immediacy of perception do not indicate physiological simplicity. Perception includes a complex set of phenomena that intervene between sensory stimulation and conscious awareness. We are aware of the last steps of this set, but all the steps that precede awareness remain unknown. They include, among others, a filtering process that allows us (a) to register some stimuli, (b) to exclude many others, (c) to organize the peripheral sensory events that are registered, and (d) to reach a gestaltic or total experience, so that (e) the perceived object has constancy—that is, it appears the same even though I may perceive it from nearby or afar.

Some of these points have to be clarified. The ways of experiencing through perception cannot match the flux of the physical world. At the same time that perception puts us in contact with the present physical world, it is also a reductive system. Every form of perception is a little window facing a universe of potentially numberless stimuli. To begin with, what we see or hear is only a small fraction of the influx of electromagnetic radiation. Secondly, we tend to perceive what we can subsequently understand or place in some category, and we tend to overlook all the rest. If we did not do so, we would be overwhelmed by a flood of irrelevant stimulation. The newborn infant experiences nothing but sensations. The world around is still a buzzing and blooming awareness of unorganized stimuli. That is why we cannot remember our infant experiences. As Schachtel has described (1959), the child gradually learns to select, to organize, to form patterns of experiences, to recognize them, and to borrow categories from other people.

Other aspects of perception have to be considered because they are important for our main topic. Let us assume that we are in a room where two mirrors face each other on opposite walls. We see the image of ourselves reflected in the mirror, but also the image of ourselves reflected in the second mirror, which is again reflected in the first mirror, and so forth. We could see ourselves reflected many times as our eyesight permits. When we look at one of the two mirrors, we see a static picture, and yet the images of ourselves are constantly moving from one mirror to the other to be repeatedly reflected. The velocity of light is so great that our nervous system cannot perceive it. Thus we have the impression of no movement, when in actuality we are in the presence of the fastest possible movement.

Other movements, which are much slower, are registered by our nervous system, but are not slow enough to reach the threshold of our consciousness. They are the early steps of the phenomenon perception, to which I shall return shortly.

So far I want to stress that perception arrests the flux of the world, gives a static picture of what may be in a state of continuous, perhaps infinite movement.

Under the influence of the Gestalt school, we have learned to stress that we see things in wholes. Most recent investigations, however, lead us to conclude that the perception of a whole has been preceded by pre-gestaltic stages, which are too rapid to be perceived, or which exist only during the period in which the infant "learns" to perceive. There is no doubt that when we look around us, we see unities, or wholes. A tree is a unity, although it may contain many branches and leaves; an animal is an organism, although it consists of the various parts of its body; and so forth. A perception of unity occurs first of all when a given figure is discriminated from the background. Such discrimination is probably innate (Hebb 1949). What- ever is experienced deeply and leads to the main response is part of the figure; whatever is less strongly perceived and leads to weaker responses is part of the background. The figure, in contrast to the background, seems to have a compelling or a releasing quality, inasmuch as it elicits the stronger response on the part of the observer.

In *The Intrapsychic Self* (Chapter 4) I have shown that one of the most arduous struggles of animal evolution is to determine what belongs to a given unity and has to be differentiated from a more or less undefined background. In fact, many species of animals respond to what to us seem parts and not unities or wholes. Tinbergen (1951) has illustrated some interesting mechanisms among animals. For instance, certain fish such as the sticklebacks, when fighting competitor males who invade their territory, react only to the red color of the competitors' bellies. Since they react to only a part of the total environmental situation and neglect the other parts, they can make mistakes: artificial red objects introduced by the experimenter elicit the same fighting response. Yet the sense organs of these fish are able to perceive the whole situation, and it is the total situation that is important for the fish: the chasing away of male competitors. Nevertheless, it is a part of the whole—the red color—that is perceived, recognized and identified, and responded to with fighting behavior. Here, the perception of the stimulus "red" as a unity seems certain. It would be too much to ascribe to the fish the capacity to abstract the red from the environment. These animals do not abstract; they are only responding in a primitive way to a simple stimulus that is differentiated from the background.

In animal psychology there are many examples of responses to a fragment of a situation, or to a quality of the background, with disregard to the situation as a whole. We are familiar with the fact that moths are attracted by light even though they may burn themselves to death in contact with powerful electric bulbs. Such reactivity to a single part of the environment is often used to trick and kill insects. In the case of flypaper, the fly reacts only to the sweetness of the paper and not to the ensnaring stickiness. It would seem that, early in the evolutionary scale, the animal organism reacts predominantly to a releasing element that is seen as a whole; it reacts in a very weak fashion to the rest, which is experienced as undifferentiated. What appears to these lowly animals as undifferentiated would appear to us as if fragmented. Actually, something similar may occur in human infancy: the perceptual background may consist not only of undifferentiated parts but also of parts that have not been organized to form wholes. These parts might appear to adults as fragments. In higher species the perceived object becomes more complicated, consisting of more than the releasing element, although the releasing element still has the most important perceptual role. Additional parts are detached from the background and become part of the figure or of the whole. Finally, the releasing element is perceived as only one of the many parts of the unity.

Thus objects that appear to us as unities, or wholes, have not always been experienced as such, either in the evolution of the animal kingdom or in the development of the individual. Spitz (1965) has convincingly demonstrated that a three-month-old human infant does not perceive the whole face of its mother, but only her forehead, eyes, and nose. These form one sign, a pre-object, of mother. Riesen (1947) raised mammals in darkness. When these animals were eventually exposed to light, they could not recognize objects in their totality, but had to become acquainted with each part one by one. Von Senden (1960) examined adult humans who had been blind from birth because of congenital cataracts. When they were operated on and were learning to see, they did not recognize whole objects such as chairs, tables, and so forth, but had to examine and become familiar with many parts

Figure 3-1

of an object in order to realize later that these parts formed a whole. The shortest time in which a congenitally blind person approximated normal perception was about a month.

Many other experimenters (Pötzl 1917; Pritchard, Heron, and Hebb 1960; Fisher 1954; Fisher and Paul 1959) have demonstrated that perception consists of part-perception at first. It becomes total perception when we are fully aware of it: at the end of previous processes which last a fraction of a second. Thus perception, which appears so simple to us, is a complicated phenomenon that has undergone differentiation in the course of evolution.

In neurological diseases such as those described by Goldstein and

Gelb (1920) and by Alexandra Adler (1944, 1950), an opposite mechanism occurs: *dedifferentiation*. The total or normal perception disintegrates; the individual sees either fragments of the whole, or parts, or only the salient points. Figure 3-1 represents a picture made by a regressed schizophrenic, reported in my book *Interpretation of Schizophrenia* (1974, Chapter 20). Whereas beforehand the patient had been able to paint and draw in a satisfactory way, at the time she made that drawing she was no longer able to perceive and draw wholes. The profiles of women that she wanted to portray underwent fragmentation and were hardly recognizable. In some of them, however, the salient parts of the face are still identifiable. I would not have spent so much time in describing these precursors of perception (along with regression of perception to early stages in abnormal conditions), did not these phenomena also occur in creativity or were they not connected with other aspects of creativity, as we shall see later in this book.

At this point we can conclude that the function of perception, although not symbolic, is not simple. It is a simplifying phenomenon that attempts to make us aware of a simple and stable picture of a very complex reality.

The Image

CONTRARY TO PERCEPTION, which relies on the external senses and apparatuses, the image is purely a mental representation. Let us examine the *visual* type of image, which is the easiest to describe and understand. We could say that it is "the mind's eye." For instance, I close my eyes and visualize my mother. She may not be present, but her image is with me; it stands for her. The image is obviously based on the memory traces of previous perceptions of my mother. Because I have an image of her, my mother acquires a psychological reality that is not tied to her physical presence.

An image not only re-evokes what is not present, it also enables a human being to retain an emotional disposition toward an absent object. For example, the image of my mother may evoke the love I feel for her; were my mother to die, her image would remain with me, and so would my love for her. Thus the image becomes a substitute for the external object. It is actually an inner object, that is, a product of my mind. It is true that in order for me to have a visual image of my mother I must have seen my mother in the external world; but when the image is formed, that image is part of me, of my inner life.

Although we cannot deny that at least rudimentary images occur in other animals, images are undoubtedly a predominantly human characteristic. Human beings themselves are not born with the capacity to form images. In the first six months of life a baby responds only to perceptions and to signs. Not until the seventh or eighth month of life is the baby able to have images (see Arieti 1967, 1974). For instance, if he is to look for a rattle when the rattle has been hidden under a pillow, presumably he can carry the image of the rattle in his mind. This the child is able to do from the seventh month of life onward.

Images soon constitute the foundation of the inner reality, which in human psychology is as important as (and in some respects more important than) external reality. Imagery not only helps the individual to understand the world better, it also helps him to create a surrogate for the world. Whatever is known or experienced, by means of images and subsequent cognitive processes, tends to become a part of the individual who knows and experiences it. Visual images attempt to reproduce the appearance of the object they stand for. However, images do not have the ability to evoke the same kind of behavior that the corresponding perceptions do. They generally elicit a more delayed and less direct action. For a number of reasons (Arieti 1967, Chapter 5), only sexual images can evoke instinctual urges that approximate in intensity those elicited by the presence of the sexual object.

As we have already mentioned, images are connected with past perceptions; they are elaborations of memory traces. Unfortunately, we know practically nothing of the neurophysiologic mechanisms that retain memory traces and elaborate them to the level of images. We know, however, that they are formed in some areas of the brain that are different from those where perception takes place. Visual perceptions occur in the occipital lobe, in Brodmann cortical area 17, around the calcarine fissure; but images used also in voluntary recall seem to occur in area 19.

When psychology was a young science, the study of images received great consideration. Since then, however, images have lost the important position they occupied in psychological thinking and research. This loss of popularity was due partially to the fact that psychology has been dominated by the behavioristic school, which studies only external behavior.* But images are subjective experiences, that is, they can be appreciated only by the person who experiences them. Therefore they are not very suitable for behavioristic research. The lack of interest in the study of images was also due to the fact that the most important functions of images (maintenance of motivation for absent objects, transformations of emotions, symbolic formation, building of inner reality) had not yet been recognized (Arieti 1967, Chapter 5). Their study consisted purely of static description, which did not lead to fruitful results. Not only were they more difficult to study than sensations and perceptions; when they seemed valuable for the understanding of the psyche, they also proved to be accompanied by other mental processes, such as thinking and language, that could be examined independently with clearer results. Even the emotions that accompany images were found impossible to study unless the subject was able to verbalize his introspections.

I believe that the phenomenon of imagery can no longer be ignored in this way. It plays a crucial role in the process of creativity. People differ greatly in their ability to produce images. Some persons resort to intoxication; for instance, they use mescaline and lysergic acid in order to have the most primitive and intense forms of imagery. However, these harmful methods are not necessary. Imagery is a common function of the mind. Images occur spontaneously, but they are made to occur more easily if the person refrains from action and if external stimuli are reduced or eliminated. Rest, solitude, darkness, and meditation facilitate their occurrence.

In special cases images appear in unusual forms. They may be so vivid as to look like photographic reproductions of previously perceived objects: these vivid forms are the *eidetic* images, first described by Jaensch (1930), which occur especially in children. Among other types are the *hypnagogic*, often wrongly called hallucinations: these are the fleeting auditory or visual images that occur in some persons while they are about to fall asleep. *Hypnopompic* images are those that occur to some people while awakening from deep sleep.

---

* An important exception is the book by M. J. Horowitz (1970).

Imagery

There are many types of images, as many as there are types of sensations. The two prevailing types, however, are the visual and the auditory, and in most persons one type predominates. In the latter respect, however, the role played by language in human mental activity complicates the study of imagery, since most people think in words that are generally experienced as auditory images. For instance, suppose I think "George Washington was the first President of the United States." In "my mind's ear" I almost hear my voice, or a faint reproduction of it, saying that sentence. If we eliminate verbal images, then, we can readily recognize that in most people the visual type plays the predominant role.

Images are fleeting. A person can retain an image for only a short period of time. When he re-evokes the image, it appears in a slightly different form. With the exception of some special forms such as the eidetic, the hallucinatory, and, at times, those appearing in dreams, images are hazy, vague, and shadowy. Unless a strong voluntary effort is made, images cannot reproduce total representations. For instance, if a person tries to revisualize his kitchen, he may first reproduce the breakfast table, then a wall of the room, then the stove. It would be very difficult and often impossible for most people to visualize the whole room at once.

The last characteristic is very important because it seems to indicate that in images, just as in the pre-stages of perception and other psychological processes (which we shall take into consideration later), a partial representation is a major factor. Consciousness shifts rapidly from one part of the image to another, with an uncertain visualization of the whole. In the mind of the person, however, there is no doubt that although he focuses on only one part, he is mentally in a total situation. For instance, in the kitchen example above, the person knows that he is visualizing his kitchen, the part he "sees" being sufficient for him to infer the whole.

Images undergo many private alterations; only eidetic images are similar to photographic reproductions. This alterability or volatile character of images makes them difficult to express in words, at times. They may also be difficult to express because they do not correspond to definite representations accepted by a social group or by the individual's social milieu. Furthermore, the fluid changes that they undergo make them dissimilar to previous occurrences. Thus they are difficult to commit to memory.

Images do not have the relative stability that is characteristic of perceptions. As we have seen in the preceding section of this chapter, perceptions that have not become arrested during their formation assume a considerable objective value and seem stable and reliable in most cases. But when the memory traces of perceptions are activated into the form of images, these traces do not prove to be immutable historical archives. The images resume a state of flux that appears to be even more unstable than that of the external world. Furthermore, whereas perceptions are projected onto the external world, images are experienced as occurring inwardly. The normal person knows that they are produced by his own mind and that they do not necessarily mirror simultaneous equivalents in the external world.

It is obvious to the individual that his images attempt to reproduce past perceptions, but that the reproduction is far from perfect. He may try to see the face of a sweetheart he had in his adolescence, but he does not see her as clearly as if she were present or as if he were looking at her picture. The image is not a faithful reproduction but a defective representation, satisfying only to the extent that it makes the individual experience a feeling related to the one he had toward the original object.

The inexact reproduction may be evaluated in various ways. We may conclude that the image is inferior to the original perception. The perception apparatus had the benefit of being under the influence of a stimulus present and available for reproduction, whereas the image is like the work of a historian who tries to retrace the remnants of the past in the best ways he can, without tangible evidence.

No matter how extensive the discrepancy is between the original perception and the image, we must say that the discrepancy is just as important as the similarity to the original perception. If we can say that images deform or distort, we can also say that images liberate us from a punctilious reproduction of reality and introduce something new: the first elements of creativity. Imagery is thus poor history or a poor keeping of archives, but it shows the first germs of creativity. Whereas perception subtracts, imagery adds, but whether it succeeds in recapturing that which perception left out can be determined only by a very subjective and therefore inaccurate evaluation.

Most images rapidly associate with other images through the mechanism of spatial or temporal contiguity. That is, they tend to reproduce the images of the objects that were in spatial proximity with the stimulus of the previous image. For instance, if I am experiencing the image of a tree, that image tends to elicit in me the image of other parts of the wood or garden where that tree was, or of the landscape at the location, or of the people who were with me when I visited that particular place where the tree was located. In some images there is a *salient part*, and that salient element may lead to other images which have the same salient part. For instance, the image of a crescent may lead to the image of the moon, or of a coast shaped like a moon, or of a banana. In other images there may be no salient element, but rather a concatenation of parts that can easily displace one another. And in other images there is a condensation, or fusion, of previous images that were separate in the real world. For instance, an image may represent a person as half woman and half fish, like a siren. Images are always in movement, going in one direction or another; they are in a state of constant becoming. They represent the unceasing activity of the human mind.

Imagery thus emerges not only as the first or most primitive process of reproducing or substituting for *the real*, but also as the first or most primitive process of creating *the unreal*. A French philosopher, Gaston Bachelard (1960, 1971), who has written many books and essays on "imagination," has stressed this point repeatedly. (However, he seems to confuse imagination with images and imagery.) To the extent that the image makes an error in reproducing reality it becomes the concern of other fields, especially neurophysiology, neuropsychology, and psychiatry. We shall not deal with this aspect of imagery in this book. But to the extent that the image, by not faithfully reproducing reality, is an innovation, a state of becoming, and a force of transcendence, we shall be very much concerned with it.

Function and Outcome of Imagery

WHAT MOTIVATES the mind to experience images? How do they come to be? Classic psychoanalysis has attempted to answer this question. It states that when the desired object is absent and the individual cannot gratify his wish (for instance, when the individual is hungry and there is no food, or when he has a sexual desire and there is no sexual partner), the image of the desired absent thing is likely to appear. Classic psychoanalysis holds that any cognitive process (other than perception) is a deviation from activity directed toward immediate gratification. In other words, according to this interpretation, images would be brought about by a need or by an unsatisfied desire.

There is, in fact, no doubt that many images are stimulated by needs and desires. But other circumstances must also be taken into account. For instance, it is the image itself that renews the desire and creates a need. It is true that if the need is a physiological one, such as hunger or thirst, one does not need images of food or water to stimulate his sense of neediness further. But many other desires and psychological needs would not continue to exist if images did not renew and sustain them. For instance, I would not have the desire to revisit a lake that I had liked very much when I first saw it, were I not able to retain the image of that lake in my mind as a memory ready to be recalled.

Most important of all, imagery becomes an end to itself. It is as though the human being had images for the sake of having them. Images play a major role in daydreaming. The individual wants to remove himself from reality, wants to have an alternative, even if only hypothetical; he wants to visualize things in different ways. Together with the desire to reproduce what is absent, but was present in reality at a different time or place, the individual wants to produce what was never present. This point has to be stressed, because it is a crucial one: imagery is a way of dealing with the "absent," of giving it a psychological presence or existence. Here the word "absent" can mean two different things. It can mean something that exists (a friend, food, an object) but is not available at the present time because it is located elsewhere. But the word can also mean that which does not exist and has to be created in order to exist. That is, although imagery has the function of reproducing what is not available, it also acquires the function—at least in its earliest rudimentary forms—of producing what was never present. To possess the absent in the form of a mental representation may be wish-fulfilling in both cases. It may be not only an attempt to gratify a longing for that which is not available, but also a springboard to creativity. Imagery is thus the first function that permits the human being not to adapt passively to reality, not to be forced to accept the limitations of reality.

If images reproduce something desirable that exists but that is not available, the individual may be motivated to act, to search, and to find the desired object. If the desired object does not exist, the individual may be motivated to create it. If the individual cannot find it or create it, he may daydream about it. The daydream, however, is not always fullfilling. The individual may then try again to search for or to create. When imagery is used too much or too intensely, it may lead to *adualism*—an inability to distinguish the two realities, that of the mind and that of the external world. Baldwin (1929) was the first to describe adualism in very young normal children. However, when adualism occurs in older children and in adults, in situations other than dreams, it is indicative of pathological conditions. In these cases the wish-fulfillment quality of the mental representation reached its culmination. To experience a wish becomes equivalent to its actualization. This state of affairs often occurs in schizophrenia. Unchecked imagery thus may provoke unbearable frustration; in some cases it may lead to psychotic delusions and hallucinations.

In those times when the evolving human mind had not yet achieved those cognitive stages it subsequently has, it must have gone through periods of great turmoil. It was thus necessary for the psyche, in evolving, to find ways (or to select those mechanisms) that repress imagery to a large extent or make it unconscious. Repression of imagery is a very common phenomenon. To varying degrees we repress our capacity for imagery, which may then resume a greater role when we dream, when we daydream, when we are intoxicated, or when we want to create. In the creative process, too, the image, which is the first ingredient, tends to produce frustration unless an attempt is made to externalize it in the creative product. But the attempt will be unsuccessful unless (as we shall see in subsequent chapters) the imagery, which may have arisen spontaneously, is reinforced, weakened, altered, and used in many ways. This modification and externalization of the creative image will be possible because the individual, who is able to use various levels of mental activity, can go back and forth from the highest to the lowest order of these levels. It is one of the major properties of the mind, especially in the creative process, to use all the levels of activity, whether in succession, in a given sequence, or in simultaneous activation.

Imagery is often used as a temporary escape from the highest levels of mental activity, or from the meanings of the highest levels that are not accepted or returned to until they are accompanied by a greater insight provided by the experiencing of an image. For instance, a person all of a sudden visualizes mentally clouds and clouds moving in the sky. Does he thereby escape from a storm that he thinks is approaching—not a meteorological storm, but one of feelings and ideas? Similarly, another person may dream that he is looking for a key. In waking life he may be concerned with finding a solution so that he can open his way toward a certain path of life.

Freudian psychoanalysis, but not that of the neo-Freudian schools, has tried to explain images in terms of a so-called economic–energetic frame of reference. A certain amount of libido, or of energy, is needed for the production of images as well as for all the other mental processes. But in images and other primary process phenomena the energy is free (that is, it shifts rapidly from one image to another), whereas in secondary process mechanisms it remains tied to the object on which the attention of the individual is focused.

As for such outlook, there is no doubt about the mobility of images; however, the hypothesis of libido is not necessary here. Many authors, including the present one, think that it is more relevant to try to explain the mechanism of image production in terms of what we know about the physiology of the nervous system, and of the propagation of the nervous impulse from neuron to neuron.

Chapter 4

Amorphous Cognition: The Endocept

The Nonrepresentational Activity of the Psyche

IN THE PREVIOUS CHAPTER we have seen how the image alone, without any subsequent mental elaboration, or as an end in itself, may lead to inactivity, dissatisfaction, and even frustration. Although it is a frequent and very important ingredient of the creative process, imagery cannot in itself constitute a creative product. But when the nervous excitement that produces an image is inhibited—that is, when it is kept from activating the brain areas that mediate images—it changes its direction.

In the evolution of the human cerebral cortex, areas of the cortex came to exist that were not committed to specific functions. These areas permitted cognitive events to be detoured in ways which eventually proved advantageous to human development. Therefore the expanded cortex was selected by evolution. The detours it provides mediate stages of cognition which extend from the level of the image to that of the highest concepts. These intermediary stages reappear in the development of each human being (Arieti 1967). Although some of them are not frequently used by healthy normal adults, they are available to them, and they can be used in special conditions. One of these conditions is the creative process. Here, of course, we shall focus on the use of these intermediary stages in the act of creativity rather than in normal conditions or in a state of illness or in dreams. Obviously, however, it will not be possible to sharply separate their occurrence and manifestations in creativity from their occurrence in phylogeny, ontogeny, and health and disease. These states are all related to one another, as the comparative developmental psychologist Heinz Werner (1957) has illustrated. Thus references to these other states will also be made, especially for the purpose of clarification.

In this chapter we shall examine *amorphous cognition*, a kind of cognition that occurs without representation—that is, without being expressed in images, words, thoughts, or actions of any kind. Since it remains an internal, private occurrence, I have called its specific function the *endocept* (from the Greek *endo*, inside), to distinguish it from the concept, a mature form of cognition that can be expressed to other people by the person who experiences or produces it (Arieti 1965; 1967, Chapter 5). The endocept has also been referred to by other authors as nonverbal, unconscious, or preconscious cognition.

The workers of the German school of Würzburg were among the first to indicate that there are some mental processes that occur without representation (that is, without images) but that are not at the level of mature thoughts. Surprise, hesitation, and doubtfulness were depicted by Marbe as "experiences which cannot be closely analyzed" (*Bewusssteinslage*, 1901), and Ach wrote of "the actual presence of knowing without images" (1935).

At the same time that the Würzburgers were drawing these conclusions, the French psychologist Binet had developed a similar point of view (1903, 1911). According to Binet, some forms of thought are completely without images: in fact the intention, not the image, is the foundation of psychic life. This "intention" is related to what the Würzburgers called the *Aufgabe* of thought.

The endocept is a primitive organization of past experiences, perceptions, memory traces, and images of things and movements. These previous experiences, which are repressed and not brought back to consciousness, continue to have an indirect influence. The endocept goes beyond the cognitive stage of the image, but inasmuch as it does not reproduce anything similar to perceptions, it is not easily recognizable. Also, it does not lead to prompt action. Nor can it be transformed into a verbal expression; it remains at a preverbal level. Although it has an emotional component, it does not expand into a clearly felt emotion.

As indicated, the endocept cannot be shared. We may consider it as a disposition to feel, to act, to think, which occurs after simpler mental activity has been inhibited. The awareness of experiencing an endocept is also extremely vague, uncertain, or partial at best. Relative to the image, the endocept involves considerable cognitive expansion, but this expansion occurs at the expense of subjective awareness, which is decreased in intensity.

The content of an endocept can be communicated to other people only when it is translated into expressions belonging to other levels: for instance, into words, music, drawings, and so forth. Expressing endocepts as such, without such translation, is probably an impossible task—although often attempted, as we shall see. The difficulty is due to the fact that the endocept is an intermediary construct of the brain; it is not equivalent to actions, words, images, or clearly felt emotions.

At the present stage of our knowledge, we cannot obtain certain proof of the existence of the endocept. It remains the least clear and the least scientifically verifiable of the ideas presented in this book. However, in the course of this chapter we shall see that there is some evidence for its existence, both from logical inference and from clinical observations. Perhaps an endocept will eventually be found to consist of numerous steps or mechanisms that are even susceptible of neurophysiological interpretation.

Although the endocept does not reach the verbal level, we do give names to experiences that retain mostly endoceptual characteristics. At times the endocept seems to be completely unconscious. At other times the individual may refer to the endocept as to something that is felt as an atmosphere, an intention, a "global" experience that cannot be divided into parts or words—something similar to what Freud called "oceanic" feeling. At still other times there is no sharp demarcation to be drawn between endocepts, subliminal experiences that have not yet reached the level of consciousness, and some vague, primitive feelings. And on other occasions, endocepts are accompanied by strong but unverbalized emotions.

Some individuals refer to endoceptual experiences as being very diffuse and abstract. We may indeed call them abstract, but only provided we are aware that the word "abstract" has two almost opposite meanings, and that in reference to the endocept we mean only one. In one use of the word, "abstract" refers to what is separated or differentiated from many objects or situations. For instance, I see many red objects, and I abstract from them the quality "redness." Redness is an abstraction, a Platonic universal, of whose existence I become aware after I have seen many particular red things. This is a very high mental mechanism in the hierarchy of cognitive processes; it is not an endocept. The word "abstract," when used in speaking of amorphous cognition, refers instead to something that has not yet found embodiment in any particular object, something whose existence is suspected but not proved, something whose characteristics cannot be clearly described with words.

Creativity often consists of changing the latter, primitive form of abstraction into the former type. For instance, a diffuse, vague, abstract feeling may eventually find its embodiment in a poem, play, and so forth. On the other hand, the opposite process may occur, as in music and abstract painting. Particulars, specific objects, as experienced in daily life, are lost; what remains is an endoceptually-derived composition, auditory or visual, that is totally removed or very distant from any natural sound or shape.

A person not only cannot compare his endoceptual knowledge with that of other people, he cannot even compare it with his own other types of psychological processes. No test of validity, no dialogue with oneself, is possible at an endoceptual level. In special cases some endocepts retain or acquire some awareness, but the awareness is dim and has a global or diffuse quality that does not lead to fine discrimination. All these characteristics sharply limit our knowledge and understanding of this mental function.

People vary in relation to their endocepts: some persons deny that they occur; others easily admit this. As in the case of imagery, we find that, with the exception of what happens in periods of creativity, people devoted to scientific work or to the application of logical thinking focus on concepts and are hardly aware of endocepts. People with "artistic temperaments" are more given to endoceptual experiences. At times we encounter intelligent and well-educated people, inclined to logical, deductive thinking, who nevertheless seem "two-dimensional," lacking in depth. These people stick to fact; they are indeed *factual*. Their intelligence shows a mechanical quality that has a pragmatic value in some aspects of life but that is disagreeable in many others. Since early life these people have been trained (or because of

(56)

the nature of their anxiety have trained themselves) to experience only concepts and to suppress and repress endocepts totally. Actually their conceptual life, too, is limited, as we shall see later, because it is not enriched by endoceptual sources. Endoceptual processes, although indefinite, tend to accrue. They are self-enlarging and self-enriching; they add new dimensions, even when higher levels of mentation are present. To a large degree, however, endocepts, as we shall see, are repressed or suppressed in every adult human being.

Patients under psychoanalytic treatment often mention some endoceptual experiences that occurred in early childhood, from ages two to four, before the acquisition of adult language. The following is an example:

> In my grandparents' home there was an extra living room, "the red living room," reserved for big occasions—parties, celebrations, and so on. We children were not allowed to go into that room. Occasionally I would sneak into it, to give a quick look, afraid of being caught there. The room had an aura of solemnity. It was like a sacred, holy room. There were the pictures of our great grandparents—pictures to revere, like those of saints. The furniture was covered in gold and had red upholstery. There was a red carpet on the floor. The wallpaper was red. The whole room had an aspect of austerity.

This is a memory from the third to the fourth year of life, when the patient probably had not yet acquired the concepts or the words "aura," "sacred," and "solemnity." How is one to interpret this memory? The first interpretation, of course, is that it is a retrospective falsification: the patient attributes to his memory concepts and words that were not available at the time of the original experience. But if such concepts were not available, how was the memory of the experience carried through the years? Obviously the memory consisted of more than a conservation of visual images; the patient also remembered an affective state and a certain behavior or at least a motor disposition: a desire to sneak into the room, and an inhibition of actions because of the fear of being caught. In other words, in addition to visual images, endocepts were retained. During the analytic session the original endocepts were translated into words congruous with the patient's present understanding of the memory. He said that he had experienced the feeling of "sanctity, austerity," and so forth. "Sanctity" means the state of being sacred or free of impurity. The child knew that the room was only for big occasions, and he experienced that situation as an inner state, a state that he later attributed to the room and called "sanctity." He also described the room as having an aura of austerity, although it was richly furnished, the walls were red, and the furniture was beautiful. According to Webster, *austere* means "severe, stern, harsh, rigorous, morally strict; abstinent, ascetic, lacking ornament." Apparently the fact that the room was restricted to adults made the child experience something which he later referred to as its "austerity." These inner experiences that could not be verbalized presumably were endocepts. We do not deny here the possibility that the childhood experience of the "red living room" provoked related reveries and daydreams later in childhood. On the contrary, this was certainly the case. But before the original experiences were transformed into reveries, fantasies, and daydreams, they were endocepts.

Endoceptual phenomena also occur in dreams. In several types of dreams, verbal expressions and other kinds of communications are present and may even play an important role. We are all aware, however, of another large group of dreams into which language does not enter. The dreamer experiences the dream in an intense way, yet with no words. When he is asked by the psychoanalyst to give details or to describe what he felt in the dream, the patient uses many words of which he was not conscious while he was dreaming. For instance, he may say that he was experiencing a mixture of joy, fear, surprise, and anxiety such as he has never felt in waking life. He may describe the dream as having an atmosphere of mysteriousness and yet of hope that everything would turn out all right. Thus the patient who is now awake tries to translate into words the experience of the dream or, rather, the memory of the experience. But while he was dreaming, he was not thinking in words; his experiences were endocepts. As a matter of fact, the dreamer often states that his account of the dream is at best approximate. It is difficult and always inaccurate to translate endocepts into concepts.

In reference to dreams, we must mention at this point that a reverse mechanism is much more frequent: unconscious ideas that were kept in the psyche in mute and invisible ways become transformed, in dreams, into a representational form—namely, visual or predominantly visual images. It is one of the major tasks of psychoanalysis to study how and why unconscious cognition manifests itself in dream life. If an endocept follows the direct and shorter route to dreams, it seems to have, at least for the time being, less chance of following the tortuous road to creativity.

There are other situations in which the person is aware of the discrepancy between the endocepts and his verbal explanations. He says, "I know what I mean and feel, but I can't explain." In certain situations with intense emotional content, such as being in the company of a loved person or in a state of intense artistic appreciation, endocepts play an important role. Often people who try to verbalize these experiences say that "words spoil the feeling." Some lovers, in the midst of their loving experiences, like to say and hear endearing words and other expressions exalting the beauty of the shared feelings. Other lovers, however, do not want any verbal accompaniment to their physical or spiritual pleasure. Again the feeling is that words "spoil everything. Beauty must remain unsaid." In some poetry, the words that are used suggest much more that remains unsaid and is experienced endoceptually. Another feeling is that words "put a strait jacket on" or "deaden" the experience. The experience tends to be an otherwise "unending" phenomenon to which "words put an end." Indeed, endoceptual experiences, as clusters of nonverbalized associations, tend to expand in indefinite ways. All this is reminiscent of artistic or aesthetic experience, as we shall see in Chapter 8.

Psychoanalytic studies not only of dreams but also of life situations reveal that endocepts do not derive necessarily from childhood experiences or from preverbal cognitive components alone. They may also derive from high-level concepts that have regressed to an immature status. Again and again we discover that the psyche functions in two ways, from a low level to a high and from a high level to a low. To give clinical examples: Psychoanalytic practice affords opportunities to study men who always become romantically involved with women whom they want to "rescue," "save," "rehabilitate." It takes long analytic work to bring about insight into these patients' behavior. In each of these cases the patient claims that he is in love with these women, and he may indeed be really sincere and have experienced love; but he does not realize that an unconscious motivation directed him to search for and love a woman whom he believes would benefit from or actually be "saved" or "redeemed" by his love. These attitudes are generally connected with childhood fantasies of saving one's mother from the "terrible" father or from other circumstances. Inasmuch as this motivation remains unconscious and nonverbal, it is endoceptual until it is transformed into conscious actions. Although it might have originated in early childhood, it also consists of elements that must have been conceptual. For instance, the patient in some way must have appraised the situation—that is, that the woman was in a position from which she needed to be "rescued" or on account of which she had to be "helped." These evaluations could have been made only by concepts, by logical thinking, which became unconscious and remained so until treatment restored them to consciousness. Incidentally, the reported example has many variants. At times the analysand unconsciously selects a woman who will mother him; or a woman who will subjugate him; or, on the contrary, a woman whom he will always be able to put in a state of submission.

What we want to stress is not that our motivation can be unconscious—a well-known fact since the time of Freud's great work—but that a major part of our cognitive activity exists in a nonrepresentational, endoceptual state. To repeat, this nonrepresentational activity has two sources: (1) the primitive, which may derive from a repressed image or from other mental work that is not yet differentiated; and (2) the content of higher levels of mentation, which escapes from consciousness or well-organized behavior, or searches for different media and returns to primitive levels for other reasons. (In this second group we must add cognition that is not attended to.) Often it is difficult to distinguish the two sources. In many cases, especially those leading to creativity, the two sources converge and weld.

The Outcome of Endoceptual Experience and Its Relation to Creativity

ENDOCEPTS may remain endocepts. However, they tend to undergo various transformations: (1) into communicable symbols, that is, into various preconceptual and conceptual forms (the symbols are generally words but may also be drawings, numbers, sounds, and so forth); (2) into actions; (3) into more definite feelings; (4) into images; and (5) into dreams, fantasies, daydreams, reveries, and so forth. In all these cases they may constitute the springboard to creativity.

Empathy is a type of communication based to a large extent on a primitive understanding of one another's endocepts. Some people who operate at a predominantly endoceptual level experience strong empathy for others. Some situations involve typically empathic–endoceptual communications: for instance, the relation between a mother and her baby. Of course, the baby can also communicate in other ways, with his motions and his smile. While it is pleasant and appealing to the basic emotions, empathic communication is unreliable; but it is one of the ways by which one can overcome the difficulty inherent in expressing endocepts.

Some individuals who operate endoceptually—including some creative people—appear to be uninterested in relating to people, or indeed in any real-life situation. Such an individual is not really indifferent, but he seems unmotivated because he has a temporary difficulty in experiencing images or in attaching himself to external objects or inner representations. Before he acts, or starts his creative work, he goes through the stage of the endocept. When he is finally ready to perform, he changes radically. In some creative moments an endocept is immediately converted into a verbalized statement or into some kind of visual art (for instance, a painting or sculpture). We then speak of "intuition" or "inspiration." Intuition appears as a kind of knowledge that is revealed without preparation, or as an immediate method of obtaining knowledge. Actually there is no such thing as an immediate acquisition of knowledge, in the sense of not having had any preparation, information, or elaboration of any sort. The reason why the new knowing or understanding does not seem to have been prepared is that the subject was unaware of the antecedent stages. It is my belief that at least part of the "intuitional" knowledge on which Spinoza and Bergson have placed so much importance is endoceptual knowledge that is promptly translated into a conceptual form. (We must remember, however, that "intuition" and "inspiration" do not spring from endoceptual sources only; between the endocept and the "inspiration" that originates the creative product there may be many intermediary stages.)

In the previous section of this chapter we saw how some patterns of life pre-existed in many individuals in endoceptual forms before they became actualized in external behavior. We also saw how a large part of our conceptual life tends to fuse with an endoceptual counterpart, or to transmute into endoceptual forms. We must go on to say that the same things hold true for much cognitive activity that eventually unfolds into the creative process. We should not believe that the conceptual life that returns to an endoceptual level does so only because a person needs to escape from anxiety, neurosis, or danger; the creative person also needs to escape from established or reputedly valid systems of order. That is, he has sensed a defect, or incompleteness, in the usual order of concepts, or has some other motive for dissatisfaction with it. Thus he brings part of his mental activity back to the stage of amorphous cognition, to that great melting pot where suspense and indeterminacy reign, where simultaneity fuses with sequential time and unsuspected transmutations occur.

Creative (and to a lesser extent, noncreative) people have stated that they were aware of the existence of some fundamental endoceptual organizations even before they had any idea what these organizations were about. Some people have spoken of unconscious premises—even in sociology Gouldner (1970) described the unconscious domain assumptions that regulate life; and in my psychoanalytic work I have found that not only specific patterns of living but also unconscious philosophies of life regulate the existence of people who are not aware (at least verbally) of this phenomenon. These philosophies often consist of cardinal concepts, such as those defining the relation between parents and children; authority and individuality; duty and self-assertion; desire and reason; love and hate; irresistible fury and the search for peace; love for men, for women, for God; or the longing for the infinite, for power, for immanence or transcendence, for mathematical certainty or mystical mystery, for the secret harmony of the universe, or for the aesthetic aspect of life. These philosophies often remain in a nebulous, ineffable form unless or until the individual matures to the point of reaching insight into them, spontaneously or with treatment.

In creative persons this endoceptual cognition is an indeterminate activity in search of a form, a groping for some definite structure. When a suitable form is found, this activity is transformed into a creative work, at a more or less advanced stage of production. In some cases the creative work tends to retain an endoceptual character. Wanting to express artistically what is ineffable brings about a paradoxical situation. Thus in certain fields creative work is rarely expressed in quasi-endoceptual forms. Perhaps the forms of creativity closest to the endoceptual stage of cognition are music and abstract visual art. Music does not have to imitate sounds, like the murmuring of a brook or the chirping of birds. Similarly, colors, lines, and form in abstract art may not reproduce anything existing in nature, but they may be an attempt to give expression to the inner endoceptual life of the artist.

Some artists and musicians return to an endoceptual level when they want to liberate themselves or escape from forms, or from whatever is external and has impinged upon the individuality of their inner life. Their individuality thus seems to be expressed in pure forms, in something that cannot be shared. But of course the artist must have a secret wish that his inner experience be shared; otherwise he would not present his work to others. He does present it, and sooner or later people understand it. Thus the attempt has been victorious and the ineffability of the endocept has been defeated. An addition has been made to what can be communicated between human beings and appreciated by them.

The quasi-musical character of what emerges from endoceptual cognition has been discovered by creative minds who, although not musicians, have referred to music in describing their creative work. Thus Nietzsche speaks of music in reference to the endoceptual stage of his work *Zarathustra* (1927). In the Italian village of Recoaro, near Vicenza, on a day in February 1883, he experienced what he likened to "a warning sign in the form of an abrupt and profoundly decisive change . . . in music." On that day he discovered that "the phoenix bird of music hovered over us, decked in more beautiful and brilliant plumage than it had ever before exhibited." In the same essay from which these quotations are taken, he wrote that "Zarathustra may be classified as music." What he referred to was nothing but the endoceptual stage, which transmutes and returns to new life—like the phoenix. At that stage Nietzsche actually did not yet have any idea of what Zarathustra was about; the incubation period lasted several months. We shall consider subsequent stages of the creation of Zarathustra in other chapters. But just as in the case of Nietzsche, the majority of creative persons proceed beyond the endoceptual stage so that their work shows no resemblance to endoceptual cognition.

At times a fragment of the endocept may appear in dream form, or take the easier-to-grasp form of an image, in order to be promptly expressed creatively. At other times there may be a state of suspension and indecision, after which a dim, clouded idea emerges. Playwrights or fiction writers often mentally see a vision that erupts from nowhere. The play is later built around this crucial scene; but the whole play is a concrete, external, verbal representation of the endocepts that accrued to and surrounded this image in a state of unconsciousness. At other times the scene that produces the nucleus of the endocept, or mobilizes the endocept, comes from life. Thus Henry James (1908) beautifully described the germ of his work *The Spoils of Poynton* as a "single small seed, a seed as minute and windblown" as a "casual hint . . . dropped unwitting" by his neighbor. His lady friend spoke of a lady she knew who was in litigation with her son over the ownership of furniture left by the dead father of the young man. This was the germ. James "saw clumsy Life again at her stupid work." This was the germ, or the image, over which many endocepts accrued over a long period of incubation. As James beautifully put it, the seed had to be "transplanted to richer soil."

The playwright Peter Shaffer, author of the remarkable play *Equus*, wrote that two years before the play was completed he was driving with a friend through a bleak countryside. They passed a stable. Suddenly the friend was reminded of a crime that he had heard about recently at a dinner party in London. The friend knew only one horrible detail of the crime, and the account of it given to Shaffer lasted less than a minute. The friend, who gave no name, no place, and no time of the crime, died a few months later, and Shaffer could not find out more about the dreadful event. But that brief mention was the germ of the play-to-be. Obviously the mention of the dreadful event was the external stimulus that permitted a great deal of material already existing within Shaffer, at an endoceptual level, to become reorganized and eventually to assume an artistic form. Thus, there was nothing in the account given by the friend of the relation between the boy who committed the crime and the boy's parents.

I do not want to convey the erroneous idea that the endocept is like an embryo, containing in potentiality everything that will become fully developed in the child. Not at all. The endocept of a future creative work contains no more than possibilities of what can be actualized in different ways, according to what the author may choose to do.

The content of the endocept is unintended, unplanned. What is unintended would seem to be due to chance; and it may very well be so considered from the point of view of the consciously creative person and of all of us who will witness and assess his work later on. However, it seems plausible that in fact the content of the endocept is determined by a combination of past experiences, present unconscious feelings, and neuronal or intrapsychic organizations. (However, the possibility that a degree of actual indeterminacy may also enter into the picture will be discussed in Chapter 17.)

Once the creative urge goes beyond the endocept it will continue to grow on its own, sometimes in unintended directions, bringing up unsuspected connections, and resorting to other mental processes that we shall study later. However, we must not believe that in subsequent stages the creative person will remain passive, a mere spectator of what goes on in his brain or in the medium before him. He must make conscious choices; he must accept and reject and bring to bear additional concepts of which he is fully conscious, to judge whether they do or do not fit with what is emerging. Even in the cases when the conscious concepts do not fit, he must choose whether or not to accept his tentative work in spite of seeming incongruities.

In some creative people the endoceptual stage is not retraceable in any form even of dim awareness; it seems to be absent. Other people pass from the stage of imagery to that of logical thought. For instance, Einstein, in a letter to Jacques Hadamard, stated that words as used in written or spoken language did not play any role in his thought mechanisms. His cognitive process started with images of a visual and muscular type. Words later intervened, but purely in auditory forms. Einstein wrote that he could voluntarily reproduce and combine these images. He did use imagery to a large extent and was able to go directly from imagery to the most abstract thought. However, it is noteworthy that he could voluntarily reproduce and combine the images. Thus they did not have the characteristics common to the images of ordinary people. They constituted a language, one which presumably had already undergone or was undergoing the thought processes that follow the image or the repression of the image in the average person.

I believe that in at least part of the stage some authors call incubation, there is a great deal of endoceptual activity. Preparation—the earliest stage characterized by a conscious effort to master several subjects and connect them with the direct lessons from life—is followed by that period of incubation, during which even what used to be clear becomes less distinct and confused with something else, and is at times regressed to the endoceptual stage. Eventually something new reemerges, perhaps a clear-cut new product, or an abstract concept that could not easily have been anticipated from the known material. When this occurs, the endoceptual stage has been outgrown.

Chapter 5

Primitive Cognition

Introductory Remarks

WHEN the creative process proceeds to a stage of differentiation that permits the use of words and ideas, two types of thinking assume prominent roles. As mentioned, one type can be included in the broad category that Freud called the primary process, and the other in the category of the secondary process. In this chapter we shall study the first type, a way of thinking that in different terminologies has been designated as primitive, immature, obsolete, archaic, dedifferentiated, abnormal, defective, first-signalling, concrete, mythic, and so forth.

I must stress from the beginning that, in terms of the creative process, this type of immature thought is used not just in art and myths but in every creative process, including science. Jung was correct in pointing out that the great work of art is not the exclusive result of the life experiences of the artist, or of the usual cognitive ways, but that primordial processes are also involved. In my opinion, however, these primordial processes do not derive from the Jungian collective unconscious and have little to do with *content*, no matter to what field of creativity they are applied. They deal with *processes* and *forms*.

These primordial mechanisms appear also in dreams and in mental illness, especially schizophrenia. They also emerge spontaneously in the healthy human being when he is overcome by emotions, prejudice, or anger, or when he is indoctrinated by ancient mores or habits of his culture. This is one of the major reasons why psychiatry and psychoanalysis can make important contributions to the study of creativity. By no means ought the reader to infer here that we should associate creativity with mental illness and, in particular, with schizophrenia or schizophrenic tendencies. Such associations are only in rare exceptions. What is meant here is that some thought processes that occur frequently in the mentally ill also become available to the creative person. But whereas the mentally ill person directs his life in accordance with these unusual ways of thinking, the creative person uses them in his creative work, either in the original form in which they occur or, more frequently, after having modified them in accordance with normal ways of thinking.

These primitive thought processes have been studied intensely. They are of various kinds and present numerous characteristics.* In this chapter I shall illustrate only those of which knowledge is needed for the understanding of the creative process. (The specific modalities by which they become parts of the creative product will be discussed in Part Three.) The fact that these primitive mechanisms are used in creativity by no means indicates that any creative work is invalid or suspected of being invalid from the point of view of logic and rationality. It simply indicates that creativity can draw from all the cognitive methods that are available to the human being, even those that are usually discarded.

Because of its archaic nature I have called the main form of immature thinking "paleologic" (from the Greek *paleo*, meaning old). This form of thinking is not illogical or alogical, but it does follow a logic different from that used by the human being who is awake and healthy. The normal human being as a rule uses the ordinary logic of the secondary process—the kind of thinking that in Western civilization is generally called Aristotelian logic, because Aristotle was the first to formulate its laws. But whereas imagery and endocept (the cognitive forms already studied) constitute a considerable amount of the mental life of every human being, paleologic thinking is present in normal or average people only to a minimal degree. In order to study it in almost pure form, we have to observe it in schizophrenic patients.

---

* The reader with a special interest in them is referred to other writings of mine (Arieti 1948, 1950b, 1955, 1956a, 1961, 1962, 1965, 1967, 1968, 1974). They represent one of the major areas of my research.

That is what we shall do in this chapter; schizophrenia will be like a laboratory where we can observe paleologic thinking almost as if under experimental conditions. We shall take into consideration only three of its characteristics, as discussed below.

Identification Based upon Similarity

THE SERIOUSLY ILL schizophrenic, especially at the beginning of his illness, lives in a state of utter confusion. The world makes no sense; and this lack of understanding is often experienced as panic, anguish, turmoil, a desperate search for some meaning. At times some understanding does arrive, as a sudden illumination. Such an insight seems deceptive to us, but the patient feels extremely lucid and has at least a transitory feeling of exuberance, similar to that of a person who has made an important discovery. Now he "puts two and two together;" now he is able to "solve the big jigsaw puzzle." Things that had appeared strange, confused, and peculiar now acquire sense, and the patient succeeds in recapturing some understanding and in giving some organization to his fragmented universe. But he does so by resorting to a faulty way of thinking, the thinking of the primary process.

As a first example: a red-haired young woman in a schizophrenic post-partum psychosis developed an infection in one of her fingers. The finger's terminal phalanx was swollen and red. She told the therapist a few times, "This finger is me." Pointing to its final phalanx she said, "This is my red and rotten head." She did not mean that her finger in some way represented her; she saw it either as a duplicate of herself or, in a way that is incomprehensible to the normal person, literally herself. Another patient believed that the two men she loved in her life were actually the same person, although one lived in Mexico City and the other in New York because both of them played the guitar and both of them loved her. And another patient thought that she was the Virgin Mary. Asked why she thought so, she replied, "I am a virgin. The Virgin Mary was a virgin; I am the Virgin Mary." Obviously the patient had a great need to identify with the Virgin Mary, who was her ideal of feminine perfection and to whom she felt very close. At the same time she needed to deny her own feelings of unworthiness and inadequacy.

From these examples it can be seen that patients who adopt paleologic thinking succeed in identifying with objects that otherwise can hardly be used in this way. A patient identifies with her finger; she becomes her finger. A second lover of another patient is transformed into the first lover. Another patient becomes the Virgin Mary. *The patient succeeds in finding at least one element in common between two or more things or persons, and that is enough to warrant the identification.* Obviously this type of thinking is absurd from the point of view of a normal person. The patient focuses on the common element and ignores the rest, which does not count. What should be only a similarity becomes the basis for making a total identification. The patient who identifies in this way often indulges in what I have called an orgy of identifications (Arieti 1974). He may see similarities and identifications everywhere. His capacity to do so probably derives not only from the fact that he is particularly receptive to similarities, but also to the fact that he is more capable than the average person of dividing or fragmenting wholes so that the single parts can stand out by themselves. As we shall see later, the same mechanisms occur in the creative process.

The first psychiatrist who studied this anomaly of schizophrenic thinking and attempted a logical formulation was. Eilhard Von Domarus (1944). He enunciated a principle which, in slightly different form, reads, "Whereas in normal (or secondary process) thinking identity is based only upon the basis of identical subjects, in paleologic (or primary process) thinking identity is accepted upon the basis of identical predicates." The predicate that leads to the identification is called the identifying link or identifying predicate. Obviously this type of thinking does not follow Aristotelian logic, in which only like subjects are identified. The subjects are fixed; therefore, only a limited number of deductions are possible. For instance, an apple is identified with another apple (both recognized as belonging to the class "apple"). But in paleologic thinking the apple might be identified with the breast of the person's mother, because the breast and the apple have a similar shape. The breast and the apple become equivalent. In other words, in paleologic thinking, A also becomes non-A—that is, B—provided A and B have a predicate (or element) in common. It is the predicate that leads to identification and equivalence.

Here is the important point. Since the predicates of a subject are numerous, it is not possible to *predict* what type of identification will take place. Who could have predicted that a patient would have focused on her red hair and identified with her finger? Who could have predicted that a patient would have ignored all her other attributes, concentrated on being a virgin, and thereby think she is the Virgin Mary? Of course, if a psychiatrist knows a patient well—knows the conflicts, motivation, and desires of the patient—he can understand, in *retrospect*, why a given identification took place. The choice of the predicate that led to the identification will then be seen to have been psychodynamically determined by conscious or unconscious needs and desires. The important thing for our discussion of creativity is that this type of thinking diverges from ordinary paths and opens up a larger number of possibilities. One can find hundreds of predicates in a single subject. Thus the possibilities for originality are enormous.

We are reminded again of that openness that prevailed in imagery. One image led to another because they had a common element, or because their corresponding original perceptions had occurred at the same time or in the same place. But whereas in imagery, different images are only associated by some such common or associative link, in paleologic thinking different subjects are actually identified as one. What should be only an associative link that reminds us of A when we see B becomes an identifying link; A and B become the same. (In Part Three we shall be examining in detail the tremendous role played in creativity by paleologic thinking based on Von Domarus's principle.)

Incidentally, this type of thinking occurs not only in schizophrenia; it is at the root of every type of Freudian symbolism. For instance, as Freud demonstrated, in a dream a stick or a pen may stand for a penis. Here the common predicate that leads to the equivalence is the elongated shape. Similarly, a box may stand for a vagina, because both box and vagina are able to contain something in their cavity. A gorilla may symbolize a dreamer's father, because the dreamer attributes a common quality to the father and the gorilla: a wild, bestial attitude toward life. Thus, in dreams, images are not just associated; in the process of symbolization they replace each other. The replacement is not casual. It is based on a cognitive relation: the kind of equivalence described by Von Domarus's principle. In this matter Freud, who did so much to reveal the symbolic activity of the primary process, did not clearly elucidate its cognitive foundation. He was interested almost exclusively in its motivational aspect and in the accompanying desire to deny the motivation.

Paleologic thinking also occurs in children, between the ages of one and a half and three and a half. There is a great variation from child to child, however, in the amount of paleologic thinking. Some children around two years of age will quite often say "Daddy" if shown a picture of a man and will say "Mommy" if shown a picture of a woman, no matter whom the pictures represent. Any man has features like daddy and becomes daddy; any woman has features like mommy and becomes mommy. Somebody could object to this interpretation by saying that the child makes a mistake because not all the facts are available to him yet, namely, the facts that would enable him to arrive at the concept "father" or "mother." This is true; but it is equally true that even with his limited knowledge the child tries to give meaning to what he sees, and in doing so he follows Von Domarus's principle. Even errors are not casual but follow a certain organization.

The cognitive organization of this primitive thinking can be interpreted in ways that are apparently different from those so far presented. In reality, all that differs is the terminology. We may, for instance, state that primary-process thinking organizes classes or categories that differ from those of secondary-process thinking, or of Aristotelian logic. In secondary-process thinking and in standard Aristotelian logic, a class is a collection of objects to which a concept applies. For instance, Washington, Lincoln, Roosevelt, Jefferson, and so on form a class to which the concept "President of the United States" applies. But in paleologic or primary-process thinking, a class is a collection of objects that have a predicate or a part in common (as, in the above instance, the state of being virgin), and that become identical or equivalent by virtue of this common part or predicate. The formulation of a primary-process class is often an unconscious mechanism. Whereas the members of a secondary-process class are recognized as being similar (and it is in fact on their similarity that their classification is based), the members of a primary-process class are freely interchanged: for instance, the above patient becomes the Virgin Mary.

A world paleologically-interpreted corresponds in many ways to the mythical world of ancient people and to many cultural repertories of various aboriginal societies today. The eighteenth-century philosopher Vico (1725) and the twentieth-century philosopher Cassirer (1955, Volumes 1 and 2) have given us the best descriptions of the mythical world of the ancients, which was characterized by metamorphoses, the equivalence of part and whole, and the interchangeability of objects. And anthropologists have at various times reported that in some aboriginal cultures, paleologic thinking prevails over other types, and that in general it is much more common in primitive societies than in Western cultures. Paleologic thinking seems to be the foundation of many societal or collective manifestations—rituals, magic, customs, and beliefs—that are transmitted from generation to generation and accepted without questions being raised as to their validity (Arieti 1956a).

These findings mean only that some cultures tend to retain paleologic characteristics in some forms of collective behavior. In Western societies, too, collective manifestations of paleologic thinking can be found, even in our times. Paleologic processes also occur in several habits of Western men and are much better recognized as such by non-Westerners. To give a down-to-earth example, in some Western restaurants waiters are reluctant to serve white wine with meat and red wine with fish. They feel that red wine "belongs" with meat, white wine with fish. Actually there is no biochemical or other scientific reason for these associations. Meat can taste well with white wine, too, and fish with red wine. The association is purely due to a paleologic type of identification with the redness of the meat and the whiteness of the fish. We are so indoctrinated by this custom that we, too, may feel ill at ease or may develop a stomachache if we drink red wine with fish, in spite of there being no biochemical counterindication.

In a not too distant past, the Western world was permeated by paleologic thinking in every manifestation of life. In his admirably scholarly book, *The Waning of the Middle Ages* (1924), Huizinga clearly described the prevalence of this type of thinking in medieval Europe, although, of course, he did not use the terminology followed here. Differences in the amount of paleologic thinking in various eras and various countries are due to different historical, not biological, factors. Even Lévy-Bruhl, one of the most misunderstood authors in this field, referred only to collective manifestations and not to the individual native when he was describing "the prelogical functions" of aboriginal societies (1910, 1922). We could advance the hypothetical possibility that some species of hominids that preceded our species *Homo Sapiens*, such as *Homo Erectus*, were obligated by the limitations of their nervous systems to think paleologically when they bypassed immediate learning, based on perceptions and conditioned reflexes, and adventured into symbolic thinking. These prehuman species thus presumably had two choices. The first was to use psychological functions in a framework that included stimulus–response, or perception–action, together with learning based on associations, trial and error, and imitation. This meant living a nonsymbolic psychological life, limited to the immediately given, the concrete: a very realistic life. The second choice was to adventure into paleologic thinking. We could advance the hypothesis that these prehuman species did use paleologic thinking to a large extent, and that it is on account of this use that they eventually perished. In fact, a life regulated according to paleologic thinking is not sufficiently equipped to deal with reality. We must conclude that although the appearance of symbolic thinking was an evolutionary improvement that led to what is specifically human in man, it was a dangerous improvement, because at first it emerged in the form of paleologic thinking.

No man living today belongs to a species other than *sapiens*, and every existing man who is in a state of health and more than three years old is at least potentially capable of thinking in accordance with the Aristotelian laws of thought. Thus two important points must be kept in mind: (1) The frequency of paleologic thinking in some human societies neither implies, nor calls into question, the moral and spiritual equality of man; (2) the fact that paleologic thinking may have first appeared in some prehuman species and may have remained the preponderant form of thinking for those extinct species of hominids does not mean that people who think or act paleologically are in other respects like such hominids. Moreover, from a biological point of view, a structure or function that appeared earlier in phylogeny may be of the same evolutionary relevance as one that appeared later. The chronological order is not necessarily an order of value (Arieti 1950b, 1956a). Moreover, as we have already stated and shall illustrate in Part Three, paleologic thinking plays an important role in the creative process.

An additional point is in order. In some aboriginal societies, the individual (who is potentially capable of Aristotelian thinking) adopts the primitive or paleological mode of cognition in order to conform to and comply with his society, tribe, or culture. In contrast, the person who uses paleologic thinking in the midst of his creativity does so—at least at a certain stage—in order to separate himself from the commonplace thinking of his community.

At the paleologic level the individual starts to think categorically, or in terms of classes; but these categories are not reliable. Being primary, they are at the mercy of emotions or random associations and do not respect the Aristotelian law of identity: that A is always A, never B. In fact, according to Von Domarus's principle, B may be A, provided B has a quality of A. The Aristotelian law of contradiction states that A cannot both be and not be A at the same time and place. If a person follows Von Domarus's principle, he may see A as A and at the same time as B (that is, non-A) if he concentrates on a quality that A and B have in common. The Aristotelian law of the excluded middle states that A must either be or not be A; there cannot be an intermediate state. In its tendency to condense several subjects, paleologic thinking neglects this law. Things are often seen as a composite of A and B. For instance, in schizophrenic drawings one often sees a human figure that is half man and half woman (see Chapter 9).

Primary categories do not lead to platonic universals but to transmutability. Benedetto Croce (1947) wrote that Vico, in his conclusions about the studies of the thoughts, myths, and poetry of ancient people, had changed Plato's universals into "phantasmic universals" (corresponding approximately to the contents of our primary classes). Incredible as it may seem, the creative person tries to find the phantasmic universal and transform it into a platonic universal. But it is premature at this point to pursue this subject, which will be better understood in Part Three.

At this point we must justify why we have spent so much time describing paleologic thinking. The reason is that it occurs as a transient stage in the large majority of creative processes. At first the creative person tends to identify disparate subjects, not just in the fields of literature and art, but also in science. This tendency is arrested whenever he succeeds in controlling himself, and only similes or metaphors result. As we shall see in greater detail in Chapter 8, similes and metaphors are formed through the sharing of predicates. Nietzsche, whom we have quoted in reference to the endoceptual stage of *Zarathustra*, also described a subsequent stage of his work in which paleologic thinking and its derivatives prevailed (1927). He wrote: "If I may recall a phrase of Zarathustra's, it actually seems as if the things themselves came to one, and offered themselves as similes.

(Here do all things come caressingly to thy discourse and flatter thee, for they would fain ride upon thy back. On every simile thou ridest here to every truth. Here fly open before thee all the speech and word shrines of existence, here all existence would become speech, here all Becoming would learn of thee how to speak.)" At times during this stage of creativity, the urge to identify is so rapid that metaphors or similes overlap to the point that it is not possible to accept all of them logically, although aesthetically they may still be valuable.

Consider the following passage from Pirandello's *The Late Mattia Pascal.* "Are we or are we not on an invisible little spinning top, whipped by a beam of the sun, over a mad little grain of sand, that spins and spins without knowing why, without ever reaching a destination, almost as if it got pleasure in spinning in that way, making us feel now rather warm, now rather cold, making us die?" (Translation mine.) In the turbulent moments of his life Mattia Pascal, the hero of the book, personifies the author himself. He undergoes an irresistible urge to find similes and metaphors. Obviously the spinning top is the planet earth; but so is the little grain of sand, which has gone mad. The earth spins without ever reaching a destination; so is our life, which is compelled to be spent on this planet, also compelled to share the planet's crazy ways. The beautiful concatenation of metaphors is logically untenable; but Pirandello has grasped a particular stage of the creative process and has remained with it to give a generalized image of our aimless journey.

The appearance—in the development of the species and the individual and during the creative process—of a type of thinking that follows Von Domarus's principle and not Aristotelian logic, explains how the power of imagination is extended. As great as that power was at the cognitive level of the image, it becomes much greater with paleologic thinking. As a rule paleologic thinking uses language, of course, thus taking advantage of the symbolic essence of language. (The reader is referred again to my book *The Intrapsychic Self.*) However, it is not only because of the symbolic use of language that paleologic thinking increases the power of imagination. Imagination is also increased in dreams in which language plays a secondary role but paleologic cognition prevails. The increase is the result of identification through similarity, which permits the stream of thought to proceed in a large number of directions.

One of the major mechanisms of the process of creativity consists of the disciplining of this imagination. If imagination were left to the free realm of paleologic thinking, it would lead to formulations that the logical mind could not accept. It is for this reason that imagination was often condemned by rationalistic thinkers. Saisselin (1970) reminds us that in the classic period of French civilization (the seventeenth and eighteenth centuries), "imagination was associated with instinct, blindness, caprice, rebelliousness, vagueness, divagation, wandering, folly . . . and [the] source of madness." He quotes Pascal, who defined imagination as a deceiving part of man, a mistress of error and falsity, and yet a shrew, because while it would be the infallible proof of lying, it would also be the infallible proof of the truth. Apparently what Pascal meant is that one does not know when imagination portrays the truth and when it portrays the false, since it gives the same character to both. According to Saisselin, Pascal, unlike Descartes, thought that the imagination was more powerful than the will. "Imagination is indeed too strong for the reason, and men, in fact, aspire to be deceived because this is easier than facing the truth of our own human condition" (Saisselin 1970, p. 103). And Condillac "thought of imagination as a power capable of combining ideas and creating fictions. It is still a double-edged tool: a help to knowledge and understanding, but also a danger because of its power to deceive." In our imagination, according to Condillac (1746, Chapter 18, 75), there is nothing that cannot assume a new form. Through imagination, the qualities of many subjects can be carried by a single one. Such powers of combination may be creative, but they are also dangerous if not controlled. Condillac further distinguished two phases of imagination, voluntary and involuntary; the difference between involuntary imagination and folly, he said, is only one of degree.

The reader is referred to Saissellin's book for a more accurate account of how imagination was considered in this classic period of French history. In spite of some exceptions such as that of Bossuet in the seventeenth century, imagination was feared as a source of error; but in the eighteenth century the fear diminished. Several authors, and especially Marmontel (1787), assigned it a major role in creativity.

The Altered Relation Between Word and Meaning

AN ALTERED RELATION between the word and its meaning is the second characteristic of paleologic thought. At this point it may be worthwhile to review what is generally meant by the terms "connotation," "denotation," "verbalization," and related expressions. As an example let us take the word *table*. The connotation of table is the meaning, or definition, of the word: namely, an article of furniture with a plane top that is supported by legs. The denotation of it is the signified object: the table as a physical object. That is, the word can mean either "table" in general, or any specific table. But there is another aspect to take into consideration: the word "table" as a sound or phoneme, irrespective of its meaning. Thus the term can be considered from three points of view: of the connotation, when we refer to its meaning; of the denotation, when we refer to the meant object; of the verbalization, when we refer to the word table, independently of the symbolic value given to it. Table can be an idea (the concept or definition of table), a thing (the table in its physical entity); a sound (the word table).

A healthy person in a wakened state is mainly concerned with the connotation and denotation of a verbal symbol. He wants to be understood when he uses the word "table." He wants his listeners to understand that he refers to the general concept or to a particular table. At the same time, he is also able to shift his attention from one to another of the three aspects of the word. In the person who thinks paleologically, on the other hand, the relation between connotation, denotation, and verbalization is altered. He undergoes two important modifications in the use of language: the first consists in his different way of connoting; the second in his focusing on the denotation and verbalization and giving less importance to the connotation.

Let us consider the first modification. The individual seems unable to connote in the usual way. Words do not stand for classes any longer, but for specific embodiments of a class. For instance, the individual may not use the word "dog" in relation to all members of the canine genus but only in reference to a specific dog, as in "the dog sitting in that corner."

The Psychological Components of Creativity

As already mentioned, schizophrenic patients offer almost typical laboratory reproductions of such impairments or changes in connotation. One schizophrenic woman who was asked to explain what the word "table" means replied, "What kind of tables? A wooden table, a porcelain table, a surgical table, or a table you want to have a meal on?" She was unable to define the word table in general, and she attempted to simplify the problem by inquiring whether she had to define various subgroups of tables. Other patients, when asked to express a general or categorical definition, have replied by giving specific embodiments of the definition. A patient who was asked to define "chair" said, "I sit on a chair now. I am not a carpenter." Another patient answered the same question with "A throne." He restricted the meaning to that particular type of chair because of a connection with his delusions: he believed that he was an angel and was sitting on a throne in heaven. At times these definitions reveal not only a constriction to one instance, or a few specific instances, of the class, but also the prominence of bizarre associations. Correct but uncommon definitions are also given. For instance, a patient who was asked to define the word "bird" replied, "A feathered fowl." Another patient answered, "A winged creature."

These examples are instances of what J. P. Guilford would call divergent thinking. In these cases the mode of thinking is due to illness; nevertheless the examples illustrate the phenomenon of divergence. In other cases the individual stresses the denotations of words, but his effort is frustrated; and, since his concepts of things have changed through divergent thinking, he misidentifies. That is, when he loses the socially accepted connotations of words, he tends to think paleologically. He misidentifies himself or other people or things, but the misidentification is due to the abandonment of Aristotelian classes and the adoption of primary classes. For instance, when one regressed schizophrenic, a beautiful woman, was asked who she was, she replied, "A flower." She thought she was a flower because she had a predicate in common with a flower: being beautiful. This manner of denoting is similar to that of children who have not yet acquired the ability to conceptualize properly and who therefore follow a paleologic method of cognition.

I have already mentioned that children approximately two years old respond with the word "Mommy" if shown a picture of a woman, no matter whom the picture represents. A girl three years nine months old saw two nuns walking together and told her mother,

"Look at the twins." The characteristics of being dressed alike, which twins often have, led to this identification of the nuns. These examples indicate that children may denote in a way that seems wrong to us. In fact it *is* wrong, but not haphazard. Between the right and wrong denotation and designation there is a paleologic relation, often in forms of metaphor or of divergent thinking. I hope that a personal note on this matter will not appear inappropriate to the reader. My parents were fond of telling me about a little episode that occurred when I was three years old. My father was in the army during the First World War, and my mother and I went to visit him. He was stationed near Padua, a city quite distant from Pisa, where we lived. We met in a hotel, and it was there that for the first time in my life I saw an elevator. I looked at it, going up and down in the shaft, which was protruding and visible, and I exclaimed with astonishment, "Look, look! A streetcar that flies!"* To me the elevator was a streetcar that had acquired the power to go up and down like a bird.

When the connotation of a word decreases, the emphasis shifts to its verbalization. Language acquires functions and values that are connected primarily with the formal structures of words instead of their meanings. At times a word evokes images and acquires a quasiperceptual quality and an emotional tone that is stronger than usual. The word becomes almost an icon of the thing it represents, and at other times it actually becomes equivalent to its denotation. Schizophrenics, as well as some aboriginal people, often confuse the word for the thing that it symbolizes. But the most important characteristic resides in the fact that for the schizophrenic, and perhaps for any kind of primitive mind, the phonetic sound of the word often acquires a value that is connected with the sound itself. Moreover, in some cases this particular value of the sound is added to the usual meaning of the word. I am not referring here to onomatopoetic words (words that imitate natural sounds, such as tinkle, buzz, or chickadee). Onomatopoetic words are relatively few, whereas the capacity to give a special value to their phonetic property applies potentially to all words. The examples that follow will explain this characteristic.

Schizophrenic patients often associate words according not to their meanings but to their phonetic quality, a process called "clang association." (This series of words was written by a regressed patient: "Chuck, luck, luck, buck. True, two. Frame! Name! Same! Same!

* In the original, "Guarda, guarda, un tram che vola!"

Same! Same!") Or at times the patient loses the proper denotation of a word and gives it another one that is suggested by the verbalization. For instance, a patient who was shown a pen and was asked to name the object replied, "A prison." The word "pen" elicited in him the idea of the vernacular for *pen*itentiary.

Often the verbalization is exploited to fit certain preoccupations of the patient. For instance, every time one patient heard the words "home" and "fair," he thought they were the slang words for homosexuals, "homo" and "fairy." He was very concerned with the problem of his own sexual identification and believed that people were subtly referring to his alleged homosexuality.

In many patients, two or more objects or concepts are paleologically identified because they can be represented by the same word. The verbal symbol thus becomes the identifying predicate. This leads to what seem to be plays on words. For instance, a patient who was asked to define the word "life" started to define *Life* magazine. An Italian patient whose name was Stella thought she was a fallen star. Another patient thought she was black, like the night; her name was Laila, which means night in Hebrew.

The abnormal thoughts of schizophrenics may give the appearance of being witticisms and thereby induce listeners to laugh. Such thoughts generally result from paleologic identifications or from the extreme literalness that follows the reduction of connotative power and emphasis on verbalization. One patient, reported by Max Levin, believed that she was in a ward "for colored people" (1936). Asked why she thought so, she replied, "Because I was brought here by Miss Brown" (the nurse who had accompanied her to the hospital). A patient reported by Bychowski, asked where her husband was, replied "On our wedding picture" (1943). Another patient believed he was Jesus Christ. When he was asked why he believed so, he said, "I have drunk too much Carnation milk, and I have been reincarnated."

At times patients use series of words that are associated because of their similar verbalization, but that retain a general, vague sense or atmospheric meaning. For instance, the patient mentioned above who defined a chair as a throne and who believed he was an angel wrote the following "prayer," which he used to recite every morning:

Sweetness, angel, gentle, mild, mellow, gladness, glory, grandeur, splendor, bubbling, babbling, gurgling, handy, candy, dandy, honor, honey, sugar, frosting, guide, guiding, enormous, pure, magnificent, enchanted, blooming plumes.

Some of the words were selected because of their meaning, applicable to God and to angels. Most of them, however, were selected because of their assonance, or because in addition to a specific meaning they had an assonance. The last case is represented by the "blooming plumes" that winged angels have. It is evident that the particular meaning that this prayer acquired for the patient derived from the formal structures of its verbal components. In comparison to the usual prayers, this one manifested a semantic loss or evasion for an ordinary reader but acquired a particular one for the patient, on account of its many series of assonances. Let us take another look at them:

> an*gel*, *gen*tle
> *m*ild, *m*ellow
> *gl*adness, *glo*ry, *g*randeur.

Grandeur loses the *l*, which is reacquired in the sequence

> *g*ran*d*eur, sp*l*end*o*r.

Splendor reacquires the *l*, loses the *g*, but acquires *nd* as in grandeur:

> bu*bbl*ing, ba*bbl*ing, gu*rgl*ing.

Gurgling loses the *b* but reacquires the *g*, to which the ear was already used on account of the previous sequence: gladness, glory, grandeur.

> h*andy*, c*andy*, d*andy*
> *h*on or, *h*oney

Honey also repeats the *h* of handy. Honey and sugar are also associated semantically, probably under the influence of candy.

> *gui*de, *guid*ing

In summary, when we consider verbal expressions of primitive thinking in contrast to those of mature thinking, we are impressed by what to us seems a loss or diminution of the socially established semantic value (*semantic alteration*), and by the increased value of the verbalization (*formal pregnancy*). What seems to us a semantic loss does so only in reference to our socially accepted connotation. Both the semantic alteration and the formal pregnancy confer the characteristic of divergence.

Concretization and Perceptualization of the Concept

PALEOLOGIC, primitive, or primary-process thinking tends to give concrete representations to what often occurs in abstract forms in normal ways of thinking. This is a common occurrence in schizophrenics. When the psychosis starts, concepts become specific and concrete. The indefinite feelings become finite, the imperceptible becomes perceptible, the vague menace is transformed into a specific threat. It is no longer the whole horrible world that is against the patient; rather "they" in particular are against him. He no longer has the feeling of being under the judgmental attitude of the world; no longer does he have a mild sense of suspiciousness. Rather, the sense of suspiciousness becomes the particular conviction that "they" follow him. The conceptual and abstract are reduced to the concrete, the specific. "They" become more definitely recognized as F.B.I. agents, neighbors, or other specific persecutors. At other times the judgmental attitude or scrutiny of the world is perceived as a big eye that watches vigilantly and with condemnation, or as myriads of eyes that watch, condemn, or ridicule the patient.

One patient had the delusion that his wife put poison in his food. He actually used to feel that his wife "poisoned" his life. The abstract poisoning then became a concrete and specific one; a concept was transformed into an object, a chemical poison. In this respect the schizophrenic is similar to the dreamer, the fine artist, and the poet, all of whom transform abstract concepts into perceptual images (see Chapters 8 and 9). It is not implied that in the fine artist, the dreamer, or even the schizophrenic, the capacity to think abstractly is lost. The schizophrenic uses the concrete representation as a psychological defense, the creative person, as we shall see later, uses it for aesthetic or scientific purposes. It is beyond our purpose either to assert the superiority of the concrete over the abstract (in accordance with Hegel's philosophy) or the superiority of the abstract over the concrete, as some psychiatric studies imply. Certainly in psychiatric conditions the non-use of abstract thinking is an indication of illness, but it is not so in some fields of creativity, as we shall see in Part Three. As a matter of fact, the poet–psychiatrist André Breton put it very well when he said that the (creative) image lends to the abstract the mask of the concrete (Balakian 1970).

Chapter 6
Conceptual Cognition

IT IS BEYOND the purpose of this chapter to illustrate the numerous aspects of secondary-process cognition. We would have to review the laws of logic and study such processes as causality, deduction, induction, and the formation of concepts. We shall instead examine only three aspects of the secondary process that are particularly important in the process of creativity: (1) facing the primary process, (2) the use of the concept, and (3) the concept as an ideal. We shall conclude the chapter by examining the possibility of a unifying theory of cognition.

Facing the Primary Process

IN THE PREVIOUS CHAPTER we saw how inexhaustible the primary process is as a source of content. Whatever had been invisible, ineffable, and unpredictable may come to the surface in various ways: abruptly, unexpectedly, as a rush, a flash; during meditation, contemplation, daydreaming, relaxation, intoxication, dreams; or through an evoking effort, association, external stimulation, kinesthetic sensation, and so forth. It is up to the mental faculties that are parts of the secondary process to accept or reject this material.

The individual must affirm or deny whatever presents itself to consciousness. Freud (1925) wrote that there is no "no" or "negation" in the primary process. According to him, any absence there is translated, not into a "no" or an admission of absence, but into a fantasy or hallucination of the absent object. The baby, according to Freud, does not say to himself, "Mother is *not* here to nurse me;" instead he replaces her with a fantasy of her in the act of nursing him.

Frankly, I don't believe that the baby in the first eight to nine months of life is able to have such fantasies (Arieti 1961, 1967, 1974), but I shall not deal with this topic here. It is true, however, that primary-process cognition does not enable one to deny. After approximately the first ten months of life, the child gradually becomes able to accept or reject fantasies. His emerging secondary process enables him to test the reality of his inner life. He may understand, even without using words, that a fantasy of his mother is not really his mother. For a certain period of time, however, he may have difficulty in making such a differentiation. When he is able to deny the validity of a fantasy, he may do so by hindering its reappearance by willful suppression or by repression—that is, by unconsciously removing it from consciousness and, possibly, by preserving it in unconscious or endoceptual form.

In the creative process the mechanism is more complicated. The secondary process does not have merely the function of accepting or rejecting. First, the imagination is accepted per se, for its own sake. Second, it must be decided whether to accept it or not as an ingredient of the creative process. A painter, for instance, may have an image of a tree that is completely unlike any tree existing in nature. To begin with, he accepts the image as an inspiration. In other words, he does not dismiss it immediately from his mind as being unrealistic, something one could even fear because of its bizarreness and unreality. Instead he indulges in the fantasy, he plays with it. Then he may start to think how he can use that imagination in producing a work of art—in other words, how he can actually externalize (make an external object of) what is now an internal object; and, most important, what changes he has to perform on the original imagination in order to make of it a creative product (that is, new and desirable). In Part Three of this book we shall discuss how an artist actualizes such changes.

Suppose that which presents itself to the secondary process is in the form of diffuse, disorganized, or primitive cognition. An already existing concept or cluster of concepts of the secondary process may then adopt and use this primitive material. The primitive material that has been accepted may be used to add strength to the content of the secondary process or to give it aesthetic or ornamental characteristics, unsuspected possibilities of expansions, detours toward unusual directions, or associations that are impossible to premeditate.

As we have seen in Chapter 5, the primary process tends to divide or fragment unities and to focus on the fragment (or parts, or predicates) that these unities have in common. As a matter of fact, there is a strong tendency to identify unities that have common salient characteristics. The secondary process may accept these identifications for aesthetic reasons (see Chapters 7 and 8) or may reject them and direct the thinking process to the recognition of similarities or to the formation of a class whose members have that similarity (or some same characteristic) in common. Every time a class is formed—as, for instance, the classes of birds, reptiles, mammals, and so on—a new concept emerges that is added to the already extremely vast conceptual repertory of secondary-process cognition.

At times either the primary or secondary processes present the possibility to consciousness that there is a union or association between fact A and fact C, while at the same time no explanation can be found for such an association. Therefore a search starts for B, the link that would explain the union of A and C. The primary process may offer a series of hypothetical B's, but only one of them is the real, or desired, B; and it must ultimately be chosen by the secondary process. For instance, the English anatomist Harvey understood that venous blood (A) becomes arterial blood (C) after having passed through the lungs, but he could not know how that was possible—what the intermediary medium (B) could be that permitted such passage. He postulated a B like the capillaries, but could not prove their existence. When capillaries were discovered by Malpighi in the lungs of a frog, the existence of this B could no longer be denied; but for 33 years, from the time Harvey published his famous book (1628) to the time Malpighi made his discovery (1661), Harvey's explanation of the circulation of the blood remained unproved.

Just as the secondary process of every human being must resort to a so-called reality test, the secondary process of the creative person must resort to a so-called *creability* test, when a decision must be made whether or not to accept the newly-conceived material. If the material passes this test, it will be used for the completion of the creative product.

The Use of the Concept

CONCEPT FORMATION is a very important function of the secondary process; secondary-process thinking generally consists of the formation and use of concepts and their relations.* A concept is a general notion that embraces all the attributes common to the individual members making up a given class: for instance, the concept "table" is a notion that applies to all tables. Concepts have been studied much more by philosophers than by psychologists, with the most important ideas originating in the classic period of Greek philosophy. Aristotle (*Metaphysics*, XIII, 4) and Xenophon (*Mem*, IV, 6) attribute to Socrates the discovery of the definition of the universal—that is, the concept of the concept. For Plato, ideas, or concepts, become the ultimate reality. Thomas Aquinas believed that a knowledge of some thing is perfect to the extent to which there is a correspondence between the concept (or "essence") and the thing that is conceived (*Summa Contra Gentiles*, IV, 11).

In this book, however, the concept is considered only from a psychological point of view—that is, as a cognitive form, not as the ultimate description of reality. We can, in fact, differentiate several conceptual substages of unequal value. At times the demarcation between a preconceptual form and a conceptual form is not sharp: a concept that appears definitive at a certain stage of development is considered a preconcept later. If it is found that a concept does not include all the essential attributes of what it wants to define, it may be even recognized as a paleologic or faulty construct. What follows is a brief summary of the ways in which concepts are formed in natural rather than experimental conditions.

In the first method of concept formation, the individual collects data and recognizes a lasting association between these data. The association is often based on contiguity in space or time. All the attributes that have to be taken together form a concept. For example, the attributes of (1) being a figure that is (2) formed by three straight lines that (3) intersect by twos in three points and (4) form angles, make up the concept of "triangle."

* For many aspects of this vast and complicated subject the reader is referred to Hull (1920), Bruner et al. (1956), Vygotsky (1962), Werner (1957a, 1957b), Werner and Kaplan (1963), and Piaget (1929, 1952). In this section we shall review only a few topics particularly relevant to the creative process.

The Psychological Components of Creativity

People continuously form new concepts from old ones by discovering or adding new attributes. For instance, if we add an additional attribute to the attributes of a triangle, that of one of the lines being perpendicular to another, we have the concept of a right triangle. Similarly, we may discover that some of the objects included in the class of "animal" have a vertebral column. We thus form the class of "vertebrate," which is a subclass of the "animal" class. We may discover that some vertebrates nourish their young with milk, and we form the "mammal" class, and so on.

New concepts originate unexpectedly when apparently unrelated objects can be put into a new class by the discovery of a previously hidden attribute or predicate. For instance, the brain and the skin of an organism may seem to be different, unrelated parts until we discover that they have the common quality of originating from the ectoderm. Then we have the concept and class of "ectodermic tissue."

New concepts may be developed by a second method that is the opposite of the one just described: the subject realizes that certain attributes can be omitted, and that a different class containing only some essential attributes can be formed. For instance, primitive people have names for different types of birds, but not one which just designates "bird" as a class. More civilized people, however, have dropped all the attributes characteristic only of certain groups of birds in order to form this concept of "bird," which refers to all birds because it includes only the following attributes: that its members are (1) vertebrate, (2) warm-blooded, and (3) covered by feathers.

The production of a new concept is a difficult process. Concepts represent acquisitions of the human race attained through the ages, collectively adopted and transmitted from generation to generation. Social life imparts a large number of concepts. Formal education in schools expands our conceptual life even more. A concept is a parsimonious device, inasmuch as it permits man to respond in similar ways to various facts that are included in the concept in question. For instance, if we know that Socrates can be included in the concept "man," we also know that he will eventually die, although we may not see him do so. If a physician knows that a patient has diabetes, he also knows that the patient's glucose rate is likely to increase in his blood. In addition, the doctor can deduce that there is something wrong with the pancreas of the patient, and he may prescribe insulin.

In summary, the concept (1) offers us a more or less complete description; (2) permits us to organize, since the different attributes or parts appear logically interconnected; and (3) permits us to predict, because we can deduce what is going to happen to any member of the class covered by the concept. With time, concepts become more and more organized into higher mental constructs.

From what we have said so far, somebody might conclude that concepts are rigid, ironclad formulations from which it is difficult to escape, or whose exact meaning cannot be doubted. This is absolutely not the case. As a matter of fact, there is another, almost paradoxical, quality of the concept that makes it a particularly suitable medium for the creative process: its open-endedness. Certainly there are some concepts that seem clear, conclusive, definitive. But let us examine three such apparently clear concepts: "mother," "fire," and "Friday." The first means a woman who gives birth to a child; but generally the word carries an extra load of meaning. The mother is the woman who loves the child, nurses the child, and takes care of it. These attributes do not enter into the definition because they are not necessary ingredients; but they are generally included, and if I think of a mother, I think of them. For instance, I may even find out that the mother of a friend of mine is not his biological mother but only an adoptive mother. Although she does not possess the necessary ingredients of the definition "mother," she is still his mother for me—and, what is more important, for my friend, too. "Fire" means the act of burning, but the exclamation "Fire!" screamed in a crowded theater, acquires an additional meaning: "It is dangerous to be here; try to get out as soon as possible!" "Friday" generally means the day between Thursday and Saturday, but adventitious meanings are added, as the following example will show. Once my wife had a nice housekeeper who, on a Friday night before leaving for the weekend, told her, "Mrs. Arieti, this is Friday." That meant not only that it was Friday, but that it was the day she was supposed to be paid—a tactful reminder of what my wife had forgotten to do.

Poets, playwrights, and (to a lesser extent) fiction writers in general know very well that words often acquire great meaning not because of what they say, but because of what they don't say. What is not said, and at times is hidden, may then appear with powerful effect. The discovery of this unsaid, extra-semantic load marks one of the creative qualities of writers. In many cases—as in the above examples—the extra-meaning is dictated by interpersonal or social situations, habits, transformations of words into signals, and so forth. At times the word acquires a special meaning because of the uniqueness of the situation. Open-endedness is a characteristic of science, when new, implicit properties are discovered in some concept or thing that supposedly had been completely known. Let us take another example: the concept "three." As a number, it seems to have a clear and well-defined meaning: it is the successor of 2 and the predecessor of 4. But is not so simple a matter as this. I am not referring to the fact that numbers may acquire a superstitious, obsessive–compulsive, ritualistic meaning, although of course they do also carry that extra load. I am referring to the fact that mathematical and geometrical creativity aims at discovering those properties that are grounded in the original definition, but not apparent there. For instance, the definition of 3 does not tell us—although it implies the fact—that 3 is a divisor of 2,151. Or in the earlier definition of a triangle, it is not apparent that the sum of the angles of any triangle is 180 degrees.

The open-endedness of concepts is of particular value to the creative person. But the other qualities are extremely valuable to everybody. The ability to form and use concepts enables man to learn, use, and integrate thoughts. Culture, with its systems of knowledge, languages, beliefs, and values, bestows upon each person a patrimony of concepts that becomes part of the individual himself.

In the process of development, concepts eventually become the larger part of man's inner reality. In thinking, feeling, and even in acting, man becomes more concerned with concepts than with things. We must indeed consider every concept a product of creativity that, from the time of its origin in some period of the history of mankind, has increased the cognitive repertory of any individual who became familiar with it. The individual was enabled to interpret those parts of the world differently to which a given concept applied. Moreover, sooner or later, concepts themselves either become parts of new creative products or else a means of inquiry and evaluation by which primary-process material or other concepts are accepted or rejected.

Some existentialist writers assign great value to the particular and to the concrete and seem to belittle the abstract and conceptual. Psychologists of the self-realization and self-actualization group also minimize the role of concepts. Thus according to Maslow (1948, 1954), concepts "rubricize" our experiences—that is, put them into categories; they prevent us from making contact with the unique qualities of things. More properly, Maslow should disparage a common *wrong* use of concepts, rather than the faculty of conceptualizing itself. For instance, if I see a policeman coming toward me and I don't know why, I might imagine that he is going to arrest me or fine me for a traffic violation. Thus I respond not to him but to the class "policeman;" his uniform automatically makes me put him into the class of policemen and remove him from other classes. Actually he might be a neighbor of mine who wants to ask my opinion about a neighborhood matter. However, although I am wrong in reacting to the category of policeman rather than to him as an individual, this does not mean that I would be better off if I did not know what a policeman is and what his function should be. Possibly I made a wrong use of the concept "policeman" because of some problems of mine; say, because of my neurotic need to see people in authority or in uniform as threatening, or because of some obsessive habits of thinking of mine that are rigidly applied.

Thus the person who uses concepts is not necessarily like a museum curator who labels specimens and puts them in the proper departments to lie there forever. Again, as an example let us consider a physician who, in making his diagnosis, "rubricizes" a patient as a diabetic. The knowledge that the patient is a diabetic will help the physician to select the treatment; but the fact that he already knows many things about the patient because he has put him in the diabetic category also enables the physician to concentrate on the special, non-diabetic features of the patient's illness—that is, on what is dissimilar between him and other diabetics, and thus on what requires special care.

One of the characteristics of every normal human being and, to a more intense degree, of the creative person, is the ability to have a mental representation of the individual (the particular) and of the category (the general) at the same time. As we shall see in Part Three, the creative person in different ways succeeds in accentuating one of these two aspects without losing the other.

Some anticonceptual philosophers have enjoyed great popularity in the anti-intellectual movements of the nineteenth and twentieth centuries. One of them is Bergson, who advocated abandoning conceptual thinking and reverting to intuitional forms of knowledge that correspond to our endoceptual and paleologic levels of cognition (1912). But while it is true that these forms of cognition, if properly used, are useful in some areas, they do not exclude the conceptual. As a matter of fact, in order to evaluate the validity of our thinking, we often must determine whether or not our apparent concepts are actually disguised primitive preconcepts. It seems that many anti-intellectual writers are afraid that conceptual man may become a prisoner of reality and a captive of society's conventions. We have seen that this does happen to some people. It is not because they use concepts, however, but because of the wrong use they make of them. Concepts enable man to deal more adequately with some aspects of life, but they also transcend the empirical world. They help us see what lies beyond facts. Science, for instance, does not stop at empirical data but is concerned with the implications of these data.

Let us briefly review the ways in which concepts go beyond their immediate and apparent content. First of all, not only the highly creative person but in fact any normal human being uses and associates concepts in innumerable complex ways, in clusters and inventive derivations that are eventually transmitted to others in interpersonal relations. By using concepts in multiple and often unpredictable ways, man reacquires that originality that he temporarily lost when he assimilated concepts conveyed by others. Second, and equally important, is the fact that clusters of concepts become the repositories of intangible feelings and values. Every concept has an emotional counterpart, and concepts are necessary for high emotions as well. Faith, loyalty, patriotism, aesthetic rapture, love in the agapic or fullest sense, and anything usually referred to as pertaining to the spirit—none of these would be possible without concepts. Such conceptual emotions are more differentiated but no less intense, necessarily, than primitive emotions. I have mentioned only positive emotions, but others that we may regard as negative are also common; for instance, feelings of vanity, pride, hate, and so on.

In the course of reaching adulthood, a person's emotional and conceptual processes become more and more intimately interconnected. It is impossible to separate the two; they form a circular process. The emotional accompaniment of a cognitive process becomes the propelling drive not only toward action but also toward further cognition. Only emotions can stimulate man to overcome the hardship of some cognitive processes and lead him to complicated symbolic, interpersonal, and abstract operations. On the other hand, only cognitive processes can indefinitely extend the realm of emotions. If man studies complex mathematical problems, looks at the stars, or thinks of things that occurred in the remote past or are expected to occur in the distant future, he not only attempts to mirror events regardless of space and time, he not only searches for a coherent relationship among the apparently unrelated parts of the universe; in addition, his inner self and life are altered as a result of these endeavors. Every cognitive process becomes an inner experience. The spectator of all times and all existences is "touched inside" by all the times and by all the existences. Whatever is conceived touches the core of man. Whereas in the very primitive types of thinking there was a sense of timelessness and spacelessness, eventually groping toward the distinct experience of time and space, in conceptual thinking there may be a groping with the infinity of time and space—an attempt always frustrated, always renewed.

Concepts as Ideals

CONCEPTS are not only about "what is," but also about the possible. Concepts about the possible make us envision worlds better than the one we live in and motivate us to get closer to such ideals through our own efforts. It is through concepts that man's greatest psychological growth occurs. Concepts of concepts and symbols of symbols can continually be formed by creative people and used by the community of men.

Conceptual ability thus enables man to create or to be exposed to an unending organization of cognitive elements, an unending variety of emotions, and the possibility of moral choice (Arieti 1967, 1972). The endlessness of man can now be recognized. Man is a self-conscious finitude that challenges itself (1) by transcending facts and building an ever-increasing number of concepts and symbols; (2) by increasing the number of facts (or material things) when he gives a physical form to his new concepts and symbols; and (3) by transcending the determinism of nature by bringing about the new, the unpredictable, the possibility of moral choice and of systems of values. Because of his challenging and transcending ways, man is a product not simply of nature but also of his own making; he belongs not only to the physical cosmos but to history. He is no longer satisfied with the possible and the conditional; he now conceives the impossible, the unconditional, the infinitely bigger and the infinitely smaller, the absolute, the whole, nothingness, the real, the unreal, and the unceasing expansion of reality. These functions, present in every human being, are particularly pronounced in the creative person.

In considering the ideal, there are several possibilities that conceptual organization has to evaluate: (1) the ideal may be realizable; (2) the ideal may be realizable only as an artistic product, especially with the help of other cognitive processes; (3) the ideal cannot be realized but nevertheless remains an incentive toward progress, motivates creativity, and is thus constructive; and (4) the impossible becomes actualized in dreams, superstitions, prejudices, decadent modes of living, and psychopathologic conditions, which are within the scope of psychiatry. In these cases, too, however, the impossible can occasionally be rescued by other mental processes and transformed into myth, religion, social customs, and so forth. The ideal thus actually becomes one of the strongest motivational forces in creativity.

The Three Modes of Operation, and Unifying Hypotheses

IN another of my books (Chapter 11 of *The Intrapsychic Self*) I once posited the problem of whether we can pursue a unifying theory of cognition. Can general principles be found that apply to such different levels as perception, recognition, memory, learning, simple ideation, language, conceptual thinking, arithmetic, and so forth? In the expository framework of the present book I can offer only a brief summary of what I discussed in that earlier volume. I believed that an inquiry such as the one I proposed was worth being pursued. Following the method of Von Bertalanffy (1955), I sought a general theory that would apply to all levels of cognition. I concluded that three basic modes of operation are followed at such different levels of cognition as sensory organization and perception, learning, memory, association of ideas, class formation, and so forth.

The first mode is the mode of *contiguity*. Sense data experienced together, if they produced a single effect in the organism by the fact of being contiguous, tend to be reexperienced together. In learning, too—according to such theorists as Thorndike, Guthrie, and Pavlov—contiguity in time or space is the most important factor. In Pavlovian conditioning, for instance, the dog learns to salivate in response to the ringing of a bell. During the learning period, the bell is rung shortly before or at the same time as the food is seen. There is thus a temporal contiguity between the food (the unconditioned stimulus) and the ringing of the bell (the conditioned stimulus). Also, the first law of association of ideas is the law of contiguity, which states that when two mental processes have been active simultaneously or in immediate succession, the recurrence of one of them tends to elicit the recurrence of the other. For instance, if I think of my grandmother, I may also

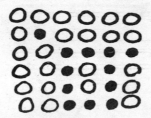

Figure 6-1

think of the home where she lived when I visited her in my childhood. In induction, the mode of contiguity makes us associate *A* (for instance, a sunset) and *B* (night) because we have observed that *B* has followed *A* many times. In arithmetical thinking, the mode of contiguity predominates in the concept of the number 1. In fact, by the contiguity of parts, a unity is formed that is separated from the rest of the world and will later be recognized as one.

The second mode is the mode of *similarity*. Figure 6-1, for example, contains dots of different shapes and colors, and the dots that are alike tend to form a separate group or to be perceived together. Similar or identical elements become associated. What psychologists call "transfer" may be viewed as an application of the mode of similarity at the level of learning. An acquired response is extended to similar situations. For instance, if I have learned to avoid certain insects—

say, wasps—I may extend my avoidance reaction to similar insects such as bees. The second law of the association of ideas, the law of similarity, is another expression of the second mode of operation. It states that if two mental representations resemble each other—that is, if they have one or more characteristics in common—the occurrence of one of them tends to elicit the occurrence of the other. For instance, I visualize the Eiffel Tower and I may think of the Empire State Building. I think of Beethoven and I may start to think of Brahms and Mozart. In induction, the mode of similarities makes us associate all A's with all B's. In arithmetic, the mode of similarity predominates, for example, in the number 2. In fact, unless objects are at the same time seen as distinct and similar, no concept of 2 or of any subsequent plurality is possible.

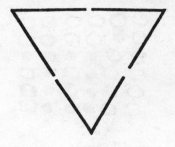

Figure 6-2

The third mode of operation is *pars pro toto*. The perception of a part has an effect upon the organism that is equivalent to that of the perception of the whole. If we look at Figure 6-2, for example, we see a triangle, in spite of the fact that there are three gaps in the picture—which technically, therefore, is not a triangle. The followers of the Gestalt school call this way of perceiving "closure." According to them the closure, as a principle of organization, permits the perception of the whole; the small gaps are filled in. They consider this tendency to close a gap the expression of a fundamental principle of brain functioning. Tension is supposed to be built up on both sides of the gap until it is closed, in the same way that an electric current will jump a small gap in the electric circuit. But let us look once more at Figure 6-2. The gaps are never closed. We continue to see the interruptions; but in spite of the gaps we perceive a triangle. The triangle of Figure 6-2 is not a whole triangle, but nevertheless stands for a whole triangle. The Gestaltists actually speak of closure because they have taken into special consideration certain experimentally-devised stimuli with small gaps. Actually very little in nature is perceived totally. More often than it may seem at first, we perceive parts that stand for wholes. For instance, I see only a crescent in the sky, yet I know I see the moon; I see only a side of the table, yet I know I see the table: I see only the facade of a cathedral, yet I know I see the cathedral. This phenomenon is not the simple Gestalt phenomenon of closure but a much more general faculty of the psyche, which permits a part to stand for the whole. Except for a few optical illusions purposely arranged, the whole is not experienced at a sensory level. The whole is instead filled in by our responses (inasmuch as we react as to wholes), or by our memories (of parts being generally associated with their respective wholes), or by symbolic processes. The third mode of operation, *pars pro toto,* operates in all types of learning, even the simplest. For instance, in conditioning, when the dog secretes gastric juice in response to the buzzing of the bell, the buzzing of the bell can be seen as a part that stands for a whole (the buzzing of the bell, plus sight of food).

At a neurophysiological level, too, the whole process of learning can be seen as an application of the third mode of operation. The activation of certain neuronal elements, through a stimulus, brings about the arousal of the whole neuronal circuit, or of patterns involved in that given learning situation (Bugelski 1956). The phenomena that Gestalt psychologists attribute to insight may be viewed as based on the concomitant application of the second and third modes of operation. The "insight" is due to the fact that the organism responds as it would to a previous situation because of the presence of identical elements in the old and new situations. The identical elements stand for the total situations.

I wish to propose the law of *pars pro toto* at the level of the association of ideas, as well, instead of the law of contrast mentioned in some old books of psychology. The few ideas that are associated by contiguity and similarity stand for a whole constellation of ideas and tend to bring about the whole constellation. For instance, the idea of my grandmother may stand for my whole childhood and bring about many memories of my childhood. This is also, in a certain way, thinking by cue. A small cue may arouse a complex pattern. A fragment of a situation may evoke the total situation; a member of a series may evoke the whole series. In induction the mode of *pars pro toto* causes us to extend to the whole series of *A*'s and *B*'s that which we have observed in a segment of that series. In arithmetic, the properties of 1 and 2, and of 1 and 2 together, and so forth, are applied by *pars pro toto* to the whole series of positive integers.

Indeed deterministic causality, considered by Kant as one of the basic a priori concepts, is actually induction: an association is made between *B* and *A* (the mode of contiguity); but the human being interprets the phenomenon as *A* being the cause of *B*. The association is extended to all the sequences $A \rightarrow B$. Inasmuch as this law will be applied to all similar data in the cosmos, it will follow the *pars pro toto* mode.

At this point we can perhaps conclude that the three basic modes of operation determine and structure our knowledge of the world.

The first mode determines *what is and what is not*. What is, is a unity.

The second mode *identifies* by discovering similarity, or identity, and permitting class formation.

The third mode *infers* the not-given from the given.

These three modes could really be considered three basic pre-experiential categories. We can, however, represent the general process of cognition with a different formulation and say that it is based on two fundamental characteristics: progressive abstraction and progressive symbolization. The first mode abstracts unities and groups from the manifold of the universe. The second mode abstracts the similarity between different unities. The third mode abstracts (that is, infers) the not-given from the given; and abstraction leads to symbolization (Arieti 1967).

PART THREE

The Creative

Product

Chapter 7
Creativity in Wit

Introductory Remarks

IT MAY SEEM SURPRISING that a study of the creative product should give first consideration to wit and the comic, which in the estimation of several people do not reach the height of other forms of creativity. Yet even for researchers as different in background and methodology as Freud and the essayist Arthur Koestler, the study of wit has been the path to a better understanding of the creative process. I, too, was prompted by some expressions of psychiatric patients to formulate some notions on wit and the comic, which I reported in an early paper (Arieti 1950a) and later extended to other forms of creativity (Arieti 1964, 1966, 1967).

Wit has aroused deep interest in a considerable number of men of letters, philosophers, psychologists, psychiatrists, and neurologists. Often it has been studied as a form of art; at times as a psychological process; occasionally as a special expression of the spirituality of man.

In his important monograph *Wit and Its Relation to the Unconscious* (1916), Freud succinctly reviewed the theories that had been previously advanced and showed their inadequacies. For instance, Fischer (quoted by Freud) had defined wit as "the ability to combine many ideas with surprising quickness," but had not shown how these ideas are combined. Freud wrote that many authors had found the basis of wit in "sense in nonsense" or in the "succession of confusion and clearness." Freud recognized the vagueness of these formulations, which in no way explained how there could be "sense in nonsense" or "clearness in confusion." *

Freud's Contribution to the Psychology of Wit

OF ALL THE DISCUSSIONS of the phenomenon of wit, the one by Freud seems to me the most illuminating and the most far-reaching in its implications. Because of their significance and because I take issue with some of them, I shall review Freud's major findings and concepts in detail.

* An important contribution that Freud overlooked is that of the neurologist Hughlings Jackson, who in 1887 delivered an address on "The Psychology of Joking" at the opening of the Medical Society of London (reprinted in 1932). Long before Freud, Jackson compared puns with dreams, but he did not pursue this comparison as far as Freud eventually did. Jackson found that in both puns and dreams "two very dissimilar mental states pretending to be stereoscopic" are in reality "diplopic"; that is, they show two different overlapping visions instead of one.

In a monograph published in 1924, J. C. Gregory added a rich bibliography to that of Freud. After reviewing the literature on the subject, Gregory came up with the interesting remark that "Wit is a quick, vivid illumination of a truth." E. Froeschels, a philosopher as well as a physician, dealt with the problem, from a philosophical point of view (1948). He considered witticisms the means by which unexpressed philosophical truths that actually have been known to us from the time of our birth become "ripe for expression."

In a philosophical journal, K. Lash (1948) wrote that "It is out of the incongruous relationship between a given norm and an object (let 'object' include person, action, situation, and concept) that laughter springs. . . . The comic object pretends to fit the norm, or in humorous naiveté believes that it does, but the intellect perceives the discrepancy between the posited and the actual, finds it incongruous, and laughs."

Koestler applied to the problem of wit his concept of "bisociation," by which he also tried to explain all forms of creativity (1949, 1964). Bisociation is "any mental occurrence simultaneously associated with two habitually incompatible contexts." This does not seem too useful a contribution. Although it is true—as we shall see later in detail—that many jokes contain a mechanism that can be called bisociation, this mechanism per se is not sufficient or specific enough to create a joke. In schizophrenic productions or drawings, for instance, we often find the simultaneous association of two or more habitually incompatible contexts. And yet it is only in rare cases that these productions are witty or comical. Incidentally, Kraepelin, quoted by Freud, advanced a similar theory. According to Kraepelin, wit is "the voluntary combination or linking of two ideas which in some ways are contrasted with each other" (Freud 1916).

In a recent book edited by Goldstein and McGhee (1972), Patricia Keith-Spiegel presents a scholarly review of theories of humor from the first half of the nineteenth century to the 1960's. This review is very informative and accurate, although some significant contributions have been

Freud opened a direct path to the understanding of the creative process with his book on the pathology of wit (1916). He became interested in the problem of wit when he noticed that certain dreams resembled jokes, especially when they were interpreted. He did not disregard this apparently accidental similarity. He studied it more and more and discovered numerous analogies between witticisms and dreams. He analyzed the various techniques of wit and found them similar to those he had described in his book on dreams as parts of the dream-work (1901). He noticed, for instance, that the formation of mixed words, or condensation, occurs in witticisms as well as in dreams. For example, in a well-known witticism by Heine, the word "famillionaire" condenses two meanings, familiar and millionaire.

Freud found double meanings or plays on words to be among the preferred techniques in jokes. This is one of his examples: *A doctor, leaving the bedside of a wife whose husband accompanied him, exclaimed doubtfully: "I do not like her looks." "I haven't liked her looks for a long time,"* was the husband's rejoinder. With the word "looks" the physician referred to the patient's condition of health; the husband, to his wife's appearance.

According to Freud, other jokes are based on ambiguity, such as the following one, which was popular during the trial of Dreyfus, the French Jew unjustly accused of treason by the French army. *"That girl reminds me of Dreyfus. The Army does not believe in her innocence."* The technique is based, Freud said, on the experienced uncertainty over the meanings attributed to the words "innocence" and "Army."

Freud realized that the technique of a witticism is very important, writing that the wit "invariably disappears when we remove the effect of these techniques in expressions." Freud divided the techniques of wit into three groups: (1) condensation, (2) application of the

---

omitted. In the same book Suls advances a two-stage theory of the appreciation of a joke. In the first stage, the perceiver finds his expectations disconfirmed by the ending of the joke—that is, he encounters an incongruity. "In the second stage, the perceiver engages in a form of problem solving to find a cognitive rule which makes the punch line follow from the main part of the joke and reconciles the incongruous parts." Suls does not explain the specific nature of the cognitive processes involved in the attempt to reconcile the incongruity, and does not explain why the attempt fails. As we shall see in this chapter, he is handicapped by his lack of knowledge of primitive forms of cognition. McGhee, one of the editors of the book just quoted, presented an article there in which he appreciated fully that "conceptual thinking is a necessary cognitive prerequisite for the experience of humor based on violation of cognitive expectancies." However, he cannot explain the nature of "the violation," nor the role of conceptual thinking when confronted with such a violation.

same material, and (3) double meaning. He then divided each of these groups into several subgroups. Conjecturing that all these techniques must have something in common that gives the expression involved its witty character, he made an attempt to find this common denominator. At first he thought it might consist of condensation, the tendency to economy, as when a single word in the witticism gathers several different or even opposite meanings. He soon realized, however, that the nature of wit does not lie in the tendency to economize in expression, because "laconism is not necessarily wit." Indeed, the intellectual work required in putting together several meanings in order to make a witticism often requires more energy than is saved by the economy of expression.

Freud then turned his attention to puns. Whereas in a play on words, both meanings are expressed in the identical word, in the pun only a certain phonetic similarity or structure is necessary. A pun reported by A. Brill (1938) is quoted as typical. *At a party someone spoke disparagingly of a certain play and said, "It was so poor that the first act had to be rewritten." "And now it is rerotten," added the punster.*

Freud also examined other forms of wit whose techniques he could not classify under the three groups mentioned. He found that a displacement of the focus of attention from the original theme to another, as he had described in dreams, is a technical aspect of some jokes. He gave the following example: *A needy man borrowed twenty-five dollars from a wealthy acquaintance. The same day his creditor found him in a restaurant eating a dish of salmon with mayonnaise. The creditor reproached him, "You borrow money from me and then order salmon with mayonnaise. Is that what you needed the money for?" "I don't understand you," responded the debtor. "When I have no money I can't eat salmon with mayonnaise. When I have money, I mustn't eat it. Well then, when shall I ever eat salmon with mayonnaise?"*

According to Freud the technique of this joke does not lie in words or a play on words, but in the displacement of the psychic accent. The creditor does not blame the debtor for eating salmon *on the day* he borrowed the money, but reminds him that he has no right to think of such luxuries at any time.

Another common technique, according to Freud, is that of "representation through the opposite," as in the following example from Heine: *This woman resembles the Venus de Milo in many ways: Like her, she is extremely old, has no teeth, and has white spots on the yellow surface of her body*. In this case, ugliness is depicted by making it agree with something very beautiful.

It is not necessary to report here all the possible techniques described by Freud. He described them accurately, but in spite of his attempts he failed to find their common and essential characteristic. His conclusion was that the same techniques are to be found in dreams. Since he could not reach a complete understanding of the forms or techniques responsible for transforming an expression into a joke, he directed his interest toward the study of the content and motivation of wit, hoping to repeat the great contributions that he had made in the field of dreams. Thus he proceeded to study the *tendencies* and the content of wit. Freud pointed out that wit may be harmless when it has no hidden meanings and its pleasurable effect is due only to its technique. However, he stressed that tendency wit permits expression of feelings and ideas which otherwise would be repressed, as in hostile and obscene jokes. He showed clearly how sexual exhibitionism, invective, and rebellion against authority are made possible by the technique of wit.

Freud then reached the conclusion, which is one of the most significant of his contributions on this subject, that the pleasure derived from the above tendency of wit results from the fact that the tendency whose gratification would otherwise remain unfulfilled is actually gratified. In other words, it is only by resorting to wit—a usually acceptable medium—that a person can more or less safely express hostility, resentment, rebellion, and a wished-for invasion of sexual privacy. Freud tried to demonstrate that the search for and discovery of an outlet for hindered motivation was the main aim of the joke, just as it was for the dream. The joke permits release of the inhibition and sets free some repressing energy. Freud, however, could not find any economy of psychic expenditure in "harmless witticisms," in which he could not recognize any repressed tendency in need of gratification. After evaluating a number of doubtful hypotheses, he expressed the idea that pleasure derived from some "harmless" witticisms is due to the discovery or recognition of the familiar, where one had expected to find something new instead. Recognition of the familiar occurs, for instance, in witticisms that use unification, assonance, antonyms, and words with double meanings as techniques. Freud thought that the source of pleasure in rhyme, alliteration, refrains, or assonance in poetry is also the discovery of the familiar.

However, it seems to me that if this were so, there would still have to be some other fundamental characteristics that mark the difference between the pleasure derived from a poem and the pleasure obtained from a joke.

Freud did not focus on the fact that, in some forms of thinking and language, the formal structures of words acquire special values not necessarily connected with the meaning of these words. He had to admit that, in some cases, the gratification of a forbidden tendency is not the mechanism responsible for the pleasure experienced in hearing a witticism. However, motivation in wit remained his main preoccupation, as it had been in his studies of dreams and neuroses. Thus he saw witticisms as more related to dreams than to works of art. And indeed they are something intermediary between dreams and other works of art.

Paleologic and Faulty Logic in Wit

SOME OF the primitive mechanisms described in Chapter 5 form an integral part of many jokes. Let us reconsider some of the examples from Freud; for instance, the witticism of the poet Heine, who, in talking about a lady, said: "This woman reminds me of the Venus de Milo in many ways. Like her she is extremely old, has no teeth, and has white spots on the yellow surface of her body." Heine in reality wanted to say that the lady was ugly; but to say that would have been an act of hostility. Heine therefore resorted to a witticism, that is to a method that would allow him to gratify this hostility, although not too overtly. The method he resorted to is indeed unpredictable and bizarre: he identified the ugly woman with an accepted ideal of beauty—the Venus de Milo.

How could this logically impossible identification be made? Namely, by abandoning Aristotelian logic and reverting to the paleologic of the primary process for the sake of wit. The woman and the statue of Venus are identified because they have some predicates in common—namely, being old, having no teeth, and having white spots on the yellow body. Freud believed that the technique of this joke consists of "representation through the opposite." Ugliness is made to agree with the most beautiful. Trying to identify a subject with its opposite is, in fact, a skillful device for reinforcing the effect of a joke; but in my opinion the fundamental factor in such a joke is the *possibility of an impossible identification*, through the application of the Von Domarus principle, according to which two different subjects are identified just because they have one or more predicates in common. Thus, in Heine's witticism, we enjoy the impossible fact that the same kind of descriptive identifications can apply to a beautiful and a nonbeautiful subject. This logical mechanism, which is commonly found in schizophrenic thinking, also appears in the witticisms of normal people.

To take another of the quoted examples from Freud: *The doctor leaving the bedside of a woman says to her husband, "I do not like her looks." The husband of the woman adds, "I have not liked her looks for a long time."* In this little joke, a conflict is portrayed in an unusual fashion. The husband experiences some feelings of aversion for his wife— feelings that he has to repress until an unpredictable opportunity presents itself for letting off steam in a more acceptable manner. The physician gives him the opportunity. The physician uses the word "looks" as a symbol of the concept "physical appearance as indicative of a state of health." The husband accepts the word "looks" and uses it as a symbol of the concept "physical appearance as indicative of a state of attractiveness." The two concepts are identified because they have the same verbal symbol. The identification here is made possible by the application of the mechanisms already described: Von Domarus's principle, and altered connotation–verbalization balance.

Another of Freud's examples is "That girl reminds me of Dreyfus. The Army does not believe in her innocence." Freud reasoned that this joke mainly utilizes the technique of ambiguity; but it is obvious that here again an improbable identification is made, with the application of the Von Domarus principle and of altered connotation–verbalization balance. Dreyfus and the girl are identified because they have a common predicate: that is, "innocence not believed in by the Army." The predicate is common to both subjects only in that the same verbalization is applied to two different concepts. In the case of Dreyfus, "innocence" means "the state of not being guilty of treason"; in the case of the girl, it means "lack of sexual experience." Also, the word "Army" has two different meanings here. In the case of Dreyfus it means "general staff"; in the case of the girl it means "group of men," with the emphasis on their being male. The ambiguity of this joke, which was the quality emphasized by Freud, is due to the difficulty encountered in making the three or four paleological identifications; it certainly adds charm to the joke, but it is not the fundamental ingredient.

An example with a more complicated mechanism is the joke reported by Freud about the man who had borrowed twenty-five dollars and who was found by his creditor in the act of eating salmon with mayonnaise. When the creditor reproaches the debtor and asks him whether that meal was what he needed the money for, the latter answers, as reported: "I don't understand you. When I have no money I can't eat salmon with mayonnaise. When I have money, I musn't eat it. Well then, when shall I ever eat salmon with mayonnaise?" What is the latent meaning of this joke? Here is the problem of a poor fellow who, being human, thinks he too is entitled to eat salmon with mayonnaise occasionally, in spite of his economic condition. When the debtor is reproached by the creditor, he has to find a way to justify himself. He cannot find an acceptable logical justification and resorts to paleologic: if he is not allowed to eat salmon when *he has no money*, he should be allowed to eat salmon when *he has money*. This reasoning would be correct if the statement "to have money" were identical with "to have borrowed money," but it is not. It is generally assumed that borrowed money should not be spent so freely. The debtor has conveniently identified the two types of money, just because they can be spent.

In other jokes the mechanism can become even more complicated. It is not founded on "pure" paleologic but consists of transitional stages from paleologic to logic, or of discarded and obsolete ways of thinking, as in the following example (not from Freud): *A mother goes for a walk with her little boy. They come to a nudist camp surrounded by a high board fence. The little fellow peeps through a low hole. Mother asks: "What do you see? Boy: "A lot of people." Mother: "What are they, men or women?" Boy: "I don't know; nobody's got any clothes on."*

In order to justify his ignorance, the child resorts to childish reasoning. He thinks, as very young children occasionally do, that people wearing masculine garments are necessarily men and people wearing feminine garments are necessarily women. The child could have another source of information, which is the most reliable and which in this case is unexpectedly available: the direct observation of the anatomical characteristics of the nudists. However, he is not able to resort to this method because he is not familiar with (or because he wants to deny) the anatomical differences between the two sexes. From his point of view his answer is logical; but it is in decided contrast with the adult way of approaching the question. Furthermore, by answering as he does, the child reveals naiveté (or according to another interpretation, his repression of the facts of life). Many other factors are involved in this joke, such as the contrast between the surprising availability of the source of information and the nonuse of it. And obviously there is a sexual tinge as well.

The transition from paleologic to logic is almost complete in the following contemporary joke: *A woman sues a man by whom she claims she has been raped. The plaintiff and the defendant are in front of the judge. The judge looks at both of them and sees that the woman is tall and stout, the man short and thin. With some astonishment he asks the woman, "Is this the man who raped you? How did he do it?" The woman answers, "He pushed me against a wall and he raped me." "How is it possible?" asks the perplexed judge. "You are so tall and he is so short!" "Well," says the woman, "I bent my knees a little bit."*

The woman is logical. If she bends her knees, the sexual act is possible. In the attempt to use logic in self-defense, however, she accuses herself, because the bending of the knees implies her willingness to be a partner and automatically excludes the act of rape. Though in this case no paleologic is involved, it is still the logical mechanism that is the basis of the joke—a logical mechanism that is used by the woman in self-defense and that, on the contrary, turns out to be a self-accusation.

In some jokes the mechanism consists of comparing two different ways of thinking and of discarding one of them, or of accepting an absurd way of thinking such as that of mental patients. For example: *A deluded patient visits a psychiatrist. "Doctor, Doctor, help me!" he says. "Look, I am full of bugs," and tries to brush off the parasites from his clothes. "Be careful," replies the psychiatrist, quickly recoiling, "Don't brush them on me."* The story is witty because the psychiatrist accepts the patient's way of thinking, whereas he is expected to reject it. The meaning of the joke is obviously this: "Psychiatrists are not necessarily superior to or healthier than their patients. Like their patients they may be fooled—and may also be unbalanced."

Some jokes rely more on a nonverbal medium, but they are still based on the same formal mechanisms. For example, a cartoon that appeared some time ago in a periodical showed a middle-aged couple arriving at a railroad station. On his shoulders and in both hands a porter carries the luggage, consisting of so many heavy bags as to make it hardly believable that one man could carry so much. The wife tells the husband, "Darling, keep an eye on the porter. See that he doesn't run away." The woman's attitude is somewhat logical: she wants to make sure that the porter, a man whose honesty has not yet been proved, does not rob her of her belongings. In the circumstances, however, the remark is absurd, because the porter could not run away with such a heavy load.

From all these examples it is apparent that if for the time being we overlook their emotional tendency, which seeks gratification, we can conclude that jokes require apparent ways of proving something, such as sustaining an allegation, a hostile attitude, or a desire. *The sustaining of the story is made possible by the adoption of special cognitive mechanisms*. At times these mechanisms consist of primary processes—often, the paleological type of cognitive organization; at other times of logical processes with false premises, or of ways of thinking that (although logical) imply some additional facts that would automatically invalidate the allegation. These are the same mechanisms that occur in psychopathological processes. In special cases, the technique consists of comparing two different ways of secondary-process thinking and rejecting one of them.

Just as the mentally ill person or the dreamer resorts to primitive cognitive processes to sustain wishes or hostile attitudes or to avoid anxieties, so does the joker resort to these regressive mechanisms. Their degree of regression varies. At times they are based on the principle of Von Domarus; at other times, on the principle of altered connotation–verbalization balance; at still other times, on mechanisms that are logical per se, but whose premises are false.

The Nature and Perception of Wittiness

ALTHOUGH the previous section discussed the special cognitive mechanisms that must be used in forming a joke, it did not intend to suggest that the *wittiness* of a joke is due simply to the use of primary-process paleologic or of faulty logic. More than that is necessary. Let us examine again the Dreyfus joke, and let us assume that the girl who was identified with Dreyfus was Jewish. If a person said, "This girl has something in common with Dreyfus; she is Jewish," this would be a logically correct statement but platitudinous. It would be a statement made with a secondary-process mechanism. Or if a schizophrenic patient said, "This girl is Dreyfus; she is Jewish," this would be a paleologic primary-process identification because of a common predicate (being Jewish). It would be delusional but not witty.

Thus it is not the use of primary-process paleologic or of faulty logic that confers wittiness to a joke. *One perceives a stimulus as witty when he is set to react to logic and then realizes that he is instead reacting to paleologic or faulty logic.* The listener is temporarily deceived because he first apprehends the intellectual process of the joke as logical. A fraction of a second later, however, he realizes that the cognitive process is not logical at all, and he laughs. He discovers that he is not reacting to logic but either to paleologic or to faulty logic. Logic, faulty logic, and paleologic may be very similar and, when they are put together as they are in a joke, they may deceive us as identical twins do. It is just a fleeting deception, however. As soon as we become aware of it, we laugh. We could imagine that when, at the time of Dreyfus's trial, Europeans heard the joke "That girl reminds me of Dreyfus. The Army does not believe in her innocence," for a brief fraction of a second the statement did not yet appear illogical to them. But as soon as they realized the divergent meanings given to the words "innocence" and "Army," they laughed—or at least they perceived the witticism.

If we know that we are going to listen to a joke, we prepare ourselves to be temporarily deceived. At the same time, we are invaded by curiosity; how will the raconteur be able to solve the difficult situation in which he has put himself? (How will he, for example, prove that an ugly woman is like the Venus de Milo?) We then experience surprise when we realize that such proof is based on unsuspected modes of thinking. Surprise confers charm to the witticism. The confusion between similarity and identity, which we have dealt with in Chapter 5, may occur *twice* in the joke; the first time, when the joke is based on the paleologic of the Von Domarus principle (and this principle leads to a mistaken identity); the second time, when paleologic or faulty logic is confused with logic. To take the example we have again just referred to: (1) the first identification is based on the fact that the lady in question and the Venus de Milo have characteristics in common (being old, having yellow spots, and so forth); and (2) the second characteristic is based on the fact that a statement that was only paleologic was for a very rapid fraction of a second taken for logic.

In the creation of a joke, the creative process is based on the following: (1) primary-process mechanisms, or cognitive mechanisms that are usually discarded because of their faults, become available to the creative person; and (2) out of the primary-process and/or faulty cognitive mechanisms that have become available, the creative person is able to select those which give the fleeting impression of being valid secondary-process mechanisms. The amused response on the part of the listener occurs when he realizes the invalidity of the thought processes—that is, when he recognizes the logic–paleologic discordance.* The creative process of wit consists of putting together the primary- and secondary-process mechanisms and automatically comparing them. The comparison reveals the discordance and provokes laughter. The discovery by a creative person of an apparent concordance in a logic–paleologic discordance constitutes the tertiary process of the wit he creates. It constitutes the creative process of the joke. Of course, additional factors may enter into and increase the value of the joke, which may no longer be just a joke but also an unusual work of art. For instance, only a creative mind like that of Heine could find an apparent concordance between an ugly lady and her presumed opposite: the Venus de Milo.

I have stated that the perception of wit—or more specifically, the typical response to the perception of wit—consists in the discovery of a logic–paleologic discordance in what for a brief interval seemed a concordance. The extremely brief concordance, together with the following recognition of the discordance, forms a temporal and also an artistic unity: a joke is born. This unity, to which we have already referred in Chapter 1, is very important. The oneness, made up of diverse elements, is organized as a structure that has the purpose of making us laugh. Were this state of unity not achieved, the creative product would not make us do so.

---

* If faulty logic is used instead of paleologic, then there will be a logic–faulty logic discordance. In the following discussion in this chapter we shall take into consideration only logic versus paleologic and the secondary versus the primary process, because these seem the most typical and most frequent combinations in the creativity of wit. However, the same notions could be repeated for logic versus faulty logic and the secondary versus the faulty-secondary process.

To have recognized these crucial points is a very important step in the psychological understanding of wit. However, we have not yet understood the *reasons* for the subjective response to wit. That is, we have not yet come to understand why the recognition of a logic–paleologic discordance in an apparent concordance is followed physiologically by a pleasant subjective experience or reaction. This reaction, which is more or less specific, entails a feeling of amusement and tends to make the listener smile or laugh—at times even very forcibly.

Here we have reached the border between objectivity and subjectivity—that border between body and psyche which, at this stage of our knowledge, we are unable to cross. In some ways we are like the physicist, who knows that a certain wavelength of light is in fact perceived by the mind as the color red, but who cannot know *why* such a wavelength leads to such a subjective experience as "redness." Or we can compare ourselves to the chemist who knows that compounds such as glucose and saccharin are perceived as sweet, but does not know *why*. It is true that many authors (for instance, Langevin and Day 1972) have studied the physiological correlates of humor, especially the galvanic skin response (GSR). However, these studies deal with the bodily effects of humor and not with the psychological experience of wit and the comic. In many psychological phenomena it is easy to obtain a degree of understanding similar to the one that we have reached in the study of wit. For instance, we know that embarrassing stimuli make people blush—although again, we do not know why the experience of embarrassment is accompanied by a dilation of the capillaries of the facial region. In the case of wit, it has been much more difficult to determine the specificity of the wit-producing constellation of stimuli, since this consists of a relatively complicated cognitive construct.

However, in terms of what has been said here, it is possible to understand why most paleologic expressions of schizophrenics (and occasionally of other psychiatric patients) are bizarre but not witty. The language of the schizophrenic is often so remote from reality that no similarity or possibility of confusion with logic is left. The logic–paleologic discordance cannot be confused for concordance even for a fraction of a second. Thus the comic unity we have referred to is not achieved. Expressions are witty only when a confusion between concordance and discordance becomes possible for the listener. Occasionally schizophrenic language *is* witty. (As a matter of fact, it is to some witty expressions of schizophrenic patients that I owe the origin of my interest in the psychology of creativity.*) For instance, a patient examined many years ago had the habit of oiling her body. Asked why she did so, she replied: "The human body is a machine and has to be lubricated." The word "machine," applied in a figurative sense to the human body, had led to her identification with man-made machines. But the creative process, as it has been described in this chapter, was not involved in what this patient said. She did not know that what she was saying was witty; she meant what she said quite literally. Her delusional remark is witty only for us; we, not the patient, create the joke, because we recognize the illogicality in her apparent logicality. Such apparent witticisms of schizophrenics, which have been reported in the literature, generally result from paleological identifications or from extreme literalness, which result in turn from a reduction of the power of connotation and an emphasis on verbalization.

The Comic

THE INDIVIDUAL who perceives wit undergoes a pleasant experience, as said, which entails a feeling of amusement and tends to make him smile or laugh. Actually, this response occurs not only to witty stimuli but also to a much larger category, *comical stimuli*, of which the witty ones constitute only one subgroup. Before proceeding, therefore, we must try to determine the nature of the comic and to distinguish it from wit. Many philosophers since ancient times, and a considerable number of contemporary psychologists, have investigated the nature of the comic: that is, the nature of that form of amusement to which we tend to respond with laughter, smiles, and a merry attitude. In this chapter, perhaps helped by what we have already es-

---

* In Chapter 5 we reported several apparent witticisms made by schizophrenic patients (p. 80). Apparent witticisms are also found in nonschizophrenic psychotics. In organic patients they generally represent attempts to cover the inadequacy or deficit due to the illness. Witty expressions were particularly numerous in expansive cases of general paresis, which have now become extremely rare (Arieti 1950). They also occur in Korsakoff's psychosis, senile psychosis, cerebral arteriosclerosis, brain tumors (especially of the frontal lobes), epilepsy (especially in twilight states), mental deficiencies, and the cerebral type of Buerger's disease (Arieti 1950).

tablished about the nature of wit, we ourselves shall be in better position to examine the nature of the comic. (Since wit is a special subgroup of the comic, what we shall determine about the comic must also apply to wit; but the reverse does not hold true.)

An observation made several decades ago in Italy led me to the formulation of a theory about the nature of the comic: when Italians hear or read something Spanish for the first time in their lives, they laugh or smile—that is, they react as though they are perceiving a comic stimulus. Obviously, there is nothing comical per se in the beautiful Spanish language. There must be something else in the situation that makes Italians react in this way. I propose that an Italian who listens to Spanish for the first time recognizes that he is listening to a foreign language with a different grammar and vocabulary. Yet in some expressions the two languages are so similar that the Italian is often able to understand the meaning of what is said. In other words, he often understands the meaning, not because he has studied Spanish, but because he knows Italian. He is prepared to respond to Spanish, but instead he finds himself responding to Italian—the Italian which appears in the Spanish. And he experiences this confusion as a comical sensation. This observation and subsequent similar ones led me to formulate the following hypothesis: *The subject perceives a comical stimulus when he is set to react to* A *and then finds himself reacting to* B, *because of a confusion between the identity and similarity of* A *and* B (Arieti 1950).

To test this theory, let us consider a common situation in comedy: that of mistaken identities. For example, in Shakespeare's *Comedy of Errors* two brothers, unknown to each other, are identical twins and are continuously confused with one another, even by their wives. To increase the confusion they have the same name, one being referred to as Antipholus of Ephesus and the other as Antipholus of Syracuse. And each Antipholus has a servant, called Dromio, who is an identical twin of his brother's servant. The resulting situations are extremely comical. Thus, the wife of one of the twins allows certain intimate expressions to a man she thinks is her husband, but in fact the man does not even know her. Such scenes cause the audience to roar with laughter, because when an onlooker thinks he is reacting to the presence of Antipholus of Ephesus, he finds he is instead reacting to Antipholus of Syracuse, and vice versa. Or when he thinks one servant is on stage, it turns out to be the other. And even when the onlooker recognizes the confusion for what it is, he still laughs at the confusion of the characters on stage.

This comedy by Shakespeare is a very close imitation of the comedy *Menaechmi* by the Latin Plautus (254–184 B.C.). Plautus in his turn imitated the Greek Menander (343–291 B.C.). Thus from ancient times, the misidentification of persons has been one of the most powerful comical stimuli. The simplest form of mistaken identity occurs in the case of two persons who look very much alike, as with identical twins. Even today in plays, movies, and vaudeville shows, twins appear frequently as a source of the comic. The comical element is maintained if the two persons are identified not only because they look alike, but, for instance, because they also have a predicate in common, as when A has the same name or dress as B, or is located geographically in a place where B is supposed to be. The audience then tends to laugh when a character C, in a theatrical performance, is set to react to A and instead reacts to B, thinking that B is A. The spectators do not accept C's apparent identification of A and B, however, and are compelled to laugh. Even the spectators themselves, who are set to react to A, may in fact find themselves reacting to B; when they become aware of the mistaken identity, they are equally amused. The performer C, however, allegedly does not know that the person whom he thinks is A is in reality B, so he cannot show such a reaction. He continues to identify paleologically—somewhat like the schizophrenic. It is because the audience cannot accept the identification that it continues to laugh.

Let us examine what happens in other comical situations. When A and B are the same person, the intensity of the comic persists but is diminished. For instance, there is a tenuous comical element in plays and masquerades when we know that the person who acts or is dressed like A is not A but B. In the old vaudevillian "horse act" we laugh because we pretend to react to a horse and instead find ourselves reacting to two men functioning as the legs of the horse. In a caricature we look at an anatomically distorted and yet recognizable picture of a person, and we recognize the similarity in the dissimilar. Caricature uses the exaggeration of traits to make a B of an A—generally a distorted and often an undesirable B—but in spite of the deformation we recognize A and we smile. Images seen in distorting mirrors produce the same effect. We may also get a comical effect from a photograph that had not turned out well.

Generally we find the inadequate comic, but only when the inadequate has unconsciously deceived us in the paleological identification. For instance, a child who uses big words like a grown-up makes us smile, because at first we react to him as to a man, in the sense that he is the source of grown-up words. Then we realize and are amused by the incongruity of words and source. Yet in a certain way we feel that there is indeed a man within the child, because we know that any child is potentially a grown-up. We are subliminally taken over by his adult ways until we focus our attention on the fact that he is a child. Using a different formulation, we can say that we experience a comical effect when we recognize the inappropriate in the seemingly appropriate. The inappropriate is so similar to the appropriate that a confusion is possible. Moreover we know that in most cases if a person wanted to elicit a sense of the comic in us, he did not really want to deceive us. If indeed he produced this effect voluntarily, he wanted to confuse us, but only playfully and temporarily. He knew that a *comic unity* would result from the extremely rapid succession of confusion and then dissolution of that confused state.

The concepts of identity and similarity, which I have mentioned so many times, again appear very important. We may look at the problem in a different way. A principle that logicians generally call Leibniz's law states: "X is identical to Y if X has every property that Y has and Y has every property that X has." The Von Domarus law or principle followed by the person who thinks paleologically can then be reformulated in this way: "X is identical to Y if X has at least one property that Y has and Y has at least one property that X has."

My theory of the comic, as advanced for the first time in 1950 (Arieti 1950), can be stated as follows: "A subject is a perceiver of a comical stimulus when he realizes that he tends to identify X with Y, not in accordance with Leibniz' law, but in accordance with Von Domarus' law." For such a realization, the person does not need to know what Leibniz and Von Domarus' laws are, of course, just as he does not need to know that he adopts Aristotle's laws of thought whenever he thinks logically. These "laws" are formulations of mental mechanisms, devised for practical purposes, and probably can be designated as Kantian, or a priori, categories.

Wit is a particular form of the comic, inasmuch as the required confusion between similarity and identity necessarily occurs in the field of cognition. The two subjects that are unwarrantably identified are logic and paleologic (or faulty logic). The listener at first is prone to identify the faulty logic of the joke with valid logic by virtue of Leibniz' law. Very shortly thereafter, however, it would be found that he identifies the two forms of thinking in accordance with Von Domarus' law. We therefore repeat that the confusion between similarity and identity may occur twice in a witticism: at first, when the joke is based on Von Domarus' principle (and Von Domarus' principle leads to mistaken identity); and after that, when paleologic or faulty logic is confused with logic (that is, when Von Domarus' principle is confused with Leibniz' principle).

Some readers may think that in my views on paleologic thinking and on the comic I attribute too much importance to the concepts of identity and similarity. But it is exclusively on the ability to compare and to identify that logical thought is based. James wrote: "Logic has been defined as the 'substitution of similar,' and in general one may say that the perception of likeness and unlikeness generates the whole of 'rational' or 'necessary' truth" (James 1911).

Gratification of Tendencies in Wit

THE PREVIOUS SECTIONS have investigated the formal cognitive mechanisms of wit. We shall now consider the aspect of wit in which Freud was particularly interested and to which he devoted the most study: the gratification of tendencies in relation to the content of the wit. We shall consider also the present author's views.

A joke, according to Freud, does not try to impart new knowledge. It has a special aim, which is disguised under the obvious aim of amusing the listener: it attempts to gratify that which is generally suppressed or inhibited. The joke is an attempted gratification or pseudogratification—or at least a partial or vicarious gratification—obtained by resorting to special cognitive mechanisms. These mechanisms represent the wit-work, which, like dream-work, transforms the content of the joke into one that is more acceptable; but neither the repression nor the gratification achieved in jokes are as marked as in dreams. Gratification in joking arises from the fact that verbal expression of the forbidden becomes permissible, and with such expression a certain excitement and release of emotions is obtained.

There are several tendencies whose gratification is sought by means of witticisms. One of the most common is sexual in nature. Frank admission of sexual drives, as well as of sexual exposure and consummation, is made possible in telling a joke. That sexual jokes are extremely numerous is understandable because of the repression to which sexual drives are subjected by society. However, since the repression in the joke is very weak, sexual jokes, too, are forbidden in numerous milieus and, of course, not all of them can be published. Homosexual jokes are less common because the repression in the joke is indeed too feeble to compensate for the ostracism to which this form of sexuality is subjected even in our own time.

As far as the technique is concerned, sexual jokes do not differ from others. Often they resort to very primitive paleological laws, as in the following example taken from Freud: *A wealthy but elderly gentleman showed his devotion to a young actress by many lavish gifts. Being a respectable girl, she tried to discourage his attentions by telling him that her heart was already given to another man. "I never aspired as high as that," was his polite answer.* The technique of this joke consists of the paleological identification of two concepts, because they have the same verbalization in the word "high." The gentleman used the word in an anatomical sense, not in a figurative sense, as he pretends. The latent meaning of the joke is obviously this: "Let's do away with this false sentimentality. My attentions are caused only by my sexual desire for you."

A second group of jokes, perhaps even larger than the group with sexual content, consists of what may be called hostile jokes. In these jokes the tendency is toward the expression of anger, enmity, disparagement, and denigration. It is not surprising to find so many hostile jokes, since civilization requires repression of hostility as much as of sexuality. The target of hostility in the joke is not attacked directly, but through wit-work. The reader will remember the witticism about the husband who shows his feeling toward his wife by agreeing with the physician about her looks. Heine's joke about the Venus de Milo has a similar tendency. Jokes expressing rebellion against socially recognized authority may be included under this category. The jokes about psychiatrists that appear so frequently in the American press express resentment of the prominent position that psychiatry has attained. "Psychiatrists are human like their patients and may be unbalanced too," most of these jokes imply. In many situations the hostile joke becomes an actual act of hostility, ranging from bland teasing to vitriolic expression. The individual with a schizoid personality, who is particularly sensitized to environmental hostility, is often said to have no sense of humor. This is because the schizoid person, alert as he is to external antagonism, is not deceived by wit-work and recognizes the hostile element in much wit (Arieti 1955, 1974).

I might mention that some parents and teachers who disapprove of physical punishment punish children instead by using witticisms or by emphasizing the comical aspects of a situation. However, unless the humor is of a very bland type and accompanied by affectionate concern, it may have even more disturbing effects on children than other types of punishment, as has been disclosed by patients under intensive psychotherapy.

Hostility engendered by prejudice may also be ventilated through jokes, as in the following example: *A Jewish gardener answered an advertisement for a job in a nunnery. The Mother Superior told him that since he was Jewish she'd have to give him a week of trial service. At the end of the week the Mother Superior came up to the gardener and said, "Well, you've done pretty well, but there are several habits I want you to lose. I don't mind so much your lighting cigarettes from the holy candles, or washing your hands in the holy water, but for God's sake, stop calling me 'Mother Shapiro.' "*

This joke, apparently innocent and harmless, has a tiny touch of anti-Semitism. Its latent meaning lies in the reticence to accept the fact that some Jews may not be so prone to lose their habits and traditions, even when they are sharply different from those of the majority. Moreover, there is a disguised apprehension that they may want to spread their habits or ideas to others. The gardener should be very grateful to the Mother Superior. He has found employment in a Catholic cloister, a place where it is hardly conceivable that a Jew would be hired. He should feel a sense of obligation and try to conform as much as possible. What does he do instead? He lights his cigarettes from the holy candles and washes his hands in the holy water. These habits are overlooked by the Mother Superior because they disclose only the gardener's poor judgment. What the Mother Superior cannot tolerate is being called "Mother Shapiro." Shapiro is a common Jewish name, and the gardener, who is used to pronouncing it, confuses it paleologically with "Superior." Even in the cloister that has been so generous to him, he remains a typical Jew, a Jew who bestows some of his Jewishness on the Mother Superior by calling her Mother Shapiro.

In a third important (though somewhat smaller) group of jokes, the tendency that is expressed is the frank admission of human frailty as a truth that has to be accepted and defended. This tendency, though justified, has to be repressed generally because of the ways of living that civilization imposes upon us. Typical of this group is the joke described earlier, about the man who was caught by the creditor in the act of eating salmon with mayonnaise. The debtor had to resort to wit-work in order to assert his human rights and defend his wish to eat salmon with mayonnaise once in a while. To him this desire had the validity of a truth. Several jokes, especially those belonging to this group, assert what may be considered "natural truths." In a certain way they are reminiscent of those dreams that do not express the fulfillment of irrational and immoral wishes but rather, the fulfillment of some of our good impulses that have to be repressed for social reasons. They also show that, at least in some cases, the assertion of Gregory (1924), that "wit is a quick, vivid illumination of a truth" is correct. And they support the plausibility of Froeschels's statement (1948), that witticisms are means by which philosophical truths congenitally known but not yet expressed become "ripe for expression."

A fourth group that is quite common consists of jokes expressing the unrealistic effort of the inadequate man to cover his own inadequacy. This effort is not really fulfilled in the joke, which therefore in a certain way becomes a hostile joke. Nevertheless, since it is especially the covering of one's own inadequacy that is emphasized in these jokes, they deserve to be classified separately. The following example is from Koestler (1949): *Mr. Dupont, an elderly notary, has for years suffered from the annoying habits of his clerk, Jules. Returning home unexpectedly from a journey he finds Jules in bed with his wife. Mr. Dupont surveys the scene with a mournful eye and says, "That's enough, Jules! Once more and you're fired!"* According to one way of thinking, the notary's action is logical. The clerk is warned; one more infraction and he will be fired. However, another way of thinking, more acceptable in our society, requires that Mr. Dupont be more energetic in seeking immediate and drastic retaliation against Jules. But Mr. Dupont is a weak, inadequate person, a man unwilling to defend his honor with strong action. What he really wishes is to find a method to keep peace and save his face.

In my opinion, these four tendencies are the principal ones expressed in jokes, but probably there are many more. Often several tendencies are combined in the same joke; at times even all four appear. An example is found, for instance, in the joke about the tall woman who sues the short man on the charge of rape. In this joke there is certainly an element that satisfies the sexual tendency. There is also some hostility toward women, since the joke illustrates very well what many men wish to think of rape charges made by women: that sexual intercourse with conscious adult females is almost impossible without their consent, or at least without a certain degree of acquiescence.* From the point of view of the man, there is the assertion of his own rights; he is unfairly accused of having raped the woman. Finally, the joke portrays a woman attempting to cover up her own inadequacy, or the inadequacy of her story.

The aim to gratify these forbidden tendencies in jokes does not preclude the coexistence of other motivations, some semiconscious and others fully conscious. Together with the four tendencies described above (but especially with the fourth) we also find an attempt to sympathize with our fellow men for their inadequate attempts to get out one or another of the many kinds of human predicaments. Quite often we find an attempt, as well, to enlighten one another about the helplessness of man's condition on earth. The main character of the joke, even if he is the victim of his sexual desire, greediness, or inadequacy, is often a poor fellow like the rest of us. He is caught like a fly in the web of a complicated situation and tries to disentangle himself, often by using illicit or inappropriate means. Let us not condemn him too quickly or too harshly, say such jokes; let us just laugh at him. Let us look with indulgence at his contradictions, absurdities, or paradoxical ways, and make an attempt to transform what is hard to accept into a little pleasantry. The main character in the joke is one of us; in laughing at him, we laugh at ourselves—since we cannot escape from our human limitations. This type of gratification often appears not only in witticisms but also in more generally comical situations.

We must thus revise Freud's point of view that a joke does not try to impart new knowledge. It is still correct to say that in most jokes the main motivation is the gratification of a generally inhibited wish. But in a considerable number of jokes—as in other literary forms—there can also be observed an attempt to restate an old truth in a new

---

* Except, of course, under threat of violence. But how could some men, like the one reported in this joke, physically less endowed than the woman, and without any weapon, threaten her?

way, or to show a new aspect of a habitual situation, or even to lead people to experience brotherhood and compassion.

In addition to all the motivations and tendencies that I have mentioned, there are also other fully (or almost fully) conscious reasons for witticisms. Prominent among them is that of simple enjoyment. We *enjoy* laughing or smiling, in addition to the other gratifications that a joke offers us. In this, wit is similar to other art media, which confer an aesthetic pleasure not necessarily related to the content involved. In wit, however, the hidden tendency is stronger than in other art forms. This fact, as well as others that will be mentioned here later place the joke in an intermediary position between other art forms and dreams.

Various authors have stressed that humor in all its aspects has a healthy influence on the human organism. This influence would again place it close to dreams, which also have salutary physiological and psychological effects. Patricia Keith-Spiegel (1972), summarizing the views of authors ranging from Spencer (1860) and Darwin (1872) to Menon (1931), concludes, "Laughter and humor have been hailed as 'good for the body' because they restore homeostasis, stabilize blood pressure, oxygenate the blood, massage the vital organs, stimulate circulation, facilitate digestion, relax the system, and produce a feeling of well being."

Sociological Aspects of Jokes

A FURTHER fully conscious motivation for jokes must be added to those so far described: their social function. Since this subject has been widely discussed, I shall be very brief on this topic and will deal only with some points with which I am more familiar.*

The interpersonal aspects of wit and the comic were studied by Freud (1916). He made an important observation in comparing the two: whereas in a comical situation only two persons are necessary (the observer, and the object in which the observer finds something

---

* For a clear review of the literature on this subject the reader is referred to the article by Martineau (1972).

comical), in wit an interplay of at least three persons generally occurs (the person who tells the joke, the hero in the joke, and at least a third person who is the listener). Although it is true that a person may enjoy reading a joke with nobody present, in the typical situation there are at least three people. Freud did not adequately explain why this third person (or group of people) is, if not essential, at least important in a "wit" situation. I think that the reason must lie in the nature of wit itself. In wit, much more than in other forms of humor, an attempt is made to demonstrate something by resorting to some kind of cognitive process. This "something," the theme of the joke, has to be demonstrated to a "somebody," the third person or group of persons. When the third person explodes with laughter, he shows that for a moment he was deceived by the logic of the joke and has corrected the deception.

To continue, then. When we discussed the various tendencies or motivations of jokes, it became obvious that in addition to producing enjoyment, a joke conveys a message. In fulfilling this double role, it thus becomes a social and cultural manifestation.

National literary traditions influence the ways in which wit and the comic are used. Ignoring Aristotle's principles about the classic drama, Shakespeare mixed comic scenes in the context of his tragic dramas and, as it was said, mingled kings with clowns. Neither the French Corneille and Racine nor the Italian Alfieri would have dared to do so. This English tradition has continued, and in English-speaking countries a joke is often interpolated as comic relief in a serious situation—as in a lecture, political speech, diplomatic discussion, and so on. Until very recently this has not been possible in other milieus such as the French and the Italian.

In English-speaking countries humor is also frequently used in political campaigns. Political jokes follow the usual wit techniques. Many of us remember the use of wit made by President Truman in his unexpectedly victorious campaign against Dewey in 1948. The following is an example. Referring to the fact that during the campaign Governor Dewey seemed to go to each city where Truman had been shortly before, the President said in one of his speeches, "I went into consultation with the White House physician, and I told him that I keep having the feeling that wherever I went there was somebody following behind me. The White House physician told me not to worry. He said, 'You keep right on your way. There's one place where that

fellow's not going to follow you and that's into the White House.' " *
Here Truman pretends to accept a psychotic way of thinking in order
to prove something. He assumes the role of a deluded patient who ex-
hibits a common characteristic of such patients—the feeling that
somebody is following them. In the joke the doctor reassures the patient that the follower will not come into the White House (a statement that proved to be prophetic).

Jokes have been frequently used in political campaigns. Among
many other examples in this area, Sperber cites (1955) the jokes made
about General Lewis Cass, an American statesman who was born in
1782 and died in 1866, and who was a Democratic candidate for
various offices, including the presidency. These jokes used the phonetic likeness of Cass' name with a certain derogatory word that can
be used in an abusive sense. The following is an example:

> And he who still for Cass would be,
> He is a Cass without the C.

Another example:

> Why is it necessary to go to Europe to understand the true character of
> Lewis Cass? Because it is necessary to pass over the C.

The reader is familiar with these mechanisms, which we have described in this chapter.

Local historical factors play an important role. For instance,
when Germany and Italy were under Fascist rule, a large number of
jokes were secretly circulated that expressed hostility against the
tyrannies. The social use of wit as an expression of ethnic or religious
prejudice is also important. The common use of Jewish jokes as a
manifestation of anti-Semitism has already been mentioned. This
problem is complicated by the fact that Jews themselves have created
anti-Jewish jokes. How is this to be explained? Freud attempted an interpretation. He thought that Jewish jokes made up by non-Jews are
nearly all brutal, whereas Jewish jokes originating with Jews are sincere admittances of one's real shortcomings. Freud then added, "I do
not know whether one often finds a people that makes merry so unre-
servedly over its own shortcomings." But this explanation of Freud

---

* Speech delivered in New York City, October 28, 1948.

seems unsatisfactory to me. Granted that Jewish jokes originated by non-Jews are more offensive than those originated by Jews, the fact remains that even the latter may be offensive. Jews know that even mild jokes dealing with dirtiness and thriftiness may be disparaging.

I believe that this habit of the Jews is paradoxically an unconscious defense against anti-Semitism. Surrounded for centuries by a hostile environment, the Jews have tried to make the members of the majority discharge their hostility by means of such relatively harmless jokes. It is better to be accused of stinginess and dirtiness than of deicide and ritual murder. It is better to be laughed at than to be massacred. Freud was right in being surprised at this tendency of the Jews, but this peculiarity is connected with the history of the Jewish people.

I have noted something similar to this, though on a much lesser scale, among Italians in New York City. In some sectors of New York City where there was a prejudice against Italians, I saw vaudeville shows, performed by Italians, in which characteristics such as the excessive eating of spaghetti and the poor pronunciation of English were made fun of. Again, it is better to be accused of eating too much spaghetti than of being gangsters. Similar jokes about Italians would disturb an audience in Italy. If my impression is correct, Jewish jokes should have already started becoming unpopular in the state of Israel. As I wrote elsewhere (1950), "Just as a psychiatric patient may accuse himself in order to placate his cruel superego, so may social groups under environmental stress resort to the neurotic social defense of creating self-accusatory jokes."

Bieber (1974) has recently described the similar use of humor by masochists. He writes, "Humor, especially masochist humor, is an effective technique for coping with aggression. If one can manage to be a target for laughter, one is not likely to be a target for hostility. Laughter extinguishes anger, hostility, and allied affects, at least for the period during which the laughter continues. Many comedians use masochistic techniques to evoke laughter, particularly when an audience is being unresponsive."

The Comic, Playing Games, and Children's Play

IS THERE a relation between wit, the comic in general, playing games, and human children's play? (Although other animals play too, they do so in a much simpler way that consists mostly of nonaggressive motor activities.) Comic situations, games, and children's play seem related in some respects. They are all pleasant and imply a special attitude toward life, one that promotes an evasion of reality. In this respect they again show their similarity to dreams. Games and playing, however, are not just an evasion. They substitute a bit of creativity for what they replace or temporarily suspend from the focus of consciousness.

The child who assumes in play the role of a parent, a general, a builder, or a fireman, abandons the reality of being a small, obedient child and becomes what he would like to be. Play, like the dream, has a wish-fulfilling quality: the fantasy is lived. The main characteristic common to both children's play and wit, then is that of make-believe. The child knows that he is not a fireman, but he makes believe that he is. Heine knows that a certain lady is not like the Venus de Milo, but for a fraction of a second he makes believe that she is.

However, these two make-believes are based on different mechanisms. In children's play, reality is suspended or kept at the periphery for the duration of the playing, and the fantasy acquires the power of reality. (Not completely, however. If the mother of the role-playing child calls him for one reason or another, the child can stop the fantasy, although reluctantly, and resume the role of being his mother's child.) In wit, the make-believe is of much shorter duration. First of all, it is based on the presumed acceptance of faulty logic. But as soon as the valid logic reacquires the upper hand, the make-believe disappears. When it disappears, it leaves a wake of laughter. The wake of laughter is due to the recognition that we almost believed the make-believe. The pleasure lies not in enacting a fantasy but in arousing from one, in realizing how astounding it would have been had we been able to accept the story—which soon proved to be a pretension.

The Relation between Content and Form

WE MUST now take into consideration another aspect of jokes that makes them particularly suitable as an introduction to the study of the creative process: the relation between form and content.

In jokes we can easily recognize an almost perfect harmony between form and content. It is hard to imagine a different product that, in waking life, would permit the gratification and (practically at the same time) the rejection of a forbidden tendency. In a dream, the visual hallucination transports the dreamer into a world of illusion that exists as long as the dream lasts. In the joke the illusion can exist in waking life, too, but it is even more fleeting. It is because we know in advance that our intellect will soon reject what the joke asserts that we allow ourselves to hear it and momentarily believe it.

In wit there is a *going backward*, or regression, of part of the cognitive faculties. However, this cognitive regression is temporarily accompanied by the assumption of *going forward* (sustaining a new point). At this point we can re-examine the statement that jokes occupy an intermediate position between dreams and other works of art. They do; nevertheless they are genuine works of art, even if their purposes or tendencies are similar to those of dreams. Whereas the dream is only for the dreamer or for the dreamer's dream life, the joke is understood by others and accepted socially. Whereas the dream consists mostly of primary-process mechanisms and does not substantially reach the secondary process, the joke attains an overlapping of the two processes that is necessary for the evolving of the tertiary one. We must remember, however, that in the joke also, the two processes are not fused or integrated. One of the two, generally the primary, is soon rejected.

Although jokes, too, like other forms of art, have high aims and social purposes and may use refined techniques, as a group they are less advanced than other forms of creativity. In fact, primitive cognitive mechanisms undergo relatively little elaboration in jokes. Among all the motivations, *the propelling need to gratify a non-admitted emotional drive, at least for a fleeting instant*, stands out, almost as it does in dreams. In other forms of art this gratification is not so direct. It is attenuated by the effort to create an independent life for a new object, the work of art; to maintain an "aesthetic distance" from it (see Chapter 7); and most of all, to experience aesthetic pleasure, independently from, or less related to, emotional needs.

Accessory Factors

THE EMPHASIS given in this chapter to the use of some special cognitive mechanisms in the formal structure of witticisms should not obscure the existence of certain other factors that are part of the technique of jokes. Some of these factors were first recognized by Freud, but whereas he believed that they constituted the basis of wit, I think they are merely accessory mechanisms. They are not essential to eliciting a comic response, but they lend additional charm to the joke. The ability to find them and to unite them is an expression of the artistic level of the person who developed the joke.

Some of these secondary factors have been implied or even referred to in the previous discussion. For instance, what Freud calls *ambiguity* can be interpreted as the suspense and effort necessary to make the paleologic identification. We remember, in this respect, the ambiguity of the sentence, "I never aspired as high as that," in the answer that the elderly gentleman gave to the actress who "had already given her heart to another man."

The device of *displacing the psychological accent* is based on the fact that often the paleologic identification needs a predicate or a characteristic that is secondary, adventitious, or loosely associated with the original meaning.

Representation through the opposite also confers charm and beauty to a joke. We can again take as examples the joke of the ugly woman who was identified with the Venus de Milo, and the joke about the young child who could not determine the sexual identity of people because they were naked.* In these cases representation through the opposite increases the element of surprise; but the intellectual element—the demonstration of something that cannot be demonstrated by the usual cognitive mechanisms—is the fundamental factor. In many jokes

* In some ways not yet clarified, representation through the opposite may be connected with the origin of opposite meanings described in *The Intrapsychic Self*, Chapter 7, pp. 101–103.

these secondary characteristics are elaborate and sometimes exaggerated in order to increase the suspense and the element of surprise. A good example is the following:

There were twins, about seven years of age. One had been born a pessimist, the other an optimist. Came Christmas, and their father gave the pessimist a nice little automatic plane that would do all sorts of tricks; and he filled the optimist's shoe with some horse manure. On Christmas morning an uncle came to visit and asked the pessimist, "Well, how did Santa treat you?" "Terrible," was the answer. "I got a plane that does everything by itself—no fun for me, nothing to do." "And you?" asked the uncle of the optimist, "How was Santa to you?" "Couldn't have been nicer," said the little boy. "He brought me a real live pony; only before I got up, unfortunately the pony ran away!"

The emphasis on the opposite attitudes of the twins gives considerable charm to this joke. However, most of the content is technically unnecessary. The really witty part consists not in the attitude of the pessimist, mention of whom may even be completely eliminated, but in the attitude of the optimist—that is, in the optimist's interpretation of the presence of manure as proof that he had received a pony as a gift. At a latent level this joke is a pessimistic one, inasmuch as it shows how unfounded the optimism is of one of the twins. At a less latent level we see the drama of man, who tries to escape from an unpleasant situation in which he is caught.

Another characteristic mentioned by Freud, *condensation*, is an important accessory factor, just as it is in dreams. The more condensed the latent meaning, the more significant the joke is. This condensation is due to the paleological identifications or compositions mentioned before. Condensation also occurs in the emotional content of a joke. For instance, at least four different tendencies and emotional drives are condensed in the joke about the tall woman and the short man who was accused of raping her.

In extremely rare jokes the cognitive technique is more complicated or is even at variance with the ones commonly encountered. Let us consider the following unusual example: *A young man by the name of Peter went to his mother in a very agitated, mournful state. "What happened?" asked the mother. "Mother," replied Peter, "I am in love with the daughter of Mr. Smith, our neighbor, and I cannot marry her." "Why?" asked the mother. "I went to father," said the son, "and told him of my love, but he replied, 'You cannot marry Mr. Smith's daughter. Mr. Smith's daugh-*

ter is my daughter.' " "*Is that all?*" replied the mother. "*My son, don't worry. You can marry Mr. Smith's daughter.*" "*How is it possible?*" asked Peter, perplexed. "*Very possible, son. You are not your father's son.*"

There is some humor in this joke, but not much, as the mechanism is the reverse of the one usually adopted. The young woman who is at first identified as a sister is then discovered not to be a sister after all, and therefore eligible for marriage. The joke is unusual because it is the information given by the mother that permits the logical (not paleological) possibility for the gratification. The mechanism thus is the reverse of the one usually adopted. The humor is consequently diminished, although the two unexpected confessions of the parents make the story "interesting."

Puns, Proverbs, and Parables

ONE EXAMPLE of a pun—about the play that had to be rewritten and was "rerotten"—has already been mentioned. Another example may be taken from a speech by President Truman, delivered during his 1948 political campaign.* Alluding to the fact that the Gallup and other private polls, which had predicted the victory of his opponent, discouraged Democrats from going to vote on election day, he called them "sleeping polls." He obviously meant that they could have the effect of sleeping *pills*. Other examples, mentioned by Freud, are the Latin *amantes–amentes* (lovers–lunatics) and the Italian *traduttore–traditore* (translator–traitor).

All these examples are witty; and yet, in the order presented here, they decrease in comic power. What meanings do these expressions really convey? The play is both rewritten and "rerotten;" the polls are in a certain way (sleeping) pills; the lovers (*amantes*) act foolishly and therefore are like lunatics (*amentes*); the translator (*traduttore*) does not convey the real meaning of the original text, and he is therefore a traitor (*traditore*).

It is obvious that in these examples the latent meaning is not sustained by paleological identification alone. In other words, there is no

* Speech given in Cleveland, October 26, 1948.

contrast between the logical and the paleological form. The paleological identification is used either to add something to the logical meaning or to give additional support to it. These witticisms are not like the one about the woman who was identified with the Venus de Milo, for such an identification is possible only in an exclusively paleological way. It is true that in the case of the rewritten and "rerotten" play, the meaning of the expression is still mainly sustained by paleological identification, so that there is still a considerable amount of humor. But in fact, the punster was more interested in conveying the notion that the play was "rerotten" than the notion that it was rewritten.

The ability to make puns derives from an increased emphasis on verbalization: a characteristic which, in its original form, is prominent in primitive cognition. We have seen how many schizophrenic patients "discover" puns. Some of these puns are connected with delusional thinking. A patient of mine thought that when people used the word "candy," they were referring to her former boy friend whom she had "given up." When I asked how she could interpret the word "candy" in that way, she replied, "I am on a diet, and I have given up eating candy." Thus the quality "something which I gave up" led to the identification and to the pun—that is, in effect, the "play" on different applications of the same word. On the door of the office where this patient worked there was a sign "O.B." The patient felt that these letters referred to her: maybe they meant that she was an *old b*ag; or to the fact that she was pregnant, although not married, and should consult an *ob*stetrician. She had conveniently overlooked the fact that she was working in the department "Orders and Billing." The schizophrenic pun, as a rule, has meaning only in relation to the patient; It resorts almost exclusively to paleologic. This is not true of the pun created as a form of art. In the pun as a creative product, the more the logical meaning is accepted, the less need there is for paleological sustenance. The humor decreases, but the expression acquires greater effectiveness. *When the logical thought is entirely accepted, there is very little, if any, witty effect.* Thus the use of paleologic does not have the purpose of confusing for the sake of humor, but of conveying the message through a stronger medium. Modern advertisements often use this paleological reinforcement.

Puns and proverbs, in which the paleological meaning mainly reinforces the logical one, may be compared to those rare dreams whose manifest content coincides with their latent content. A beautiful example of paleological reinforcement is found in Benjamin Franklin's historical statement, "We must all hang together, or assuredly we shall all hang separately." This sentence has great vigor and effect because it follows both logic and paleologic. It has practically no comical effect, because the meaning is not sustained by paleologic alone. Franklin wanted to convey the message, "We must remain united," but he did not use this ordinary phrase. He said instead something like this: "One way or another we're going to hang; so let's hang together rather than separately." But "hang together" also means "remain united," and "hang separately" means to be executed on the gallows. In a fleeting preconscious moment, all the meanings of the word "hang" are identified. When they are recognized as being different, the artistic effect is experienced; although these meanings are different, they do not exclude each other.

We may take another example that has been considered with veneration through the centuries. In the Gospels it is written that people who wanted to confuse Jesus asked him whether it was proper to pay taxes to Caesar. Jesus requested that money be shown to him and then asked whose image was on the coin. They replied, "Caesar's." Jesus then said, "Render therefore unto Caesar the things that are Caesar's, and to God the things that are God's." The Gospels say that the people were astonished at such an unexpected answer, just as people have been throughout the centuries.

Jesus' answer is enigmatic and has been interpreted in many ways. And yet we immediately perceive its great vigor and sense that it conveys a great meaning. Why is this so? It is difficult to examine Jesus' sentence from an exclusively formal, strictly literal, concrete point of view, because as soon as we hear it we become inundated by its various and deep abstract meanings. Nevertheless, it seems that if we make an effort, we can recognize in this sentence a concrete and literal basis, as we do in parables in general. The image on the coin was Caesar's only as it represented the likeness of Caesar, not because it belonged to Caesar. In other words, only the image was Caesar's, not the ownership of the coin. Therefore, if we take this sentence in an extremely literal, concrete sense, Jesus would be wrong; he would then have based his statement merely on a play on words, on the fact that the expression "Caesar's" would paleologically acquire the meaning "being the property of Caesar." The coin, then, would have to be given back (rendered) to Caesar, its rightful owner. (But taxes would have to be paid even if the coins did not show the image of Caesar.)

Why, then, does the story appear unhumorous, in spite of having a partially paleologic foundation? Because the expression reinforced the important message that Jesus wanted to convey to the people: that money *did* belong to Caesar, not in a literal but in a metaphorical sense. Money meant material things. Such things belonged more to Caesar and to the materialistic world of Rome than to the spiritual world of Jerusalem. Jesus' followers should not be concerned with such things, but only with "things which are God's and must be rendered to God." Jesus was trying to counter the discontent of the people by showing, in an unusual, unpredictable way, that it was acceptable to pay the unfair tribute to Caesar. With these words he did not take a pro-Roman attitude, nor did he come out against payment of taxes. This would have been a rebellious position. At the same time, in a new and highly artistic way, he supported the old religious Hebrew tradition which stressed the antithesis between God and Moloch. "Moloch" is a contemptuous word for "king," a king being interested in temporal, earthly values only. In Jesus' parable, Caesar is Moloch.

In this example we can see the fusion or contemporaneous occurrence of several levels of meaning. Had Jesus simply resorted to a play on words, his remarks would have been witty but not epoch-making. Had he tried to mitigate the sorrow of the discontented taxpayers, his intent would have been a noble one but not a revelation. Jesus wanted to reveal what, for him, was a highest truth. His revelation was made not through a scientific demonstration but through paleologic reinforcement. Paleologic reinforcement is the opposite of logic–paleologic discordance. It does not pertain to the comic but to the general realm of art—and occasionally of science, as shall be demonstrated in later chapters.

Chapter 8

Poetry and the Aesthetic Process[*]

FOR MANY PEOPLE the work of art is a perfect and indissoluble unity, capable in its totality of evoking a particular and beautiful experience. These people follow Croce's tenet that it is impossible to separate form from content. Such "dissection" would actually destroy the aesthetic value.

This point of view is understandable in aestheticians as well as in admirers of art, inasmuch as they are interested in the end result of the creative process—the only one that elicits the aesthetic effect. Such an approach, however, does not lead to a psychological understanding of the creative process. The psychologically oriented student of creativity does not deny that the work of art constitutes a unity, where the content is indissolubly intertwined with a particular form. But he is aware that this intertwining is completed at the last stages of the process of creativity, and that these stages are preceded by many others— some conscious, others unconscious—that at times unfold in rapid and at other times in slow succession. The psychological analysis of a work of art may temporarily suspend the aesthetic appreciation, but eventually it should lead to a deeper understanding and more intense experiencing of that work.

* Unless otherwise indicated, the translations are the author's.

Clive Bell called the aesthetic form "significant" (1913). With this term he strongly emphasized that the quality which confers to a work of art its artistic essence is the "significance" of the form. But Bell's concept, although important, does not greatly increase our understanding; it does not *explain* what makes a form aesthetically "significant." This chapter will illustrate how the tertiary process does in fact add aesthetic significance to form and content. I shall take as my central example the tertiary process as it evolves in poetry, but my aim is to clarify the aesthetic process in literature in general. Thus some consideration will be given to other literary forms as well.

The Similar in the Dissimilar: The Metaphor

WE HAVE repeatedly seen that one of the mainstays of human cognition is the ability to associate similar things and then to distinguish similarity from identity. The person who creates a witticism sees a similarity between a logical statement and a paleological one; by momentarily making the listener believe that this similarity is an identity, he creates a joke.

A poet also sees similarities in the dissimilar, in the process of creating a metaphor.* Aristotle wrote, "The greatest thing by far is to be a master of metaphor; it is the one thing that cannot be learnt from others; and it is also a sign of genius, since a good metaphor implies an intuitive perception of the similarity in the dissimilar" (*Poetics*, 1459a).

Poetry, of course, is not based exclusively on metaphor, but metaphorical language is one of its fundamental components. I shall take as an example Blake's beautiful poem, "The Sick Rose."

> *O Rose, thou art sick!*
> *The invisible worm*
> *That flies in the night,*
> *In the howling storm,*

* The grammarian's distinction between metaphor and simile is unnecessary in a psychological study and will not be retained in this book.

> *Has found out thy bed*
> *Of crimson joy,*
> *And his dark secret love*
> *Does thy life destroy.*

Ostensibly the poem is about a beautiful flower that has been invaded and soon will be destroyed by an ugly worm. But there are many more levels of metaphorical meaning. What comes easily to mind is that the rose stands for a beautiful woman and that the worm stands for a fatal illness that soon will destroy her.* In fact, the poet addresses the rose as a person. He says: "Thou art sick!" Such comparisons between flowers and women, and between worms and illnesses, occur not only in poetry but also in dreams and in schizophrenic ideation.†

We have seen earlier that, in psychopathological conditions and in dreams, common predicates lead to metamorphosis—to identifications of what seem dissimilar subjects to normal or waking people. In poetry there is no *metamorphosis*, but *metaphor*. The poet knows that the rose is not a woman, but he feels the woman is like a rose.

In order to compare the sick flower to the sick woman, the poet has access to the formation of a primary class. As described in Chapter 5, a primary class consists of equivalent or interchangeable members. Now, is a primary class involved in the making of a poetic metaphor? Yes and no.

The poet does not *actually* substitute the sick rose for the sick woman. The sick rose is not the sick woman; but in the sick rose he sees the sick woman. In schizophrenia the interchangeability or displacement is complete instead of partial: in one of the examples given in Chapter 5, the patient becomes the Virgin Mary.

In poetry, the displacement—for instance, from the woman to the rose—is conscious. The poet wants to react to the sick woman as he would to a sick rose. Whereas in psychopathologic conditions and in dreams the displacement is from the real object to the symbolic, in poetry it is from the symbolic object (the rose) to the real (the woman).

The difference is deeper than that. Let us take Blake's poem

---

* For a similar interpretation see E. Drew (1959).

† Names for women often denote flowers, of course. With the image of the "invisible worm," it could be said that Blake's creativity prophesied the bacteriological era in science, which discovered "invisible" germs in sick animals and plants.

again. As we have already mentioned, the rose does not *replace* the woman (as the Virgin Mary replaces the patient, who is no longer the patient but who has undergone the delusional metamorphosis of becoming the Virgin Mary). In the poem we see the woman *in* the rose. The woman and the rose are fused; but it is not that bizarre fusion that we see in schizophrenic drawings and delusions. The woman and the rose, though fused, retain their individuality. The retention of their individuality permits a comparison, yet does not lead to identification. How is this possible? It is possible because by putting the sick rose and the sick woman together, we become at least partially *conscious* of a class: the class of "beautiful life destroyed by illness." As a matter of fact, it is enough for the human cognitive faculties to be aware of only two members of a class to become aware of the whole class, or to grasp the meaning of the class.

But is this class primary or secondary? Both, and in a certain way, neither. In the act of being created, the class is primary. Finding common predicates among different subjects and identifying by virtue of these common predicates is a primary-process mechanism. The primary process tends to remain primary: the rose and the woman tend to interchange or to remain together, but as the concept of the class "beautiful life destroyed by illness" emerges, their fusion does not become, so to speak, consummated. They remain distinct. However, the level of the secondary class is not reached completely in the poem, or does not remain independent of the primary-process origin. The poet does not deal on a cognitive level with "beauty destroyed by illness." Only the student of literature may translate the poem into a secondary-level content. The poem itself oscillates between a primary level and a secondary level, which is inferred. Here, thus, is an important difference between art and psychopathology: *Whereas in the psychopathologic use of the primary process there is no consciousness of abstraction* (as a matter of fact, the power of abstraction is impaired, and the mind has to find concrete channels), *in art the use of the primary process does not eliminate the abstract. On the contrary, it is through the medium of the primary process that the abstract concept emerges.* *

A physician would not compare a woman to a rose in order to clarify the outcome of a fatal illness or in order to lead to the formation of a new class. Why does a poet need a rose invaded by a worm to tell

---

* In some forms of art the abstract concept is not immediately available. We shall discuss this important topic later.

us that fatal sickness in a beautiful woman is a horrible thing? Why does he need to resort to his unusual accessibility to primary classes?

The poet discovers that things abound in similarities. New similarities take on new meanings because each recognized similarity is a concept and implies the formation of a new class. (One of the main ways of expanding knowledge that the aesthetic fields have in common with science is this formation of new classes or categories.) Let us remember what happens in jokes: the joke is based on the eventual recognition that logic and paleologic (or faulty logic) are not identical, only similar. The recognition of the logic–paleologic discordance leads to the comic response. In poetry, however, there is agreement between paleologic and logic; paleologic actually reinforces logic. Art, indeed, is founded to a great extent on *paleologic reinforcement*. At the same time that a work of art elicits an abstract concept, it sustains itself upon paleologic reinforcement, or identification with a concrete example. There is an almost perfect welding of the abstract concept with the concrete example, of the replaced object with its metaphor. The concrete object of the metaphor is not only a symbol, it is also a participant in producing the effect.

In paleologic mechanisms as used by the schizophrenic, the object that is replaced or symbolized fades away (at least from consciousness) or is replaced by its symbol. (In our earlier example, the virgin patient disappears and is replaced by the Virgin Mary, and so on.) In dreams, too, that which is symbolized is no longer present. For instance, a gorilla may stand for one's father in a dream. The image of the father is completely absent, and only psychoanalytic work can recapture it. In art the replaced object also fades, but not entirely. It fades away only in its concrete essence; its presence is felt in its absence. For instance, the woman is not mentioned in Blake's poem, but her presence is felt. She indeed exists in the artistic assumption. At the same time that the work of art eliminates her, she is there as a rose. Symbol and reality hold hands.

There are other factors to be considered in the study of the metaphor: (1) accessory techniques, (2) multiple meanings, and (3) the universality of metaphor in symbolism.*

In a brief poetic passage we may find only one metaphor, but in highly wrought artistic works more than one metaphor is combined.

---

* In this chapter, metaphors are studied only as aesthetic forms. However, they can be analyzed in a much larger perspective (see Foss 1949; Kaplan 1960; Wheelwright 1954, 1962).

Let us reexamine Blake's poem. We have seen that the rose stands for a beautiful woman who is sick, and that we are, so to speak, invited to pity the fate of this woman. In some respects this is a recurring theme in literature. In French literature there is the ailing woman named after the flowers she liked so much: *la dame aux camelias*. In Italian opera, Mimi of *La Bohème* is not a sick flower but a sick maker of artificial flowers. Her beauty is compared to the crimson beauty of dawn and of sunset. Something vaguely associated with this image is also found in Dante. In the first of the dreams reported in his early book *La Vita Nuova*, he describes how Beatrice appeared to him in the arms of a male figure, Eros or Love. Beatrice is partially covered by a red cloth. The whole scene takes place in a cloud red as fire. Dante knows that Beatric is going to die because of something Love has made her eat.

In Blake's poem, however, many other metaphorical meanings are suggested. As in Dante's dream, the invader is male (*his* dark secret love). The bed of crimson joy conveys the image of feminity and sexuality, from the point of view of a male (the cheeks, lips, and, perhaps, the vagina of the woman are crimson). The rose becomes more female, the worm more male. Accessory predicates that lead to more identification increase the artistic value, just as they do in jokes.

But there is much more in the poem. The invisible worm that flies in the night, in the howling storm, and that invades the bed of crimson joy and destroys life with his secret love, may suggest an evil-producing sexuality, a sadistic passion, a "dark" love inappropriate to crimson joy.

At this level of understanding the poem would represent a drama between two people, woman and man, the battle of the sexes. But the poem can be interpreted at a much more abstract level where it represents beauty and evil that must, but cannot, coexist in the same universe; for evil often destroys beauty in the end. The worm may represent the seed of spiritual decay. And yet the worm may even appear not so evil in its evil, because it is capable of loving; it is only that this love leads to destruction. Moreover, the worm, too, wants to flee from "the howling storm," that is, from the horrible and tempestuous world; but inasmuch as it is part of that world, it ends by producing evil.

We could find other levels of meaning. The rose and the woman can appear as sisters, in the sense in which Francis of Assisi saw brotherhood and sisterhood in the disparate existences of the universe. The new class or "family" to which the rose and the woman belong reasserts the universal encounter with life, love, sorrow, decay, and death. We enter, thus, into an indefinite realm of symbolism; the classes of symbolized objects accrue by a sequence of paleologic analogies that are like more and more windows, more and more doors, opening into unguessed aspects of reality, into unpredicted worlds. In great works of art we seek and find such analogical expansions; though a new object has been found, the longing and the search continue. The finiteness of the new object contrasts with the indeterminacy of the search. And yet the search itself becomes part of the newly created work, of the new unity—an aesthetic entity that appears in its totality for the first time in the universe. This is occasionally referred to as the unfinished statement of the work of art.

The person who appreciates a great work of art has the feeling that the work grows in him as he becomes involved in a prolonged capturing of emerging marginal meanings. He feels that he, too, is creative, that he himself is adding to his experience and understanding. Moreover, he wants to confront the work of art many times. He is not easily tired of it, as he would be had he read a purely logical statement. He realizes that the work of art does not merely transmit information; it produces pleasure. He also experiences each element of it as essential and unique: nothing is redundant. By reading the poem again, the reader adds further to his aesthetic understanding and again experiences pleasure. Indeed, many people enjoy and even prefer going back to well-known poems and music many times, rather than experiencing new works.

The apparent (and implied) subject matter of great poems is vast and of universal relevance. At times the poetry of an author involves one whole aspect of human existence. For instance, Homer's works deal with the heroic aspect of man. Nevertheless, in poetry the content per se plays a relatively secondary role. To refer again to Blake's poem, we have seen that its theme is a recurrent one that in itself cannot be responsible for the striking beauty of the poem. Some aestheticians have repeatedly emphasized this point. Ciardi, for instance, has titled a monograph on poetry *How Does a Poem Mean?* (1959) His asking "how" instead of "what" reveals his basic idea. Ciardi wants to demonstrate that the aesthetic meaning is inherent in the way a poem is constructed—the "how" of it—not in its content.

Again in regard to Blake's poem, we can say that all of us respond to phonetically beautiful words and to their rhythms; we pity beautiful women who become sick and die; we are concerned with evil that destroys beauty; we are receptive to the sensuous beauty of flowers and have some distaste for the "worms" that attack them. Everything was ready for the fitting together of all these elements, but somebody had to make them "click." Blake did this by harmoniously blending primary and secondary processes, as in a novel symphony of unsuspected predicates. The synthesis Blake achieved could then be easily communicated and shared. The originality of the new unity contrasts with the almost general response to such a unity.*

Can a poetic fusion of primary and secondary processes be compared to a scientific or other discovery? In a certain way, yes; but only to a special type of discovery. An aesthetic discovery, unlike its counterpart, does not inherently make us know things that we did not know before. However, it creates a new, affective experience.

Schizophrenic language and dreams, too, have different meanings and different levels of cognition. However, in dreams and in psychopathological conditions these different meanings are discordant; furthermore, often they do not co-exist with but instead replace one another. That is, the dreamer or the schizophrenic is only aware of what he sees in the dream, or of what he says, at a manifest level. He needs the therapist to recapture all or many of the meanings. If there is a unity, it is in the atmospheric quality or in a sort of primitive, affective gestalt. Although the schizophrenic experience is also a new experience, it is actually a reduction to a concrete level—a restriction, not an enlargement—unless some new understanding or the recapturing of the abstract meaning is obtained through recovery or therapy.

At times the artist has almost that capacity for imagery that the dreamer has, or that capacity for "orgies of identification" that the schizophrenic has (Chapter 5). He is able, however, to use these images in unpredictable syntheses that become works of art. For instance, in his poems Victor Hugo compares stars to diamonds and other jewels, golden clouds, golden pebbles, lamps, lighted temples, flowers of eternal summer, silvery lilies, eyes of the night, vague eyes of the twilight, embers of the sky, holes in a huge ceiling, bees that fly

* This section focuses on the use of the metaphor. The other aesthetic elements blended together in Blake's poem will be taken into consideration in subsequent sections.

in the sky, drops of Adam's blood, and even the colored spots on the tail of the peacock.* To the average person these comparisons would have been inconceivable beforehand. The ability to form metaphors reveals the richness and versatility of the poet's imagery, the potentiality of his mind, the visionary quality of his poetry. As Boase (1967) has written, the vividness of Hugo's imagery strongly suggests that in him survived the eidetic imagery observed in children (see Chapter 3). But the vividness of the imagery does not embrace the whole poetic phenomenon. The imagery is also transformed into a similarity or a metaphorical identity. Many of us have seen diamonds, jewels, clouds, pebbles, eyes, embers, holes in ceilings, and spots on the tails of peacocks, but it is most unlikely that any of us would have compared them to the stars in the sky. If their similarity to the stars had occurred to us, we probably would have rejected it as remote to an absurd degree. This similarity would not have passed our "creibility" test. Our imagery would not have become free imagination and would not have proceeded toward the completion of a creative product.

Can we call a metaphor a rejection of reality? Hardly. When Victor Hugo calls the stars flowers of eternal summer, or eyes of the night, he does not reject the reality of the stars, or the ordinary way of experiencing the stars. It is obvious that he considers the stars very beautiful; and he wants to add beauty to beauty, to give a new form to the appreciation of the firmament. Some of Victor Hugo's metaphors seem far-fetched, but they certainly do not subtract from the realistic beauty of the stars. Not all poets endorse this procedure. The surrealists following André Breton, believed that the value of the metaphor or analogy is not "in an equivalent but in the subtraction of one set of associations from the other. The greater the disparity, the more powerful the light, just as in electricity, the greater the difference in potential of the two live wires, the greater the voltage" (quoted by Balakian 1970). We must thus acknowledge that the surrealist poets used, or endeavored to use, the metaphor in a special, discordant way.

Metaphors are at times used to offer a paradoxical mode of thought. The paradox and the beauty of the imagery confer a striking effect. Consider these lines from Richard Lovelace (1618–1657):

> *Stone walls do not a prison make,*
> *Nor iron bars a cage;*

* See also Huguet (1904) and Konrad (1958).

The Creative Product

Minds innocent and quiet take
That for a hermitage.

The first two lines give a metaphorical expression of how free the mind can be under any circumstances. The thought acquires strength through paradox, because in a physical sense stone walls do make a prison and iron bars do make a cage.

Consider these verses from Thomas Gray (1716–1771):

> *Full many a gem of purest ray serene*
> *The dark unfathom'd caves of ocean bear;*
> *Full many a flower is born to blush unseen,*
> *And waste its sweetness on the desert air.*

We immediately grasp the metaphorical message. The gems and the flowers are unrecognized or unrealized beauties or talents. The expression's value results from the contrasts between the "gem of purest ray serene" and the dark underocean cave, the blushing of the flower and its being unseen, its sweetness and the desert air. The poetic paradox becomes the poet's magic. By reading these verses we do "see" the gems, although in the dark of the ocean's caves, and the blushing flowers, although in the desert.

To summarize: the successful metaphor, even when it seems to subtract from reality, adds to our understanding and confers aesthetic value. When the poet says that *A* is like *B*, whereas nobody else had been able to see that similarity, he transports us into a universe where real and unreal unite to give us a vision of unsuspected depths and dimensions. When Shakespeare, in *Macbeth*, tells us:

> *. . . Out, out, brief candle!*
> *Life's but a walking shadow, a poor player*
> *That struts and frets his hour upon the stage,*
> *And then is heard no more; it is a tale*
> *Told by an idiot, full of sound and fury,*
> *Signifying nothing. . . .*

we perceive a greater, even if a dubious, understanding. The poet purports to give us a series of definitions of life. Were we to remain in the realm of our daily reality, we could insist that life is not a "brief candle," is not a "walking shadow," is not a "poor player," is not a "tale told by an idiot." But our realistic judgment is suspended. Although these definitions of life are not those given in the dictionary or in a textbook of biology, we sense that we are getting closer to touching a special truth that only the metaphor can offer us. The metaphor seems to transport us closer to a world of absolute understanding that is more real than reality. At the same time we are conscious that these words are pronounced by Macbeth, the evil hero, certainly not a man whom we should listen to as a master of life. Is he right? Is he wrong? Is this vision of life determined by a life of crime? There is no answer to these questions. The metaphors have enlarged the realm of possibilities within our understanding.

Concretization of the Concept, or Perceptualization

IN DREAMS and in schizophrenia, when a concept cannot be sustained at an abstract level, it undergoes a transformation: it assumes a concrete representation (Chapter 5). The capacity for abstraction is not lost; otherwise there would be no abstract content to be transformed into a concrete representation. The abstract ideation, however, cannot be sustained at an abstract level. In dreams, thoughts are transformed into visual images. In schizophrenia, high mental processes are transformed into specific thoughts that have a concrete content, or into forms equivalent to perceptions—for instance, hallucinations.

The concretization of the concept at times takes the form of a metaphor. For example, if a patient believes that his wife is poisoning his food when he actually feels she is "poisoning" his life, this may be considered a metaphor. Actually, there is no displacement here from one concrete object to another, as in the case of Blake's poem. What is concretized here is an attitude or an aspect of behavior: the attitude that the patient feels his spouse has toward his life.

In the aesthetic process, too, we must speak of concretization, or perceptualization, when something that is difficult to objectify in definite terms is transformed into concrete, tangible symbols. What is transformed is generally a subjective state, a life-attitude, some general or specific behavior, a mood, or so on. In the aesthetic tertiary process, the concrete representation not only is not incongruous with the original abstract concept, it actually reinforces it.

Our terms *concretization* and *perceptualization* indicate that concepts are represented by images or imagery. For some aestheticians these words refer to something that has a wider range than the metaphor. At times the expression *metaphorical language* is used. However, in a psychological study it is preferable to maintain the distinction between metaphor and the more general phenomenon of concretization. When we speak of metaphor, we focus on the similarity between the original object and the one used in the metaphor. When we speak of concretization or perceptualization, we refer to the fact that what used to be conceived at a more conceptual or abstract level is given a concrete, specific, or perceptual representation. For instance, Victor Hugo succeeds in giving pictorial representation to a general sense of mystery and terror, as in the poem:

> *O deuil! est le bâton de cet aveugle immense*
> *Marchant dans cette immense nuit.*

In these verses, difficult to translate, the poet compares mankind to a blind giant who travels in the darkness of the night and sustains himself on a special cane: his sorrow.

At times it is indeed difficult to distinguish a metaphor from a more general concretization. Metaphors are, of course, also concretizations, but they are very limited ones: they may still be interpreted as displacements or interchanges between members of a primary class. In many cases, simple metaphors and larger areas of concretization are associated. For instance, as long as Blake compared the sick woman to a sick rose, we can speak only of metaphor, but when the woman came to represent beauty and the worm to symbolize evil, we can speak also of concretization.

Poets quite often express themselves through concretization. A typical example is the Italian poet Pascoli, who unfortunately is not well known in English-speaking countries. In some of his poems he ostensibly describes natural phenomena or countrysides, in some ways as Frost later did; but these descriptions must be interpreted as concretizations of high concepts through imagery. In one of his most celebrated poems, a fallen oak concretizes people who are ignored or hated as long as they are alive, but are recognized in their full value and even sanctified after their death. In another poem, "In the Fog," we are confronted with an allegory about the obscurity, or "fogginess," of life, while at the same time the description of countryside under fog stands on its own merits as a realistically vivid representation. The following poem is entitled "My Evening" ("La Mia Sera"):

Il giorno fu pieno di lampi;
Ma ora verranno le stelle,
Le tacite stelle. Nei campi
C'è un breve gre gre di ranelle.
Le tremule foglie dei pioppi
Trascorre una gioia leggiera.
Nel giorno, che lampi! che scoppi!
Che pace, la sera!

The day was full of lightning, but now the stars, the silent stars, will appear . . . while in the fields little frogs say gre gre. Joy moves the wavering leaves of the poplars. What lightning! What thunder in the day! What peace in the evening!

Si devono aprire le stelle
nel cielo sì tenero e vivo.
Là, presso le allegre ranelle,
singhiozza monotono un rivo.
Di tutto quel cupo tumulto,
di tutta quell'aspra bufera,
non resta che un dolce singulto
Nell'umida sera.

The stars must open up now in so alive and tender a sky.
There, close to the merry frogs, a brook sobs monotonously.
Of all that dark tumult, of all that bitter storm
Only that sweet sobbing remains in the humid evening.

È quella infinita tempesta,
finita in un rivo canoro.
Dei fulmini fragili restano
cirri di porpora e d'oro.
O stanco dolore, riposa!
La nube del giorno più nera
fu quella che vedo più rosa
nell'ultima sera.

That infinite storm ended in the singing brook.
The fragile lightnings became golden and purple clouds.
O tired sorrow, do rest! The darkest cloud in the day
Is the one which seems to me the pinkest in the evening.

Che voli di rondini intorno!
che gridi nell'aria serena!
La fame del povero giorno
prolunga la garrula cena.
La parte, sì piccola, i nidi
nel giorno non l'ebbero intera.
Nè io . . . e che voli, che gridi,
mia limpida sera!

Now the swallows fly all around; what shouts in the serene air!
The hunger of the poor day prolongs the garrulous supper.
During the day the nests did not have a small portion of food.
Nor did I; and what flights, what shouts in the limpid evening!

The Creative Product

Don . . . Don . . . *E mi dicono,*
  Dormi!
mi cantano, Dormi! sussurrano,
Dormi! bisbigliano, Dormi!
là voci, di tenebra azzurra . . .
Mi sembrano canti di culla,
che fanno ch'io torni com'era . . .
sentivo mia madre . . . poi nulla . . .
  sul far della sera.

Don . . . Don . . . *The bells say,*
  Sleep!
They sing: sleep; they whisper: sleep.
They softly repeat: sleep, over there . . .
  voices from the blue darkness.
They seem songs of the cradle, which
  make me be as I was . . .
I felt my mother . . . then nothing, while
evening was coming.

This poem cannot be interpreted, of course, merely as a description of a stormy day followed in the evening by a change in the weather. There is also an allegorical meaning. The tempest, which seemed endless (infinite), has ended in a melodious singing brook, as the sorrow of the poet has ended in the poem. At the end of the day (life), the darkest cloud becomes the pinkest one. The peace of old age is compared to the peace of a beautiful sunset after a stormy day. Now the bells of the nearby church suggest to the poet that he fall asleep: that is, that he accept death. The night will be beautiful after this reconciliation with the day; death will be agreeable if the poet has accepted life for what it is. The bells sound like a lullaby, and the image of the lullaby evokes the image of the poet's mother. It is the image of love that now makes him fully accept his past life and approaching death, as in his childhood it made him accept falling asleep.

At times a retention of conceptual expressions, an inability to fully concretize the content, decreases a poem's aesthetic value. Consider the following poem by Shelley, called "Love's Philosophy."

The fountains mingle with the river
And the rivers with the ocean;
The winds of heaven mix forever
With a sweet emotion;
Nothing in the world is single;
All things by a law divine
In one spirit meet and mingle.
Why not I with thine?

See the mountains kiss high heaven,
And the waves clasp one another;
No sister-flower would be forgiven
If it disdained its brother;

> *And the sunlight clasps the earth,*
> *And the moonbeams kiss the sea;*
> *What are all these kissings worth*
> *If thou kiss not me?*

This is a beautiful poem; however, in my opinion it does not reach a very high level, mainly because it is spoiled by lines 5–7. In these lines the poet attempts to give us a conceptual, not perceptualized, "philosophy" of love. His concept of love is represented better by the imagery of the rest of the poem.

At times a poem, conveying a relatively simple or nonpoetic thought, attains poetic effect or potentiality because of a progressive concretization. Consider Blake's poem "A Poison Tree," another *Song of Experience;* not as striking as "The Sick Rose," but still strong and memorable.

> *I was angry with my friend:*
> *I told my wrath, my wrath did end.*
> *I was angry with my foe:*
> *I told it not, my wrath did grow.*
>
> *And I water'd it in fears,*
> *Night & morning with my tears;*
> *And I sunned it with smiles,*
> *And with soft deceitful wiles.*
>
> *And it grew both day and night,*
> *Till it bore an apple bright,*
> *And my foe beheld it shine,*
> *And he knew that it was mine,*
>
> *And into my garden stole*
> *When the night had veil'd the pole:*
> *In the morning glad I see*
> *My foe outstretch'd beneath the tree.*

Blake professes to give the kind of psychological advice given nowadays by psychotherapists. If you experience an unhealthy emotional attitude, express it openly and it will clear up. If you hide it inside yourself it will grow, make you deceitful in your attempts to dissimulate, and cause you to plan a horrible revenge. The poet recounts a seemingly prosaic tale consisting of one fact after another, as expressed by the repetition of the conjunction "and." But it is not a prosaic tale, because from verse four to the end the wrath not only grows but becomes concretized into a tree, the poison tree; a tree watered with tears and sunned with smiles and wiles, a tree bearing an apple of contention. Is this apple reminiscent of the one eaten in the Garden of Eden, or of the one Paris offered to Aphrodite, thus preparing the ground for the kidnapping of Helen and the Trojan war?

The poet generally tends to abandon concepts and to return to a life dominated by the senses,—the origin, according to Aristotle, of whatever later will become part of the individual. But it is obvious that the poet reproduces a sensuous experience not just because it is sensuous, but because, further, it satisfies other aesthetic requirements. However, whereas the philosopher (or the intellectual man in general) builds from sensation to conception, the poem seems to move in the reverse direction. In other words, it is the associated conceptual overload that leads the poet to go back to the sensuous experience. If he goes back to the crimson rose, it is because he sees in it the embodiment of abstract beauty and innocence; if he goes back to the pink evening after a stormy day, it is because he sees in it the representation of his old age after a tempestuous life. Again, the poet follows a mental mechanism that is similar to one often encountered in the schizophrenic. For instance, the patient experiences hostility in the world, but this diffuse atmospheric feeling becomes concretized when he actually believes that he tastes poison in his food. Now, neither the schizophrenic nor the poet is aware of his conceptualizations, retained in endoceptual form (see Chapter 4). The schizophrenic is ready to swear that as soon as he had a bite of food, he tasted the poison. A poet may look at flowers or at the clouds of the evening, and believe that he perceives them just as he describes them, unaware of their underlying potentiality. In the case of the poet, the cognitive overload often becomes conscious, or partially conscious, during the creative act.

Concretization of the concept through imagery is found not only in poetry but in many other forms of art. It is frequently used in parables and in religious writings in general. We have already examined the parable of Jesus and the coin. Here is a poetic gem from the Talmud. "Don't make a woman cry, for God counts her tears." The meaning is obviously that God will consider individually each one of the woman's sorrows and will not forget who is responsible for them;

but the imagery of God actually counting the tears, as if they were pearls, adds strength and beauty to the expression. Proverbs often utilize the same technique. When we say, "Don't cry over spilt milk," the image of the spilt milk is employed as a symbol of something we cannot undo.

Parables and proverbs differ from poetry, however, in form and aim. Their main purpose is to give a precept of good behavior or wisdom, whereas poetry aims to create an aesthetic experience. Although parables and proverbs concretize concepts, they do not use a metric medium—which, as discussed later in this chapter, is necessary in most poetry.

Concretization of the concept is strikingly evident in the theater. Classical tragedies, for example, reproduce human emotions and situations, such as passion, ignorance, immutable destiny, conflict between moral law and the law of the land, and so on, that bring the leading character to catastrophe. In this way the playwright "concretizes" a predicament of larger significance, at times a tragic premise about man's existence. The denouement of the play often represents the unfolding of an inevitable situation. Concepts are not expressed in philosophical, discursive ways, but are concretized in action. The actions speak for themselves; the characters stand for categories of men. What happens to Macbeth, for instance, represents in part the final crumbling of the human being when he accepts evil. Evil leads not only to external catastrophe but also to the disintegration of the human being as a moral entity.

The concretization obtained in the theater is more realistic than in other forms of art. Living human beings, who are seen three-dimensionally and who move as they do in life, stand for characters and for the categories these characters represent. The drama, however, is not a documentary. It represents certain scenes only; many others are not seen. Accidents, irrelevancies, or any scenes that are not larger in significance than what they actually represent, are stripped away.

Often not only can the whole unfolding of a play be seen as a great concretization, specific scenes can also be interpreted as specific concretizations and paleologic reinforcements. For instance, *Oedipus Rex* can be said to portray the relation between good and evil, or between truth and illusion (or knowledge and ignorance). Oedipus commits evil because he *does not know:* he does not know that he is the killer of his father and the husband of his own mother. The whole drama is a series of events that leads to the discovery of the truth. When he knows the truth, Oedipus feels he has to pay the penalty for his horrendous actions; he gives up the throne and blinds himself.

Freud found in this tragedy the inspiration for his concept of the Oedipus complex, but it seems to me that the play portrays the limitation of human consciousness rather than Oedipus' incestuous desire for his mother. His "crime" was actually that of not knowing or not "seeing." He had not been perceptive enough of the many clues, some subliminal, that were in his surroundings. He certainly would not have done what he did, had he known; but the idea of using his ignorance as an alibi did not occur to him. The limitation of his consciousness did not limit the severity of his conscience. Or could it be that Freud, in addition to the idea of the Oedipus complex, found in this tragedy the inspiration for his concepts of the unconscious and of repression? That is, one could also conjecture that perhaps Oedipus did not see, because he did not *want* to see.

Oedipus' self-inflicted punishment is also a concretization, which becomes symbolic: he blinds himself. Since he would not "see" in a more abstract way, he feels he does not deserve to see. This theme of not seeing is a recurring one in the play. The only person who really "saw" and knew was the blind prophet, Tiresias.

Specific concretizations also occur in *Macbeth*. The three witches appearing at the beginning of the play are concretizations of Macbeth's emerging ambitions after his victory. Lady Macbeth is the fourth "witch" in the play, a function reinforced by her concrete role as Macbeth's wife. Another reinforcing concretization of great power occurs toward the end of the play. The witches had predicted that Macbeth would fall only when Birnam Wood itself marched against him. Macbeth interpreted this statement as an assurance that he would never fall, because woods do not move. But in one of the last scenes it was reported to Macbeth that the wood was indeed moving toward him. The enemy on the march was carrying bushes as screens, thus giving the impression from a distance that the wood was moving. At one level this scene may be interpreted as a comic device of the witches and of Shakespeare, a trick to deceive poor Macbeth (an acted-out witticism, like those described in Chapter 7). But of course the scene has a far deeper meaning. The crimes of Macbeth are so horrendous as to make even the immovable woods move in horror. The immensity of the crimes is equalled by the stupendousness of the phenomenon. At times the abstract and the concrete are merged and at other times they are separated, so that at times we have the simultaneous and at other times the subsequent occurrence of contrasting levels of cognition, functioning harmoniously.

Another example from Shakespeare is found in *King Lear*. The king, after having been rejected and betrayed by two daughters, finds himself in the open in the middle of the night, while a terrible storm rages. The darkness of the night, the inhospitable wilderness of the land, the fury of the storm are actual concretizations of King Lear's tragic predicament. They portray not only the misdeeds of the daughters but also the king's situation and state of mind. These paleologic concretizations do not reduce the status of the king; on the contrary, they enrich it aesthetically. Up to now the concrete and the abstract converge. Up to this point Shakespeare is a great poet. But, when he actually undoes the fusion of the abstract and of the concrete, he reaches the sublime. King Lear cannot externalize or project his concern to the realistic tempest and his own physical survival. The two persons who are with him, the fool and Kent, want to make him aware of the tempest; he should take care of himself, go under cover. But the king is concerned only with the tempest of his mind. He says:

> *Spit fire! Spout rain!*
> *Nor rain, wind, thunder, fire are my daughters.*
> *I tax not you, you elements with unkindness;*
> *I never gave you kingdom, call'd you children;*
> *You owe me no subscription. Then let fall*
> *Your horrible pleasure. Here I stand your slave,*
> *A poor, infirm, weak and despis'd old man* . . .

Shortly afterward, however, King Lear again matches the concrete with the abstract; he recognizes that the tempest of feelings and thoughts joins the tempest of the elements. He says to the elements:

> *But yet I call you servile ministers,*
> *That will with two pernicious daughters join*
> *Your high-engender'd battles, 'gainst a head*
> *So old and white as this.*

This alliance—of the fury of the external and inner worlds—intensifies and preannounces the tragic development and tragic ending. Like Oedipus, the king of old, Lear failed to see the truth in a crucial situation, and this mistake unchained a series of events that could not be checked. However, this alliance of the external and inner worlds resulted not in suffering and doom alone, but in a victory of the spirit as well. At the end of his life, Lear loses his arrogance and pride, feels bound to the poor and the afflicted, and reunites with Cordelia in an act of parental love.

"As If" and Adualism

THE INCIDENT of the moving woods in *Macbeth* leads us to the study of more complicated forms of concretization, such as the phenomena of "as if" and adualism. In one of the most beautiful cantos of the *Inferno* (Canto xxxiii), for example, Dante describes his encounter with Ugolino, a count who had betrayed his fatherland, the city-state of Pisa, which was consequently defeated in war. Count Ugolino describes how the Pisans punished him for his crime: they jailed him and all his family in a tower prison and kept them there without food, until all of them died of starvation. The count describes to Dante the heart-breaking agony of his whole family. His children died one by one. He was the last to die.

After hearing Ugolino's account, Dante hurls one of his strongest invectives against the city of Pisa, for he was horrified that the city had not limited its punishment to the traitor, Ugolino, but had included his innocent children. Dante says:

Ah, Pisa, vituperio delle genti
del bel paese là dove il sì suona,
poichè i vicini a te punir son lenti

Ah, Pisa! Shame to the people of that fair [Tuscan] land where "si" * resounds,
since thy neighbors are slow to punish thee,

Muovasi la Capraia e la Gorgona,
e faccian siepe ad Arno in su la foce,
si ch'egli anneghi in te ogni persona.

The islands of Capraia and Gorgona must move
and hedge up the Arno River at its mouth,
so that every living soul be crowned in thee.

* *Si* is a symbol for the Tuscan [Italian] language, like *oui*, *oc*, and *oi'l* for other Romance languages.

Chè se il conte Ugolino aveva voce   For, *if Count Ugolino had the fame*
d'aver tradita te delle castella,   *of having betrayed thee of thy castles,*
non dovei tu i figliuoi porre a tal croce: *thou oughtest not have put his sons*
    into such torture:

innocenti facea l'età novella.   *Their youthful age made them innocent.*

No translation can reproduce the terse style of Dante, the beauty of his images, and the intensity of his emotions. Capraia and Gorgona are two small islands in the Tyrrhenian Sea, not too far from the mouth of the Arno River, beside which the city of Pisa lies. Dante is perturbed by the terrible crime that had been committed in Pisa and expresses the wish that these two islands would move and close the mouth of the Arno, so that every person in the city would drown.

During my adolescent years, I admired the beauty of this passage, but I was also somewhat irritated by it. Born and raised myself in Pisa, I resented Dante's zest for having the whole town perish—for inflicting a punishment like that of Sodom and Gomorrah on the city that was to become the birthplace of Galileo. In fact, I used to go to great lengths to demonstrate that Dante's invective here is an example of poetic incongruity and self-contradiction. He is horrified by the murder of Ugolino's innocent children, yet he seems to propose a similar crime on a scale many times greater.

What the literalness and crusading zeal of adolescence prevented me from seeing was that Dante in this passage did not want to give us a piece of juridical wisdom. He knew that no matter how intensely he wished that the islands of Capraia and Gorgona would move, they would stay where they were. Dante was not a Greek god, endowed with cosmic power, and he was aware of it. Had he really possessed the power to move them (the kind of power actually held by some people today, who could push a button and initiate a cataclysm), he would not have contemplated using it.

What Dante actually did was to resort to an artistic technique: the "as if" phenomenon. This is *artistic potentiality*, which becomes *artistic reality*. Nobody could make the islands move, but in the poetry we see them move and cause thousands of people to drown in an apocalyptic deluge. Dante did not want to destroy a city and its inhabitants, but to transform his intense rage into a titanic *image*. He succeeded in concretizing his feeling in an image fit for a supernatural power; that is, he was able to transform an impossibility into an actual image that has a real artistic effect.

The Creative Product

The operation of adualism in schizophrenia and in dreams was discussed in Chapter 3. This mechanism causes a person to be unable to distinguish between acts of consciousness and objects; that is, between the world of the mind and the external world. Obviously the creative person knows that what he creates is fiction. However, what is being created comes to exist in its own right—that is, as something having artistic value and effect. Thus at the same time that an artistic work is fiction, it is also reality: artistic reality. The "as if," which logically involves a possibility, becomes an artistic actuality as an expression. When Shakespeare, by resorting to a trick, makes Birnam Wood move in *Macbeth*, he creates an "as if" phenomenon. The woods did not really move spontaneously, but the effect is as if they had really moved. The spectator understands that Macbeth is doomed. Here the theatrical medium permits an acted-out "as if" phenomenon.

As described in Chapter 3, the dreamer or the schizophrenic may think, "If this would happen . . . if I were king . . ." and immediately this emerging possibility becomes transformed into a dream or a delusion in which he *is* a king. In a similar way a poet may think, "If islands were to move . . ." and in the mind of the poet and of his readers, the islands *move*. This phenomenon is found not only in literature, but in other arts as well. For instance, in painting and sculpture, movement may appear as an artistically actualized potentiality. The artist is not dreaming or delusional; he knows that there is a difference and therefore a dualism between art and reality, but his artistic work, by being both fictitious and real, becomes adualistic. Its life is a life *sui generis*, as is best exemplified in the theater. The work of art belongs to a *second reality*, which maintains a certain distance from the first reality. It differs from the delusional "reality" of the psychotic, which is fused with and therefore belongs to the first reality. During the creative act the artist sees his work as independent of him and as already having a life of its own. A playwright often feels that the characters of his play are directing him in constructing it. Jung wrote (1933) that it was not Goethe who created Faust, but Faust who created Goethe.

The Positive Aspect of Negation

ANOTHER characteristic that primitive cognition and poetry have in common is the positive aspect of negation. I have already mentioned this phenomenon in Chapter 6, together with the fact that Freud has described it in dreams. Susanne Langer (1953) has also described it in relation to poetry, although, if I understand her correctly, she does not connect it with primitive cognition. She quotes the last stanza of Swinburne's "The Garden of Proserpine," in which almost every line is a denial.

> *Then star nor sun shall waken,*
> *Nor any change of light;*
> *Nor sound of waters shaken,*
> *Nor any sound or sight:*
> *Nor wintry leaves nor vernal;*
> *Not days nor things diurnal;*
> *Only the sleep eternal*
> *In an eternal night.*

Langer correctly states that in a literal sense the poem is a constant rejection of the emerging ideas. But what is denied acquires artistic reality: the imagery of the sun, stars, light, waters, leaves, and so on, is present.

Emphasis on Verbalization

WE HAVE already provided a detailed discussion of the altered balance between connotation, verbalization, and denotation in Chapter 5, where we saw how schizophrenic thinking entails a reduction of connotative power and an emphasis on verbalization. We have shown that the same phenomenon occurs in witticisms, as well. In the literary arts, especially poetry, there is also an emphasis on verbalization: words acquire importance as phonetic entities or sounds. As demonstrated, emphasis on verbalization rather than connotation can definitely be a regressive phenomenon. In poetry, however, contrary to what happens in schizophrenia, there is no reduction in connotation. Instead of decreasing connotative power, the emphasized verbalization increases or accentuates some aspects of it. This is another phenomenon of creativity that belongs to the tertiary, not the primary, process.

In some other fields of art, such as painting and sculpture, verbalization does not exist; it is the denotation that acquires emphasis and significance. In other words, it is the work of art itself, in its physical entity—connected, of course, with its connotative value. In poetry, denotation is not absent; but it assumes an unusual form. The word acquires special denotative qualities, so that in a certain way it becomes the thing that it symbolizes. The word is not just a symbol of the object; it often *embodies* the thing symbolized. It may become an actual portrait or image of the thing that it represents—a verbal icon, as it has been called by Wimsatt (1954). With this emphasis on denotation, language becomes a more vivid mirror of reality, not because it provides a sequence of meanings, but because it reproduces or evokes images of aspects of reality. Here too, however, the phenomenon is not the primitive or regressive mechanism described in Chapter 5; rather, it belongs to the tertiary process. The connotation is not eliminated but reinforced or expanded in unusual ways by this special type of denotation.

The topic of verbalization in poetry has been the subject of much study and research by literary men of every age. This discussion will not include everything that is important from a literary point of view, but will stress the aspects that are relevant to our study.

In ordinary language, words are predominantly carriers of meanings to be communicated to others. In poetry, words have additional qualities. Many phonetic characteristics exploited in poetry are well known. We shall review six of them here very quickly in order to pass on to three additional ones that are of particular relevance to our major topic. (1) *Onomatopoeia*. There are a certain number of words in every language whose sounds suggest their meaning. Thus words like *hiss*, *bang*, *crackle*, and *whisper* are onomatopoeic. (2) *Quantitative aspect of the syllable*. Although this characteristic was particularly emphasized in Latin and ancient Greek poetry, it has been fairly important in modern languages, too. Some words convey a quick and others a slow tempo. (3) *Euphony or cacophony*. A word that has an agreeable (euphonious) sound reinforces an agreeable meaning. A disagreeable (cacophonous) sound reinforces a disagreeable content. (4) *Versification*. The words are distributed in such a way as to produce a rhythm, or verbal music. They constitute a combination of sounds that is cyclical and agreeable to the ear. (5) *Rhyme*. A correspondence of terminal sounds, rhyme is agreeable to the ear. The rhyme may be perfect or imperfect. Assonance, consonance, and alliteration are forms of partial rhyme. (6) *Archaic, obsolete, or childlike forms*. One example would be the use of the archaic "thou" and "thy" in Blake's poem "The Sick Rose." (The use of archaic terms will be discussed in Chapter 9, in reference to religious experiences.)

EMERGING MEANING IN THE PHONETIC By resorting to the first five characteristics listed above, the poet, in addition to conveying the meaning of the words, appeals to our phonetic sense. We perceive a pleasant and rhythmic sound, something reminiscent of music. This melodious phonetic quality is obvious in any poem in its entirety. Often even isolated verses acquire a majestic beauty because of it. I shall mention two examples, one from Italian and the other from French literature. The first is a verse from Petrarch, the poet who introduced this emphasis on the formal structure of words into European literature.

Primavera per me pur non è mai.

No translation can adequately reproduce this verse, which has been defined by Contini (1951) as enjoying "supreme ineffability;" that is, a quality that cannot be expressed in any other way. A literal, prosaic translation is: "Spring never is for me." Because of his sorrow the poet will no longer be able to enjoy spring. The concept is rather commonplace, but the way in which it is expressed is unique. The verse starts with the word *primavera*, "spring," placed there to indicate one of the most desirable parts of life, and ends with the word *mai*, never. Spring will no longer exist for the poet. The verse starts with a noun, the only one in the verse; the rest consists of monosyllabic words (preposition, adverbs, pronouns, and so on).

It is also difficult to describe the beauty of the following verse by Racine (*Phèdre* IV, II).

Le jour n'est pas plus pur que le fond de mon coeur.

Prosaically translated as "The day is not more pure than the bottom of my heart," the verse consists of monosyllables only. It can be divided into three feet: *Le jour/ n'est pas plus pur/ que le fond de mon coeur.* Each foot ends with the sound *r*. As Agosti points out (1972), the verse relies for its effect on the phonetic similarity between the three words with which the feet end: *jour, pur, coeur.*

What I wish to give special consideration to here is that the formal structure, or special sounds such as assonance, consonance, and alliteration, do not appear in a poem merely to increase or improve the phonetic effect, but also to permit the emergence of a special meaning. At times an assonance is used to emphasize a connection, not apparent but residing in the depth of the human soul, between two different and seemingly contrasting meanings. The most typical example of this mechanism that I know of is in Shakespeare, when Othello says in reference to Desdemona, "I kissed thee ere I killed thee." Kissing is generally associated with love and killing with hate; the two words, which are almost opposite in connotation, are united by the assonance, but this union symbolizes that they have been united by Othello's mad passion. Thus by resorting to special verbalization, this sentence includes the whole theme of the tragedy.

In many other cases, special phonetic structures become carriers of a special meaning that is hidden or not immediately apparent. I shall take as an example the marvelous poem by Tennyson:

> *There has fallen a splendid tear*
> *From the passion-flower at the gate.*
> *She is coming, my dove, my dear;*
> *She is coming, my life, my fate;*
> *The red rose cries, "She is near, she is near";*
> *And the white rose weeps, "She is late";*
> *The larkspur listens, "I hear, I hear";*
> *And the lily whispers, "I wait."*

The poem describes the poet's exultation because his beloved is about to arrive. All the flowers in the garden join him in this joyful expectation. The expectation consists of two different, antithetical thoughts that are both expressions of a great, impatient love: (1) soon she will be here; and (2) she will not be here soon enough. The red rose and the larkspur stress how close she is; the white rose and the lily complain that she is not yet here. All this is semantically expressed in a clear way. What is not easily apparent is how these two different thoughts are expressed phonetically in two different ways. The thought "Soon she will be here" relies on the sound *ear*, which ends the first, third, fifth, and seventh lines (tear, dear, near, hear). With this ending the words emphasize the closeness, the undisputed pleasure of the thought. Even the word "tear," which is generally associated with sorrow, is transformed into a "splendid tear," the dew. The thought which stresses that the beloved will not be here soon enough relies instead on the sound *ate* (gate, fate, late, wait). In verse four the beloved is called "my life, my fate," but these two words, although endearing, indicate the prolongation in time and are different from the other endearing words, "my dove, my dear."

The antithesis between the two thoughts is, however, overcome or blended by other phonetic devices. The possessive pronominal adjective *my* is put before dove, dear, life, fate. The beloved is the poet's no matter whether or not she arrives soon enough. The other device is the repeated use of the pronoun *she*, which appears five times in the brief poem. The other pronoun, *I*, appears only three times. The flowers that talk represent the contrasting voices coming from the poet's heart. Since prominence is given to the loved one, not to the lover, *she* appears more frequently than *I*. Although both contrasting thoughts are very well represented, the positive one is stressed more than the negative one. In fact, both the red rose and the larkspur twice repeat their positive statements "She is near, she is near" and "I hear, I hear," whereas the white rose and the lily only once make their negative statements "She is late" and "I wait." Perhaps it is also of some significance that the "negative" flowers are white, whereas the fully positive flowers are of different colors.

While the poet was composing the poem, he was following a complicated formalism of which he was probably fully unconscious. The emphasis on verbalization expands the meaning beyond the one established by conventional language. Whereas, in ordinary language, words have a meaning almost always unrelated to the sound, the affinity and similarity of sounds in much poetry superimposes a special value to sequences of words. As a rule, phonetic similarities and equivalences strengthen the equivalences in meanings. At times semantic differences are diminished or abolished by such similarities. Often this formalism, which carries a hidden but nevertheless felt additional value, does not participate in a progressive unfolding or evolution of meaning but instead produces an atmospheric meaning or a "main effect."

In schizophrenic language, thinking, and writing, one can also recognize an increased formalism based on phonetic affinities and similarities (see prayer of a regressed patient in Chapter 5, and many other examples in Arieti 1974). However, in schizophrenics, the accentuated formalism goes together with a semantic evasion. The patient seems to be less and less concerned with the conventional meaning, or with any meaning at all that can be conveyed to other people. Thus we have no reinforcement of primary and secondary processes. Instead we have discordance; any additional meaning, if there, is only for the sake of the patient—the only person who accepts the discordance. Thus the creative person and the schizophrenic obtain different results. However, they both use primary process and other primitive mechanisms, and this fact is relevant. In fact, it proves that the poet uses a faculty that does not come from "nowhere" but from a basic source inherent in every human being. The poet rediscovers that source and puts it to good use.

REPETITION, VERBAL PARALLELISM, AND PATTERNS OF SOUND Repetitions of the same word, combinations of words, verbal parallelisms, and patterns of sound are very important in poetry. They are probably related to the stereotypes and perseverations that are typical of the primary process and that occur in advanced schizophrenia and aphasia. In schizophrenia the stereotyping, although due to the automatic prevailing of the primary process, acquires a practical motivation. The patient feels that his message is not heard (and generally it is true that people disregard the message because, rightly or wrongly, it seems absurd); therefore he often repeats it in a stereotyped manner, hoping that eventually it will be heard (Arieti 1974, Chapter 23). In poetry and poetic prose, repetition of words or of special patterns of words increases the semantic effect. It indicates that the matter dealt with should penetrate the heart of the reader. The Bible, both in the Old and in the New Testaments, offers many splendid examples. Think of David's lament for his son in Samuel 2:

> O my son Absalom, my son, my son
> Absalom! Would God I had died
> for thee, O Absalom, my son, my son!

Consider also the song of Deborah in Judges 5.

> At her feet he bowed, he fell, he lay
> down: at her feet he bowed, he fell;
> where he bowed, there he fell down
> dead.

In Ecclesiastes there are many repetitions and parallelisms. In Chapter 3 (verses 1–8) the repetitive pattern indicates that there is a time for everything one can imagine:

> 1) *To everything there is a season, and a time*
> *to every purpose under the heaven:*
> 2) *A time to be born, and a time to die;*
> *a time to plant, and a time to pluck*
> *up that which is planted;*
> 3) *A time to kill, and a time to heal;*
> *a time to break down, and a time*
> *to build up;*
> 4) *A time to weep, and a time to laugh;*
> *a time to mourn, and a time to dance;*
> 5) *A time to cast away stones, and a time*
> *to gather stones together; a time to*
> *embrace, and a time to refrain from*
> *embracing;*
> 6) *A time to get, and a time to lose; a*
> *time to keep, and a time to cast away;*
> 7) *A time to rend, and a time to sew; a*
> *time to keep silence, and a time to speak;*
> 8) *A time to love, and a time to hate; a*
> *time of war, and a time of peace.*

Famous for the efficacy of its redundancy is verse 2 of chapter 4.

> *. . . I praised the dead which are already*
> *dead more than the living which are yet alive.*

In Matthew 5 we read:

> *Blessed are the poor in spirit: for theirs*
> *is the kingdom of heaven.*
> *Blessed are they that mourn: for they shall*
> *be comforted.*
> *Blessed are the meek: for they shall*
> *inherit the earth.*

The repetition of the pattern has an almost hypnotic, spellbinding effect, appropriate to the grandeur of the content. The reader can scarcely help but be persuaded, at least for the moment.

The Creative Product

Verlaine also makes a large use of repetition. Let's examine some verses from one of his well known poems.

> O mon Dieu, vous m'avez blessé d'amour
> Et la blessure est encore vibrant,
> O mon Dieu, vous m'avez blessé d'amour.
>
> . . . . .
>
> Voici mon sang que je n'ai pas versé,
> Voici ma chair indigne de souffrance,
> Voici mon sang que je n'ai pas versé.
>
> O my God, you have wounded me with love
> and the wound is still vibrant,
> O my God, you have wounded me with love.
>
> . . . . .
>
> Here is my blood that I have not shed,
> Here is my flesh unworthy of suffering,
> Here is my blood that I have not shed.

The whole poem consists of stanzas of three lines. The third line is always an exact repetition of the first line, producing a very unusual and intensely felt atmosphere.

At times the repetition adds a special meaning or leads to innumerable paths of association. Consider Robert Frost's "Stopping by Woods on a Snowy Evening": *

> Whose woods these are I think I know
> His house is in the village though;
> He will not see me stopping here
> To watch his woods fill up with snow.
>
> My little horse must think it queer
> To stop without a farmhouse near
> Between the woods and frozen lake
> The darkest evening of the year.
>
> He gives his harness bells a shake
> To ask if there is some mistake.

* From *Complete Poems of Robert Frost*. Copyright © 1923 by Holt, Rinehart and Winston, Inc. Copyright © 1951 by Robert Frost. Reprinted by permission of Holt, Rinehart and Winston, Inc.

> *The only other sound's the sweep*
> *Of easy wind and downy flake.*
>
> *The woods are lovely, dark and deep.*
> *But I have promises to keep,*
> *And miles to go before I sleep,*
> *And miles to go before I sleep.*

This poem embodies an intensely lived drama. At first the conflict is between three categories of people: one represented by Frost himself, the unpractical poet who wants to absorb the beauty and mystery of nature, no matter how inconvenient it is to do so; the second represented by the owner of the land, who is interested only in owning and not admiring his property; the third represented by the little horse, a realistic-unpoetic organism. The conflict then acquires momentum within Frost himself: it becomes intrapsychic. The poet soon will have to follow the suggestion of the horse. He cannot indulge in poetic contemplation; he has "promises to keep," he must face the obligations of life and the miles to go before he sleeps (perhaps a long and hurried life before he can rest with nature).

The repetition of the last line, in my opinion, concretizes or embodies a multiplicity of meanings. It portrays a sense of distance: miles and miles to go. It stresses the necessity of interrupting the poetic interlude and proceeding with a sense of urgency. At the same time there is an almost opposite meaning: in the repetition lies a vague association with the anticipated sleep. Often verbal repetition evokes the thought of lullabies and of the act of falling asleep. To be noticed also is the fact that all the lines of the last stanza end with the sound *eep*, accentuating the repetition.

HOMONYMS AND SIMILARITIES OF VERBALIZATION   These devices are used as springboards to unusual thought processes. We have seen (in Chapters 5 and 7) how often homonymous words are employed in schizophrenic thinking and in witticisms to bring about paleologic identifications. We have also seen, in schizophrenic thinking, that similarities of words frequently lead to unusual mental processes.

The same mechanism is found in literature, especially in poetry. We shall start with a classic example from Shakespeare. His Othello is a black man, a Moor. Actually, in the original Italian story written by Giovanni Battista Giraldi Cintio (from which Shakespeare took the plot) Othello was a white man, a Venetian patrician who served as a lieutenant in Cyprus in the year 1508. Giraldi's story gives no names, but historical documents indicate that the episodes he reported really took place and that the family name of this lieutenant was *Moro*. *Moro* in Italian means Negro or Moor; in the case of this lieutenant, however, Moro was his last name and had no connection with his race or color. It could be that Shakespeare mistook a family name for a name referring to the color of the person involved. I am more inclined to believe that the coincidence stimulated Shakespeare's mental associations. Shakespeare may have had the inspiration that if Othello were really a Moor, or black, the story would be given an uncommon artistic twist, and the contrast with the fair, "divine" Desdemona would be accentuated. A real pun was made from the name *Moro*.

Similar puns, quasi-puns, and strange plays on words are common in literature, especially in poetry. A typical one is from Petrarch, who plays on the word *Laura*:

> *L'aura che 'l verde lauro e l'aureo crine*
> *soavemente sospirando move . . .*

Here the name Laura is felt and heard in three different words (*l'aura*, the zephyr; *lauro*, the laurel; *l'aureo crine*, the golden hair).

Dante, too, utilizes plays on words. At first impression the examples are reminiscent of schizophrenic cognition. In *La Vita Nuova*, a book consisting of poems and poetic prose, he wrote that he saw Beatrice walking on the street *preceded* by her girl friend Giovanna, who was once the beloved of Dante's friend and fellow poet Cavalcanti. Dante wrote that Giovanna was often called *Primavera* (which in Italian means spring) because of her beauty. Dante then makes a peculiar play on words. *Primavera* signifies for him *prima verra*, which in Italian means "She will come first, before"—that is, before or preceding Beatrice, while walking. But his second pun is even more revealing. Dante stresses the fact that the real name of Beatrice's friend is Giovanna (the feminine of Giovanni, or John). Dante then compares her to John the Baptist, who *came before* or *preceded* the coming of Christ.

The underlying unconscious motivation, appearing several times in Dante's works, resides in his wish to identify Beatrice (whom he also calls "daughter of God") with Jesus Christ. He wants to make this identification not only in order to glorify the object of his love—in real life a woman named Beatrice—but in order to transform his profane or earthly love into a sacred or divine love. Dante must resort to the ambiguity of primary-process thinking in order to make this identification possible. But he knows that this way of thinking, which he follows, is not logical. He knows that if people believed that he accepted these ideas as true, they would consider him insane, but he manages to pass the reality test, so to speak, by using an opportunity made available to him by his secondary-process mechanism. He says that he does not really believe in these ideas. He writes "It seemed that Love spoke in my heart" to say such things. He tells the reader that this is fantasy, but there seems to be little doubt that he would like to believe at least part of this fantasy. As a matter of fact, the whole *La Vita Nuova* and *The Divine Comedy* are suffused with a mysticism that is not simply part of an aesthetic technique. As we have already mentioned, this mysticism is in fact, a special kind of reality for the poet.

In conclusion, the phonetic devices that are common in schizophrenic languages are also exploited by poets for artistic effect. But whereas in schizophrenic language these mechanisms contrast with the common meanings of the words and thereby confer bizarreness, in poetry they add charm and significance and agree with the meaning, which is carried by secondary-process mechanisms. In art, these phonetic mechanisms do not represent a regression to the primary process, but the emergence of the tertiary process. To paraphrase Hughlings Jackson once again, the several meanings are stereoscopic, not dyplopic. The poetic work may show many and unexpected dimensions, some belonging to the primary and some to the secondary process; but they are concordant, not discordant, and the whole attains new and unexpected results.

Before proceeding to examine more complicated examples, we must stress that we are now in a position to dismiss a common assumption. Often plays on words, assonances, alliterations, and so on are considered artificial techniques; poets are thought to indulge in these technical refinements at the cost of losing spontaneity and interest in the content. Nothing could be farther from the truth. Inasmuch as the poet has much easier access to these primary or archaic mechanisms, compared to the average person, special phonetic structures occur spontaneously to him. He does not search for them. As a matter of fact, he has the opposite problem to contend with. Since they come to his mind in such large numbers, he has to actively reject and eliminate most of them. Whereas the schizophrenic often accepts all of them, the poet chooses only those that fit with his secondary process and with the general need of his tertiary process.

In some complicated cases, homonymies and metaphors blend together. Let's take as an example the beautiful poem by the French poet Ronsard:

> Comme on voit sur la branche au mois de mai la rose,
> En sa belle jeunesse, en sa première fleur,
> Rendre le ciel jaloux de sa vive couleur,
> Quand l'Aube de ses pleurs au poinct du jour l'arrose;
>
> La grace dans sa fueille, et l'amour se repose,
> Embasmant les jardins et les arbres d'odeur;
> Mais batue ou de pluye, ou d'excessive ardeur,
> Languissante elle meurt, fueille à fueille déclose
>
> Ainsi en ta première et jeune nouveauté,
> Quand la Terre et la Ciel honoroient ta beauté,
> La Parque t'a tuée, et cendre tu reposes.
>
> Pour obseques reçoy mes larmes et mes pleurs,
> Ce vase plein de laict, ce panier plein de fleurs,
> Afin que vif et mort ton corps ne soit que roses.

> As one sees on the branch in the month of May the rose,
> in her beautiful youth, in her first blossoming,
> When the dawn at the beginning of the day bathes
> her with her tears, making the sky jealous of her vivid color,
>
> Grace lingers in her leaf and love rests there,
> irradiating fragrance to the gardens and the trees,
> but beaten or by the rain or by the sun's excessive ardor,
> languishing she dies, petal by petal.
>
> Thus in thy first and young newness,
> When Earth and Heaven honored thy beauty,
> Atropos has killed thee and as ash thou reposest.
>
> Receive for obsequies my tears and laments,
> This vase filled with milk, this basket full of flowers,
> so that alive or dead thy body be only roses.

Like the poem by Blake analyzed earlier in this chapter, a woman is compared to a rose, but she is further identified; she is the poet's beloved (Marie), who recently died. Agosti (1972) has analyzed the intricate phonetic mechanisms used in this poem. At first reading these mechanisms are immediately appreciated as part of the poem's aesthetic beauty, although at least some of them are not consciously differentiated. The phonemes by which the first two verses end (*rose*, *fleur*) are repeated in reverse order in the last two verses. *Repose*, which ends the first line of the second stanza, reappears in the last verse of the first tercet. The second part of the poem, which consists of the tercets, is addressed to a person, *tu*, and the *t* of the *tu* (thou) is heard all over again in many words of the tercet to emphasize the individuality of the addressee as a person. Agosti points out that repetition of words, with the same or different meanings, is one of the characteristics of the poem. The *rose* of the first line is repeated in the 14th; *fleur* of the second line is repeated as *fleurs* in the 13th; *ciel* of the third is repeated in the 10th *pleurs* of the fourth is repeated in the 12th; *fueille* of the fifth becomes *fueille à fueille* of the 8th; and *se repose* of the fifth becomes *tu reposes* in the 11th. *En sa belle jeunesse, en sa première fleur* of the second line becomes *Ainsi en ta première et jeune nouveauté* in the 9th line. Often the word which has been used twice is in one instance used metaphorically, metonymically, or in a way intermediary between the literal and the metaphorical. Thus *rose*, which is used literally in the first line as the object of comparison, in the plural form *roses* at the end of the sonnet becomes, metonymically and metaphorically, the body of the beloved, which is seen as a fragrance of roses. *Fleur* in the second line seems to be literally used, but actually means "in the first blossoming stage," or when the rose starts to blossom. In the 13th verse *fleurs* (flowers) seems to be used literally, but actually the *fleurs* symbolically represent Ronsard's poem, which by remaining in the French literature will permit the survival of the beloved. (The beautiful poem *does* make Marie survive: we are at this moment thinking of her, long after her death.) The *ciel* (sky) of the third line has a different meaning from the *Ciel* (Heaven), with a capital *C*, of the 10th verse. *Pleurs* in the fourth verse is metaphorically used for dew, but *pleurs* (crying) in the 12th verse, after *larmes* (tears), refers literally to weeping, as tears can be represented in a literary form by the poem.

The poem has the purpose of immortalizing the beloved, transforming her into roses after her death, since she was like a rose when she was alive. Ronsard is conscious of having succeeded; he feels that Marie will always be remembered in connection with roses: "Alive or dead thy body be only roses." It is beyond the purpose of this chapter to analyze further the intricacies of the French language used by the poet, that permit him to achieve the artistic fusion of roses and Marie.

It is an astonishing surprise to discover how language has many hidden meanings connected with phonetic sounds, with the possibility of shifting from the literal to the metaphorical and from the semantic to the phonetic. Since these hidden characteristics frequently occur in the language of schizophrenics who have never written poetry or studied poetics before they became ill, we must conclude that the possibility of resorting to these formal structures exists in many persons. In such disparate conditions as poetic creativity and schizophrenia, in which the usual ways of thinking and of using language are partially suspended, these phonetic structures—and what results from them—attain unexpected and in some cases unsuspected prominence. Again we must stress that whereas the poet is able to integrate them fully with the secondary process to such an extent that they are not immediately apparent except to the learned reader, they are apparent, and discordant with the context, in the patient's productions.

We have mentioned how spontaneously these phonetic characteristics occur to poets, and how unexpectedly the beauty emerges. Because of the particular characteristic of language it is extremely difficult to reproduce in a different language the beauty found in the original. Nevertheless exceptions occur, which also demonstrate to what an extent these devices can be learned in the form of a technique. Readers who know both Italian and English may be astonished at reading the following two passages, dealing again with a rose compared to a woman whose beauty will soon fade away. The first is by Edmund Spenser, the English poet, who was born in 1552 and died in 1599, from a section known as The Bower of Bliss in "The Faerie Queene."

> *Ah see, who so faire thing doest faine to see,*
> *In springing flowre the image of thy day;*
> *Ah see the Virgin Rose, how sweetly shee*
> *Doth first peepe forth with bashfull modestee,*
> *That fairer seemes, the lesse ye see her may;*
> *Lo, see soone after, how more bold and free*
> *Her bared bosome she doth broad display;*
> *Loe, see soone after, how she fades, and falles away.*

> *So passeth, in the passing of a day,*
> *Of mortall life the leafe, the bud, the flowre,*

Ne more doth flourish after first decay,
That earst was sought to decke both bed and bowre,
Of many a Ladie, and many a Paramowre:
Gather therefore the rose, whilest yet is prime,
For soone comes age, that will her pride deflowre:
Gather the Rose of love, whilest yet is time,
Whilest loving thou mayst loved be with equall crime.

The second is from *La Gerusalemme Liberata* by Torquato Tasso, an Italian poet who lived from 1544 to 1595. *La Gerusalemme Liberata* was finished in 1575. Spenser's passage is almost an exact translation of Tasso's passage and retains its original beauty. Spenser never acknowledged, as far as I know, his indebtedness to Tasso. Nevertheless, the content is almost identical, so that we can conclude that it is beyond statistical possibility that the two poets independently envisioned the same content with the same terms. Another amazing fact is that both passages possess great aesthetic finesse.*

Deh, mira, egli cantò, spuntar la rosa
Dal verde suo modesta e verginella,
Che mezzo aperta ancora e mezzo ascosa,
Quanto si mostra men, tanto è più bella.
Ecco poi nudo il sen già baldanzosa
Dispiega; ecco poi langue, e non par quella;
Quella non par che desiata avanti
Fu da mille donzelle e mille amanti.

Cosi trapassa al trapassar d'un giorno
De la vita mortale il fiore e il verde;
Nè, perchè faccia indietro april ritorno,
Si rinfiora ella mai nè si rinverde.
Cogliam la rosa in sul mattino adorno
Di questo dì, che tosto il seren perde;
Cogliam d'amor la rosa; amiamo or quando
Esser si puote riamati amando.

Tacque; e concorde de gli augelli il coro, . . .

---

* I am grateful to Dr. Henry Brill, an eminent psychiatrist, linguist, and scholar, for discovering and pointing out to me the amazing closeness between Tasso's and Spenser's passages.

Aesthetic Pleasure in General, and Specifically in Poetry

IN EXAMINING the nature of the aesthetic pleasure elicited by the appreciation of a work of art, I shall omit some issues that are predominantly philosophical: for instance, the question of whether aesthetic value is identifiable or commensurate with aesthetic pleasure. In the case of wit and the comic, it is relatively easy to determine the nature of the comical or witty experience. Our organism is equipped to respond to wit with laughter, smiles, or an easily expressed feeling of merriment. It is much more difficult to analyze the nature of aesthetic pleasure. Some authors define it as a pleasant emotion or state of satisfaction that occurs when one contemplates a work of art. This statement is vague and circular. Other formulations are equally tautological. For instance, if we say, "We enjoy this work of art because it is beautiful," we add nothing to our understanding, since the word "beautiful" in this context means "having the property of eliciting aesthetic pleasure." Some authors find the essence of aesthetic pleasure in experiencing the perceptual aspects of a work of art; others in experiencing the emotional component. In what follows we shall examine these two possibilities.

The word "aesthetic," which was coined by the German philosopher Baumgarten about the year 1750 from the Greek word *aestheticos*, etymologically refers to what is "perceptive and sensuous." Indeed, there is an attempt in a work of art to reduce everything to sensuous or perceptual impressions. This is obviously so in painting, sculpture, and music, where, as already mentioned, denotation becomes predominant. In poetry the attempt to perceptualize—that is, the attempt to reduce the object of contemplation to a perceptual level—is made in at least two ways: (1) by placing the emphasis on the verbalization, so that the phonetic aspects of the word (sound, onomatopoeia, rhyme, rhythm, assonance, and so on) acquire prominence; and (2) by transforming concepts into imagery. The images cannot be reproduced as in dreams, paintings, or movies, but they are represented by words and metaphors. Words become icons or images by proxy.

We must first recognize that not all types of perception are apt to produce an aesthetic effect. Selection is necessary. For instance, perceptions involving taste and smell may be pleasant, but they are not conducive to aesthetic pleasure, presumably because they are not associated with abstract conceptions and cannot assume a significance that transcends the perceptual, except through other senses. In the human cerebral cortex, olfactory and gustatory stimuli receive relatively little elaboration.

It is visual and auditory perceptions, in particular, that are important in aesthetics. Such perceptions, of course, can be easily divided into pleasant and unpleasant ones. Not all noises can become music. As a rule a chord pleases the ear only when the frequencies of its component sounds are in a simple mathematical ratio to one another. We also know that colors of certain wavelengths are more pleasing to the eye. We do not know yet why certain physical characteristics of a stimulus produce pleasure or displeasure in the human organism, but we know that they have that effect. At times a perceptual stimulus is not pleasant per se, but its repetition or combination with others is. The repetition or the regular distribution of the same stimulus, as in architecture, poetry, dance, and music, produces a pleasant perceptual effect. Consider also the kaleidoscope—an instrument, often used by children as a toy, which contains loose bits of colored glass. These bits are reflected by mirrors many times, so that even the most inartistic combination of bits of glass produces a beautiful symmetrical design when it is repeated again and again.

Another perceptual quality frequently utilized to create an aesthetic effect is art's capacity to stimulate the sexual instinct—as, for instance, when nudes are portrayed. An artistic representation of a nude obviously transcends sexual stimulation and is not pornographic. The sexual element nevertheless plays a prominent role; the nude attracts and gratifies our sexual instinct. Other types of art resort to less obvious but equally effective sexual stimulation; for instance, literature with an erotic content.

We may conclude that art requires a pleasant sensory-perceptual background, generally of a visual, auditory, or sexual nature.* These sense perceptions are like the bricks on which the aesthetic edifice is built.

Contrary to the perceptualization that occurs in psychopathologi-

* Some apparent exceptions, like cacophonic music, arhythmic poetry, and so on, do not concern us here. These forms have departed from the original pleasant perceptual elements by complicated processes of aesthetic proxy, or for purposes of creating a contrast.

cal processes, a special selection is made in art: only physiologically pleasant perceptual stimuli, or spatiotemporal combinations of stimuli, directly or by proxy, are allowed to enter into the aesthetic work. Does this mean that a work of art consists only of these pleasant elements? Fechner (1876) attributed the whole of aesthetic pleasure to them. With his experimental or "scientific" method, he tried to track down the elements and the "supreme formal principles" on which aesthetic pleasure is based. For a while his experiments reached a worldwide audience, but their limitations were afterward recognized. Obviously something very important was missing in his formulations. The sublime cannot be reduced to these elementary facts.

Yet it is true that perceptual elements are particularly accentuated in art. Their selection and combination often increase their perceptual quality. For instance in reading or listening to poetry one becomes more than usually aware of the auditory aspect of words; in looking at paintings one becomes more aware of forms and colors; and so on. It seems that in order to carry the aesthetic message, the stimulus has to accentuate its perceptual quality or to actualize its perceptual potentiality.

As I have described elsewhere (Arieti 1967, Chapter 2), sensations lose some of their perceptual vividness when they assume a cognitive meaning. The child in his eidetic possibilities, primitive people, and some unusual persons who are said to be "in touch with themselves" have a greater ability than the majority of people to experience the perceptual nature of things. Apparently this is a faculty that the majority of modern men have lost. Giambattista Vico was one of the first to describe this sensuous or perceptual way of experiencing that is retained by primitive people and children (1725 and 1744).

Existentialists and Zen Buddhists point out how Western man, by indulging in the cognitive aspect of life, has lost touch with himself and with the intimate nature and perceptual richness of things. These philosophical schools are unfair not only to Western man but to *Homo sapiens* in general. As I have discussed elsewhere (Arieti 1967), man has really had no choice but to follow the expansion of his symbolic functions. Although it has led him to intellectual mastery of the world, this expansion occurred to a certain extent at the expense of the "experience of inner states" and of immediate subjectivity. It is one of the aims of art (or of some philosophies) to recapture the perceptual richness that has been lost. Art can do so, but to think that perceptual richness can be reintroduced into the daily life of every man, as many existentialists and Zen Buddhists assume, is utopian, to say the least.

As a matter of fact, perceptual vividness is recaptured in some pathological conditions. A few people who have undergone cerebral concussions experience vivid perceptual experiences for several minutes after they reacquire consciousness. Objects appear vague and indistinct, yet more beautiful and "more real" than in reality. Also at the onset of some acute schizophrenic episodes as well as during acute toxic states, for instance from ingestion of LSD, there is an accentuation of the perceptual characteristics of objects; to the patient, everything seems to be in technicolor. Such increases in perceptual qualities probably occur because the higher levels of cognition are impaired and decrease their inhibitory influences. However, these perceptual alterations undergo secondary or restitutional elaborations. In very primitive people and in children, the perceptual qualities of things have not yet been muffled by the enormous expansion of cognitive processes.

In my opinion it is incorrect to attribute aesthetic pleasure exclusively or predominantly to mere perceptual experience or accentuation. The admirer of a work of art is not an empiricist who approaches the world by way of sensory perceptions. Perceptual enrichment is related more to decoration than to real art. Aesthetic pleasure is indeed much more than perceptual enjoyment; it occurs when the enriched perceptions are pregnant with abstract and categorical concepts, which in their turn evoke unusual feelings. In fact, a great part of the aesthetic meaning involves the attuning of the abstract to the perceptual.

As already discussed in the section on the metaphor, the perceptual level to which we return in art, so to speak, reinforces the work of art's abstract level, just as in puns the paleological level reinforces the logical. Although based on perception, art does not rely on mere perception. To be specific, we have seen how the use of metaphor, the concretization of content, the emphasis on denotation and especially on verbalization, the use of the positive aspect of negation, and so on, are all archaic methods employed in the aesthetic process. Contrary to what happens in psychopathological conditions, dreams, and witticisms, concordance, not discordance, exists between these different mechanisms. Each borrows something from the others, so that the content seems to possess the beauty of the medium, and the medium the beauty of the content. In our first example, Blake's poem "The

Sick Rose," the abstract concept of beauty versus evil borrows significance from the concept of the beautiful woman and a man who destroys her; the concept of the woman and of the man borrows perceptual vividness from the images of the rose and the worm; and the images of the rose and the worm borrow sensuous beauty from the rhythm, rhyme, and pleasing combinations of sounds.

So far we have shown how each level borrows from a lower one. Now let us adopt a reverse process and see how each level borrows from a higher one. The medium consisting of "oral noises" is enriched by rhythm and rhyme. This phonetic pleasure is transcended because the oral sounds have not only a meaning, but a special meaning: the rose in the crimson bed. The beauty of the words fuses with the beauty of the imagery; then the image of the rose acquires further power from the fact that it may refer to a woman; but the concept of the woman acquires strength from the fact that it stands for beauty in general, or for the unfulfilled promise of a beautiful life. Similar remarks could be made about the image of the worm, who is invisible at first (in contrast to the rose's abundant crimson joy), but victorious in the end. Thus the simple words of the poem, reinforced by their sound, rhythm, and rhyme, come to carry an expanding load of meaning.

In contrast to the writers who have said that the basis of aesthetic pleasure lies in the perceptual aspects of a work of art, some important authors, such as the Russian novelist Tolstoy (1898) and the aesthetician Ducasse (1929), have propounded an emotional theory of art. According to them, the essence of art is the expression or sharing of emotion. The relation between art and emotion was studied long ago by Aristotle, who developed the concept of catharsis (from which Freud derived his psychoanalytic theory of catharsis). Aristotle felt that during an aesthetic experience, such as seeing the theatrical performance of a tragedy, painful emotions are first aroused and then "purged" or eliminated. Turbulent emotions are transformed into serene or calm ones. Aristotle thus saw catharsis almost as a medical procedure, that of taking a purgative medication. He failed to explain why catharsis is enjoyable. (In fact, purging is useful but almost never enjoyable.) An aesthetic experience is certainly an emotional experience, but not just any emotional experience. Some emotional experiences can be very anti-aesthetic. Even psychoanalytic catharsis, which purges and may cure in a medical sense, is not an aesthetic experience.

Perhaps we can understand the problem better if we compare the ways in which emotional and cognitive elements enter into the work of art. We have seen that the cognitive content consists not only of secondary-process mechanisms but also of lower-level mechanisms, often belonging to the primary process. Can we make the same statement about the emotions that enter into a work of art? Not at all. These emotions are not primitive experiences of inner states, nor are they simple emotions that we share with other animals; often they are on man's highest emotional level.

Strivings toward fulfillment of love, of a mission, of an ideal, or of an ethical demand; conflicts between the aspirations and the limited power of man, between the dictates of society and those of the inner self, between truth and illusion, or between the tendency toward symbolic infinity and the finitude of man—these are the emotions that often enter into a work of art. Even if primitive emotions occur in art, like the passion that leads to sexual assault or the greediness that leads to murder, they stand for the states of imperfection of human existence. In ordinary life, high emotions are frequently elicited by conceptual constructs, general statements, universal maxims, and so on. In the work of art, they retain the majesty of universally shared emotions and concepts but acquire the vividness of a specific and generally personal instance. This vividness is modified and made more acceptable by the pleasing perceptual medium.

The listener or observer identifies with the content of the work of art only inasmuch as he or she is a man or a woman and the work of art portrays a human situation. In other words, he is involved merely as an element of a larger class that includes not only the actual but also the possible. The possibility at times is merely theoretical—for instance, the possibility of finding oneself exactly in the position of King Lear, betrayed by his daughters; or of Ulysses, who decides not to return to Ithaca but to go "beyond the sunset;" or of being the inhabitant of another planet, as in science fiction. Thus the cognitive elements and the emotions, although profound, are dispersed into a class or category that has only a theoretical reality—what I have called a *second reality*.

In the act of being attached to a hypothetical class, the emotion is experienced as not affecting the observer directly. This is tantamount to saying that the adualism of art is transformed into *aesthetic distance*. The artist, or the admirer of the work of art, in a certain way recognizes that the creative product has its own life, independent of the life of the artist and that of the admirer. The admirer is not detached, but he is involved only to the extent that he is a member of a hypothetical class to which his life and the content of the work of art both belong. Thus in my opinion aesthetic distance, to which Bullough (1957) has attributed great importance, is related to art's adualism and to the formation of hypothetical classes. We have on one side the emotional vividness of the specific event portrayed, on the other side the distance conferred by adualism and the formation of a hypothetical class. And all this is expressed through a pleasing perceptual medium. In the theater, the aesthetic distance itself is concretized by the physical distance between the stage and the audience. Some people do not want seats in the first few rows of the orchestra, because from there they can see the actors as real entities and not exclusively as the characters they impersonate.

We must spend a few more words on these hypothetical classes. Although capable of producing a distance between us and the content of the work of art, they should bring about in us not a sense of alienation but of participation. For instance, although it is extremely improbable that we shall find ourselves in the position of King Lear, many of us have experienced ingratitude from people whom we considered close to us. Although it is improbable that we will find ourselves in the position of Ulysses, we, too, at times daydream of adventuring into the unknown rather than returning to the protective environment of our home. Although we shall never be inhabitants of other planets, we can envision people somewhat related to us in a strange environment. Thus, in spite of the differences and of the aesthetic distance, a tie to our condition can be recognized.

The opposite of a sense of distance can also occur. At times, spectators who recognize something in a play that is very similar to what they too have experienced identify closely with the characters and are deeply moved. In this case the response is not so much an aesthetic one as it is a mere emotion caused by identification.

(Some schizophrenic patients cannot visualize an artistic hypothetical category and cannot experience a "second reality." These patients have great difficulty when they see a theatrical performance. Aesthetic distance in the theater is as important as it is in poetry or novels, and yet it is more difficult to retain. But although aesthetic appreciation is diminished in these pathological cases, it is not totally absent. Thus it would seem that aesthetic distance enriches the aesthetic potentiality but is not a prerequisite for a moderate appreciation of art.)

At this point let us review all the elements that participate in the formation of an aesthetic product or in the aesthetic experience:

1. An abstract ideation or constellation of concepts is to a considerable extent sustained by low cognitive forms and mechanisms: formation of primary classes, perceptualization and concretization of the concept, use of the positive aspects of negative, emphasis on verbalization, and so on. A special type of concretization of the concept is the particularization of a universal, whether a principle or a recurring human situation—a perennial conflict of man. For instance, Robert Frost's poem "The Road Not Taken" refers to a type of life that was rejected when the road "less traveled by" was chosen. The characters of a play or of a novel stand for human characters, types, or human conditions. Don Quixote is a way of facing life. Isabel Archer in Henry James's *Portrait of a Lady* is the representative of the recurrent conflict of women who dream of freedom and nobleness but are stuck in a conventional life.

2. Contrary to what occurs in witticisms, the low cognitive forms and mechanisms that are used are concordant with the abstract meaning and reinforce it. A paleological reinforcement often takes place.

3. The fusion of the different levels of cognition is mediated by a perceptual medium. In the process of perceptualization, the perceptions that have a pleasant physiological effect on the human organism are almost always selected. When unpleasant ones are selected, it is generally done in order to stress a contrast.

4. With the use of lower levels of cognition and of special types of perceptualizations, there is a strong tendency to transform an act of cognition into an experience (namely, a deeply felt subjective status) at the same time that the cognitive meaning is retained. As a matter of fact, the cognitive meaning is generally enlarged by newly emerging classes, associative levels, marginal ideas, and—as we shall see in the next section—a return of endoceptual constructs.

5. The emotional content belongs not to the lowest but to the highest levels. Even in the cases where primitive emotions are portrayed, their expression tends to reassert the highest levels of cognition. This is true even when these levels seem to have disappeared because of the use of low cognitive forms. The formation of hypothetical cognitive classes and the presence of artistic adualism produce a

sense of psychic distance. Thus the emotional effect, no matter how intense, is not experienced as something that refers personally to the admirer of the work of art.

6. Aesthetic value and aesthetic pleasure emerge from the fusion or concomitant occurrence of all the factors named above.* How aesthetic pleasure emerges from this fusion is difficult to substantiate. In fact we cannot offer quantitative measurements of the various elements that enter into the work of art, as exact science would require; nor can we explain *why* the fusion of these elements causes the human organism to experience aesthetic pleasure.† Again we have reached that border between soma and psyche, psychology and physiology, which we are unable to cross. Aesthetic pleasure is not a mere act of cognition, but predominantly a pleasant experience.

Aesthetic Work and Aesthetic Synthesis

THE CREATIVE PERSON seems to have special access to the primary process, just as do the dreamer and the schizophrenic patient. Dreamers generally lose their entrée to the primary process as soon as they wake up. Schizophrenics, as a rule, cannot coordinate the two

---

* In a poem entitled "Poetry," the Italian poet and writer Niccolò Tommaseo (1802–1874) listed the different ingredients of the creative process involved in the writing of a poem:

Non la raggiante immagine,	*Not the radiating image,*
non la riposta idea,	*Nor the hidden idea,*
non l'armonia de' numeri,	*Nor the rhythmical harmony,*
non e' l'amor che crea.	*Nor love create.*
Idea, concento, immagine,	*Idea, rhythm, image, air of fecund love,*
aura d'amor fecondo,	*Merge into one form*
formansi in uno, e n' escono	*From which the verse, the flower,*
il verso, il fiore, il mondo.	*The world come out.*

Incidentally, it is worth noticing in the first stanza of this poem the aesthetically positive aspect of negation, described in a preceding section. Tommaseo's use of negation is aesthetically inferior to that of Swinburne given earlier, because the negated entities are abstract concepts that do not evoke concrete images.

† For a scientific method in aesthetics, see the interesting book by Munro (1956).

processes for creative purposes. Some recovering schizophrenics, however, retain a greater accessibility to the primary process than normal persons and are nevertheless in a position to use the secondary process. The study of these patients is useful for the understanding of creative activity. Reports of such cases are rare, because the examiner has to see them during a special transitional stage that lasts a short time and is easily missed if not looked for.

Such a patient was a 13-year-old schizophrenic girl who was admitted to the hospital following an acute psychotic episode in which she experienced hallucinations, delusions, and the idea that nearby people referred to her when they were talking.

Three days after admission, during a routine mental examination, she was asked to explain the difference between character and reputation. She replied: "Character is your personality. Reputation is stamped on, and can never be erased. Your reputation is a bed, and when you get in, you can't get out of it. Character is like a bedspread which can be taken off, or character is like dirt on a sheet which, if you wash it, can be removed." The patient was asked to define the word despair. She answered, "Despair is like a wall covered with thick grease, and a person is trying to climb up this wall by digging his fingers in. Down below is a deep, bottomless pit. Up at the top of the wall on the ceiling is a big, black spider. I have been in this deep pit during the past year, but now I am climbing up a rope, trying to get out of it." When she was asked to tell the difference between idleness and laziness, she said, "Both have to be present for one to be present. You have to be idle to be lazy, but you don't have to be lazy to be idle. When you're idle, you are living physically, but not really living. Laziness is when you give up." When she was asked the difference between poverty and misery, she replied, "Poverty is poor; misery is agony."

It is very unusual for a 13-year-old to express herself with such depth. She was not physically mature for her age; on the contrary, she looked younger than 13. Although bright, she did not give the impression of being exceptionally intelligent. And yet her expressions often revealed that uncommon faculties were at her disposal. Her definitions of character, personality, and despair are not those to be found in a dictionary. She did not explain the concept or the connotation of these words. She defined them by transforming the concept into a constellation of perceptual images. Webster defines despair, for example, as loss of hope—an accurate but also a circular and prosaic definition in comparison with that of the patient, who resorted to a sequence of vivid images: the wall covered with thick grease, the person who tries to climb up and digs his fingers in, the bottomless pit, the black spider. The girl's definition is a poetic definition; so are her definitions of character and reputation.

Was the girl's illness at least partially responsible for her ability to translate concepts into images? Most probably. As a matter of fact, as far as it was possible to determine, she was not given to the use of rich imagery prior to her illness. When she became ill, she was in a rare condition where both primary and secondary processes were accessible and could be coordinated.* This state permitted her to change from a language of classification (or of concepts) to a language of experience, when she was giving definitions such as those of character and despair. Her language was certainly not based on classifications validated by society; but could we say that it was based on experience? The girl had never climbed a wall covered with thick grease, had never dug her fingers into it while she observed a bottomless pit below and a black spider on the top. She was capable of having these experiences only by verbal proxy, as we, reading her remarks, can by proxy see and feel as she did.

This automatic translation into imagery is a potentiality of the human psyche. It is an attempted return to the level of imagery that preceded the verbal level (see Chapter 3). The imagery, however, is represented by verbal proxy. As Giambattista Vico (1725) described, very ancient people resorted to this type of thinking more than modern people, because in ancient times abstract concepts were not yet developed to a high degree. Primitive life retains a quality of freshness, genuineness, and perceptual vividness that imparts an aesthetic or artistic flavor. There is some question, however, whether it is correct to think of primitive life as always being "lived poetry." Although that life may be richer than ours in imagery, in many circumstances it may not have the concomitant abstract counterpart. In other words, it possesses the concrete and the particular but not always the universal

* Some poets and artists have tried to obtain similar states through alcoholic intoxication, smoking opium or marijuana, or the use of other drugs. Mescaline or lysergic acid intoxication may also produce states vaguely related to the one experienced by the girl. However, in these artificially induced conditions, people either do not regress to a primary process, or, if they do, they lose the use of the secondary process or cannot coordinate it with the primary.

(at a conscious and verbalized stage). When we observe the primitive life of aborigines, we automatically imprint on it our abstract concepts, so that such a life becomes artistic for us.

A few more words are necessary to avoid misunderstanding. Primitive life may be very poetic, but not *just because* it is primitive. Freshness, genuineness, and perceptual vividness are usually pleasant qualities, but they are not sufficient to make life poetic. Primitive life is poetic if it at least implies the abstract in a way in which it can be appreciated.

If primitive life is not necessarily artistic in its totality, however, primitive art is real art (Chapter 9). Although primitives express themselves more easily in imagery, concepts are created in primitive societies, too. The rarity of concepts seems more pronounced than it is, because of the lack of words corresponding to ours. Concepts are actually budding in primitive art, and probably reach a full conceptual level mostly because of the realizations achieved by artistic means. It is likely that the transformation of icons into ideas is more important for primitive man than for other men. Other primitive realizations are achieved through religious means, as Chapter 10 will demonstrate.

Returning to our 13-year-old girl, we find other aesthetic characteristics in addition to her visual imagery. One is the emphasis on verbalization that appeared, for instance, when she explained the difference between idleness and laziness. As she started to define these words, she had the idea (which she later discarded) that idleness and laziness are correlational terms—that is, that one cannot exist without the other (for example, the words "husband" and "wife"). Bertrand Russell (1919) in his *Introduction to Mathematical Philosophy*, calls this relation a one–one relation. How much more beautiful is the girl's definition: "Both have to be present for one to be present." The contrast between the words "both" and "one" and the repetition of the words "to be present" confer aesthetic qualities to her expression.

The girl actually contradicts herself almost immediately, when she states correctly that "You have to be idle to be lazy, but you don't have to be lazy to be idle." Here again the repetition of the same words gives rhetorical emphasis. In the rest of her reply, "When you're idle, you are living physically, but not really living," she achieves an aesthetic effect by repeating the word "living," which assumes a different meaning. "Really living" means to her a full living— one not compatible with idleness, which permits living in a vegetative way. When she was asked what the difference is between poverty and misery, again she gave an artistic definition. The usual dictionary definitions are "a state of being poor" for poverty and "a state of great distress" for misery. The girl includes these definitions in hers, but offers much more: she succeeds in accentuating the contrast between poverty and misery. "Poverty" is a *poor* word in comparison with "misery," which has much stronger affective associations evoked by the word *agony*.

It is not enough to conclude that this girl had greater accessibility to the mechanisms of the primary process. We must recognize that she was also able to make good selections among the various possibilities offered by her primary process and that she could coordinate them with secondary-process mechanisms.

Another patient, a poetess, occasionally experienced quasi-schizophrenic episodes that were elusive in nature; often it was difficult to determine whether she was in a psychotic state or not. At times her poems almost resembled schizophrenic word-salads; at other times they had a genuine beauty. They were nevertheless always difficult to understand, like much contemporary poetry.

At the beginning of this woman's treatment she used to speak of human beings as worms, and she wrote poems in which they were represented as worms. Her ideas could have been accepted at a metaphorical level, except that she insisted people really were worms. It was impossible to determine whether the statement was made in a metaphorical sense or not. There was a flavor of literalness in her remarks; even if she meant "worms" metaphorically, there was a resolute attachment to this metaphor, as if it literally represented reality. Her expressions seemed to me to belong to an intermediary stage, hard to delineate, between metamorphosis and metaphor. As her condition improved, she wrote poems in which the metaphorical meaning of the word *worm* could no longer be doubted.

As has been said, the creative person—for some reasons not fully understood—maintains a greater than average accessibility to imagery, metaphor, emphatic verbalization, and other forms related to the primary process.* According to Croce (1909), art is intuition (or intu-

---

* When a poet or a playwright resorts to symbols that are purely intellectual or that come from his knowledge of previous literature or of psychoanalysis, high aesthetic levels are not reached. Even great poets like Dante resort in their weakest moments to allegories and metaphors that are the result of erudition and not of contact with the primary process. On the other hand, others (see Spenser earlier in this chapter) are able to renew beauties by imitation.

itive knowledge) that produces "images," not concepts. In this chapter I have in effect tried to analyze Croce's assumptions psychologically. Intuition remains an obscure concept unless the underlying psychological process is clarified. "Inspiration" is the faculty by which the creative person finds a primary-process form that will hold the content of the secondary process. This accessibility to the primary process may require a state of passivity similar to that of dreaming; but the passivity cannot involve the artist's whole psyche. On the contrary, it contrasts with the increased alertness on the part of the psyche that deals with the secondary process and presides over the artistic synthesis. Thus in the act of aesthetic creation, a complicated mental mechanism takes place that combines greater than usual passivity and greater than usual activity.

The artist must put together many elements of different origins to make syntheses of higher orders—that is, to create artistic unities. The word "poet" derives from the Greek *poietes*, the maker. And yet often the artist seems to uncover unities rather than to make new ones. People have the impression that they were potentially able to appreciate the poet's strange harmony and unusual meaning even before he revealed them. In other words, since we often respond so promptly to an aesthetic work, we feel that the artist is simply pointing out what we already knew in an unclear or unverbalized way. The artist is seen in a role similar to that of the psychoanalyst, when the analyst gives interpretations to the patient.

This point of view is valid only to a limited degree. It is true that on many occasions we have had ready in us the elements needed to form or appreciate a work of art. However, only the creative person could fit all the elements together in order to create the new unity. Once the unity is formed by the artist, it is easily apprehended by others. The concordance of various elements, or the confluence of the various levels of cognition and affects, makes it easy to grasp the unity or at least to respond aesthetically to it. The new unity enlarges our world and our capacity for experience. Without it, life seems impoverished. Thus there are essential differences between the uncovering made by the creative person and that made by the psychoanalyst. Whereas the psychoanalyst analyzes or separates the various elements, the creative person puts those disparate elements together. Whereas the analyst is interested in the meaning of what is uncovered and in the feelings that will ensue as a result of the uncovering, the artist wants to offer a special feeling: aesthetic pleasure.

The Creative Product

In psychological terms, the aesthetic unity often pre-existed in us in a state of potentiality, as an unconscious endocept or as a loose aggregation (see Chapters 4 and 5). The union of disparate elements in a primitive grouping and diffuse emotional tones is found in primitive endocepts. In the act of inspiration, the creative person is able to change the totality of the endocept into a conscious conceptual experience. He becomes aware of the unpremeditated interconnectedness among a relatively large number of different items of experience. An aesthetic design is thus discovered. This by no means implies a Platonic theory of knowledge. The new unity is actually new in the universe, but the formation of an aesthetic whole from disparate elements is facilitated by the diffuseness of endoceptual and other disconnected cognitive constructs. Artistic inspiration is perhaps the sudden discovery of a way to translate an endocept and disparate elements into an aesthetic unit.

The experience of aesthetic insight—that is, of creating an aesthetic unity—is a strong emotional experience in some ways comparable to what Maslow has called "peak experiences" (1959, 1961). The artist feels almost as if he had touched the universal. The particular, or the new unity that he has created, seems to have incorporated the universal, to have become a "concrete universal" that transcends space and time. As already mentioned, the quality of universality seems to come from two achievements: the enlargement of reality that everybody will acknowledge; and the transformation of an endocept into a conscious and vivid experience in the inner reality of man. The creation of the aesthetic unity thus results from a reservoir of unpredictable and incommensurable imagination, and also from an understanding that seems incommensurable and unpredictable because it derives from the potentially infinite symbolic process of man.

The primary process offers the artist the imagination—that is, the faculty of presentation which provides the basic matter, as well as a loose form of organization such as the emergence of similarities, suggestions, and partial representations. The secondary process provides the screening and elimination of many suggestions and partial representations, whether in verbal, pictorial, or other forms. The tertiary process ultimately comes into being as a "click," or match, between the primary and secondary processes, which brings about an accepted emerging representation. Eureka! The new unity is created!

In wit and the comic, it was relatively easy to determine the formation of the new unity. It came into being when the logic–paleologic discordance was suddenly recognized, a short interval after an assumed concordance. The opposite occurs in the formation of an aesthetic unity. When the paleologic or unusual representation is added to the realistic representation, not only is it not rejected, it is *fused* with it, to give us a deeper or new appreciation of the object.

Obviously it is much more difficult to define a paleological or any other reinforcing formal characteristic than it is to define those that produce a discordance. Again, at this stage, we cannot do better than to repeat that all the six elements we mentioned in the previous section concur in the formation of the unity. In wit it is generally almost impossible to divide the creative product into parts. As a rule, a fragment of a joke is not a joke anymore. In the aesthetic unity there is much more freedom. The unity may be a total epic, like the *Iliad* and the *Divine Comedy*, or it may be an excerpt. A statue may be admired in its entirety, or as a fragment preserved through the passage of time. In relation to aesthetic products, the appreciation of a unity does not prevent the artist or the admirer from shifting his attention from the part to the whole or from the whole to the part. Each subsequent part contributes its share, so that finally the whole gestalt appears in its aesthetic sequence. Once the whole is appreciated, each part will acquire new significance because of the significance of the whole. It is inherent in the aesthetic experience to recognize the affinity and interrelation of the parts, how each part affects the whole, and, finally, how the whole affects each part.

At this point we can state that the formation of an aesthetic unity satisfies three cognitive modes of operation: * (1) The material necessary to form the artistic unity consists of elements that are connected in external reality or are put together by the artist in the work of art (the mode of contiguity). (2) A work of art aims at imitating an aspect of life, as Aristotle thought, or consists of elements put together because of their similarity, as in metaphors, concretizations, and so on (the mode of similarity). (3) A work of art stands for a class of objects, situations, events, or meanings (the mode of *pars pro toto*).

---

* These are described in *The Intrapsychic Self* (Arieti 1967, Chapter 2) and also briefly in Chapter 6 of this book.

The Role of Poetry

ALL LITERARY FORMS are major forms of creativity, but the limitations established for this book necessitated that we make a choice. Focusing on poetry seemed the natural choice, not only because poetry discloses more clearly than other literary media the relation between the components of the primary and secondary processes, but also because poetry makes the deepest impact in general. No other literary medium has played such an important role from antiquity to our days. When we think of literary geniuses or of the persons who stand out in a given body of literature, most of the time the names of poets come to mind. If we think of the ancient Greeks, the name of Homer stands out; of the Romans, Virgil; of the Italians, Dante; of the English, Shakespeare; of the Germans, Goethe. This is not always so. For instance, if we think of Spanish literature, the one who comes to mind first of all is Cervantes with his *Don Quixote*. But as a rule the statement is valid. Whereas in other literary genres a moderate degree of creativity is readily acceptable, it is only with a certain degree of reluctance that we accept poets who are less than great. Horace, a great Latin poet himself, reminds us in his *Ars Poetica* (verses 377–378) that:

> . . . *Mediocribus esse poetis*
> *non homines, non di, non concessere columnae.*
>
> *Neither men, nor gods, nor booksellers allow*
> *poets to be mediocre.*

The great value of poetry, transcending the field of aesthetics, has been stressed by poets themselves. The message of the poet comes from the primary sources of the soul of man through the primary process, and from the highest ideas and ideals of the secondary process, to offer to mankind a message of beauty, goodness, and hope. The last few pages of this chapter will be devoted to showing how the poets themselves appreciated the great and multiform value of poetry. Incidentally, poetry has recently been used by some psychiatrists (for example, Leedy 1969, 1973; Pietropinto 1973) as a form of therapy, and the results are very satisfactory. Indeed, poetry has been seen for a long time as having a salutary effect. *The Divine Comedy* can be viewed as a form of psychotherapy or self-analysis. Dante's conflicts, represented metaphorically by his going through Hell and Purgatory, are finally solved by his having access to Paradise in the company of his beloved Beatrice. But before he can be free from earthly conflicts and reach a state of bliss, he has to submit himself to the terrible events of Hell and to the climbing of the purgatorial mountain. During this metaphorical journey he has a very good therapist, Virgil; and some critics have written that Virgil represents wisdom, or knowledge, in contrast to love, represented by Beatrice.

But we should not forget that Virgil was first of all a great poet. Thus he represents poetry, too. And it is with the help of poetry that Dante cleanses his soul and becomes capable of receiving real love; the love of a woman, Beatrice, and the love of God in Paradise. When, at the beginning of the Inferno, Dante recognizes Virgil, who was sent to his rescue, he exclaims (*Inferno*, Canto I, verses 79–84):

> *O degli altri poeti onore e lume,*
> *Vagliami il lungo studio e 'l grande amore,*
> *Che m'han fatto cercar lo tuo volume.*
>
> *Tu se' lo mio maestro e 'l mio autore:*
> *Tu se' solo colui, da cui io tolsi*
> *Lo bello stile, che m'ha fatto onore.*

> *O honor and light of the other poets,*
> *May the long study and the great love, which have*
> *Made me search thy volume, be helpful to me.*
>
> *Thou art my teacher and my author;*
> *Thou alone art he from whom I took*
> *The fair style that has done me honor.*

The word "style" generally refers mainly to literary style, but in this special context we may interpret it as a life style that Dante imitates, a poetic life style second only to love in obtaining liberation from conflicts and in pursuing peace of mind and happiness.

Dante's great regard for poetry is disclosed also by the homage that his characters in Purgatory pay to Virgil, the symbol as well as the incorporation of poetry. The characters of the Inferno are much concerned with unredeemable evil and their sorrow, and therefore unable at having to pay attention to such matters; the characters of Paradise are involved only with the divine and celestial. But in Purgatory, where the shadows undergo purification, poetry's value is fully acknowledged. When Sordello, a minor poet born in Mantua (the same city where Virgil was born), finds out that the shadow who is talking to him is Virgil's, an intensely emotional episode emerges (*Purgatory*, Canto VII, verses 10–19):

> *Qual è colui che cosa innanzi a sè*
> *Subita vede ond' è si maraviglia,*
> *che crede e non, dicendo "Ella è . . . non è . . .*
>
> *tal parve quelli; e poi chinò le ciglia*
> *e umilmente ritornò ver lui*
> *e abbracciol là 've 'l minor s'appiglia.*
>
> *"O gloria de' Latin" disse "per cui*
> *mostrò ciò che potea la lingua nostra,*
> *o pregio etterno del loco ond' io fui*
> *qual merito o qual grazia mi ti mostra?"*

"Like one who sees suddenly before him a thing he marvels at, who believes, and believes not, saying, 'It is, it is not;' such seemed he, there bent his brow and humbly turned back towards him and embraced him where the inferior clasps. 'O glory of the Latins,' he said, 'by whom our tongue showed forth its power, O eternal praise of the place from which I come, what merit or what favor showeth thee to me?' "

When later in the Purgatorial journey another Latin poet, Statius, discovers that the shadow in front of him is Virgil's, his full affection and reverence also come forth. Statius was bending to embrace Virgil's feet, but the Latin poet reminded him that they were only evanescent shadows and could not embrace each other. "Brother, do not so, for thou art a shade and a shade thou seest."

Many other poets, too many to be represented adequately here, attempted to clarify in poetic forms the role of poetry. Théophile Gautier (1811–1872), a French painter who became a poet, wrote a poem entitled "L'Art" that came to be accepted by many people as a guideline for the artist. In this not exceptionally beautiful poem, Gautier says that inspiration is not much in itself, unless transformed and made permanent as an art product. A perfect mastery of a difficult medium must be achieved; and as a matter of fact, it is the difficulty of the medium that gives new and lasting inspiration to the poet. The hard medium makes art indestructible.

> *Tout passe . . . L'art robuste*
> *Seul à l'eternité,*
> *Le buste*
> *Survit à la cité.*

> *Everything comes and goes. Only*
> *strong art is eternal.*
> *The bust*
> *survives the city.*

"Bust" is used metaphorically here for anything made through hard work.

Giosué Carducci (1835–1907), an Italian poet, ended his beautiful book *Rime Nuove* with the poem "Congedo" ("Farewell"), in which he describes the work of the poet. The poet is *un grande artiere,* a great artisan, made strong by his works. His muscles become iron. He is a smith who strikes the anvil. On the incandescent mass of metal he throws memories and glories of the past, he makes swords, armor, garlands for the glorious, and diadems for the beautiful ladies. For himself he makes a dart, throws it toward the sun, and then he looks up to see how high it will go and how brightly it will shine.

For the Italian poet and Nobel laureate Salvatore Quasimodo (1901–1968), the birth of a poet is an act of disorder and presupposes a new method of adhering to life. The poet never denies life, even if through his desperation he recognizes its aridity (1960). He sees men made half of gold and half of blood, poured in their constant dialogue with death. He sees poetry as a position of the spirit, as an act of faith—or rather of trust—in what man does.

For the present writer, poetry is one of those magic syntheses that make us bypass daily life and find undreamed beauties and unsuspected truths. This bypassing does not mean rejecting the world. The magic makes us rediscover the world, retrace with Thomas Gray the gems in the dark unfathomed caves of the ocean, and dispel with Richard Lovelace the bars of the cages and the walls of the prisons. It is the magic that enacts a sublime metamorphosis—when, with the Bard of Stratford-on-Avon, any of us "could be bounded in a nut-shell and count [himself] a king of infinite space."

Chapter 9
Painting
(with a Note on Music)

Preperception, Visual Perception, and Imagery

FINE ART has played a fundamental role in the growth of civilization. According to Herbert Read (1955), the icon precedes the idea; it is the new image, portrayed artistically, that leads to new concepts in human history. If the parallelism is valid, Read's conception finds support in human development. We have seen in Chapter 3 that the image is a function of the nervous system that occurs before the acquisition of language. In this chapter we shall discuss visual art and specifically painting, that is, images made on external objects by human beings. Contrary to the method of exposition followed in the previous chapter, we shall focus not on single works but on long periods of human history, as representatives of the psychological processes involved. We shall terminate the chapter with some brief comments on music.

What is a pictorial image? An imitation of nature, as Aristotle thought? A return to the mental level of imagery—that is, a regression comparable to dreams, which consist predominantly of visual images? Or is visual art a creation of new forms and combinations of colors?

It is all these things together. If we consider in its immense totality that period of approximately 2,500 years of Western culture that extends from the beginning of the classic Greek era to the end of the nineteenth century, we are impressed by the recurring attempts made by the artist to imitate nature. It is an imitation that selects, recreates, constructs, beautifies; but nevertheless it is a human endeavor that expresses an adherence to reality, a concern with the impression that the external world has made upon the retina. In some centuries, especially in the Middle Ages, such imitation was less strictly observed, but as a rule a more or less accurate reproduction of reality was the aim. In this historical period the observer of a work of art would first of all be involved in the problem of recognition. No matter how it was chosen, stylized, or beautified, the image was immediately associated mentally with the object it represented. At no time in history could an artistic image be compared to a photographic image of today; but nevertheless, during these twenty-five centuries, representation was essentially an altered reproduction of reality. A woman could be recognized as a woman, even if idealized as Aphrodite.

The recognition of reality and the endeavor to organize reality in symmetrical order, as the Greeks did, are perceptual phenomena as well as phenomena pertaining to the secondary process. When we recognize, we automatically classify; we give a known meaning to what we observe. To do otherwise would be like living in a chaotic and incomprehensible world, in a perennial state of flux. The known meanings that we give to what we recognize are those that we have learned from others, our parents, peers, contemporaries, and our culture in general.

Does this mean that in visual art, in contrast to other creative fields, we pass from perception to the secondary process, bypassing the primary? As a rule, no. First of all, in almost every work of art—even in those works in which the secondary process retains undisputed supremacy—unconscious and primary-process mechanisms can be recognized. Second, and most important, this historical period of 2,500 years during which the secondary process prevailed is a *short* period in relation to the history of humanity on the planet, although long relative to the life of an individual human. This period is like a big parenthesis wedged between pre-Greek art and the advent of modern art. Prior to the classic Greek period and after Cézanne, the primary process is in a state of harmonious rivalry with the secondary process. (For the sake of accuracy, we must add that another important realistic parenthesis occurred during the paleolithic period, as we shall discuss later.)

Let us examine what a person does when he paints. He may look at the object that he wishes to portray—a tree, a human being, an animal—and attempt to reproduce by some graphic method the likeness of what he sees. In this case he relies on his *perception*. Or he may paint the tree, the human being, or the animal not by looking at the object but by relying on his memory. In this case he must resort to his *imagery*. He must evoke the image of the absent object that he wants to portray. As a matter of fact, the earliest expressions of art that have been preserved, such as those of the caves of Lascaux in southern France or in the caves of northern Spain, were made by artists who relied on their own images. The animals portrayed were not in the caves. Thus we have an important dichotomy that affects all the periods of art history. It would seem correct to assume that work based on perception is closer to nature than work based on imagery. To a large extent this is true; but it is not as well established as it might seem.

First of all, the artist, who relies on imagery, has to perceive the object before he can evoke it through imagery. Second, he can always check what he is doing through imagery by getting to see the object in reality and reexperiencing the original perception. Thus cave-dwellers, in the course of their painting, could have gone out of the cave and re-observed the animals they were in the process of representing graphically. But even the painter who relies on direct perception goes through complicated processes. First of all, preceding thoughts and feelings about an object affect the way he perceives it directly. In other words, past experiences of the object—everything he knows and feels about it—influence the way he sees that object. Even more important, perception per se is neither such a simple neurophysiological nor psychological process as it might seem to be. Rudolph Arnheim (1969) has gone to great lengths to show that perception is not a passive impression, but that it selects the targets of vision with eye movements and then organizes them.

In Chapter 3 we saw how conscious perception is preceded by unconscious mechanisms such as gestalt-free perception, part-perception, and the perception of salient parts. We also saw that these necessary stages are suppressed or repressed during the last stages of perception. They are repressed even in imageries and dreams, although not actually as much as it would seem. One of the reasons why these early stages seem to be so rare in imagery and dreams is that we cannot remember them. We cannot recall them because we cannot give meaning to them, just as those of us who do not know the Turkish language could not remember a passage of Turkish literature read to us. We could not connect the sounds of the words with their meanings. The painter, like the creative person in other fields, probably has greater access than the average person to preperception or to gestalt-free perception, but he has learned to repress it because it is deprived of ordinary meaning. Let us remember that these preperceptual and early perceptual stages are even more primitive than the primary process, unless they are associated with meaning.

Ehrenzweig is an author who has stressed the importance of the unconscious, gestalt-free level of expression (1957, 1967). What we are accustomed to see in an art object, according to Ehrenzweig, is a surface order. But beneath this order there is a hidden order. (Ehrenzweig is apparently influenced by Nietzsche in recognizing in art both the expression of a Dionysian urge and an Apollonian love of order. As we shall see later, this is a recurring theme in the history of aesthetics. Many aestheticians have seen such a duality of principles operating simultaneously in art.) Ehrenzweig believes that there are two fundamentally different types of perception: depth perception and surface perception. Surface perception is gestalt-bound; depth perception is gestalt-free and includes those perceptual stages that we discussed earlier. Ehrenzweig says that gestalt-free perception in art is inarticulate, chaotic, undifferentiated, and vague. The traditional artist forgets the gestalt-free vision as soon as definite formative ideas emerge; the secret unconscious struggle between surface and depth perception animates the surface gestalt and adds artistic grace. Ehrenzweig seems to confirm the point of view expressed here previously when he says that the creative process serves two masters, the irrational id and the rational ego. He goes on to say that unconscious scanning occurs in the deeper levels of the mind. In this chaotic registration of perceptual content, apparently, a mode of operation prevails that Ehrenzweig calls *syncretistic*. The artist or viewer has a syncretistic grasp of the total object. He abandons precise visualization and experiences an unclear vision of the whole. Ehrenzweig says that "a mysterious syncretistic vision can be precise in grasping a total structure, the components of which are interchangeable" (1967, p. 38).

Probably this state of organization is comparable to what, at a cognitive level, I call an endocept (see Chapter 4), or perhaps a primary aggregation (Arieti 1967). At other times this primitive preperceptual faculty grasps or sees only fragments or fragmentations of wholes. Several schizophrenics whom I have treated have described to me this phenomenon of fragmentation that occurs in acute or advanced stages of their illnesses (see Arieti 1974, and Chapter 3 of this book). However, artists generally deny these pre-gestalt stages. Some state that at times they focus on a fragment, or detached fragments, or salient points, after they have seen or imagined the whole. It could be that pre-gestalt perception does not have a specific role in art work, or—and this second possibility seems more likely—most artists may be completely unconscious of this process and sincerely deny its existence. It is also true that many aspects of visual art unfold at a mature perceptual level. For instance, students of art know that colors do not have a certain perceptual value only in themselves, but in relation to other colors as well. The same patch of red can appear lighter or darker according to the colors by which it is surrounded. A form also changes aesthetic value according to other forms with which it is associated. The form may have a special value because it is unique and stands out from the others, or because it is repeated several times.

All these and many more principles and laws are familiar to the student of art; yet they originate at a preconceptual level. They are inherent in the phenomenon of perception. Whatever thinking goes into them is implied or exists only in a potential form.

The Vital and the Schematic Styles and Eras

CAVE DWELLERS made drawings that were both stylized and realistic. According to Read (1955), the general character of this work is "best described by the word vitalistic, for the effect of the drawing, if not the intention, is to enhance the vital potentiality of the animals." The men's figures, however, are highly stylized, always two-dimensional, and generally painted in only one color. Thus it is obvious that paleolithic men were able to use two styles separately or conjointly:

the vital and the schematic of which we shall take the second—the stylized-abstract—into consideration later.

It is indeed extremely interesting to notice how naturalistic the representation of animals is in paleolithic art. How is it possible that the most primitive art is in some cases almost realistic, much more so than the art extending from the neolithic to the preclassic Greek period? If we try to compare the most primitive paleolithic art to children's first stages of artistic development, we find no correspondence. A very young child would not be able to draw animals as realistically as a paleolithic man. However, this discrepancy does not by itself eliminate comparative considerations. The young child does not have complete control over his body, nor coordination of his movements, and therefore has not yet acquired a refined technique. Even if he perceives animals as vividly and as vitally as paleolithic men, he would not be able to reproduce them graphically. Perhaps this stage would correspond ontogenetically to that stage called the "scribbling" stage in children's artistic development. During this stage the child cannot reproduce real pictures; but it is important to note that he gives a name to his scribblings. The things that appear as scribbles to us are called "a man," "a dog," "mommy," and so on by the child. Thus he makes an attempt to refer his scribbling to mental pictures. According to Lowenfeld (1951, 1959), the naming of scribblings represents one of the most important stages in human development. "It indicates a change of thinking from a mere kinaesthetic to an imaginative." Thus the lack of correspondence between the realism of the most primitive art and that of very young children is not a proof that a developmental parallelism is not possible. On the other hand, the fact that the cave dwellers could, relatively speaking, so realistically portray animals that were not present in the caves and could not be used as models indicates that these primitives might have experienced an eidetic type of imagery, similar to that of many children. The hypothesis is not to be a priori discarded: that if young children had the muscular coordination of adults, they might draw in a way similar to that of paleolithic men.

When the child is a little older and still not able to imitate nature as accurately as he would like, he resorts to another method: simplification of forms and reduction of the object to essentials. For instance, the human body is reduced to a schema: two dots represent the eyes, two lines the arms, two other lines the legs, and so on. An adult who looks at these drawings of children can often recognize what they represent. Thus it is obvious that the child is able to abstract important relations. The figure, reduced to the essential, tends to assume a geometrical form; mathematical proportions are respected, although biased by the concept (a child is represented as very small, a daddy is very big). For instance, one leg is of the same size as the other leg, and the same is true of arms, ears, eyes, and so on.

It is between three and four years of age that the child starts to represent the human figure. First of all, two big eyes are represented, because the face and the eyes attract the child more than anything else (Spitz 1965). At four and a half the child schematically draws the trunk, in which he often includes the navel (Ferrari 1973). At five, the schema of the whole person can be easily recognized, with arms and legs. At the age of six the schema is complete and the height is four times the width (Gesell 1940, Ferrari 1973). The child feels frustrated that he has to resort to the schema and envies the adult who can reproduce a picture closer to perceptual reality. However, we could repeat here what we said about images in Chapter 3: although images are imperfect in comparison to perception, their imperfection leads to creativity. The power to abstract the essential and the potentiality for a mathematical, geometrical interpretation of reality are already present in the schematic representations of the child.

This tendency toward simplification, repetition of form, bilateral symmetry in the human figure, and (in some cases) stereotypy and ornamental simplification cannot be considered just as a defect, an inability to reproduce reality. We may call it *stylization*, provided we give a psychological meaning to this term. Stylization is a mental process that modifies the appearance of objects of the external world in accordance with certain tendencies or faculties of the mind. These faculties are by no means removed from the external object; their definite involvement with it is apparent. However, the external object is represented (1) by what seems the object's essential morphological character; (2) by a very simple way of reproducing that essential character; (3) by a tendency, in the case of the human form, to make it bilaterally symmetrical; and (4) by repetition or stereotypy. The child is not able to reproduce the whole; but he does not want to reproduce a part either. He has not reached the degree of symbolism in which a fragment stands for the whole; or at least, if he has reached that degree of symbolism, he does not know how to use it graphically. He wants to use a whole, but it is a whole that is formed only by the salient or essential elements.

From Schema to Beauty

IT IS of exceptional interest that the characteristics that we have described in the art of children, especially those between four and six and a half years old, are also prominent in the art of the neolithic period. Read (1955, p. 35) writes that "to most students of the history of art, the transition from the paleolithic to the neolithic period has every appearance of a catastrophic decline. Instead of the accurate depiction of animals in drawings of great variety, we find geometrical designs which tend to degenerate into dull repetitive patterns; instead of a vital naturalism, a deadly monotony of abstraction." However, abstraction represents a tremendous mental advance, a prerequisite for the progress made by neolithic man in relation to the paleolithic. No longer was he a hunter of wild beasts. Instead he became an agriculturist, he domesticated animals, he made pottery, and he even became interested in astronomy. It is no wonder that the New Stone Age is considered the cradle of the ancient great civilizations.

Abstraction or schematization requires imagination, inasmuch as it is a transformation of reality. But this imagination does not rely on images *as* images. If images are used, it is in order to abstract a schema from them. A linear symbol now replaces the image, but obviously this linear symbol is related to the image. It need retain only the essential components of the image, thus transforming the image into a schema. These primitive schemata are very distant from the eidetic imagery that reproduces reality almost photographically. Yet inasmuch as schemata are common in children's art, and in the art of the mentally ill, we must recognize that they are the work of relatively primitive processes of the mind. They are perhaps the most archaic forms of the secondary process. But it is on this archaic structure that more advanced mechanisms are based, as we shall see later in this chapter.

According to Read (1955), it is in the neolithic period that *form* itself originated. I assume that by form he means a *formal* entity, an abstraction from practical life. As suggested by Raphael (1947), the neo-lithic form achieves a synthesis. It indicates a disposition, or determination to create a unity of several elements: *simplicity*, the desire to build a complex structure from few elements; *formal necessity*, since it implies a determination to represent some content and conceal others; *detachment*, as the artist is determined to rise above the content of his product; *definiteness*, embodied in the self-evidence of the form; *energy*, often expressed in the will to transcend the physical powers of life; and *connection of content and meaning*. Read believes that adoption by neolithic men of this schematic style did not signify the abandon-ment of the previous vital style. The two coexisted.

According to Read, the discovery of artistic beauty is grounded in the discovery of form itself. He realizes, however, that mere geo-metrical proportions are not sufficient requirements for beauty. Most children's drawings are far from beautiful; the primitive drawings represented in Figure 9-1 and Figure 9-2 are definitely ugly. On the

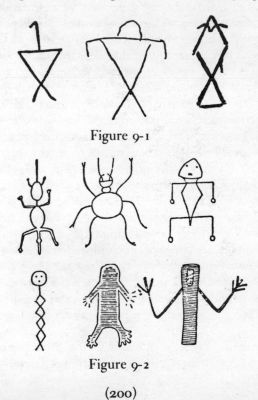

Figure 9-1

Figure 9-2

Figure 9-3

other hand, geometrical-schematic art has played an important role, to a varying degree, in all subsequent ages. The giant statues of Easter Island are an interesting example of Polynesian art (Figure 9-3). These strange figures are 40 feet high; they have long heads and sketchy bodies. They are almost identical to one another. In many Egyptian and Assyrian paintings, sculptures, and carved plaques, repetition and stereotypy are seen in the multiple and almost identical representations of workers, slaves, soldiers, and animals, repeated almost identically. At times the repetition of the multitude is on both sides of a central figure.

Figure 9-4 represents the fervid activity of an Egyptian estate. The same forms are repeated many times.

And yet these forms convey feelings of alacrity, composure, order, organization and class system. In fact we find great beauty not only in the stylized ancient Egyptian and Assyrian works of art but also in such relatively recent works as the Byzantine mosaics of the ninth century. The Byzantine mosaics exhibit repetition of forms to the point of stereotypy, as well as stylization in the elongated human forms. And yet—Read stresses the fact—the creator of geometrical-schematic art introduces irregularities into his repetitive design. In fact, if we observe the classic Byzantine mosaics in Ravenna, we discover that the repeated human figure in each instance shows some important variations, although following a general pattern. In

(201)

geometrical-schematic art, according to Read, "a subtler intuition of relation of parts to a whole was needed for the maintenance of aesthetic vitality, and this was found in the principle of *balance*. Fundamentally, balance is no more than the achievement of perceptual ease in a formal design; it is the discovery of a '*good*' Gestalt."

In such ways, suggests Read, schematization and repetitiveness to the point of stereotypy can yet produce an image of beauty. I would agree that whereas a paleolithic drawing manifests a sense of vitality, geometrical-schematic art discloses coherence. And it is relatively easy to understand why vitalistic art should evoke a feeling of aesthetic pleasure in the observer: there is the intense visual emotion of seeing the animal itself; and the movements and positions of the represented figures portray not only a vivid eidetic image but also the excitement of the hunt, the conflict of man and animal. But what about geometrical-schematic art? Why should it produce aesthetic pleasure? The introduction of irregularities into the repetitive design, mentioned by Read, does not seem to me a sufficient factor, although it is certainly effective. The sense of balance also suggested by Read is important as well; but balance is present in every type of art, including the paleolithic. I suggest that geometric-schematic art stops the flux of the world. The intensity of paleolithic art is replaced by relaxing symmetry and the repetition of forms. The vitality becomes much less intense; but it becomes indelible in other ways, by being repeated and repeated to the point of stereotypy. The impact of something forcefully expressed is replaced by or mixed with the impact of an art that permits pause, contemplation, meditation, excursions into depth. The many complexities, irregularities, and variations of life are now seen in a simpler way, opening the way to that mathematic geometrical vision of the world that will in turn open the human mind to the realm of science and to an understanding of the order of the universe.

Stereotypy or any kind of repetition or rhythm may be used in high art, in purely decorative or ornamental fashion, or in modern advertising. In modern advertising, the repetition of the same figure or design may lack aesthetic appeal but serve the purpose of becoming imprinted in the consumer, who will not forget that special product. At other times, especially in book stores and newsstands, the display of many copies of the same book or magazine will have a striking and even aesthetic effect on the passer-by.

My studies in that laboratory of the human mind which is schizo-

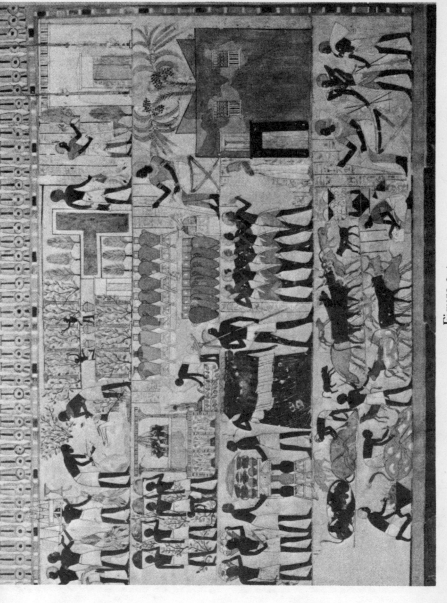

Figure 9-4

Figure 9-5

phrenia support some of the views expressed in this section. In the beginning of the illness, the drawings and paintings of schizophrenics disclose an eruption of conflicts and the supremacy of feelings. But at a more advanced stage of the illness, stereotypy is resorted to as an attempt to arrest the frightening flux of the world. Reality has to be stated and restated many times—in some instances in agreeable ways, as in Figure 9-5.* But the schizophrenic must do much more than stereotype in order to escape from the anxiety-provoking input from the world. He must also simplify and therefore impoverish the world that he perceives. Figure 9-6, made by a very regressed adult schizophrenic, shows how she sees her family. Each human member is represented in the way that a young child or a nonartistically-endowed neolithic man would represent them. Figure 9-7 also represents impoverishment of reality, stereotypy, and schematization.

It seems to me a reasonable assumption at this point to state that geometrical-schematic visual representation is an expression of a level of mental functioning. It appears ontogenetically at a stage of normal human development; while in the development of the human race as a whole, it appears in the neolithic era. It reacquires supremacy in several mental disorders, such as advanced schizophrenia. However, as a style to be integrated with other styles, it often participates in beautiful compositional syntheses. In geometric-schematic art the image has become an abstraction, a thought; the vitality has become order, crystallized form, symmetry, harmony.

Read considers "beauty"—discovered in neolithic times in the balanced composition of the art work—the second principle of art, in contrast to the principle of vitality discovered during paleolithic times. According to him, these two principles have been adopted by all subsequent modes of art. Read identifies the vitalistic tendency with what Nietzsche (1872), in *The Birth of Tragedy*, called the Dionysian force, and the principle of beauty with what Nietzsche called the Apollonian force. These two principles—at times called the two types, two styles, two aims, or two laws—have been contrasted by many aestheticians. Schiller called vitalistic art "sentimental" and geometrical art "naive." Verworn (1914) spoke of "physioplastic" and "ideoplastic" art; Danzel (1924) of dynamic and static art; Kühn (1923) of "sensorial" art, which is concerned with what surrounds the artist,

---

* Reproduced with permission from the collection of Dr. Enzo Gabrici.

Figure 9-6

Figure 9-7

and "imaginative" art, which departs from life. The artist P. Mondrian (1914) spoke of the two aims of art. The first aim, by representing reality objectively, strives toward the direct creation of universal beauty. The second aim, by representing reality subjectively, strives toward the aesthetic expression of oneself. According to Mondrian "the only problem" in art is to achieve a balance between the subjective and the objective. . . . Art has shown that universal expression can only be created by a real equation of the universal and the individual."

In agreement with Mondrian and disagreement with Nietzsche, Read believes that great art, or at least great Greek art, is not just a taming of the wild Dionysian force, but a synthesis or balance of the two principles. I agree, and therefore I am reluctant to call the second principle of art (the geometric-schematic style) the principle or discovery of beauty, as Read does. Beauty should be reserved for the proper matching of the two principles. Here, too, we could use our concept of the tertiary process to represent the harmonious matching of the first and second principles. It is true that the vitalistic principle does not correspond to the primary process, but only to a sensuous-perceptual appreciation and reproduction of reality. It is also true that the schematizations appearing in some drawings may vary from a primitive organization to a rather complicated mathematical order. But in their basic structures, these artistic principles do in fact indicate modalities of functions of the primary process or of the archaic ego. Thus in visual art, too, we have the fusion of two levels of cognition.

Fusion, Diffusion, and Misidentification

IN THE ART of schizophrenic patients a stage of "fusion, diffusion, and misidentification" generally evolves at a less advanced stage of illness than the ones in which the geometric-schematic is likely to prevail. In young children too, as a rule, it occurs for a brief period of time before the onset of geometric-schematic art. The ability of children to see faces or grotesque figures in walls, clouds, and so on is very well known. These generally two-dimensional perceptions provide a form of primitive, natural Rorschach test. Children are also prone to combine or fuse objects or parts or objects that are not ordinarily considered together. Thus a three-year-old child may say that a boat has eyes in order to see where it is going, and try to draw human eyes on the boat. In primitive art, the style of fusion and condensation may appear before, during, or after the geometric-schematic stage. It represents composite figures that do not exist in the real world. According to Preuss (1914)—quoted by Kretschmer (1934)—the Huicho Indians of Mexico, by virtue of some remote associational link, put together a stag, a certain kind of cactus, and the morning star to form graphic condensations of these disparate elements. Strange half-human, half-animal figures such as sphinxes, centaurs, fauns, and angels are very common in ancient art. Combinations of animals and plants, or of different animals such as lions and eagles, birds, and snakes, were used to make up fantastic figures.

The possibility of this type of art may depend on the following factors:

1. *Imagery*. It is obvious that the individual parts of the composite work are based on images of objects that the artist has seen in external reality or in previous works of art.

2. *Imagination*. Imagery is not enough. The artist must have imagination—that is, the ability to transcend reality and put together parts mentally that are not together in the external world.

3. *Primitive cognition*. Imagination is not whimsical. Such compositions and fusions are not due to chance or to aesthetic requirements alone. The very fact that a few combinations recur frequently means that they have special meanings. Thus a special cognitive process is at the basis of these compositions. A primitive type of cognition that follows the primary process and, in particular, the paleologic laws of thought discussed in Chapter 5, is at the basis of this type of art. Suppose the artist wishes to confer to the man that he graphically represents the qualities of a lion, such as strength and courage. To do so he portrays this man as having some physical characteristics of a lion. If the artist conceives a god as being strong, he may also represent this deity in a form that is half human and half lion, or half man and half horse. He cannot abstract the qualities or predicates (for instance, being strong) from the wholes (for instance, lions and horses). Therefore he condenses the wholes, giving origin to unusual unities. Representations of Egyptian gods reveal the way of thinking of the ancient

Figure 9-8

Egyptians very well. Ra, the sun god, is often represented as a combination of a disk (the sun), a human figure, and a falcon. Figure 9-8 represents the Egyptian goddess Bast, worshipped during the Second Dynasty, as long ago as 3200 B.C. In early historical times, wild cats took readily to domestication, killing the snakes that were common in the region of the Delta and infested gardens and homes. Thus Bast, the cat goddess, who is represented with the features of both woman and cat, could easily be identified or conceived of as the protector of the home. Figure 9-9 represents Tauret, another goddess, protector of expectant mothers and of a woman in childbirth. She is shaped like a hippopotamus, an animal that on account of its size is easily associated with the abdomen of a pregnant woman.

Schizophrenic drawings and studies of schizophrenic thought can reveal to us the structure of the type of cognition that made this art possible. Here it is important to recall Von Domarus' principle (discussed in Chapter 5), on which primitive cognition is to a large extent based. Von Domarus' principle states that "whereas the person who thinks in usual ways accepts identity only upon the basis of identical subjects, the schizophrenic (or whoever thinks in this primitive fashion) accepts identity based upon an identical predicate (or part)." Thus, by adopting this principle, if I think that you are as strong as a lion, I could conclude that you *are* a lion and portray you graphically as such. In doing so, the contradictory evidence of reality would be suspended either by illness, or by my religious belief, or my artistic impulses. This type of thinking leads to multiple identification, because the same character, trait, predicate, shape, form, or part may be possessed by different people or things. According to standard logic, multiple identification is misidentification and therefore error. The schizophrenic suffers from delusions, illusions, or hallucinations.

In schizophrenic art, more often than in schizophrenic thought, Von Domarus' principle is only partially applied; that is, some partial identity among the subjects is based upon partial or total identity of a predicate or part. Thus we have no total identification, but the fusion or condensation of the two subjects. Figure 9-10 represents the drawing of a female patient with unresolved homosexual conflicts. She sees herself as a devil. The tail may be a phallic symbol. Figure 9-11 represents the drawing of another patient who sees herself as beautiful, like a flower—a flower nobody plucked or smelled. Figure 9-12 represents a girl with the head of a cat, was drawn by a patient shortly before de-

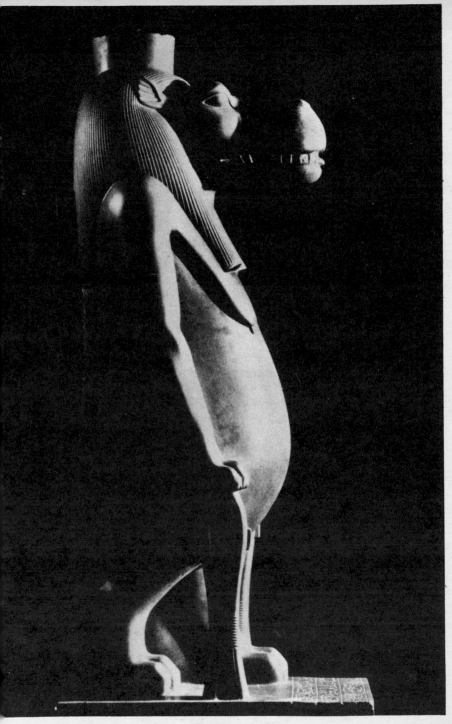

Figure 9-9

Figure 9-10

Figure 9-11

Figure 9-12

Figure 9-13

veloping an acute schizophrenic psychosis. Condensation assumes more bizarre forms in schizophrenic drawings in which no unity is reached; that is, when different subjects, although fused, fail to identify with each other or to converge into a unity. The disparate elements do not produce a harmonious combination but a bizarre product, as in Figure 9-13. I shall focus on the main part of this picture. Because they are all strong, an ancient warrior, a horse, a mythical bird, mountains, and people are partially identified and fused. The patient wants to convey an ideal of grandeur and strength. Somehow the artist fails to convince us; his inner world does not evoke in us a sense of participation. However, although no universal chord is struck, the work is not without merit. We sense in it mysteriousness and grandeur. We would be willing to accept the mysteriousness and grandeur, but not the related pathology. That which is private, pertaining only to the artist's way of seeing the world, is more prominent here than that which achieves a collective resonance. The patient has failed to convince us, because he has not been able to control the eruption of primary-process mechanisms. Their emergence was so strong that the various elements of the art work became fused, in spite of the fact that such fusion was unacceptable to mental mechanisms that follow the secondary process.

Schizophrenics soon learn the technique of fusing numerous subjects; the results at times are most strange and unpredictable. Figure 9-14 * shows how, with the progressive fusion of six original words and images (the fish, the girl, the nipple, the caterpillar, the cow, and the steam engine), a patient produced an amazing list of neologisms and neomorphisms. Here Von Domarus' principle and primary process mechanisms reach extreme supremacy, and the result is completely unacceptable to the secondary process of the normal observer.

We may draw some conclusions at this point. This multiple identification, fusion, or permutation is a way of transcending reality, of bypassing the restrictions of reality in spite of using pieces of reality. This fusion leads to the creation of unpredictable new forms, new concepts, and new images. At times the fusions are to be rejected—like the drawing represented in Figure 9-12, which is not acceptable as a representation of a girl or a cat or as creative synthesis. What a difference from Figure 9-8, which although representing a deity unac-

---

* Reproduced with permission from a work by Bobon and Maccagnani (1962).

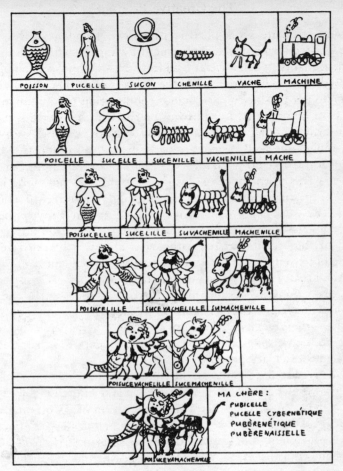

Figure 9-14

ceptable to us, impresses us with its artistic distinction and its ability to evoke a feeling consonant with a specific culture and religious belief!

These mixed compositions have recurred throughout the centuries, although in decreasing number, from the famous centaurs of the Greeks to the fantastic figures of Hieronymus Bosch. Figure 9-15 represents a masterpiece of Japanese art, the "Peacock King," made in the first half of the twelfth century. In a way that a modern Western

Figure 9-15

mind has difficulty in understanding, the divinity with four arms is seated on the back of a peacock and becomes fused with the peacock. According to a religious belief prevalent in Japan in the Heian period (794–1185), in an earlier life Buddha appeared in the form of a peacock. The composite king–peacock–Buddha became a benevolent divinity, endowed with the power of ending calamities. Even though most of us, as modern Westerners, cannot embrace or fully understand the religious meaning that animates such a concept and pervades this composition, we cannot refrain from admiring the magnificence of the synthesis. Something new and of spectacular beauty emerges. The unnatural union of a human figure and of a peacock does not appear to us unnatural or perverse, but a harmonious union from which peace, relaxation, activity and composure, and rhythm and balance emerge. The wisdom and serenity of the Buddha are enriched in the most unpredictable way by the colors and plumage of the peacock. The peacock adds a chromatic festivity to Buddha's wisdom and deep serenity. The inactive wings of the peacock, generally used graphically for display, produce here an harmonious contrast to the four arms, which are in different positions and represent perennial action and multiple powers. We do not reach the conclusion that the peacock is Buddha or Buddha is a peacock, but an unusually intense tertiary process enables us to experience a unique synthesis, a sublime and concrete representation of a profound religious belief.

It will be more the aesthetician's job than ours to determine why such compositions are at times unacceptable or bizarre concoctions and at other times great works of art. We know that in the great work of art the fusion is accepted visually and conceptually; an element of pleasure is experienced, and whatever seems unnatural from a biological or physical point of view seems very natural in the realm of art.

Idealism in Art

IN THE WESTERN WORLD the journey from primitive art to realistic art was a long one. The latter reached a peak period with the development of classic Greek art. A somewhat more than superficial examination will reveal, however, that Greek art—as exemplified especially by the sculptures—is not so much realistic as idealistic. The artist did not aim at portraying nature, especially the human being as he is, but at idealizing forms. The Greeks were realistic to the extent that they wanted to reproduce the human body even when the statues represented gods and goddesses; so the gods and goddesses were presented as human beings, but in forms that had reached as high a degree of perfection as the artist could conceive. For instance, the Aphrodite of Knidos made by Praxiteles around 350 B.C. is an ideal of female beauty. Women this beautiful and gracious, exhibiting such balance and harmony of form, do not exist in nature. The statue, inasmuch as it aims at perfection, embodies the concept of a goddess more than that of a living woman.

But how is the ideal pursued? After all, in spite of its beauty, anyone could recognize in Praxiteles' Aphrodite a body similar to that of an earthly woman. The Greeks, too, like neolithic men, used a schema, but not a schema that was just a primitive abstraction representing the essential qualities of the subject in a few linear forms. To the primitive and spontaneous neolithic schema the Greeks applied their mathematical knowledge, their ability to measure, and the geometrical proportions they were able to conceive. According to Read (1964), the geometrical proportion known as the Golden Section was the foundation of Greek art. It is founded on two propositions of Euclid (Book 2, Proposition 2; Book 6, Proposition 30): "To cut a finite line so that the shorter part is to the longer part as the longer part is to the whole." Euclid, with his formula for cutting a given finite line in extreme and mean ratios, gives a ratio of approximately 8:5 to produce harmony between the longer and shorter parts. Kenneth Clark writes (1956), "One of the few classical canons of proportion of which we can be certain is that which, in a female nude, took the same unit of measurement for the distance between the breasts, the distance from the lower breast to the navel, and again from the navel to the division of the legs."

The Greeks thus had an elaborate schema, a product of high-level secondary-process thinking. But this schema is reincarnated. The ideal abstraction, applied to a human body, becomes the desirable norm. Reality and idealism fuse and match to produce Greek beauty. The primary process is defeated. The irrationality of the pre-Greek periods, as well as the naked schematism of the neolithic, are silenced for centuries by this new, harmonious fusion. Perception and mathematics fuse; any symbolism, any elevation beyond terrestrial values, comes from the high concept of the mind. The Platonic victory of the rational over the irrational, and of the conscious over the unconscious, includes fine art too. To be exact: Greek art also reproduces irrational or mythological materials; these, however, follow idealistic aims. Greek religious art is not transcendental. Gods are made in the image of man—the reverse of the Hebrew concept that man is made in the image of God. And whereas in Hebrew culture the image of God in man was representative of love, knowledge, and the ability to choose between good and evil, without reference to physical attributes, the images of Greek gods were concretized in human forms.

With the advent of Christianity, the Western world found itself in a serious predicament as far as art was concerned. Accepting the transcendence of the monotheistic Hebrew God would mean giving up visual representations of any kind. Greek civilization did not permit the revival of old, unrealistic forms; on the other hand, reproduction of religious themes in realistic forms repeated pagan customs. The Christian tenet of the incarnation of God, however, permitted the representation of the divinity in human form. But if this form were to receive not human but divine perfection, how was it to be represented? The Middle Ages struggled with all these problems, with no perfect solutions. However, the stylization and schematization produced in Byzantine and Gothic art were great achievements. The Byzantines were much more concerned with the spiritual and transcendental than with the corporeal. The body becomes a symbol, a schema adapted to be a human body for the reason that only a body can contain the soul of a living person. Thus we have a return to a schematic-geometric style, but one with hardly any resemblance to the primitive style of the neolithic period. In Byzantine art, too, the beauty of the human flesh is not reproduced. On the contrary, a certain iconoclasm of the body has been effected in order to stress the spiritual and transcendental quality of man.

It was only with the Italian Renaissance that a fusion of Greek realistic idealism with Christian transcendence became possible. This did not come about easily. The figure of Francis of Assisi, in all his spiritual transcendental quality, emerged at first almost as much as that of Christ. Early Renaissance men such as Berlinghieri, who were eager to represent the saint, portrayed him not as he presumably was in real life but as a sort of spiritual, Byzantine abstraction. Cimabue, who in his *Crucifix* and *St. Francis and Madonna Enthroned* gradually gave up the abstraction of the Byzantine period and retained human forms, nevertheless achieved transcendental and sublime qualities by representing extreme (and yet composed) grief as well as celestial splendor. Francis of Assisi, as the greatest of all saints, had demonstrated to the Italians that the ways of Christ could really be reenacted on earth. Thus the divine moral spirit could enter into a Greek human body and make him a saint—a man who, although mortal, could transcend mortal ways of living. The famous pupil of Cimabue, Giotto, in the frescoes he made in Assisi and especially in Padua, was the first to achieve in visual form a sublime synthesis of idealism and transcendence.

At this point we could conclude that from the Greek classic period to the advent of modern art, visual art fused together the cognitive tendencies and styles that belong to the secondary process. Even the schematic-geometric style of Byzantine art has very few connections left with the style of the neolithic period. However, in visual art—as a matter of fact, more so in visual art than in any other form of creativity—we also have that fundamental mechanism of primary-process cognition: the perceptualization (or concretization) of the concept. Connotation, denotation, and the denoted object are transformed into visual perception (see Chapter 5).

How can visual perceptions concretize emotions and meanings? In his book *Art and Visual Perception* (1954), Arnheim attempts to answer this question without using the concept of the primary process, as I do. Arnheim illustrates how such basic concepts (or human motives) as rising and falling, dominance and submission, weakness and strength, harmony and discord, struggle and conformance, expansion and contraction, and approach and withdrawal, which underlie all existence, are expressed by concrete visual methods. The conceptual motives are translated into a visual language consisting of shapes, colors, light arrangements, and so on. In different historical periods, different modes of stylization have been developed that have enlarged this visual language. The artist and the admirer of the work perceive the harmonious concordance between the concrete perceptual expression and the meaning.

To give some of Arnheim's examples, in Giotto's painting *Lamentation* the upsurge of the diagonal expresses the dynamic motif of resurrection, and the retreat and rise of the curve formed by the row of the mourners express awe and despair. In discussing the dome that Michelangelo designed for St. Peter's in Rome, Arnheim points out that the two contours that make up the section of the outer cupola are parts of circles and possess the firmness of circular curves. But they are not parts of the same circle; they are parts of two circles having different centers. Thus a Gothic effect is superimposed. At the same time that the symbolic image of weight is maintained, the expression of spiritual liberation dominates the construction.

Modern Art

AS I WROTE long ago (Arietj 1952), the year 1895 represents a milestone in the history of Western civilization. It was in that year that Western culture expressed in various ways a reappraisal of that rationalistic philosophy which had started with the great Greek era and had for so long diverted the interest of people from the irrational, specific, and objective. It was in 1895 that Freud and Breuer published their book on hysteria, which marked the beginning of the psychoanalytic era and opened the road to the study of the unconscious and of the primary process (Breuer and Freud, 1895). It is in 1895 that in Paris Paul Cézanne had the first one-man show of modern paintings, the first show of modern art in the whole world. The *Journal des Artistes* called the exhibition "an apparition of atrocious nightmares." People were shocked, as they were at Freud's interpretation of neurotic symptoms. Cézanne was called a primitive, and in a certain way he was: he disregarded the Greek laws of aesthetics. He was going back to the "primitive" times of pre-Greek art.

Cézanne said, in an apparently simple sentence, that he did not try to reproduce nature: he represented it. But that word "representation" condensed a huge ensemble of concepts and feelings. Cézanne meant that he was not offering a mechanical or mirror-like reproduction of nature, as it was conventionally done. He allowed a special subjective element to enter into his work, so that such work would not reproduce but "represent" nature. In comparison to what was to develop later, Cézanne's works appear to us still very close to nature; but he remains very important in the history of art not only for the undisputable aesthetic value of his works, but because after a long period of realism and presumed objectivity he opened the door to subjectivity. Obviously every artist prior to Cézanne had expressed some subjective elements in his work, but with Cézanne a special type of subjectivity enters, one which will respect the dictates of the secondary process less and less and will lean on those of the primary more and more. The influence of Plato, who gave prominence to the rational over the irrational and to the universal over the particular, started to be reversed. As I explain later, this did not mean that the rational and the universal would not be considered by the modern artist, but that the irrational and the particular would forcefully increase their participation in the artistic conception.

The rehabilitation of the irrational during this period of history, not only in art and psychoanalysis but also in music, mathematics, and other areas of human endeavor, is too vast a topic to be discussed here (Arieti 1952). Allowing free access to the primary process meant many other things. First of all, it meant relying much more on imagery and imagination than on perception and memory; in the second place, it meant allowing the uniqueness of the subjective experience, whether originated inside or outside, to be fully expressed. Thus different levels of the human spirit could now be shown at the same time. Although such groups as the impressionists, expressionists, cubists, abstract artists, and so on have developed in a comparatively small period of time, all of these different approaches are ways of allowing the emergence of the unconscious and of the unreal. The appearance at approximately the same time, or at brief intervals, of seemingly innumerable styles, schools, and subschools, produces a marked plurality and diversity in art. This is in contrast to the previous history of Western art, which in a given country at a given time was represented almost exclusively by a given style or school (for instance, the Byzantine, Gothic, Renaissance styles, and so on). The artist is no longer the prisoner of his perceptions or his time. He roams freely. Needless to say, this freedom from perception, society, and history is only relative. Everyone is to some extent influenced by his contemporaries and by his culture. Nevertheless this freedom is now marked enough to stand out as one of the main characteristics of modern art.

Often the artist does not seem to know what he is doing. He allows himself to feel and explore within more than outside his own being. Whatever knowledge he acquires is the result of this feeling and exploring. Certainly he conforms very little or not at all to the dictates of his retina. He seems to see more with his fantasy than with his eyes. He listens more to his love and anger than to his thoughts. He does not want to describe or narrate but to symbolize. Oriental art, with its simple forms which make no use of perspective and chiaroscuro and do not reproduce reality photographically, had already been symbolic for a long time. It generally symbolized the eternal order and the perennial harmony of the universe. Modern Western art is more interested in man and woman than in the universe, more interested in the tumult of the soul in this unpleasant era than in eternity. It is the human element, the human transformation of reality that counts, rather than reality itself.

The comparison between modern art and the artwork of that natural laboratory of human experience which is the state of schizophrenia will put our interpretation to a test. When we examined the drawings of mental patients, it was obvious that they showed no perfect matching between the spontaneous unfolding of the primary process and the logical, geometrical, aesthetic, or consensual validation of the secondary process. Figure 9–16 reproduces a drawing of a regressed female patient who had homosexual conflicts, represents athletic women who have incongruously masculine physical features. In this picture there is no artistic blending of femininity and masculinity, no artistic synthesis and reintegration, but instead bizarre concretization and schizophrenic fusion that the observer is not going to accept. As I reported in detail in my book *Interpretation of Schizophrenia* (Arieti 1974), in the drawings of patients whose illness is progressing it is also possible to recognize a progressive mismatching of the two processes.

In modern art that appeals to our aesthetic appreciation, there is no mismatching but, rather, harmonious fusion. The matching requires a special effort and intuitive skill on the part of the artist because, contrary to traditional art, his art plunges very deeply into the primary process. But no matter how deeply it plunges, it rises again to attune with the secondary process. What at first seemed a private way of looking at the world receives collective consensus. The details merge into a unity, the parts form a whole, and the concrete becomes the incorporation of the abstract.

Let us take as an example the contemporary and well-known painter Marc Chagall. Chagall's paintings do not represent the ordinary aspects of things. They disregard the accidents of reality. They

Figure 9-16

respect neither anatomy nor perspective, nor the laws of gravity, nor those of space and time. Often animals and monsters, as well as simple human folk, are airborn or put together in unnatural relations. All this is primary process; all this bears resemblance to schizophrenia. The resemblance, however, ends here; and here Chagall's miracle starts. His language, while apparently abstruse, is actually understood the world over and achieves a seldom-reached degree of popularity. Ancient Jewish values, Russian folklore, and French innovations blend and harmonize in his work in a spirit of joy that calls forth a universal response. The Chagallian transformation permits us to recognize the world and see new meanings in it.

For instance, in Chagall's well-known painting *I and the Village*, the village where the artist grew up, Vigots, is not represented realistically but psychologically (Figure 9-17). The sequence of various scenes, neglectful of space and time, tells us what he feels about his village. The disregard for a proper sequence in space and time reminds us of what happens in a dream. Also dreamlike is the retention

Figure 9-17

of a total theme or aim in spite of a lack of logical continuity between the scenes. But obviously there are many differences between dreams and modern paintings. No matter how dynamic they are, modern paintings reproduce "stills," whereas dreams run like a movie.

Another painting of Chagall is reproduced in Figure 9-18. (It is not one of the best, but I selected it because I happen to own a signed lithographic reproduction.) The background is easily recognized as Nice, a place for honeymooners, and marriage seems to be the motive. Here, too, there is no respect for the force of gravity. Disparate elements are incongruously put together. But in this disorder we recognize a hidden order—the hidden order of the tertiary process, which has reconciled Chagall's primary and secondary processes. What is this order? It is a new combination of abstract concepts expressed by visual forms and aesthetic relations. The mixture of concepts is the celebration of love and joy. The fish jump out of the sea and human beings rotate in the air in circles of jubilation. We recognize aesthetic devices that give secondary-process structure to primary-process spontaneous organization. Crescentlike and circular forms reminiscent of partial moons, full moons, and honeymoons repeat themselves in Nice's coastline, in the fish, in the people, and in the other shapes that inhabit land and air. The symphony of crescent forms surrounds the floral beauty of love, and a sweet trepidation pulsates in the warm and purple night.

The expressionistic school of art portrays distortions, spatial and temporal, similar to those occurring in dreams. The distortions often seem to be suggested by an inner necessity rather than by a search for beauty. Although a few, like Chagall, express an enthusiasm for life, most expressionists, like Max Beckmann, Otto Dix, and George Grosz, depict either their inner turmoil or their rejection of society. However, in spite of themselves, the expressionists are like other artists in so far as they often discover universal ideas and forms even when they want to express their unique preoccupations. If the unrealistic elements of expressionistic art represented only a neurotic need or the need to express a private experience without aesthetic aim, no claim to art could be made.

The surrealistic school is not confined to visual art but also includes poetry, drama, and fiction. The founder of the surrealistic movement in literature was a French psychiatrist, André Breton, who, at a crucial stage of his life, abandoned psychiatry and became a

Figure 9-18

poet. Although very much indebted to Freud, Breton opposed some of Freud's views, both in his writings and during his personal meetings with the founder of psychoanalysis (Breton 1932, 1952; Breton and Eluard 1930). Whereas Freud made a sharp distinction between the external world and psychic reality, as well as between the rational and the irrational, which should be relegated to the id, Breton wrote that the psychotic realm comes closer to the great secrets of life and offers a reservoir of mental health to those who are restricted by a routine rationalism (Balakian 1970). Breton believed that absurdity is not just absurdity but an enrichment of reality—a "super-sensing" of reality. The transfiguration of the dream, the delusion, the hallucination, are not deformations but an enrichment of life.

Some of these statements seem in agreement with what we have repeatedly expressed in this book. However, there is an important point of disagreement. The surrealistic school does not advocate an unusual matching of primary and secondary processes but an acceptance of both as they are, one beside the other. Reality and unreality would then be united to form a "surreality," an expanded universe. But unreality does not exist in the external world; thus it must be an inner reality that is projected externally and made to fuse with the external. It is like escaping to another planet or another solar system, or to having a view of a galaxy that includes our solar system as well. In practice, however, even the surrealist searches for a matching or fusion of reality and unreality, and also often by resorting to similarity (or the multiple image).

In painting, Salvador Dali's position can be taken as one of the most representative of the surrealistic school. Not only are Dali's paintings very revealing, but his own writings too are often enlightening (1930, 1935, 1942). Dali often refers to his own paranoia, and he has written, ". . . all men are equal in their madness . . . madness constitutes the common basis of the human spirit." I believe that what he calls "the common basis of the human spirit" is the primary process; it is not Plato's universals but those fantastic universals that Giambattista Vico described. Dali seems to have access to the mechanisms of the primary process more than most other painters. One of these mechanisms is the phenomenon of the double image. An image suggests or turns into a second and possibly a third image, either instantly or after some contemplation. The phenomenon of the second image has been experienced by artists and common people throughout history. Dali has stated that he owes his interest in the double image to the Italian artists Arcimboldo and Bracelli, but we know that this is a common phenomenon of the primary process (Arieti 1974; also Chapter 5 of this book). As a matter of fact, it is one of the constant aims of the secondary process to prevent misidentification, the confusion between similarity and identity. The study of Arcimboldo's and Bracelli's works would not have impressed Dali so much if he himself had not had a strong attraction for (or easy access to) that which pertains to the primary process.

One drawing of Dali's (of which I own a signed lithographic reproduction) represents a hamlet. The drawing (Figure 9-19) portrays a group of homes, a small village, protected by predatory birds (the rest of the world). A tree in the middle beautifies this little oasis of love and harmony. However, when we look at the drawing in its totality, we discover that it represents not a hamlet but man himself. We may distinguish the vertebral column, trunk, ribs, arms, and legs. Man is identified with the hamlet because of the similar shape; each part of the hamlet is identified with a similarly-shaped part of the human form. Some observers may also see a phallus in the act of ejaculation. Here Von Domarus' principle is applied visually. We do not deal with identical predicates but with visually similar parts that lead to the identification. The result is that man is identified with his habitat or with his social nature. This phenomenon of the second or third image occurs frequently in Dali's works—for instance, in such a well known painting as *Apparition of Face and Fruit Dish on a Beach*. In *The Endless Enigma* of 1939, six different images are contained within the same painting. The mysteriousness of the metamorphosis (as made possible by the primary process) is appreciated by Dali, who rejects the phenomenon as merely a game. He suggests that the hidden image may be reality itself. In "La Femme Visible" he wrote, "I challenge materialists . . . to inquire into the more complex problem as to which of these images has the highest probability of existence if the intervention of desire is taken into account" (quoted by Soby 1946). Dali correctly believes that paranoiacs have "a special capacity for the recognition of double images inasmuch as their disordered minds are hypersensitive to hidden appearances, real or imagined." We must agree with him. The admirer of Dali's paintings is led by the artist to discover these similarities that he would not be able to notice by himself. We have seen that a poet does this too, in a different way;

Figure 9-19

and so does the scientist, as we shall see later. The process is in a certain aspect the opposite of that occurring as one listens to a joke, when the discovery of a discrepancy or of the falsity of the supposed identity provokes humor.

Is Dali paranoiac or paranoid? Not in a legal or clinical sense. As he expresses himself in his writings, he has "his own paranoia." I interpret his words as meaning that he has a very unusual accessibility to the primary process. It is true that people who have such an accessibility are generally psychotics who have partially or totally lost contact with the secondary process. But this is the artistic power of Dali: that he retains complete contact with the secondary process, so that the secondary process is able to control the primary. This control is well demonstrated in his paintings, which disclose an overall pattern of exactitude superimposed on an absurd content. This almost photographic exactitude, which gives an aspect of reality to many of his paintings, contrasts strikingly with the absurdity of the content, but it also mingles with it in an unparalleled way. The absurd is not made to match reality but to assume some aspects of reality, so that reality and absurdity join to form the same artistic world of surreality. On one hand, Dali seems to be an explorer of a primary-process land; he comes from a country where the secondary process reigns. But on the other hand, we know that this primary-process land is Dali's own psyche. Dali explores himself as an artist does, not as a scientist. What we experience in his paintings is not scientific or clinical but aesthetic distance, in the sense that no matter how naked the primary process is, it will still permit the hand that holds the brush to be guided by the secondary process.

I believe that psychiatry, and the psychology of the creative process, owe a debt of gratitude to Salvador Dali. By making "madness . . . as [a] common basis of the human spirit" available in the pictorial medium, he has reasserted the universality of the primary process. Of course, imitations of the primary process may also be carried out through the secondary process by imitators and second- and third-rate artists. Culture itself may adopt primary-process ways and use them as secondary-process cultural characteristics.

A vivid representation of metamorphoses, or permutations of forms similar to those discussed in a previous section of this chapter, is offered in modern art by the work of Maurits Cornelis Escher, a Dutch artist who died in 1972. Figure 9-20 portrays a woodcut in

Figure 9-20

three colors called "Metamorphosis II," and completed in 1940. Some transformations (like those from quadrangles into lizards, from lizards into hexagons, and from hexagons into honeycombs) are the result of similarity of form. When Escher makes bees fly out of the honey-comb, the image is suggested by associations of ideas. The observer discovers a cycle of permutations, made possible by the application of Von Domarus's principle, with the end coinciding with the beginning.

Abstract art reaches an extreme position. The imagination of the abstract artist frees the visual images from the characteristics of the external world and aims at expressing a purely internal representation. Paul Klee, for instance, uses a line to represent an excursion. Incidentally, some psychologists, such as Heinz Werner and Bernard Kaplan, have shown that it is possible for every human being to represent thoughts and even complicated actions in simple linear forms that have little or nothing to do with the meanings given to them (Werner and Kaplan, 1963). But whereas these lines used by average people have no aesthetic value, those made by people like Paul Klee are

highly artistic. We still have to determine what constitutes their aesthetic value.

Abstract art would tend to escape from imagery and become pure imagination. But inasmuch as any visual art *must* be visual, the imagination cannot really totally escape. A compromise must be reached, with the creation of an imagery that is unrelated or almost free from previous retinal experience. The work of art is an externalization of a purely inner process. It may consist of the greatest irregularities, where nothing is recognized (as in the works of Pollock). On the other hand, it may tend to use very symmetrical or geometrical figures, as in the paintings of Piet Mondrian. The geometric forms transcend geometry and tend toward a spiritual harmony found in measures and colors, not in anything associated with humanistic elements.* Even in contemporary abstract art the reader is now in a position to recognize

* In speaking about the geometric forms of some modern art, Segy (1967) states: "It is not their associated images or an assumed substance which gives the content of the work, but their functions. It is not fact we apprehend but the meaning which we experience."

either the vitalistic element, which started in the paleolithic period, or the geometric-schematic, which started in the neolithic period.

Within the limitations of this book it is impossible to take into consideration all the types of modern art or even of one of its movements, abstract art. One of the greatest exponents of modern art, Kandinsky, spoke of it as an "internal necessity." With these words he did not refer merely to a compulsive force, or an inner need to create; this is true of all types of fine, nondecorative art. He meant that in the modern artist there is a need to reproduce the harmony of his inner world. The external pattern, made of shapes and colors, reflects a pattern that exists only in the psyche. Kandinsky explores "inner space" and inner or psychic reality, just as Freud and other psychoanalysts have advocated, in contrast to those who are exclusively preoccupied with external space and external reality.

Does this mean that Kandinsky relies only on the primary process? Not at all. The "Spiritual Harmony" that he tries to achieve requires, as he himself wrote, "reason, consciousness, purpose." Even a rapid examination of his work reveals a refined calculation, a mathematical, almost scientific precision, which is superimposed on the inner impulses. He often compared painting to poetry and even more so to music, to notes without cognitive content. But here again, if we maintain extreme positions, we reach the paradox to which I have already referred. Abstract art is supposed to have no content, to be imageless and shapeless. But whatever is to be seen has *some* shape. No matter how much the abstract artist would unshape the world, he will do some shaping. If his unshaping is symbolic of a revolt, if it is the unshaping of a culture, the artist will also do some shaping of a new culture. What seems an art of denial and dissolution becomes an art of expansion, an attempt to transport the human being far beyond the reach of daily life.

Art cannot be exclusively symbolic; that is, it cannot stand for something totally not present. The work of art itself *is* present; it stands for itself, as artistic reality. Like literature, it becomes "a second reality." Its potentiality is also its power to evoke in us an aesthetic response, an aesthetic pleasure.

Beauty

THUS, again, we come back to consideration of aesthetic value. Why do some matchings of disparate processes in visual art, as in literature, produce the magic synthesis, the creative aesthetic effect, whereas others do not? The aesthetic effect is not just a powerful effect. If we see a picture of a raped and murdered child, we experience the greatest pity for the victim and the greatest indignation for the aggressor; but these potent feelings are not aesthetic. Unfortunately the gap between appreciation of art and the psychology of aesthetic pleasure is hard to fill.

In Chapter 8 a section was devoted to aesthetic pleasure as experienced in general but with reference to poetry in particular. It is much harder to study the psychology of aesthetic pleasure in reference to fine art. Many artists, aestheticians, and philosophers who have tried to do so have not gone very far. They have advanced hypotheses that seem valid for some cases but not for others. In relation to wit and the comic, the corresponding problem is relatively simple. In considering poetry (or literature in general), we have the great advantage of dealing with cognitive symbols. Thus any thought that we may have about a literary work, even when we focus on forms, is closely related to its content. But in visual art, any thought is widely separated from the perceptual aesthetic perception. Certainly we know that beauty in visual art, as in any aesthetic experience, is an encounter between something that resides in the artistic object, and a subjective feeling. In this dual quality the appreciation of beauty is not different, let us say, from the apperception of a color. When we see something green or red, the greenness or the redness exists in the external object but also in ourselves. Without us there to experience the green and the red, there would only be light waves. However, whereas it is relatively easy to determine the wave length that we will perceive as yellow, blue, or green, it is impossible to determine the "wave length" that will make us see beauty when we see an object of art.

Could we make any inroads in our understanding of this special "light wave?" Does it irradiate from the color, the form, the combination, the pattern, the content, or the structure of the object—or, as we suspect, from a special harmonious relation of all these characteristics and additional others? It does not matter whether the original inspiration comes from external or from inner life, whether the main impulse was to capture a pattern of vitality or to abstract the essential. It does not matter whether the aim was to portray reality, to idealize reality, or to transcend reality by creating something not previously existent. The result will be beauty only if a certain harmonization is achieved and a "secret power" develops as a cause of this harmonization. The secret power is—just that: the revelation of a secret. It was not known before that such a combination of forms and colors had that particular aesthetic power.

An additional point is necessary before we close this chapter. We have seen that, in poetry, images are represented by words and metaphors. Words become icons by proxy. But in painting no such proxy is necessary. The perception is the reality. Whereas poetry relies chiefly on verbalization and connotation, painting relies mostly on denotation and perceptualization—that is, on the work of art itself, as it exists. In the work of art as in poetry, however, perceptualization is accentuated too. Perceptual elements are sharpened by their particular selection and combination.

A Note on Music *

WHAT IS MUSIC? What is the origin of the elements (melody, rhythm, harmony, timbre, form) that compose the "core" of music? To have an understanding of these elements, how they are mixed, and in what proportions they are found in musical art is to know something about *all* music. Of course these questions have been asked before. But some of the answers given here are new; they add a dimension to an understanding of music, both as a form of creativity and as an aesthetic experience. What I am describing in this section has been inspired to some extent by a reading of *The Intrapsychic Self* (Arieti 1967).

Melody originated in the sounds produced by the vocal apparatus of man's forbears: sounds expressive of affect and reactive to external stimuli. This repertoire of sounds probably antedated verbalization. High primates make expressive sounds which they themselves understand; we, too, understand sounds expressive of sorrow, of satisfaction, of surprise, and so on. This understanding, at a very low level of cognition, is a universal. So, while primitive man was finger-pointing and gesturing his way toward language, concepts, and ever-increasing knowledge, he was also producing noises with his vocal apparatus that were expressive of pleasure or displeasure; wails, sighs, whimpers,

---

* This section has been written by Mr. Mortimer Cass.

growls that were understood (and are still understood) to symbol-ize—to be acoustic symbols for—his emotions. From this beginning developed what is known as "melody," but only after many interme-diate levels had been integrated.

Melody, one of the two essential components of music, has never lost its original function as *expressor of emotion*. (We must remember that music is concerned with expression rather than cognition.) Mel-ody in its purest forms certainly antecedes the development of the sec-ondary process. With its constant rising and falling and many inflec-tions, it approximates the affective component of the endocept. The "breathing" of melody approximates some of the physiological con-comitants of emotion. Finger-pointing and gesturing led to the deno-tation of objects and to language formation, the development of cogni-tion; the motivation was the need to understand and communicate. Developing in another direction, the vocal sounds made by early man were elaborated into a language of emotional expression which, in-corporating such refinements as pitch discrimination and scale, became what we call melody.

Because of this early association of vocal sounds expressive of emotion and vocal sounds denoting an external object melody al-ways implies verbalization. However, although melody is inseparable from the cognitive ingredient inherent in verbalization, this cognitive ingredient must be *expressive* in intent. When melody is used as an ac-cessory of information—as often in comic opera—the effect is hu-morous and does not stir deep emotions.

Rhythm, the other essential component of music, includes not only pulse and meter but also all the varieties of rhythmic groupings. Rhythm is the very life of music, that which gives it its vitality. Rhythm can exist without melody, but not melody without rhythm. Its origins are at least as ancient as are the vocal noises from which melody developed. Rhythm has its beginning at a sensori-motor level (see Arieti 1967, Chapter 3). In dance, exocepts (that is, inner repre-sentations that are subsequently embodied in movements) have a cen-tral role. Music's link to the dance derives from the presence of its rhythmic component; music's link to language derives from its me-lodic component. Rhythm, like melody, is a "universal." It is con-nected with the physiological properties of the organism and antedates any form of cognition, including the primary process.

Harmony, considered as "any simultaneous combination of

tones," is not nearly as ancient as melody and rhythm. It is not primordial. As chordal "dissonance-consonance," harmony approximates states of tension and release. Most important for music as an art, harmony, when organized into a mathematical relationship called "tonality," with its keys and modes, exerts a powerful, gravitational influence over an entire composition (at any rate it did so until the advent of atonality). Harmony, as the simultaneous sounding of many different tones, provides a textural element in music.

Timbre, which includes the concepts of tone-color and of sonority in general (whether the tones are produced singly or in combination), is defined as "the characteristic quality of a sound." This includes *any* sound, whether that of a falling leaf, running water, footsteps, rubbing branches, an animal, a voice, or an instrument. Timbre denotes the source of a sound acoustically. Animals recognize timbre. To man's forbears, timbre must have been vital in making inferences about the significance of external stimuli; it must have constituted a universal language. In music, timbre is the chief supplier of aural pleasure. Metaphorically expressed, the timbre-sensitive ear "feels" the quality of sound.

These four components, originating at different levels of the psyche, are fused by *form* into the mode of creativity which is music. Form, considered as the *linear* organization of the musical elements, is a function assumed mainly by melody. As such, it obeys the secondary-process principles of logic and balance. This logical property of melody stems from its original association, as vocal sound, with the connotative aspect of verbalization. Considered as the *vertical* organization of the elements, form is a function of the tonal system. As such it obeys mathematically-determined relationships. It is to the dynamic relationship of these two different logical orders—one arising out of man's secondary-process rationality, the other representing the facts of nature—that we can attribute the evolution of Western musical art from the simple folk tune to the complex structures of symphonic form.

Music is not concerned with connotation, with the defining of concepts. Neither is it interested in denoting objects, except in those cases where, for extra-musical purposes, it is employed in the imitation of sounds made by objects in the external world: the roll of thunder, the murmur of a running brook, the chug-chug of a locomotive, the chatter of newly-hatched chicks, and so on. In cases such as these a sound is used both to denote and to represent the object denoted. *Pars pro toto* is then the identifying mechanism. Representation by acoustic imitation must be as old as man's attempt to influence nature by imitative magic. There must once have been a universally shared repertoire of manmade imitative sounds. (A prehistoric cave painting of animals and a presiding shaman give us some notion of the visual aspect of such efforts to influence nature. But what were the imitative sounds that accompanied these magical rites?) But interesting as is the subject of acoustic imitation in music, as it is used to further narrative and descriptive intentions, the reader is reminded that such uses rarely figure in absolute, or pure, music. Such music is an organism that *represents and expresses itself alone.*

Before going on to a discussion of the creative process in music, it should be noted that musical creativity owes much to inventions—for instance, to the "valve and piston" system, which facilitated the execution of rapid chromatic passages on brass instruments; to the keyboard, which permitted a single player to depress many different keys at the same time; and to the damper pedal of the piano that, by permitting the prolongation and mixing of hitherto separate harmonies, opened a new world of coloristic possibility. Many composers have been pianists who discovered and developed their ideas at the keyboard. They were not slow to exploit these newly-found acoustic resources, thus greatly enriching the texture of musical sound.

The creative process involved in many musical compositions seems to be as follows:

1. The composer receives an acoustic idea from an external source (often from experimentation at the keyboard), in the shape of a phrase that he perceives as lending itself to his compositional purposes.

2. Of no intrinsic significance, this acoustic shape is soon objectified. The percept becomes an appercept, a construct to which he relates with affect.

3. This acoustic phrase, or sentence, in effect asks the composer "What next?" To find the "right" answer—one that is aesthetically acceptable and that does not violate the endoceptual character objectified in the other acoustic constructs—constitutes one of the major tasks of musical composition. Like Poincaré in mathematics (see Chapter 11), the composer must reject the multitude of alternative suggestions inherited from previous practitioners of musical language.

He must use only those constructs that further the formal requirements and expand the endoceptual expression. Depending on the complexity of the formal structure involved, this process of selection can take considerable effort (as is evident, for example, in Beethoven's sketchbooks). The judgments as to what is "right" are made subliminally. The form *itself* carries an affective significance for the composer.

The three foregoing psychological processes can be reformulated in the following way: (1) a perception of an evocative acoustic phrase—an aesthetic shape; (2) objectification of this construct, to which the composer relates with affect; and (3) a search for an acoustic construct to succeed the previous one in a cause–effect relationship. In a sense, an entire composition can often be seen as a chain of cause–effect, question–answer relationships.

The judgment as to what constitutes the "right" succession is a matter of the composer's individuality. It involves his previous experience and personal aesthetic preferences. The first point in the above outline of the creative process in music need not apply in all cases. The initial step is not always the perception of a short tonal pattern originating at a keyboard. But this does seem to fit one type of procedure—for example, the four note motif of the first movement of Beethoven's Fifth Symphony. The second movement is built on a long song-like theme of thirty-two notes. This theme did not satisfy Beethoven until he had made fourteen revisions over a period of eight years. The first movement is rhythmic in character, the second is melodic.

The point is that the creative process in music is influenced by the status of the basic elements of music as they are fused in that particular composition. In Debussy, for example, *color* is often very important; in Beethoven there is often a powerful sense of "pulse;" in Mozart, melody predominates; contemporary music often features rich chordal textures. However, with the exception of the first point (the derivation and shape of the musical "idea"), the rest of the formula often seems to apply, particularly in art music of an introspective character.

In conclusion, we can state that music is an *acoustic medium that can approximate, objectify, convey, and evoke content of endoceptual significance.* When this content is acoustically represented by a composer, performed by an interpreter, and empathetically invoked in a listener then the sum of these processes brings about a gratifying experience.

A total musical event implies an acoustic system of messages whose meaning is shared by these three figures. The composer has to have the capacity to reproduce and aesthetically objectify the contents of his endoceptual sphere, or better, of his inner world of imagery. The interpreter needs to have empathetic insight into the composer's affective intentions and aesthetic concepts, along with the musical ability to project these in sounds that are sensually agreeable. The listener must be ready to empathetically *endoceive while remaining in auditory contact with the sound source from which the stimuli issue.* The ideal listener is he who neither permits his mind to regress totally to the inner world of fantasy (which is being stimulated by the endoceptual acoustic elements) or allows his attention to be diverted by other stimuli (often visual) to the world of secondary process, of everyday practicality.

A total musical experience involves in addition to an unforced but steady sensuous contact with the sound source psychological reactivity to the emotional and sensori-motor musical stimuli, and an awareness of the shaping logic that is unfolding the design of the composition. If the first is present, the others will follow.

Historically, music has always responded to the need for new expressivity by making changes in its formal structure and in the status of its elements. Since the year 1900, this process has been greatly accelerated to meet the expressive and aesthetic needs of the contemporary psyche. But what has been said here about the nature of the basic elements is still true, for the most part, in contemporary music. Rhythm is still the vital force it has always been; timbre has greatly increased its role; melody, too, no longer restricted to the diatonic scale, has a wider field of expressivity; harmony as texture, as the simultaneous combination of tones, has increased in density; the "dissonance–consonance" distinction has vanished. Finally, Key-centered tonality has been replaced by other systems of organization—a principle source of the difficulty experienced by many in appreciating contemporary music.

Chapter 10
Religious and
Mystical Experiences

IN THIS CHAPTER we shall deal with the psychology of the creative process, as it finds expression in religious and mystical experiences. Any evaluation of religion as a norm for contemporary man, or any appraisal of the reality value of the objects of religion, is beyond the scope of this book.

Many religions, and especially the major ones in recorded history, have cultural components that may be studied psychologically but that do not strictly pertain to the realm of religious or mystical experience: for instance, social, philosophical, legal, political, and artistic norms, tenets, and mores. Some religious leaders in particular have had a multiple impact on their followers; they were not only religious innovators, but also political chiefs, legislators, philosophers, and so on. These collateral aspects of religion also will not be considered here.

The essence of religion as a psychological experience is to be found in the mystical aspect (that quality called *kadosh* in Hebrew and *sacer* in Latin), which includes the immediacy and primacy of direct divinity-consciousness (Schleirmacher 1958). Modern European languages (for instance, English, in spite of the word *holy*) do not have suitable terms to represent this mystical experience in its potential intensity. To obviate the difficulty, Otto (1923) coined the adjective *numinous* to serve this function.

From the standpoint of the religious innovator, religion consists of at least one of the following three aspects: (1) an apprehension of supernatural powers, which influence events affecting men; (2) a contact with these powers; and (3) a visualization of norms for special ways of living that will affect the totality of man and that have transcendental meanings. From the viewpoint of the religious person who is not an innovator, religion consists of the following three aspects, or at least one of them: (1) a set of beliefs in the existence of supernatural powers; (2) attempted contacts with or efforts to affect these powers, by means of prayers or rituals of various sorts; and (3) the adoption of special ways of living that are reputed to affect the totality of man and to have transcendental meanings.

In this chapter as in the previous one, the collective participation in a historical frame of reference will be stressed, rather than individual contributions.

Insight into the Supernatural

RECOGNITION of supernatural forces is a more astonishing phenomenon in the modern than in the ancient world. What we usually call supernatural would not be supernatural at all for primitive man. For him, nothing transcends nature; everything is immanent in it. Actually, the appearance of the supernatural is to a large extent the result of a special application of what I have called the principle of teleological causality. According to this form of interpreting the world, *every event is willed* (Arieti 1967, Chapter 7). A willed act presupposes a person or personified entity behind it. Primitive man interprets all manifestations of nature in this way.

Cassirer, quoting Usener (1896), believed that the evolution of religious ideas started with the creation of *momentary deities*. These are fleeting mental constructs. "Every impression that man receives, every wish that stirs in him, every hope that lures him, every danger that threatens him, can affect him thus religiously. Just let spontaneous feeling invest the object before him, or his own personal condition, or some display of power that surprises him, with an air of holiness, and the momentary god has been created" (Cassirer 1946). Everything is animated and personified. However, the animated or willing entity is not usually seen; it is felt or conceived as residing in the thing or the activity in question. The brook, the tree, the rain, contain the willing elements in themselves, which become the gods.

Following Usener's concepts, Cassirer believed that the whole world of the primitive became populated with little gods who represented functions, actions, or things. The world was seen as a pantheon. Whereas Spinoza later came to believe that the whole world is God, primitive man believed that everything has a divine essence; Spinoza's is a monotheistic version of an ancient belief. Usener and Cassirer went to the extent of declaring that the creation of gods was simultaneous with the creation of names. When the name of a thing or of a function (such as hunting, plowing, or sowing) was created, the corresponding god was also conceived.

As already mentioned, the immanence of the divine in nature follows from a generalization of the principle of teleologic causality. It is an extension to the whole world of what the individual observes in his early and immediate interpersonal relations. The human baby realizes that things and their appearances and disappearances—that is, events—are generally willed by people: specifically, the significant adults in his life. Mother *wills* to give the baby her breast, to fondle him, to hold him on her lap, and so on. Later the child attributes all the events he observes to acts of will. But while some acts of will are good, some are bad. Mother is there to will good things that will keep the child fed, warm, and alive. Thus a feeling of hope or trust originates in the child's association with his mother. The feeling of hope and trust is later extended to those parts of nature that are seen as animated by good gods. The concept of physical causality (A brings about B) is not yet developed; the child believes that natural object or event A must be *animated* to bring about—or rather to will—B. Thus also thinks primitive man.

Soon, however, primitive man becomes aware of the precariousness of his existence: scarcity of food, inclement weather, epidemics, invasions, and wild animals are there to endanger his survival. But if things are conceived as animated by good gods who have good intentions, the feeling of hope that originated with the contact with the good mother is experienced again in a larger context. At this level, female deities predominate. Bad events are conceived as willed by bad gods, predominantly male, who have to be placated.

Thus religion can be seen from its origin as a set of cognitive constructs that prolong hope in the survival of the individual and of the small social group to which he belongs. Later, of course, hope is expanded further and embraces the survival of the tribe, state, nation, or human race; or it is focused on the eternal survival (immortality) of at least a part of the individual (the soul), or on general human progress and so on. Faith comes to mean two things: not only belief in the existence of the divinity, but also trust or confidence. Religion is thus not just a way of interpreting the world, but of *hoping* as well. This hope is based on something that is conceived at the level of teleologic causality and is accepted as truth. What is believed becomes truth; the unknowable becomes known. We may see in this phenomenon a form of adualism (described in Chapter 3). However, except for the experiences to be recounted in the next section, this adualism originates from others and is shared with them.

The perceptual vividness of impressions, the scarcity of logical elaborations, and the elements of surprise it offers give primitive life a picturesque and fervid atmosphere that is particularly conducive to the conception of innumerable deities. The primitive feels that the god is within the physical object, be it a tree, an animal, or a stone; but somehow he does not fully understand the divine mysterious essence in the object. Thus he makes an effort to concretize it: he transforms the object, so that the tree, the animal, the stone become gods. Idolatry is a form of escaping from something vaguely perceived as too abstract and therefore threatening. This abstract "something" has to be concretized, made part of the concrete aspect of life. The world then becomes full of numberless little, concrete gods.

Life, however, changes in the course of thousands and thousands of years of history. The greater the conceptual development of psychological life, the less pronounced the perceptual vividness and the smaller the number of gods. Eventually the same god becomes responsible for many things or actions. In this way a gradual diminution in the number of gods takes place with the passage of time. And whereas in early periods the deities are within objects or belong to the same natural world as men, a gradual abstraction of the deity takes place with time. The gods are no longer inside objects. They are expelled from the things in which they were incorporated and may even be relegated to a distant Olympus. From there, however, they continue to rule the things with which they were originally fused. Thus we have a change from idolatry to paganism.

In some religions, cosmogonies are created at this stage. The origin of the world is explained by teleologic causality applied to the divinity. "The world is this way because the gods willed it this way." The gods, however, are seen more and more as being separate from the reality of man. They live in some heaven such as Olympus; they belong, so to speak, to a *third reality* that is different from the reality of human life and the reality of art. But although, in paganism, high processes of abstraction have permitted the separation of the gods from the things and events originally endowed with divine properties, the process of abstraction does not go beyond a certain level. The god is concretized again; he is anthropomorphized. That is, most of his attributes are human, although he may be endowed with some superhuman qualities such as great power and immortality.

In the Greek pagan world, the three realities—the immanent, the artistic, and the religious—exist side by side, each of them having its own place in the cosmos. There is no absolute supremacy of the third reality. In paganism, moreover, entities are conceived that transcend or are even more powerful than the gods. The gods did not always exist; they originated from a primordial realm. There are two realms: that of the divine powers and the greater one of the *metadivine* (Kaufmann 1960).* The gods are immanent in or part of these greater, metadivine things. In the religion of the ancient Greeks the greater order of things—greater than the gods, indeed the ultimate arbiter—is *ananke* (necessity) or *moira* (fate). Even Zeus, the king of gods, is incapable of altering ananke or moira. Ananke is not seen as a physical law or an order of nature but as an ultimate will, the personified essence of teleologic causality.

It is impossible today to account for the innovating insights that were responsible for the change from idolatry to paganism, or for the numerous variations of paganism that developed among peoples who were later considered as belonging to Western civilization. They probably occurred in prehistoric and very early historical time, and no trace of them has remained.

What is much better known is the change from paganism to

* "Divine" means pertaining to divinities; "metadivine" means transcending the divinities.

monotheism effected by Judaism. This religious revolution, later adopted by the whole Western world, consisted of further removals from concretization. Primitive religions tended toward the primitive mechanisms of concretizations, paleologic transformations, and imagery, whereas Judaism, as a rule, emerged as a revolt against these trends. According to the Biblical account, Abraham was the first man who had the revelation that God is one and invisible. What some consider revelation, others consider insight. Of course, we have no historical proof of the existence of Abraham, the "first Jew." His myth, however, represents the beginning of a very long trend in Judaism against religious concretization and other primitive mechanisms. One of the themes of the Pentateuch is this fight against the concrete gods. The gods of the surrounding polytheistic people are stigmatized as being "wood and stone" or "silver and gold." The Hebrew God loses human characteristics, becomes incorporeal and abstract. The third reality becomes superior by far to any other reality. The third reality is conceived as having preceded any other reality—as a matter of fact, as having created everything else in existence.

It is this intense opposition to concretization, I think, that accounts for the often-observed unpopularity of the Jewish religion both in ancient and modern times. Concretization obviously appeals to the masses, and as a rule it is needed to give an artistic aspect to religion. For that matter, the fight against concretization is not absolute in the rites or in the myths of the Jewish religion, either. Paradoxically, even the revolt against concretization is "concretized" in one of the myths about Abraham. As reported in the Midrash, Abraham was the son of a man who carved and sold idols. One morning Abraham got up, went to his father's store, and broke all the idols. This episode represents a new era in religious history: the fight against concrete gods.

The attitude of the Jewish religion and people against concretization goes beyond the objection to making physical gods. If a god can be made or represented in a concrete form, he can be visualized even when he is absent. Imagery may indeed have a religious content; and as long as it is religious, it is welcomed by most people. But for the Jews, God was and still is an abstract incorporeal entity. If any image is rejected, it has to be substituted promptly by cognitive processes higher than the level of imagery. Thus the divine presence may be experienced endoceptually; God may be referred to with words, and especially with words that tend to have a more and more abstract content. According to Jack Bemporad (1974), "the contrast between God as a force in nature and God as a transcendent spiritual being is clearly illustrated by an incident in the life of Elijah, the prophet [as reported in the Old Testament]. Elijah went up upon the mountain to seek God and was confronted by a shattering wind and then an earthquake and after that a fire. But God was not to be found in any of these, for God was not a force of nature. After all these natural forces there came a still, small voice. The still, small voice, the inner voice that is the conscience of man, this was Elijah's communication with God."

The attitude of the Jews toward the divinity and the later (at least partial) acceptance of this attitude in the Western world, together with the Platonic concept of the universal, promoted abstract thinking in Western civilization. The opposition to concretization stimulated Jews throughout the centuries to advance and contribute greatly in fields of abstract thought. However, until recently, it prevented them from participating to more than a minimal degree in the fine arts; in modern times, a less strict adherence to this attitude toward the abstract has permitted them to do so. Indeed, Jews have made important contributions to modern art—especially abstract art, because the visual reproduction of realistic images is minimized or completely abolished in it.

Another important revolution occurred later in the Jewish religion, during the prophetic period. Starting with Amos, religion becomes intimately fused with moral life; the third reality becomes the moral guidance of man. Although the association between religion and morality existed in pre-prophetic Judaism, it becomes predominant in this period.

Christianity followed the general pattern of Judaism, but with some fundamental variations made by the founders of Christianity in order to adapt the Jewish religion to the Greco-Roman world. Although in Christianity as in Judaism, God transcends nature and is the creator of nature, the separation of God from nature is, in one aspect, not as complete. For God can appear concretely as a man—as Jesus, the Christ, the incarnated son of God. In Christian theology, immanence and transcendence unite in the life on earth of Jesus Christ. Furthermore, in many Christian denominations, the representation of the divinity in concrete artistic ways is not only not forbidden but encouraged. Christianity, however, goes further than Judaism in abstracting "the soul" from the body and in disregarding man's physical concrete body. The mind–body problem becomes accentuated.

A third, philosophical revolution occurred later in both Judaism and Christianity, with Maimonides (1135–1204) and Thomas Aquinas (1225–1274), respectively. This development consisted mainly of an attempt to reconcile the two religions with Aristotelian philosophy.

Contact with the Supernatural

THE PREVIOUS SECTION dealt with religion as the apprehension of the existence of supernatural forces. This apprehension or insight was seen as based on tendencies toward concretization and abstraction competing among themselves. Over long periods of time, abstraction progressively gained the ascendancy. Another important aspect of religion seems almost opposite to this trend toward abstraction: *the return to primitive methods of cognition in order to support the newly acquired abstract insights.* Religion too, like art, resorts to mechanisms of the primary process or to earlier mechanisms of the secondary process to give a structure to abstract concepts.

The religious innovator or leader does not consciously *infer* the existence of the divinity as, let us say, a philosopher or a scientist would infer a concept or make a discovery. The religious leader establishes a direct contact with the divinity, through the experience usually called *revelation.* But direct contact or revelation is not possible if the religious innovator relies exclusively on secondary-process mechanisms or Aristotelian logic. He must resort to the primary process or to earlier levels of cognition. Obviously, not everybody is in a position to summon up the primary process in order to establish contact with supernatural powers. Special conditions are necessary. Such conditions have been described by William James, in a book that marked the official entrance of the field of psychology into the study of religion (1902). For James, mystical experiences have four qualities. One is ineffability, which he calls a negative characteristic: no words can adequately describe the mystical experience. This characteristic corresponds to what I have called an endoceptual experience. The second is a noetic quality: new knowledge is gained as a result of the experience. The other two qualities, transiency and passivity, are less significant.

In an important book (1961), Marganita Laski describes ecstasy as "a range of experiences characterized by being joyful, transitory, unexpected, rare, valued, and extraordinary to the point of often seeming as if derived from a praeternatural source." The ecstatic (or mystical) experience thus has many characteristics in common with the aesthetic experience. However, it has the additional quality of appearing to be derived from a "praeternatural" source, which the subject interprets as supernatural. How can an unusually enriching experience (perhaps an aesthetic experience or a peak experience, as described by Maslow 1959b, 1961) become an ecstatic one? First of all, the mystical person experiences what Laski calls *overbelief*. The person believes in the supreme value of what he wishes to see realized—a principle, an accomplishment, a special answer to a challenge or question—and he assumes that the supernatural powers are in favor of the actualization of his wish. His emotions become so intense as to compel him to become a fanatic doer and to carry out his mission without delay. The evidence that the supernatural powers favor his mission is provided by unusual experiences that are based on primary-process mechanisms.

For instance, the belief that God wants the person to carry out a certain mission becomes concretized: the mystic actually sees or hears the divinity in the act of giving him that mission. He feels that a contact has been established between the divinity and himself. The insight or illumination is now projected to the divinity: it becomes a revelation. The insight must assume the form of a divine revelation in order to gain access to the person's consciousness and stimulate him to action. For a rather strong conflict or resistance existed in him before the revelation: many prophets, leaders, and saints are reported as at first repressing the inner knowledge of their mission. Realistic facts, such as the hostile attitude of authorities or the indifference or hostility of an incredulous population, do not permit the mystic to become fully aware of his insights. At times he is only half aware of his inner impulses. The inner battle is won when a mystical experience at the level of consciousness gives him the determination to overpower his realistic reluctance and the anticipated opposition of the external world.

Thus we have here, too, what Kris would call a regression in the service of the ego (1952), and what I prefer to call a use of the primary process to sustain the secondary. The secondary process has undoubtedly formulated or worked out all the preparatory mental steps necessary for the insight. But the insight will occur only when mechanisms that are part of the primary process support what has been worked out at the secondary level. The subject realizes, obviously, that these primary-process experiences are not usual or common, but he does not interpret them as pathological. On the contrary, he believes they are the evidence that a contact with the divinity has been established. He has a feeling of absolute lucidity and absolute certainty. *Now* he sees, *now* he must move, *now* he must face the crowds—no matter what the price.

These mystical experiences seem to correspond to what are called hallucinations and delusions in psychiatric terms. Must we then conclude that people who have such experiences are suffering from schizophrenia, paranoia, or other psychoses? Not necessarily. It is easy to confuse religious mystics with psychotic patients, especially those psychotics who have hallucinations and delusions with religious content, but in my opinion this can and should be avoided. The following discussion of religious hallucinations and how they differ from schizophrenic ones is drawn mostly from an article published some years ago (Arieti 1961).

1. Religious hallucinations are predominantly visual, not auditory. Most of the time they have the aspect of apparitions. If there is an auditory component, it is as a rule secondary to the visual.

2. In their content they often involve old people, parent substitutes; but they are benevolent parents who guide the person to whom they appear.

3. Their content is gratifying in a manifest way.

4. The individual who experiences them has a marked rise in self-esteem and a sense of his being or becoming a worthwhile and very active person. He has been given a mission or a special insight, and from now on he must be on the move doing something important—more important than his own life. Although the message is experienced as an order, the subject does not feel that he is the victim of tyranny or a passive agent, but that he has been chosen to perform something of stupendous proportions.

The whole personalities and behavior of the people who experience religious hallucinations are not such as to warrant the diagnosis of psychosis. Mystics are fanatic, but not in the same way as the paranoid. They lack the bitterness and resentment or the calm resignation and disdain of the unjustly accused. They show instead a serene optimism, like that of people who have been blessed by the love of a good mother. Moreover, the hallucinatory and delusional experiences of the schizophrenic are generally accompanied by a more or less apparent disintegration of the whole person. Religious and mystical experiences seem instead to result in a strengthening and enriching of the personality.

These differential charactcristics may be difficult to recognize in cases of pure paranoia or well-systematized paranoid syndromes. In such conditions the secondary process is used in the service of the regression or of the regressive forces. Some wrong premises are accepted as correct, and the secondary process is summoned to demonstrate their alleged validity. Sooner or later it will be evident that the patient's personality has not been enriched but impoverished. His motivation will be recognized as grounded in hostility, not in a desire to help others. Another important diagnostic characteristic is that whereas hallucinations are rare in paranoia and well-systematized paranoid conditions, they are common in mystical experiences.

If people who have mystical experiences are not psychotic, then what are they? There is no doubt that hallucinations and delusions of any sort, religious or not, are abnormal phenomena. Must we share Freud's point of view, expressed in *The Future of an Illusion* (1928), that religion is based on unconscious, primitive, and irrational psychic processes? Must we accept the idea that in some of its beliefs religion is a form of collective schizophrenia, and in some of its practices a form of obsessive-compulsive psychoneurosis, different from the psychiatric syndromes because it is socially acceptable?

These are possibilities that we cannot easily dismiss just because we do not like them. However, another point of view, not mentioned by Freud, is suggested by our study of the aesthetic process. We have seen that one of the bases of the work of art is the use of the primary process, and yet few would deny that art has value and merit. But aesthetic methods, results, and values are certainly different from those obtained by pure secondary-process mechanisms.

In a similar way we may state that religious methods, results, and values are different from those derived from pure secondary processes. The religious value consists in giving people faith in the survival of man and man's ideals, in assuming that life has a meaning and that when such meaning is not immediately apparent, we must search for it. Religion becomes an incentive to greatness of the spirit.* It offers new insights, such as those described in the previous section, which open up new dimensions of understandings and feelings.† These new

---

* See also Slonimsky (1956).

† See also Tillich (1957).

dimensions, although they are abstractions constructed at higher psychological levels, need the support of lower mechanisms. We should not make the common mistake of considering the new insights and aims of religion irrational or primitive, just because they are partially founded on primary-process mechanisms.

How do the primary-process mechanisms become available to the mystical person, and how are they used? As already mentioned, the person who undergoes mystical experiences must be in a state of overbelief and must be expecting divine revelation.* But what are the phenomena that bring about hallucinations and delusions, in the absence of intoxication or of psychosis? They seem to me to be related to hysterical and hypnotic mechanisms. In hypnosis the subject retains the use of the secondary process but is under the influence of another person to whom he attributes great power. Gill and Brennan (1959) consider hypnosis, too, a regression in the service of the ego, but a regression that is time-limited and totally reversible.

In mystical experiences we have a condition of autohypnosis: the subject puts himself into a state of trance and projects power to the divinity. The state of trance permits the resurgence of primitive mechanisms. These mechanisms, however, are not used as they are in schizophrenia and dreams, since there is no abandonment of Aristotelian logic and no acceptance of the rule of the primary process. In religious experiences as in the aesthetic process, the various levels of mentation are concordant. This concordance leads to religious value; that is, to the establishment of faith, or to the transformation of a belief into absolute certainty. The new insights trigger the action necessary to their realization.

The subject does not believe his will is involved. He feels that he is the recipient of an experience, a passive agent: he undergoes the experience as he would undergo a dream. A strong force that he attributes to a supernatural power compels him to act. This strong religious force is the result, first, of religious preparation, then of a state of overbelief, and finally of a state of autohypnosis.

As mentioned, not only does the adopted primary process reinforce the secondary process, at times it actually makes possible an in-

---

* Collective phenomena consisting of religious hallucinations and delusions occurred during the Middle Ages and continue to occur in some societies (Hecker 1832; Ferrio 1948; Arieti and Bemporad 1974). In these environments, the abnormal manifestations are acceptable to the crowd. Their acceptance, like that of a benevolent Freudian superego, enhances their occurrence.

sight that is in contrast to the conventional attitudes of that period and that therefore had tended to be repressed or dismissed from the person's center of consciousness. For instance, the prophets of the Old Testament had the conviction that they must convey a great message of justice and love to the people. Only a mystical experience, however, could convince them that their mission was a call from God. The mystical experience transforms uncertainty into certitude, confusion into clarity, hesitation and cautiousness into courage and determination. The mystical experience becomes a "revelation" and is accepted as "reality" by the subject. Therefore, of all creative processes, it is the one that seems closest to the psychotic experience. It is a loss of "reality" but—as we have seen—it is a loss that helps open up new dimensions of reality. Furthermore, it is experienced as a "third reality," a reality distant from the first in its attributes and yet always in contact with the first.

As instances of mystical experiences I shall take two examples from my previous article (Arieti 1961), one concerning the Christian and the other the Jewish religion.

Constantine was the first Roman emperor who was converted to Christianity. He made Christianity the official religion of the Empire and thus opened the path of Christianity to the Western world. The historian Eusebius, who was a contemporary and friend of Constantine, wrote that the Emperor attributed his conversion to a hallucinatory experience. According to Eusebius, Constantine was preparing for a battle against Maxentius at Saxa Rubra, a few miles from Rome. On the afternoon before the battle, and exactly on October 27 of the year 312 A.D., Constantine saw a flaming cross in the sky with the following words: "In this sign thou shalt conquer." Constantine interpreted the vision as a divine order: he should become a Christian and he would win. He was converted, and from that time until his death his life was a series of triumphs, though the Roman Empire was already in a state of advanced decadence.

Now, Constantine was strongly predisposed to become a Christian, owing to the influence of his Christian mother. He also knew that many Christians were in Maxentius' army. If he became a convert they would rally to his support, or at least they would not fight with so much will against him. The pagan majority was disorganized and divided into many creeds. The Christians were well organized and disciplined. It would be good strategy to join forces with this strong and militant minority. But Constantine, who had to carry the burden of the long Imperial pagan tradition, could not bring himself to take this momentous step. Only a mystical experience in the form of a hallucination could give him, at a conscious level, the insight and the impetuous determination that he required.

This hallucination shows the familiar mechanism of the concretization of the concept: the cross stands for conversion to Christianity. It also exemplifed the mechanism of projection to the external world: the message that Constantine did not dare give to himself now came from God. Unlike schizophrenic hallucinations, but like the world's great myths and some dreams, this hallucination carried a deep insight that also had a great practical value. The secondary process was in accord with the primary process.

The other example of religious hallucinations or possible delusions comes from the interesting and scholarly book by Gordon concerning Joseph Caro (1949).* A famous figure in Judaism, Caro was the author of the book and code for religious Jews, *Shulhan Aruk*, or *The Prepared Table*. He lived eighty-seven years (from 1488 to 1575); and for about fifty-two of them he heard a voice, the voice of the "Maggid"—an invisible messenger from heaven, a familiar spirit, and a divine mentor. "While Caro was bent over his sacred tomes in search of deeper meanings, grave fears and daring ambitions would rise in his soul. The spirit would then enter Caro's mouth, articulate his tongue, and reveal his destiny, unveil the coming events of his life." Caro described these experiences in a book called *Maggid Mesharim*. It is uncertain from a technical point of view whether they should be called hallucinations or delusions. Caro states that the Maggid was using his (Caro's) mouth in order to speak. Thus, if Caro was hearing his own voice, used by the Maggid, the phenomenon would be more delusional than hallucinatory. In some passages, however, Caro refers to the voice of the Maggid as the "Voice of My Beloved" which "began to resound again in my mouth." At any rate, whether or not these experiences are predominantly delusional and only occasionally hallucinatory, it does not matter very much. The important point is that no matter how we classify them, they are usually found in psychotics. According to Werblowsky (1962), who ranks among the greatest scholars of Caro, "The Maggid was undoubtedly a case of motor

* At times the name is spelled Karo.

(speech) automatism, but everything he said was well within the normal range of Caro's knowledge and intellect, which . . . were of a rare calibre."

In his book Gordon, who was both a rabbi and a psychiatrist, asked whether Caro was mentally ill, and if so, what psychiatric syndrome he had. We know many things about the life and work of Caro; Gordon, reviewing them, rightly concluded that he was not psychotic. It is obvious that Caro's abnormal experiences of 52 years' duration occurred while he was in religious ecstasies or in states of autohypnosis. They did not have a harmful but on the contrary a constructive effect, inasmuch as it was during these experiences that Caro could conceive and write the *Shulhan Aruk*, a book honored for centuries.

One difficulty that Gordon did not fully consider arises from the fact that, as we have seen, religious hallucinations are predominantly visual. Caro's experiences were auditory and were therefore more like those experienced by schizophrenics than is usual with mystic phenomena. It is true that the voice seemed to come from a parental symbol, but it was the voice of a disembodied entity using Caro's mouth. Perhaps this predominantly auditory character can be explained by the fact that in the Jewish religion the divinity is represented as an abstract entity that must not be represented by a visual image. According to Werblowsky, the psychodynamic mechanisms of Caro unconsciously chose to express themselves in a chronic hallucinatory state shaped by kabbalistic patterns. Werblowsky concludes that Caro's "mystical states were a means to an end. The means were visible testimonies of divine election and favour in the form of celestial messages according to the conventional kabbalistic pattern of 'mighty promises' and 'revelations of the mysteries of *Torah*.' The end was the maintenance of a psychological equilibrium throughout a life dominated by a tremendous intellectual and spiritual ambition, calling for extraordinary energy and discipline of abnegation in addition to the 'normal' rigours of ascetic piety as imposed by kabbalistic theology. In the kabbalistically transformed mother-image of his celestial mentor Karo found the divine, inspiring, reproving, chiding, encouraging, but above all loving, spiritual agency that on the one hand confirmed his heart's most cherished desires and ambitions, and on the other hand acted as the personified pressure of conscience, urging him to persevere in his ascetic life and in the pursuit of his high aims. Considering Karo's colossal intellectual and social achievement, we are certainly entitled to speak of a psychological equilibrium rather than of a disturbance, and to understand the Maggid's influence as the compensatory function of a complex mother-symbol." *

The whole idea that the mystical experience is a source of potential enrichment for humanity could be objected to on grounds that religious "illuminations and revelations" have often led to wars, persecutions, hate, prejudices. Results such as these are obviously not to be valued. It must be said that when religion leads to these results, it fails, just as bad poetry fails—except that in the failure of religion the consequences are much more harmful. On the other hand, good religious insights become norms for generations to come. By promoting the survival of man or of his ideals, they are recognized as valid by the higher levels of the psyche.

To give an example: the precept of the Sabbath—that is, of the observance of rest one day in every seven—was once considered a wasteful practice not only by the masses but also by the intellectuals. For instance, Seneca, probably the best thinker of his generation, considered this custom of the Jews absurd. He felt that it was unpractical to discontinue all activities; it was a waste of a seventh of one's life; and furthermore, it was against nature, because the sun, the stars, and the rivers do not arrest their course one day in every seven. In a certain way, to rest is indeed to regress; yet actually it is a physiological regression, like sleep, necessary to the organism.

This chapter has repeatedly mentioned the similarities between the aesthetic and the religious processes. These similarities often confer a poetic or artistic aspect to religion. Moreover, religious ceremonies often add some artistic features such as music, poetry, pageantry, and so on, to increase the intensity of the experience.

A characteristic common to religion and to poetry is the tendency to resort to or at least to retain archaic modes. In many religious services it has become the tradition to use languages no longer spoken. For many centuries services in synagogues have been held in Hebrew, a language which, until its recent revival in Israel, was known only to an elite and was almost ignored by the masses. Services in Catholic churches were held in Latin until recently; services in Greek Orthodox churches are held in Hellenistic–Byzantine Greek; the extinct Pali

* Reproduced with permission from Werblowsky (1962).

language is used in Buddhist ceremonies. Congregations have accepted these linguistic practices, perhaps because the obscurity of the ritual gives concrete representation to the religious mystery, adding the flavor of the arcanum.

Poetry—as exemplified at least by the poetic techniques and mechanisms described in Chapter 8—is often introduced in religious practices. Religious parables often consist of metaphors or of short stories or events that are intended to represent certain aspects of life, or to enlighten some of the complexities of human existence. In Chapter 7 we mentioned the episode of Jesus replying to people who had asked him whether taxes should be paid to Caesar. The New Testament offers many parables that have had a profound impact on generation after generation of Christians, such as the parable of the sower (Matthew, Chapter 13), the good Samaritan (John, Chapter 10), the prodigal son (Luke, Chapter 15), and Jesus and the children (Mark, Chapter 10).

The effect of repetition (discussed in Chapter 9 in relation to poetry) has one of its most striking examples in Christ's sermon on the mount (Matthew, Chapter 5):

Blessed are the poor in spirit: for theirs is the kingdom of heaven.
Blessed are they that mourn: for they shall be comforted.
Blessed are the meek: for they shall inherit the earth.
Blessed are they which do hunger and thirst after righteousness: for they shall be filled.
Blessed are the merciful: for they shall obtain mercy.
Blessed are the pure in heart: for they shall see God.
Blessed are the peacemakers: for they shall be called the children of God.
Blessed are they which are persecuted for righteousness' sake: for theirs is the kingdom of heaven.
Blessed are ye, when men shall revile you, and persecute you, and shall say all manner of evil against you falsely, for my sake.

The powerful content of this passage receives additional striking effect not only by the repetitions but also by the frequent emergence of the contrary. Jesus promises the greatest kingdom to the poor, comfort to the mournful, the inheritance of the earth to the meek, and heaven to those who are persecuted for righteousness' sake. As a result these promises, usually difficult to believe, acquire the impact of unquestionable truth in Jesus' message. In Ecclesiastes too, we find as we have already described in Chapter 8, a striking effect due to the combination of repetition and the association of contraries: "A time to be born and a time to die; . . . a time to weep, and a time to laugh; a time to mourn and a time to dance; . . . a time to embrace, and a time to be embraced. . . ." and so on. This particular combination adds additional power to the message that there is an appropriate time for different things but also that everything is transient.

Faith and poetry join together to form that form of creativity that is known as prayer. Slonimsky (1965) writes: *

> Prayer is the expression of man's needs and aspirations, addressed to a great source of help—to the Friend whom we suppose to exist behind the phenomena, the Friend who is concerned for man's needs, and for his high aspirations, and is resolved to help. . . . There are those who do not need to pray; or who disdain to pray; or who regard prayer as a pathetic human fallacy, a childlike anthropomorphism in a world of iron necessities, an attempt to impose human values on a universe which is alien to them and which has no concern or regard for man's needs.
>
> There are some who really don't need to pray: the few lonely and strong, the rare souls who are sufficient unto themselves, gods in their own right, of whom the poet Henley speaks:

> "In the fell clutch of circumstance
>   I have not winced or cried aloud,
> Under the bludgeonings of chance
>   My head is bloody but unbowed.
>
> It matters not how strait the gate,
>   How charged with punishment the scroll,
> I am the master of my fate:
>   I am the captain of my soul."

But however we may exclaim in admiration of the heroism of the man, it is a lonely cry and an unhopeful, a hopeless cry; it is at bottom a counsel of despair, heroic but enveloped in gloom; above all it can never become a philosophy for mankind because it is so utterly individualistic and self-centered—it leaves out of account altogether and says nothing of the great hopes and dreams of mankind, for which co-operative ef-

---

* Reprinted with permission from Henry Slonimsky, *Essays* (Quadrangle Books, 1967).

fort, and faith in the future, are a prime essential, co-operative effort between men, and between man and God. . . . Who can prove these things? Who can decide the rightness of the religious viewpoint? . . . It is the deepest intuition of the best of the race at all times and among all peoples: an intuition, an anticipation, an act of faith: the faith that what our heart wants the universe also wants and God wants.

I give as an example of that intuition the culminating cry at the end of Beethoven's Ninth Symphony, where the human voices suddenly emerge above the instruments. That cry expresses this jubilant and triumphant assurance: Be embraced ye millions (*seid umschlungen Millionen*), take this kiss for the whole world (*diesen Kuss der ganzen Welt*), above the stars a loving father must be present (*Brueder, ueberm Sternenzelt muss ein lieber Vater wohnen*). Musician and poet (Beethoven and Schiller) unite in this religious act of faith.

We can't all pray from our own creative resources because we are not all of us religious geniuses, and prayer and religion are as truly a form of genius, a gift from God, as poetry or music or any high endowment.

We can't all write Shakespeare's poetry or Bach's music, but we can still make it our own: we can open our hearts to it, and enrich and expand ourselves by sharing and appropriating it.

And so in prayer we must turn to the great religious geniuses, the Isaiahs and Jeremiahs and Psalmists, and make our own the visions they have seen, the communion they have established, the messages they have brought back, the words they have spoken as having been spoken for us because truly spoken for all men. And by an act of sympathetic fervor, of loving contagion, to achieve their glow and to fan the spark which is present in all of us at the fire which they have lighted.

One of the greatest prayers of all times is the following one, believed to be written by Francis of Assisi:

> *O Lord, make me an instrument of Thy peace.*
> *Where there is hatred, let me sow love,*
> *Where there is injury, pardon,*
> *Where there is darkness, light,*
> *Where there is sadness, joy,*
> *Where there is doubt, faith,*
> *And where there is despair, hope.*
>
> *O divine Master, grant that I may not so much seek*
> *To be consoled as to console,*

To be understood as to understand,
To be loved as to love.

For
It is in giving that we receive,
It is in forgiving that we are pardoned,
And it is in dying that we are born to Eternal Life.

Here, too, as in the passage from Ecclesiastes and in the Sermon on the Mount, the content, in itself powerful, derives additional effect from the union of antitheticals: hatred–love; injury–pardon; sadness–faith . . . dying–born to Eternal Life.

Scholars have not been able to ascertain whether the authorship of this prayer is really Francis of Assisi, the poor man who towered in the Christian world at the beginning of the thirteenth century (he was born in 1182 and died in 1226) and who, as we have seen in Chapter 9, was one of the major inspirational forces for the art of the Renaissance. What is beyond doubt is that Francis wrote the canticle of the sun (called also the canticle of all created things) in 1225, while he was in retreat in the village of San Damiano. This poem, the first great poem in the Italian language, is written in Umbrian dialect; it is one of the masterpieces of all times. Unfortunately no translation can reproduce the sublimity of the original.

The son of a wealthy merchant, Francis repudiated all ownership, even of those things retained for personal use. He founded a monastic order based on chastity, poverty, and obedience. In his canticle he not only praises God for all the things that He created, but for the spirit of brotherhood that unites all created things. Brother sun, sister moon, brother wind, sister water, brother fire, mother earth, join together in representing the glory of God and in helping mankind. The Lord must be praised also for those who follow Him and pursue the path of goodness.*

Cantico delle Creature

Altissimu, onnipotente, bon Signore
tue so le laude la gloria e l'honore
et onne benedictione.

* Translation reproduced with permission from G. R. Kay, ed., *The Penguin Book of Italian Verse*, (London: Penguin Books Ltd., 1958).

The Creative Product

Ad te solo, Altissimo, se confano
et nullu homo ene dignu te mentovare.

Laudato sie, mi Signore, cun tutte le tue creature
spetialmente messor lo frate sole
lo qual jorna et allumini noi per loi.
Et ellu è bellu e radiante cun grande splendore
de te, altissimo, porta significatione.

Laudato si', mi Signore, per sora luna e le stelle,
in celu l'ai formate clarite et pretiose et belle.

Laudato si', mi Signore, per frate vento
et per aere et nubilo et sereno et onne tempo,
per lo quale a le tue creature dai sustentamento.

Laudato si', mi Signore, per sor'aqua
la quale è multo utile et humile et pretiosa et casta.

Laudato si', mi Signore, per frate focu
per lo quale ennallumini la nocte
et ello è bello et iocundo et robustoso et forte.

Laudato si', mi Signore, per sora nostra matre terra,
la quale ne sustenta et governa
et produce diversi fructi con coloriti fiori et herba.

Laudato si', mi Signore, per quelli che perdonano per lo tuo amore
et sostengo infirmitate et tribulatione,
beati quelli che sosterranno in pace
ca da te, altissimo, sirano incoronati.

Laudato si', mi Signore, per sora nostra morte corporale
da la quale nullu homo vivente po scappare,
guai a quelli che morranno ne le peccata mortali,
beati quelli che trovarà ne le tue sanctissime voluntati
ca la morte secunda nol farrà male.

Laudate et benedicete mi Signore et rengratiate
et serviteli cun grande humilitate.

Canticle of All Created Things

Lord, most high, almighty, good, yours are the praises, the glory, and the honour, and every blessing. To you alone, most high, do they fittingly belong, and no man is worthy to mention you.

Be praised, my Lord, with all your creatures, especially master brother sun, who brings day, and you give us light by him. And he is fair and radiant with a great shining—he draws his meaning, most high, from you.

Be praised, my Lord, for sister moon and the stars, in heaven you have made them clear and precious and lovely.

Be praised, my Lord, for brother wind and for the air, cloudy and fair and in all weathers—by which you give sustenance to your creatures.

Be praised, my Lord, for sister water, who is very useful and humble and rare and chaste.

Be praised, my Lord, for brother fire, by whom you illuminate the night, and he is comely and joyful and vigorous and strong.

Be praised, my Lord, for sister our mother earth, who maintains and governs us and puts forth different fruits with coloured flowers and grass.

Be praised, my Lord, for those who forgive because of your love and bear infirmity and trials; blessed are those who will bear in peace, for by you, most high, they will be crowned.

Be praised, my Lord, for sister our bodily death, from which no living man can escape; woe to those who die in mortal sin; blessed are those whom it will find living by your most holy wishes, for the second death will do them no harm.

Praise and bless my Lord and give thanks to him and serve him with great humility.

Some authors do not consider the experiences that we have described in this chapter mystical. For instance, for Stace (1960), the true mystical experience does not deal with ideas or feelings. The mystical experience is "formless, shapeless, colorless, odorless, soundless." The experience is also ineffable, that is, impossible to express in words. According to Stace, "The incommensurability of the mystical with the sensory-intellectual consciousness is also the ultimate reason why we have to exclude visions and voices, telepathy, precognition, and clairvoyance from the category of the mystical." What Stace refers to is a special kind of endoceptual phenomenon (see Chapter 4) that goes beyond space and time to be with "the Eternal Now," as Eckhart wrote. It is not necessarily associated with the divinity, but with what seems emptiness or undifferentiated unity.

Rite and Magic

RELIGIOUS PRACTICES or cults consist of many rites that cannot be included in our study. Although they must have originated as acts of creativity, their individual origin is difficult to trace, and no attempt will be made to do so here. Many of these rituals have already been the object of psychoanalytic studies, among them the important work of Reik (1946). Our discussion will also omit the practices of occultism, spiritism, mediumship, metaphysics, extrasensory perception, and related subjects.

This section will examine magic, which can be considered a primitive form of rite. Magic is a method of influencing the course of events (1) by procedures aimed at permitting the deity to intervene, or (2) by the use of some principles of nature that are even more powerful than the deity itself.

Frazer devotes some of the most important chapters of *The Golden Bough* to the study of magic (1922). He finds two laws ruling magic: the first, that like produces like, or that an effect resembles its cause; the second, that things which have once been in contact with each other will continue to act on each other after the physical contiguity has been severed. As an example of the first law, Frazer mentions the "imitating of rain," a procedure that primitive peoples believe will make rain fall. As an example of the second law he refers to the common belief that a piece of clothing or a fingernail belonging to a person has all the properties of that person.

Frazer calls the first law the law of similarity, which rules imitative magic, and the second law the law of contact, which rules contagious magic. He rightly sees a connection between these two forms of magic and the laws of association of ideas (the laws of similarity and contiguity). There is also a connection between magic and the three modes of psychological operation described in *The Intrapsychic Self* (Arieti 1967, Chapter 11) and summarized in this book (Chapter 6). The law of contiguity corresponds to the mode of contiguity and the law of similarity to its mode of similarity. We can add the mode of *pars pro toto;* in fact, the performed magical act also stands for what is supposed to happen as a result of it.

According to Frazer, magic is based on a fundamental conception similar to that of modern science: an implicit faith in the order and uniformity of nature. But for Frazer, who follows Tylor (1874), magic is not science but pseudoscience, because it is based on two types of erroneous association of ideas. Religion does not assume the immutability of nature; on the contrary, it offers a method (cult) by which an attempt is made to induce the divinities to change the course of nature. Frazer thus distinguishes magic from religion and upholds the superiority of the latter. He feels that the use of magic implies the operation of elementary mental associations that also occur in subhuman animals. Frazer states, "The very beasts associate the idea of things that are like each other or that have been found together in their experience; and they could hardly survive for a day if they ceased to do so. But who attributes to the animals a belief that the phenomena of nature are worked by a multitude of invisible animals or by one enormous and prodigiously strong animal behind the scenes?" Frazer thus concludes that a belief in superior beings (religion) appears in evolution after magic.

These ideas of Frazer reflect a series of errors. The fact that subhuman animals are capable of learning does not imply that they "believe" in the uniformity of nature, a highly complicated concept that has occurred only to civilized man. It is true that by following the three modes of operation of the nervous system, subhuman animals parallel the uniformities of nature. But no animals, and not all men, are aware of such uniformities (see Arieti 1967, Chapters 11 and 12). Psychopathological observations, although they cannot be taken as absolute proof, suggest that magic develops later than the belief in the existence of gods, or at least of gods incorporated in things. Magic practices could be compared to the compulsions of neurotics—symptoms of less primitive character than the paranoid ideations (projections) found in psychoses.

In magic there is a form of depersonalization that occurs in less primitive forms of mentation. In some respects magic is the opposite of animism. It could even be that magic represents an attempt by primitive man to decrease the animistic forces of the world. If everything in nature has a will, the life of the primitive is always at the mercy of these wills residing in things. Magic may help to transform animistic objects into mere things and nature into a nonanimistic, less primitive "reality." A world dominated by what Buber calls I–Thou relations becomes transformed into a world in which I–It relations also exist. I–Thou relations, however, continue to exist, especially in religious practices. And, too, magic becomes mixed with earlier religious customs. It becomes a way of controlling the world by propitiating the gods, and also a way of influencing forces stronger than the gods.

Although magic in the life of primitive man has the role that science takes in the world of modern man, this role does not qualify it as a scientific procedure. Magic solves a need of primitive man, when he finds himself threatened by overwhelming forces. As De Martino (1948) and Tullio-Altan (1960) point out, magic has a historical role and must not be considered as something necessarily absurd, even if founded on primitive mechanisms; it is an important part of a stage in man's development. Furthermore, magic "works" at times, in spite of its inherent error, because of suggestion, or the faith it elicits. A sword reputed to be magic is likely to improve the fighting ability of its owner and lead him more easily to victory.

Magic may become organized in a system of rites. Every religion has a combination of beliefs in the supernatural and an adherence to rites. In modern ethical culture, the supernatural is eliminated and the rite tends to be replaced by ethical behavior. Faith in survival thus is based only on the ethical behavior of man and on secondary-process mechanisms. Whether the religious needs of man can be fulfilled without also resorting to the primary process is a debatable question.

Chapter 11
Science

AT THE PRESENT TIME the creative process is being studied more intensively in relation to science than to any other field. There are several reasons for this focus on science. The first is the twentieth century's bias in favor of scientific knowledge. A second reason is found in the belief held by many investigators that it is easier to study the creative process in scientists than in artists. Scientists seem to be more methodical in their observations and therefore seemingly should be more capable of reporting their inner experiences. A third reason is the assumption by many investigators that the process of scientific creativity consists of logical or mathematical steps that can easily be traced back.

As to the first reason, we must accept its historical validity. The second and third reasons, however, contain only grains of truth. The scientist's methodology is of little help in the attempt to recapture the inner experiences leading to a scientific innovation. Moreover, although the tracing back of logical steps is indeed important, it does not lead to insights into unconscious mechanisms or even into the overall modes of operation that are followed consciously.

Before examining the process of creativity in scientific discovery, we must clarify one point: discoveries are not always the result of scientific creativity. An explorer who discovers an unknown land is not necessarily endowed with creative ability. Inventions that require only the rearrangement or practical application of principles discovered by others are more properly considered as pertaining to technology than to creativity, no matter how important their practical effects are. On the other hand, some scientific principles that are among the highest products of creativity may not have practical applications for long periods of time.

The Contributions of Poincaré and Others

ONE OF THE AIMS of students of scientific creativity has been to recapture the different phases of thinking that lead to the creative act. Personal accounts given by great scientists are particularly valuable, but unfortunately only a small percentage of them have provided this information. One who did so was the physiologist Helmholtz (1896), who recognized three stages in his creative work: (1) an initial investigation carried on until it is impossible to go further; (2) a period of rest and recovery; and (3) the occurrence of a sudden and unexpected solution.

One of the best accounts of the creative process in science was given by the mathematician Poincaré (1913). In a report that has become a classic in the literature on creativity, Poincaré described the discovery of the theory of Fuchsian groups and Fuchsian functions that made him famous. He studied the problem for fifteen days, trying to reach a conclusion that later proved to be false: that no such functions existed. A sleepless night spent on this problem brought no apparent results. He had drunk black coffee and could not sleep, and he later wrote about that memorable night: "Ideas rose in crowds; I felt them collide *until pairs interlocked*, so to speak, making a stable construction." The following day, on the way to a geological excursion, he got on a bus. At the moment he put his foot on the step, the idea came to him—apparently without any conscious effort and without his even thinking about this problem—that the transformations he "had used to define the Fuchsian functions were identical with those of non-Euclidian geometry." This was the creative moment. Poincaré went on with the business of the day, but later he verified this sudden illumination. A few days later, in another sudden flash, he realized that the "arithmetic transformations of indefinite ternary quadratic forms were identical with those of non-Euclidian geometry." These breakthroughs led to a great expansion in the field of mathematics.

Poincaré added another stage to those described by Helmholtz: a second period of conscious effort, after the illumination, to validate the insight obtained. In Chapter 2 we saw how Wallas (1926) named and described the stages already individualized by Poincaré. Hadamard (1945), in his interesting book on the psychology of invention in the field of mathematics, follows Poincaré's ideas for the most part.

Poincaré carefully considered the important topic of how some connections or combinations lead to the acquisition of new knowledge, to discovery, or to the experience of sudden illumination—the "Eureka!" of Archimedes. Combinations that will lead to new knowledge are a small minority; useless combinations are potentially endless in number. How is it that "good combinations" are made during the incubation period and reach consciousness in the subsequent stage of illumination? It seems impossible to attribute good combinations to mere chance, as some authors do. For how can chance explain the fact that many creative people make more than one discovery? Poincaré in fact believed that these combinations occur in the unconscious or subliminal self, and he offered the hypothesis that the subliminal self is in no way inferior to the conscious self. He wrote: "Does it follow that the subliminal self, having divined by a delicate intuition that these combinations would be useful, has formed only these, or has it rather formed many others which were taking an interest and have remained unconscious?"

In trying to understand how the selection leading to the useful combination is made, Poincaré advanced two hypotheses. The first concerns the aesthetic quality of the combination: perhaps the mind, like a delicate sieve, lets pass through the threshold of consciousness only those combinations that are striking for their beauty and elegance. The second assumes that during the preparatory work the mind does not put into motion all possible ideas but only those that have something to do with the object of study. Poincaré says that if we think of these ideas as "atoms" hooked on the mind's walls, we can imagine the mind unhooking only those ingredients that are possible for the new ideas. The mobilized "atoms" are those from which we may reasonably expect the desired solution. Some of these "atoms" collide and enter into new combinations. A good combination is one in which at least one "atom" was freely chosen by the will.

The first hypothesis does not seem convincing. It is true that several useful mathematical formulas have the characteristics of beauty and elegance that Poincaré mentioned, but their being aesthetically attractive does not make them *valid*. Poincaré himself has stated that some false ideas can still gratify "a natural feeling for mathematical elegance." On first examination, Poincaré's second hypothesis seems more acceptable. Certainly in the preparatory stage the creative person consciously mobilizes only those ideas that have something to do with the object of his research. In many instances, however, the new combinations that emerge in the subsequent flash of illumination have been suggested by something completely unrelated to the object of inquiry. Often it is by the unpredictable application to one field of what is valid in another field that valuable new combinations have occurred. Now in the case of Poincaré, obviously he put only mathematical ideas into motion in his preparatory work, not—let us say—historical, geographical, and literary notions. This restriction, however, does not seem very important, because the field of mathematics was vast enough even in his time to permit infinite combinations.

The Process of Discovery

LET US RECONSIDER the first important illumination that Poincaré experienced. "At the moment when I put my foot on the step the idea came to me . . . that the transformations I had used to define the Fuchsian functions were identical with those of non-Euclidian geometry." The act of illumination consisted of seeing an *identity* between two transformations previously reputed to be dissimilar: those that Poincaré had used to define the Fuchsian functions, and those of non-Euclidian geometry. A later illumination came when Poincaré had the idea "with just the same characteristics of brevity, suddenness, and immediate certainty, that the arithmetic transformations of indeterminate ternary quadratic forms were identical with those of non-Euclidian geometry." Again the moment of illumination was the moment when Poincaré saw an identity between two subjects reputed to be dissimilar.

Similar instances could be multiplied endlessly in which great discoveries were made by the act of perceiving an identity among two or more things that had been thought dissimilar or unrelated. In the classic example, Newton observed an apple falling from a tree and saw a common quality in the apple attracted by the earth and the attraction between heavenly bodies. He perceived the similarity between two forces: that which causes an apple to fall to the earth, and that which holds the moon in its orbit. He validated this insight by comparing the rate at which bodies fall to earth with the rate at which the moon deviates from the path it would follow if the earth did not exist.

We could say that many scientific discoveries are the result of individualizing a common characteristic or connection between things that were deemed dissimilar or unrelated before. But of course the observation of similarity is not enough. The transformations used by Poincaré are not identical in every respect with those of non-Euclidian geometry. And an apple is very dissimilar in size, origin, and chemical structure to the moon. Yet Newton saw a similarity. In what way, then, *are* the moon and the apple similar? What does their partial identity consists of? Of being members of a class of bodies subject to gravitation. That is, when Newton saw this similarity between the apple and the moon, *a new class was formed*, to which an indefinite number of members could be added thereafter. The new object for which he was searching, and which he found, was a class. The discovery of this class revealed a new way of looking at the universe, because each member of the class came to be recognized as having similar properties.

Is this new class a primary class as we described it in Chapter 5? Obviously not. It differs on many counts. First, when Newton perceived the identical element, he did not respond to the stimulus but to the class. Had he been a regressed schizophrenic, after seeing a similarity between the moon and the apple, he could have paleologically identified the moon with the apple and thought that the moon could be eaten like an apple or sucked like the maternal breast—as Renée, a by-now-famous schizophrenic patient reported by Sechehaye, did during a stage of her illness (1951). Second, Newton's creativity consisted, after seeing a common property in the moon and the apple, not in identifying them but in seeing them as members of a new class. An increased ability to see similarities—a property of the primary process—is here connected with a concept; and the tertiary process emerges. The secondary class loses all its original connections with the primary process.

Is the new class discovered by Newton exclusively the result of secondary-process mechanisms—that is, what Reichenbach called "induction by enumeration" (1951)? (Induction by enumeration is the procedure by which a man, having observed that some sequences— say, the daily alternation of light and darkness—recur again and again, feels entitled to draw a general principle such as "night follows day".) Induction by enumeration is a simple procedure, even for the average man. Obviously this is not what Newton did. His is a case of what some authors have called "induction by intuition" and others "induction by imagination" or "induction by guessing" (Frank 1957). I shall call it *induction by creativity*, which creativity consists of (1) indi-vidualizing a common property (as, for instance, the property shared by the moon and the apple); (2) *not* identifying the objects (as, again, the moon and the apple) having some such common property by put-ting them into a primary class; and (3) recognizing that they belong to an unsuspected secondary class (such as gravitational bodies). In this type of induction, an increased ability to recognize similarities—a characteristic of the primary process—is connected with a concept; and the tertiary process emerges. *The concept of the new class is much more important than the recognition of the similarity; but the mental grasping of the similarity is necessary to evoke the concept of class at the level of consciousness.*

Once the concept of the new class is created, it will be easy to use thereafter in induction by enumeration; for instance, in recognizing that all bodies are subject to a gravitational force. It will also be easy to apply the concept in deductive procedures: since *A* is a body, it is sub-ject to a gravitational force.

From this description it can be seen that the tertiary process in scientific creativity uses mechanisms that are different from those found in aesthetic creativity. Blake's poem "The Sick Rose" (analyzed in Chapter 8) compares the sick woman to the sick rose and makes us aware of a class "beautiful life destroyed by illness." However, the rose and the woman, although not identical as they would be in schizo-phrenic thinking, are not clearly distinct either, the way the apple and the moon are. The members of a secondary class that emerges through the aesthetic process retain the tendency to fuse together, or to exchange nonessential predicates. Consequently, even the class "beautiful life destroyed by illness" is not as definite as the class of gravitational bodies is. The poet leaves things somewhat indistinct. It is part of our aesthetic appreciation first to experience the ambiguity of the unfinished statement, and then to attempt a clarification of that statement by finding psychological resonances in our feelings and ideas. The scientist instead tries to make the statement as clear as possible, leaving no room for doubts or exceptions. His new secondary class loses all its original connections with the primary process. Here, too, however, although the new class is very well defined, the search is not ended. The understanding of the Newtonian system is a prerequisite to the eventual discovery of the Einsteinian world of classes.

In many instances the process of creativity consists of discovering a similarity between one system or field of knowledge and another. One of the most important examples of this type is that of Darwin. In 1838 Darwin happened to read the book written by Malthus 40 years before, *Essay on the Principle of Population*. Malthus had advanced the idea that Rousseau's optimistic views about humanity are unsound because (1) the natural tendency of population is to increase faster than the means of subsistence; and (2) this fast increase results in a struggle for existence. Darwin, abstracting from all the observations that he had made in the Galapagos Islands, had the vision that reproductive competition between members of the same species is similar to the Malthusian competition found in human society. Thus principles formulated in relation to human society were applied by Darwin to organic life in general. According to Ghiselin (1973), he also initiated a radically new way of studying behavior.

The whole theory of evolution is based on the similarities between species, as well as on the differences interpreted as leading to greater complexity. The greatest evidence for the Darwinian theory rests on the similarities collected from anatomy, embryology, and paleontology. The more closely related the groups of animal and vegetal organisms the greater is the number of like structures and functions. The recognition of similarities often leads not only to the formation of a class, but of a class of classes, that is, to the formation of a system.

Typical is the example of the Russian chemist Dmitri Mendeleev, who in 1869 announced to the world his "Periodic Table of Elements." Prior classifications, made by Johann Döbereiner in 1829, by Jean B. Dumas in 1850, and by John Newland in 1865, had not been successful. Mendeleev had noticed that some groups of elements had common properties. His great discovery was that these common properties (or similarities) recurred periodically if the elements were arranged in order of increasing atomic weight. Thus, for instance, fluorine, chlorine, bromine, and iodine have common qualities. Their atomic weight is quite different: 18.99 for fluorine, 35.45 for chlorine, 79.90 for bromine, and 126.90 for iodine. However, if we arrange all the known elements according to their atomic weight, we find that the above-mentioned four elements fall into the same column and therefore are expected to have similar properties. The genius of Mendeleev appeared also in the fact that he was not deterred by serious obstacles. When he could not place any elements in available places in the table that he had put together, he left holes. In several cases the accepted atomic weight of some elements did not correspond to that anticipated by the periodic law. He challenged the correctness of those atomic weights and subsequent investigations proved that he was right.

The Transcendence of the Discovery

WHEN a scientific innovation results in the formation of a new class or the organization of a system, its importance transcends that of the immediate discovery. It eventually leads to the discovery of additional properties hidden in the members of the class or in the system.

Let us take as an example the fictitious discovery represented in Figures 11-1, 11-2, and 11-3. In Figure 11-1 we see four black dots, apparently located at random. They may represent atoms, planets, or whatever we would like to imagine. At first no order whatsoever is de-

Figure 11-1

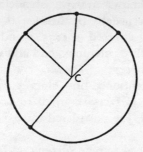

Figure 11-2

tected. But then a hypothetical discoverer recognizes a common property in the four black dots: they are equally distant from a point *C*
(Figure 11-2). Thus they belong to the class "points that are equidistant from *C*." But points that are equidistant from a given point are
part of a circumference. Thus our hypothetical person has discovered
a circumference, which always existed in potentiality. Moreover, he
can assume that if other bodies exist which have the same properties as
the four he knows, they must be placed along the same circumference.
The light dots in Figure 11-3 are the hypothetical bodies
that the discoverer will find when he travels along the potential
circumference.

A typical example of this extension beyond new findings is to be
recognized in the discovery of Mendeleev, mentioned in the previous
section. The periodic law necessitated placing in the table three ele-

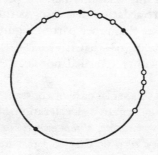

Figure 11-3

ments which were not known to exist. Mendeleev did not hesitate to
state that they would eventually be discovered, and he was fully vin-
dicated. Gallium was discovered in 1875, scandium in 1879, and ger-
manium in 1886. The three elements had almost exactly the properties predicted by Mendeleev.

In Chapter 6 we mentioned how Harvey was not deterred by the
gaps in the knowledge of facts required to prove his theory of the
circulation of the blood. He postulated the existence of the then unknown capillaries.

Many discoveries lead to new systems and new conceptions. For
instance, Galileo * discovered that the acceleration of falling bodies

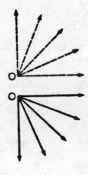

Figure 11-4

decreases consistently with their angle of inclination. From the angle
it is possible to deduce the acceleration (see the lower part of Figure
11-4). But Galileo felt this was only half the picture. When a body is
thrown upward, the retardation decreases as the angle of inclination
diminishes from 90° (see the upper part of Figure 11-4). Then what if
the body remains at point o—that is, what if the angle is zero? Obviously the body is neither retarded nor accelerated; its velocity remains constant.

Rest thus becomes a special case of constant velocity, a case of the
absence of positive or negative acceleration. Rest assumes a new
meaning; *it is no longer the absence of movement, but the absence of change in
velocity,* be the velocity zero or that of a fast-moving object. Also, a

* To a large extent this interpretation of Galileo's thinking is based on Wertheimer (1945).

body can now be seen not as something pushed from outside by an imposed force, but as a mass that is propelled by an inner force until it is affected by external forces such as friction or gravitation. Galileo did not generalize the principle to include all directions (but Newton later did so, thereby extending Galileo's findings by the concept of inertia). As a consequence of his experiments and deductions, however, Galileo could assume the presence of a completely isolated body—a body that is not under the influence of any external force. Such a body cannot exist in nature (Cassirer 1953); it is only a theoretical possibility.

This is an example of an *as if* phenomenon, but of a type different from that described in Chapter 8. The uninfluenced body would exist *if* no external forces operated on it. But every body is under the influence of some external force. An uninfluenced body, then, would seem not to exist; but as a theoretical construct, it *does* exist. In fact its properties, logically deduced, explain the empirical findings of physical dynamics. Is such a theoretical construct a fiction, like a work of art or a human device to explain complex phenomena? The temptation to consider it as such is great, since we know that the possibility of the uninfluenced body cannot be materialized. However, the majority of scientists (and in this they differ from some philosophers) do not consider such a construct fictitious at all; on the contrary, they find it much more realistic than the data and opinions that are derived from perceptions or from common-sense reasoning. We almost get the impression from them that reality is not realistic enough to live up to the theoretical construct.

Is the reality of a theoretical construct (such as the construct of Galileo) a *fourth* reality? "Not at all," would be the scientist's answer. "It belongs to the first reality." Reality *does* live up to the construct, in spite of appearances to the contrary. It cannot escape doing so. An invariable association exists between all the bodies of nature: all bodies are subject to natural laws. The scientist thinks that this alleged "fourth reality" is actually the first reality in its purest form. As a matter of fact, he may think that there is only one reality, and that all the other constructs are fictions. Some thinkers believe instead that the "fourth reality" is a creation of man. If so, we would have to explain why the first and the "fourth" realities coincide.*

* The paranoid patient, too, "discovers an underlying arrangement" in his environment, at times in everything that surrounds him. Actually he does not discover any arrangements; he

The Creative Product

This example from Galileo also shows that, in science as well as in art, the negative emerges as an important factor. What was defined, before Galileo, as a state of rest became a state of *absence* of acceleration of any kind (positive or negative).

So far we have studied examples of scientific creativity in which a perceived similarity leads to the formation of a new secondary class and to subsequent discoveries. In this type of innovation the mode of similarity, described in *The Intrapsychic Self* (Arieti 1967, Chapter 7) and in Chapter 6 of this book, is fully in effect. The *pars pro toto* mode of operation is also applied, when what is recognized as valid for a few elements is extended to the whole class. The first mode of operation occurs, too, in these great discoveries; namely, in the period of preparation or of collection of data. This collection of data is at first disorganized or poorly organized; it consists of bits of information that are loosely associated, although not disparate or completely unrelated. It probably corresponds to a primary-aggregation stage, as described in *The Intrapsychic Self*, except that it occurs at a much higher level. But when the act of discovery is completed, what had been a loose contiguity reminiscent of a primary aggregation becomes an *invariable association*. Newton's discovery may be reformulated in the following way: "Every body is associated with the force of gravity." We must, however, be aware of an important fact: in great discoveries or theories, the invariable association, or the higher unity, is reached by passing through the stage of the mode of similarity.

Many discoveries that are not of the highest creative order reach the stage of invariable association without going through the stage of similarity. And of course, it can happen that their individual practical results are more consequential than those of discoveries of the highest type. For instance, an observer is struck by an unusual sequence, never noticed before: an unusual event B occurs after an unusual occurrence of A, and he jumps to the conclusion (which later he has to confirm with other experiments) that there is an invariable association between A and B. At other times the association is a negative one: B cannot be associated with A. A great deal of medical research is based on negative association (for instance, if penicillin A is present, a certain microorganism B will not multiply).

---

creates the mental representation of an arrangement that is not in agreement with the first reality.

Many inventions and discoveries have occurred by this method of seeing an invariable association or by filling some gap between invariable associations.* When the invariable association is discovered without going through the stage of the mode of similarity, we have only a practical invention or at most an *empirical law*. The law is explained only by the empirical proof; it is not sustained by a new class or by a greater understanding of the world. It is doubtful that the tertiary process is used in discoveries made by empirical relation.

Some inventions seem to have occurred purely by accident. If Roentgen had not chanced to observe a glowing barium platinocyanide screen, X rays would not have been discovered. The creativity, if we can use that term, here consisted of not accepting the chance, the accident, the seeming anomaly, but of trying to understand the event as part of the order of the universe. In such incidents, what appears fortuitous or anomalous is recognized as an inevitable occurrence. The accidental result may immediately show itself to have great practical consequences or applications.

It is a curious fact about scientific discoveries that fortuitous incidents, such as that of Newton and the apple or that of Galileo and the lamp in the cathedral of Pisa, are frequently of importance. Many people doubt the historical validity of these episodes, which seem almost like myths that have grown up around the memory of great men. The stories have the flavor of parables, "artistic concretizations" that popular culture has created out of the ideas of these men. Early in life Galileo had neglected the study of mathematics because his father had convinced him to study medicine. In 1581, when he was seventeen, he was in the cathedral of his native city Pisa and watched the swinging of a lamp. He observed that whatever the range of the oscillations of the lamp, the time span for each remained the same. The subsequent verification of this fact led him to the discovery of the principle of the isochromism of the pendulum.

One of the most famous of these stories about creative men concerns the mathematician and inventor Archimedes, who was born at Syracuse, Sicily, in 287 B.C. Hieron, the King of Syracuse, had asked Archimedes to determine whether a crown given to him and supposed to be of gold, did not actually contain a quantity of less valu-

---

* For a more detailed discussion of the type of creativity connected with inventions, see Rossman (1931).

able silver. Archimedes did not know how to solve the problem. One day, however, while entering his bath, he noticed that he displaced a certain volume of water, and he had a sudden illumination. He realized that he would be able to solve the enigma if he put the crown and equal weights of gold and silver separately into a container of water and observed the difference in overflow. Struck by this sudden insight, he shouted "Eureka! Eureka!" an expression which throughout centuries has remained symbolic of scientific discovery.

At the risk of appearing gullible, I must say that I believe in many of these little episodes which led to great illuminations. That small, chance episodes are responsible for some inventions and discoveries is beyond doubt and has been verified by a number of observers. There is no reason why incidents such as those reported about Archimedes, Newton, and Galileo could not have occurred, thus offering a genius the opportunity to grasp a regularity he was searching for. The episode becomes a concretization of the idea, just as a work of art stands for an abstract concept. The falling apple concretizes the force of gravity. Here it is nature that does the concretizing, not man. Man's genius lies in recognizing the concretization and unraveling it by finding the universal in the particular. The particular is not just a symbol of the universal, as in art; instead it belongs to the class of the universal. Both are parts of the same reality.

Imagery

HOWEVER, it is true that many innovators have not needed some concrete episode to grasp the universal. Nor have they relied directly on seeing an identity among dissimilarities, as Poincaré did. These innovators have relied on other forms of primitive cognition, and especially on images.

In answer to a questionnaire prepared by the mathematician Hadamard (1945), Einstein wrote:

> "(A) The words or the language, as they are written or spoken, do not seem to play any role in my mechanism of thought. The psychical entities which seem to serve as elements in thought are signs and more

or less clear images which can be 'voluntarily' reproduced and combined . . .

(B) The above elements are, in my case, of visual and some of muscular types . . .

(C) According to what has been said, the play with the mentioned elements is aimed to be analogous to certain logical connections one is searching for . . ."

Hadamard himself reported that he thought creatively in visual pictures. Some authors have stressed the role of visualization in scientific creativity. For instance, Walkup (1967) writes that creative individuals, in the field of science at least, have intense visual imagery. They "almost hallucinate in the areas in which they are creative." He soon tempers his statement by adding that he uses the word "visualize" in its broadest sense to include the mental synthesizing of many sensory experiences, not just ocular experiences. He also writes that inventors with whom he talked reported "thinking visually about complex mechanisms. . . . So it appears that ideas which can be grasped when drawn on paper can be visualized without being put onto paper. . . . Also, the nature of the *seeing* or sensing is peculiar. It is almost a *feeling like* the object being visualized." (Italics in the original.) It seems to me that the "peculiar seeing" that Walkup describes is imagery.

In a very interesting article, Dreistadt (1974) examines the importance of the role of visualization in Einstein's creativity and in his discovery of the theory of relativity in particular. (Einstein was fully aware of this role. In a letter to his friend Janos Plesch (Clark 1971, p. 87), he wrote, "When I examine myself and my methods of thought, I come to the conclusion that the gift of fantasy has meant more to me than my talent for absorbing knowledge." For instance, in one of his fantasies, Einstein visualized himself as a passenger who rode on a ray of light and held a mirror in front of him. Since the light and the mirror were traveling at the same velocity in the same direction and since the mirror was a little ahead, the light could never catch up to the mirror and reflect any image. Thus Einstein could not see himself in the mirror. In another instance, Einstein fantasied some physicists in an elevator that was falling freely in a high building. The physicists, unaware of what was happening, were performing some experiments. They took coins and keys out of their pockets and let go of them. The coins and keys remained in mid-air because they were falling at the same rate of speed with the elevator and the men. The physicists might have interpreted the strange phenomenon in unusual ways. For instance, they might have thought they had been transported outside the gravitational field of the earth and were in empty space, where every body follows Newton's law of inertia and continues in its state of rest or uniform straight line.

Dreistadt aptly describes how these imaginary events, and others reported in his article, were analogous to real events. We remember that Einstein himself, in point C of his answer to Hadamard, had said that these visual elements were "*analogous* to certain logical connections one is searching for."

I believe we can go a step further and state that these fantasies had the same value that some little episodes, reported in the previous section of this chapter, had for people like Galileo and Newton. The apple in the case of Newton, the moving lamp in the case of Galileo, did not need to be imagined. They were both analogous to the logical connections implied in the physical law. They were also a particular instance of a universal phenomenon, an actual embodiment of a notion of the highest generality. The particular became identical to a potentially infinite number of cases in which the same conditions apply.

Now the problem with people like Einstein is whether the fantasy comes first, or whether it is a concretization or perceptualization of mental processes that occurred previously. Galileo and Newton saw an identity. Einstein had to create a visual identity. Einstein may be in good faith when he says that the visual part of creativity comes first, because his antecedent mental work might have been unconscious. His situation may be similar to that of a person who examines a dream he has had, and who had not been previously aware of the antecedent mental processes that gave origin to that particular dream. The difference between a person like Poincaré and a person like Einstein may be that whereas Poincaré could proceed from an endoceptual to a preconceptual and finally a conceptual level, Einstein had to go from the endoceptual back to the image level before reaching the conceptual.

Chapter 12
Philosophy and General System Theory

PHILOSOPHICAL CREATIVITY, contrary to creativity in the scientific fields, has received minimal consideration in psychological studies. And yet until two centuries ago philosophy played a much greater role than science in shaping Western civilization. The difficulty inherent in a subject that deals mostly with abstractions, and the scarcity of contributions in this field, will compel us to discuss this important topic rather briefly.

Many works have been written on the relations between philosophy, psychology, and psychoanalysis, but little on philosophical creativity per se. One important contribution, however, is an article by Money-Kyrle (1958). As he states, a discouraging factor in such studies is the difficulty in defining philosophy itself. Money-Kyrle follows Russell's definition (1945): that philosophy is something lying between science and religion. Scientific questions require empirical validation; religious questions are based on faith and revelation. Philosophical problems are not expected to be solved by empirical methods or by faith, but by reason. The fact, however, that a problem is solved by reason is not enough to characterize it as philosophical. For instance, the translation of a book from a foreign language requires the use of reason, but it is not a philosophical problem, even if philosophical premises can be found in it.

The Creative Product

Philosophy aims at transcending the other activities of man; that is, it proposes ways of going beyond the limits of man's knowledge, moral customs, and scientific achievements. Whereas science deals with the things of the world, philosophy aims at transcending these worldly things: it deals with "the first and ultimate things." As metaphysics, philosophy claims to be the only possible or valid knowledge. Philosophy can also be considered as the coordination of all the sciences or of all scientific results. It can also be seen as an evaluation of knowledge from the use man makes of it. Philosophy, however, does not offer any well-defined method by which the acceptability or nonacceptability of proposed answers to problems can be tested. On one hand, it lacks the faith of religion; on the other hand, its use of logic does not seem sufficient. In philosophical creativity there is much less reliance on primary-process mechanisms than in other fields of creativity, and yet the secondary process is inadequate to support, or convalidate, the philosophical hypothesis. A tertiary process, consisting of a well-balanced welding of primary and secondary elements, is very difficult or perhaps impossible to realize in philosophy. Either the philosopher relies too much on the primary process and thereby becomes almost mystical or an advocate of a religious doctrine, or he relies too much on the secondary, in which case his work becomes indistinguishable from logic. As a matter of fact, some parts of philosophy *have* become pure logic, such as symbolic logic.

If the philosopher would accept that the theories or the system he advocates are only hypotheses, his teachings would receive more consideration in our time (which, relatively speaking, is more refractory to philosophy than were previous eras). But, as a rule, the philosopher becomes so convinced of the validity of his own system that he presents it to the world as the ultimate truth or a way to proceed toward the ultimate truth. Were he to admit that his system is only a hypothesis—and most likely wrong, at that, since many contrasting systems have been advocated by other philosophers—he would run the risk of being considered an artist, a person so alien to the scientific method as to dare, without the minimal empirical verification, to formulate theories about the origin of the cosmos, the meaning of life, and the ultimate destiny of man. Could not a skeptical person consider philosophers' hypotheses similar to science fiction, except that instead of being expressed in a language borrowed from science, they are formulated in an abstruse network of abstract conceptualization?

Does all this mean that philosophy is useless, or that it should be discouraged? Not at all. It would be a sad state of affairs and a fatal blow to imagination and creativity if man would deal only with what is empirically verifiable. Man easily realizes that there is much more in life and the cosmos than what he knows. He feels that there is a meaning and an essence that go far beyond the fugitive character of what he is aware of. And it is part of his nature to increase his understanding, wanting to be enlightened further even though he knows that he will not achieve complete enlightenment. Man wants to know more about the precariousness of his existence, the vanity of that which is, the essence of the eternal. His attempts to learn and experience more, to *go beyond*, are not completely satisfied by such methods as common reasoning, art, literature, faith, and science. Thus he philosophizes. In philosophizing he becomes creative again, even if his philosophy comes to be proved wrong.

A pessimistic attitude toward philosophy makes us focus on the fact that, inasmuch as the various systems of philosophy contradict one another, they are all invalid (or all of them except one). But an optimistic attitude toward philosophy makes us see it as a striving: we must strive toward and settle for a closer approximation to the first and ultimate things. The creative philosopher finds a new approximation, or supposed approximation; and the noncreative but thoughtful man embraces the philosophies of the innovator. As in other fields of creativity, philosophy, although advanced by the few, becomes accessible to all human beings and soon belongs to the collective patrimony of the culture. However, several generations must sometimes pass before the abstract conceptions of a philosophy appear in concrete forms in the ideas and habits of people.

Philosophy as a Creative Product

LET US EXAMINE the difficulties inherent in the creative process of philosophy. The difficulty of philosophy in using primary processes lies in the fact that its subject matter deals with abstract concepts or categories. In philosophy, more than in any other study, there is a reluctance to "concretize." Its concepts are either general abstractions that very seldom find primary-process reinforcement, or mathematico-logical formulas that do not fit or adequately represent other aspects of the world that philosophy wants to investigate.

This reluctance to concretize is apparent in the methodology of most philosophers, and it contrasts with the attitude of most scientists. Scientists want to convalidate. Their writings are generally replete with examples. Philosophers—for instance, Kant—hate examples as illustrations of what they try to demonstrate; that's one of the reasons why their books are generally so difficult to read. The scientist offers the example as a concrete representation of the principle that he has enunciated: the example clarifies or represents or embodies the universal. But for the philosopher, any example spoils the concept, or the universal, because it is not an absolute copy or perfect representative of the concept. The philosopher is afraid of becoming "a poet"—that is, of giving only metaphorical representations—and therefore he omits examples. The fact that perfect examples do not exist is no proof, for the philosopher, that the principle is not valid.

A rare example of agreement between science and logico-mathematical philosophy could perhaps be found in the already-mentioned concept of Galileo: that of a body that moves without the influence of any external force. Such a body does not exist in nature, and yet the science of physical dynamics was founded on its theoretical existence. But Galileo reached his conclusions after empirical research. The philosopher, instead, finds universal principles through conceptualizations rather than through explorations of the external world. These conceptualizations are often reached without resorting to the concrete particulars of the physical world at all. Conceptualizations are psychological and therefore have a physiological counterpart, but philosophical conceptualizations constantly seek ways of transcending the psychological and physiological levels. Even "psychological concretizations" are discarded by philosophy. Philosophy is not interested in thoughts and feelings as functions of the psyche, but only in the *validity* of thoughts and feelings.

How the validity of intricate systems of abstract suppositions is to be tested is again hard to say. As we have already mentioned, it is either accepted by an act of faith, which often relies on primary processes, or it must be proved logico-mathematically. Both ways are imperfect. Furthermore, neither way can ever completely transcend psychology and physiology. The philosopher, by temperament, habit, and the nature of his concern, is reluctant to use perceptual data or any kind of imagery. Of course, as was the case with the British empiricists, the philosopher may be interested in perception, too, but then perception itself is the object of conceptualization. The philosopher thus in a certain way is the opposite of the poet and the artist, who resort to perceptualization of the concept in order to produce works of art. He is also far away from most scientists, who need empirical concretizations.

Philosophers, too, use images and parables, at times very beautiful ones. The most famous of them is probably the parable of the cave, written by Plato in the *Republic*. Plato compares human ideas to shadows that prisoners in a cave see projected on a wall. The prisoners are bound and can look in but a single direction. A fire is behind them, so that the prisoners, who have been chained since childhood, see nothing but the shadows of themselves and of the objects behind them cast on the wall by the light radiating from the fire. It is debatable whether, as the writer of this parable, Plato was more a philosopher or a poet; a philosopher may also be a great artist, as Plato was.

It is beyond the scope of this chapter to analyze even the most important philosophical systems. I shall only point to the fact that philosophers, too, in their innovations, resort to the three modes of operation that I have described in Chapter 6. However, they use them at a very abstract level. After having collected pertinent data—the mode of contiguity—they often see a similarity between the world and a system of conceptions: that is, they see a correspondence, or parallelism, or coincidence, between the world and their philosophical views. Plato is again the first philosopher who comes to mind. His system is founded on the great similarity between the world of particular things and the supersensible, superior world of ideas, where the real forms are perfect and unchanging. Particular things as we see them, according to Plato, are like the shadows seen in the cave by the prisoners. Plato had to create, at an abstract level, a system of ideal forms that coincides with (or is similar to) the world of particulars. I do not intend to discuss the validity of Plato's philosophy; I just want to stress that he saw a similarity between the world and a philosophical structure he conceived. Once he had envisioned (or constructed) this coincidence, he embarked upon deducing all the other facts that the system presupposed (the mode of *pars pro toto*).

Kant's creativity also consisted in seeing a similarity (or identity) between objects as they appear to us, and the transcendental a priori conditions or categories that make us see the objects in a certain way. Objects must conform to these categories. Although he was perhaps one of the least poetic of the great philosophers, he, too, resorted to a metaphor when he called his theory of knowledge a "Copernican revolution" in philosophy. As Copernicus reversed the relation between the earth and the sun, so Kant believed he had reversed the position between the world and the mind (or an abstract system of categories). In Kantian philosophy the mind does not mirror the world; instead the world is organized or actually created by the mind—or, according to other interpretations of Kant, by the system of abstract categories.

Thus we can recognize that, according to some of the greatest philosophers such as Plato and Kant, the world of reality is an analog of something else. This "something else" is, for them, the ultimate reality or the ultimate understanding. Actually it is a system of abstract thoughts which the philosophers themselves have created. They have recognized a similarity between the world and some systems of concepts that the mind has formulated. For Plato the things of the world were similarities or imperfect copies of the ideal forms; for Kant the world as we see it is a replica or a function of a priori categories.

In philosophy, more than in any other field of creativity, there is a tendency to move away from concretization. Thus the contrast with the other creative fields, which rely greatly on concretization, is very strident. The increased ability of the philosopher to see a correspondence or similarity between a system of ideas and the world is probably based on an intensified ability to see similarities; such intensified ability, however, must be accompanied by the most complicated and abstract secondary processes.

General System Theory

A NEW DISCIPLINE that lies closer to science than philosophy, but that relies more on conceptualizations than on empirical verifications, is general system theory. (Other new disciplines related to it are cybernetics, information theory, and decision theory.) General system theory is to a large extent the result of the creativity of Ludwig Von

Bertalanffy (1955, 1967, 1968). According to this author, traditional science could not account for many aspects of biological, behavioral, and social problems, which aspects therefore were declared unscientific or metaphysical. According to Von Bertalanffy, generalizations that include all these aspects and are based on interdisciplinary constructs thus became necessary. General system theory searches for these generalizations and studies their implications.

Throughout this book, as well as in *The Intrapsychic Self*, I have stressed the importance of similarities in the various levels and forms of cognition and especially of creativity; but Von Bertalanffy's theories include much more than cognition. Inasmuch as they apply to everything that exists or is organized, they are almost philosophical in content. Thus, together with mathematics, they form the bridge between philosophy and science.

Von Bertalanffy stressed the appearance of structural similarities, or *isomorphies*, in different fields. That is, the different fields of science, literature, and so on follow some corresponding principles or special laws. They do so because all these fields are systems, or complexes of interacting elements. In the words of Von Bertalanffy, "the isomorphy is a consequence of the fact that in certain aspects, corresponding abstractions and conceptual models can be applied to different phenomena" (1955). Scientific theories aim at transforming the flux of reality into simpler formulations. Nevertheless they must reproduce the essential structure of reality. Paraphrasing Laszlo (1972), we may say that whereas science, or at least Newtonian science, deals with organized simplicity, general system theory deals with organized complexities: the complexities of systems. Systems, or wholes, or ensembles, are not just things—concepts, ideas, abstractions of any kind—that are put together; they are groups of interacting parts that maintain certain relationships among themselves. Every theory generalizes (or abstracts) certain commonalities underlying individual differentiations. These commonalities, which I have called similarities in this book and which are called isomorphies by Von Bertalanffy and invariances by Laszlo, are the recurrent features of phenomena.

It is not important to analyze the tenets of general system theory here. Later we shall discuss a few of them in reference to the creative process, but in this chapter we have dealt with general system theory only as itself a creative product—of, in particular, that great innovator who was Ludwig Von Bertalanffy. Von Bertalanffy's tertiary process consisted of finding isomorphies or similarities among the various fields, or systems, and in founding the science of similarities. These isomorphies became the principles or laws of general system theory. But in the words of Boulding (1956), general system theory is itself "the skeleton of science in the sense that it aims to provide a framework or structure of systems on which to hang the flesh and blood of particular disciplines and particular subject matters in an orderly and coherent corpus of knowledge."

PART FOUR

Creativity and the Sociocultural Environment

Chapter 13
Society, Culture, and Creativity

The Occurrence of Genius

WHY DOES A GENIUS or a highly creative person appear at a certain time in history and in a certain place? Is genius a product of culture or is culture the product of geniuses? In this chapter we shall discuss what answers can be given to these questions.

According to Zielsen (1926), the use of the word "genio" started about 1550 with painter-writers like Leonardo, Vasari, and Telesio. By 1700, according to Lange-Eichbaum (1932), the word "genius" acquired the meaning of an "incomprehensible and mysterious force animating certain human beings." It was generally applied, however, to "the individuals manifesting this force." The designation genius is today usually given to a human being who has an extraordinary capacity for desirable originality, or who makes a new and profound contribution to some or all of mankind.

As is well known, such people are rare, and their appearance in given populations is extremely hard to predict. It is also well known that creative people who reach the rank of genius appear in particularly large numbers in certain periods of history in given geographical areas. This uneven distribution suggests that special environmental circumstances determine the occurrence of creativity, rather than exclusively biological factors. Four major examples will suffice: the classic Greek period; the Italian Renaissance; the time of the American revolution, during which a group of people gave the world a new concept of man; and the years since the mid-nineteenth century, with the contributions of numerous Jewish geniuses. These examples serve to show that creativity does not occur at random, but is enhanced by environmental factors. Were we to differentiate these factors, we could make an attempt to facilitate their reoccurrence and thus promote creativity.

That genius does not appear regularly but in clusters was a phenomenon known since antiquity. Valleius Paterculus, a Roman historian who lived from 19 B.C. to at least 30 A.D., wrote that distinct epochs of a few years' duration give rise to great men. The greatest Greek tragedies appeared over a short period with the work of "three men of divine inspiration," Aeschylus, Sophocles, and Euripides. Greek philosophy had a heroic era with another three men, Socrates, Plato, and Aristotle. After giving other examples, Valleius posed the question: why do men of similar talents occur exclusively in certain epochs, flock to one pursuit, and attain similar success? He concluded that he could not find any reason of whose validity he could be certain. Nevertheless he advanced some hypotheses. He suggested that genius is fostered by emulation. People want to emulate a genius who has appeared among them. Envy and admiration bring about imitations of his work. But when a given type of work reaches perfection, no further advance is possible; thus people decide to search for different pursuits. Velleius also wondered why—with the exception of Pindar, who was born in Boeotia—all the great literary men of Greek literature were Athenians.*

Since Velleius, many other authors have also pondered why creative men of the rank of genius appear in clusters in this way. But not until the work of the great American anthropologist Kroeber did we have a serious study of the problem (1944). After laboriously studying the occurrence, throughout history, of geniuses in various fields—philosophy, science, philology, sculpture, painting, drama, literature, and music—Kroeber drew the following conclusion: geniuses indicate the realization of coherent patterns of growths

---

* Another exception is Sappho, the greatest Greek poetess, who was born on the island of Lesbos.

of cultural value. For instance, at the end of the Middle Ages and the beginning of the Renaissance, Giotto and Dante appear as indicators of patterns of growth in painting and poetry. From a physiological and psychological point of view, the supply of genius "ought to remain essentially constant in any one race within any period which is not unduly long." This is not the case, however. Geniuses appear in clusters that occur at irregular and at times long intervals.

Kroeber stated that "inasmuch as even the people possessing higher civilization have produced cultural products of value only intermittently, during relatively small fractions of their time span, it follows that more individuals born with the endowment of genius have been inhibited by the cultural situations into which they were born than have been developed by other cultural situations" (1944, p. 840). He also stated that "genetics leaves only an infinitesimal possibility for the racial stock occupying England to have given birth to no geniuses at all between 1450 and 1550 and a whole series of geniuses in literature, music, science, philosophy, and politics between 1550 and 1650 . Similarly with the Germany of 1550–1650 and 1700–1800, respectively, and innumerable other instances in history" (1944, pp. 10–11). If Kroeber is correct, we must accept the fact that the possibility for the development of a large number of creative people always exists in certain populations.

Let us examine some of Kroeber's observations and conclusions in greater detail. For instance, Latin literature was characterized by four "pulses" and three recessions over a total period of 700 years. The first pulse, or formative phase (240 to 120 B.C.), contained the illustrious playwrights Naevius, Plautus, Ennius, Pacuvius, Caicilus, Terence, and Accius, and the historians Cato Censorious, Hemina, Calpurnius, and Sempronio Asellio, among others. Then there was an interval of little activity that lasted 70 years, from 120 to 70 B.C. The great golden period of Latin literature lasted 80 years, from 70 B.C. to 10 A.D. It included such great figures as Cicero, Julius Caesar, and Cornelius Nepos; the historians Sallust and Livy; and the poets Lucretius, Catullus, Horace, Tibullus, Ovid, and (greatest of all) Vergil. A second silent period followed, extending from 10 A.D. to 50 A.D., during which the only important pen was that of Seneca. The second great period, or "silver age," lasted from 50 A.D. to 120 A.D.; it included the poets Silius Italicus, Calpurnius Siculus, Persius, Statius, and Juvenal, and the historians Tacitus and Suetonius. There was then another period of decline, from 120 to 180 A.D., after which came a florescence of Christian writers, centering around 400 A.D., with such great writers as Jerome, Ambrose, Augustine, and Boethius.

Kroeber said that Italian literature began with a remarkable cluster of three giants: Dante, Petrarch, and Boccaccio. (To this I might add that this triad was never equaled in all the subsequent centuries of Italian literature.) Kroeber felt sure that he could conclude from his studies that a pattern of growth, caused by clusters of creative persons, prevailed in every field—from philosophy, science, and medicine, in particular, to sculpture, painting, music, and literature. Isolated geniuses do appear, such as the Pole Copernicus (1473–1543) and the Germans Kepler (1571–1630) and Leibniz (1646–1716), but they are the exceptions, not the rule.

Growths in different fields tend to be associated. The most typical example is that culmination of many creative activities in the relatively short, heroic period of ancient Greece. Sculpture generally precedes painting, probably because it is physically a simpler art. Kroeber stated that "the tendency toward sequence, if there is one, lies in the laws of nature rather than in some law of culture. Science possesses certain inherent relations with philosophy, and philosophy again with religion, and religion again with art. But these relations have been worked out quite diversely in their cultural manifestations. Science, philosophy, and religion impinge on one another psychologically, but their expressions in cultural growth do have manifold, and may have minimal, relations. Religion, however, in general precedes aesthetic and intellectual development of note, and a history of the arts is frequently one of gradual emancipation from religion as they attain their culmination" (1944, pp. 843–844). Kroeber also concluded that cultural growth spreads gradually from a focal region to a large area. This spreading is in accord with the specific cultural diffusions that anthropologists have studied time and again. In times of cultural decline the area shrinks upon itself. The typical example is again that of Greek civilization, which after having spread to a large part of the Roman empire, eventually drew back within its original Greek limits, while the West relapsed into barbarism.

Kroeber's important work in this field did not receive the recognition that it deserved. Two other authors, however, Sorokin and Gray, continued along the path originated by the great anthropologist. Sorokin (1951) made the following important statement about a conclusion he and Kroeber had reached: "A total, national 'civilization' displays a notable creativity in various cultural fields not necessarily once, but two or more times; in most historical total 'civilizations' there have been two, three, or even more great creative blossomings. This result contradicts Spengler's and Toynbee's claim that each civilization has only one real florescence."

The work of Charles Edward Gray (1958, 1961, 1966) is also outstanding. After having compiled a curve of creativity for Western civilization, Gray stated that the curve agreed with Kroeber's main findings; namely, "that genius emerges in clusters, that such blossomings occur several times during a civilization, that such peaks are rare and do not characterize most of a civilization's course, and that these peaks are of unequal duration" (1966). Gray also stated that Kroeber did the spade work but that—as Kroeber himself admitted (1944, p. 7)—he did not seek explanations.

Gray tried to find these explanations by advancing his *epicyclical theory*, in which history is seen as a series of concurrent cycles: an over-all economic cycle, a social cycle, and a political cycle. (For simplicity's sake I will not repeat Gray's description of a cycle, or the fact that a cycle includes subcycles—for instance, a political cycle includes four subordinate political cycles.) Each of these three cycles goes through four different stages: the formative, the developed, the florescent, and the degenerate. The stages of the economic, social, and political cycles rotate at different speeds. For instance, in the period of time during which a political cycle goes through its four stages, the social cycle may go through two stages and the economic cycle through only one. Thus while one cycle is rising, one or two others might be falling. According to Gray, this "epicyclical" theory explains why genius clustered at certain times and thinned out at others. When the florescent and developed stages of the three cycles coincide, we have clusters of creativity. Conversely, when the formative and degenerate stages of different cycles coincide, a falling off of creativity is to be expected.

Gray found accurate confirmation of his theory in his study of Western civilization. When the peaks of all three cycles—economic, social, and political—coincided, two major cultural climaxes came into being—the Developed Renaissance and Florescent Romanticism. When the peaks of the social and political cycles (but not the economic) coincided, there occurred the two minor cultural climaxes—

the Florescent Gothic and Developed Realism. The coincidence of social and economic (but not political) cycles and, again, political and economic (but not social) cycles, precipitated important periods of creativity—Formative.Renaissance, Florescent Baroque, Developed Classicism, and Degenerate Romanticism.

It is beyond the purpose of this chapter to give a longer account of the works of Kroeber and Gray; the interested reader must go back to the original works, which are impressive for their magnitude. Gray clearly spells out the criteria by which he would choose and rate highly creative men. Here are some of these criteria:

1. Have a man's creations continued to be appreciated long after his era?

2. Did his work reveal universal qualities of humanism?

3. Did he rise above the limitations of his era?

4. How influential was he on contemporary and subsequent creators?

5. How original was he?

6. How versatile and many-sided was he (that is, active in different fields)?

7. In addition to form and beauty, did his work show social consciousness?

In conclusion, it is possible to state that Gray convincingly demonstrated that favorable economical, social, political factors promote creativity.

Kroeber's and Gray's works are significant not only for their conclusions but also because they opened new paths of inquiry. Nevertheless they disclose some limitations, probably inherent in the fact that their authors have remained anthropologists, fundamentally, who are much more interested in cultural growth as a collective phenomenon than in individual creativity. If on the one hand these two authors have been very illuminating in clarifying the magnitude of the cultural factors, on the other hand they have minimized the personal ones. Kroeber and Gray frankly state that they view highly creative individuals as "manufactures" of their cultures; their achievements are stimulated by their societies. They are thus considered not as assertions of rich personalities but "as an index of the growth of their cultures" (Gray 1966, p. 1385). Kroeber wrote, "If we are interested primarily in culture and how it behaves, we can disregard personalities except as inevitable mechanisms or measures of cultural expression" (Kroeber,

1944, p. 10). But can we really see people only as "inevitable mechanisms or measures of cultural expression?" Can we see Shakespeare only as an inevitable mechanism of Elizabethan culture? Had he not been born, could another Englishman of his time have expressed the culture of his period, as well, or achieved such heights?

There is a paradoxical or ambiguous premise in Kroeber's and Gray's work. Although they seem to consider great men as the makers of clusters of high civilization, they see these men as having been shaped exclusively by economic, social, and political factors. And yet, even when the three cycles—economical, social, and political—coincide as Gray described, only a few men rise to the ranks of creativity.

Must we accept an anthropological approach exclusively and consider great men as no more than representatives of their culture? Actually, the issue of whether it is the culture that makes great men, or whether it is great men who make culture grow, was debated long before Kroeber and Gray. One of the first to participate in this great debate was Francis Galton (1870), who reached the conclusion that great men make culture, and that greatness is a hereditary characteristic. Herbert Spencer (1873), on the other hand, concluded that before the great man can make society, society must make him.

In an article published in the *Atlantic Monthly* (1880), William James sponsored the opposite point of view to that of Spencer. He wrote, "If anything is humanly certain, it is that the great man's society, properly so called, does not make him before he can remake it." In poetic, metaphoric vein, James added, "For a community to get vibrating . . . many geniuses coming together and in rapid succession are required. This is why great epochs are so rare—why the sudden bloom of a Greece, an early Rome, a Renaissance, is such a mystery. Blow must follow blow so fast that no cooling can occur in the intervals. Then the mass of the nation grows incandescent, and may continue to glow by pure inertia long after the originators of its internal movement have passed away. We often hear surprise expressed that in these high tides of human affairs not only the people should be filled with stronger life, but that individual geniuses should seem so exceptionally abundant."

James concluded that the occurrence of genius is determined by chance. He asked himself the question: why had the island of Sardinia, which in terms of material advantages was in a favorable position compared to Sicily, remained far behind Sicily in greatness and cultural development? He answered his question by saying that the disparity was "simply because no individuals were born there with patriotism and ability enough to inflame their countrymen with national pride, ambition, and a thirst for independent life."

Well, even great men like William James can occasionally give erroneous explanations. The hypothesis of chance is contradicted by the clustering phenomenon. If Sardinia fell behind Sicily, there were very good reasons. Sicily had undergone acculturation by many civilized people who invaded and conquered the island—the Greeks, the Romans, the Saracens, and the Normans, to mention just a few. Sardinia, much farther from the continent of Europe and removed from the common roads of navigation in the middle of the Mediterranean Sea, had less opportunity to be subjected to cultural influences. Moreover, Sardinia was kept in a state of servitude for many centuries, and its population was decimated by endemic malaria; only in 1951 did it become possible to eradicate malaria with DDT. After the unification of Italy, Sardinia enjoyed greater freedom than ever before and gave birth to at least two illustrious persons: the Nobel Prize winner for literature, Grazia Deledda; and the political thinker, Antonio Gramsci. As to "patriotism, ability enough to inflame their countrymen with national pride," James could not be more wrong. Everyone acquainted with Italian history knows that it was actually the little kingdom of Sardinia and Piedmont that unified Italy and fought the war of independence against the powerful oppressor, the Austrian empire.

Although James wrote that the occurrence of genius is "fortuitous," he made other statements that contradicted this hypothesis of chance. He wrote that what enhances or inhibits the appearance of a genius is not simply the environment but another, or other, geniuses as well. But the other geniuses are there in the cultural environment to form a cluster. Consider the famous psychoanalytic triad, Freud, Adler, and Jung. Although Adler and Jung opposed Freud, it is more than doubtful that they could have risen to prominence had not Freud started a new path of inquiry: namely, the field of depth-psychology. There was certainly a desire on the part of Adler and Jung to emulate Freud and go beyond him, just as the Roman historian Velleius had described. Other clusters of geniuses or quasi-geniuses in a given field can be explained as Velleius did. For instance, the group of composers of operas who were born and flourished in Italy in the nineteenth century cannot be due to chance. Such collections of names as Bellini,

Donizetti, Rossini, Verdi, Ponchielli, Giordano, Boito, Puccini, Mascagni, Leoncavallo, Cilea, and so on cannot be fortuitous. Of course the ground had been prepared by such early composers as Cimarosa and Monteverdi. Similarly, the flourishing of movie art in Italy after the Second World War cannot be due to chance. Didn't such people as Rossellini, De Sica, Fellini, Visconti, and Antonioni benefit from each other's work and from emulation?

Leslie A. White (1949) is another participant in the debate. He placed very much importance on the culture as a whole, reducing the role of the individual almost to that of a passive representative of what his time would ineluctably bring about. He stated that, just as the discoveries of Pasteur would not have been possible when Charlemagne lived, so would agriculture not have been possible at the time of Cro-Magnon man. He stated that two significant conclusions can be drawn: (1) "No invention or discovery can take place until the accumulation of culture has provided the elements—the materials and ideas—necessary for the synthesis, and (2) when the requisite materials have been made available by the process of cultural growth or diffusion, and given normal conditions of cultural interaction, the invention or discovery is bound to take place." Later in the same article White expressed the same concept in stronger words: "When the culture process has reached a point where an invention or discovery becomes possible, that invention or discovery becomes inevitable. . . . When certain factors and conditions are present and in conjunction an invention or discovery takes place; when they are not present, the invention does not occur." To prove his point White mentioned, among other things, that in 1843 Mayer formulated the law of the conservation of energy, but that in 1847 the same law was formulated by four other men working independently: Joule, Helmholz, Colding, and Thomson. The discovery of sunspots was made independently in 1611 by Galileo, Fabricius, Scheiner, and Harriot. The solution of the problem of respiration was made independently in 1777 by Priestley, Scheele, Lavoisier, Spallanzani, and Davy.

White admitted that "a given cultural tradition does not affect all brains in a given society equally." However, according to him, a genius is not a person of exceptional native endowment, but a person in whose organism a significant synthesis of cultural elements has occurred. White attempted to clarify his concepts by stating that the development of a cultural pattern is the labor of countless persons and of many generations or even centuries. However, a long pattern of thought will receive its fulfillment in the lives and work of a few persons: the Newtons, Darwins, Bachs, Beethovens, Kants, and so on.

There is no doubt that White added the weight of his arguments to those who stress the importance of culture, of "the right time and place." Very few people would believe that a Beethoven could have been raised among the Eskimos in the twelfth century, or an Einstein among the Hottentots in the fifteenth century, or an Enrico Fermi among the Bushmen of Australia even in the twentieth century. White, of course, made his whole line of reasoning easier to accept by concentrating on science, scientists, or discoveries that are based on previous scientific accomplishments and on scientific equipment. There is no doubt that if Columbus had not been born, sooner or later somebody would have discovered America; and that if Galileo, Fabricius, Scheiner, and Harriot had not discovered the sunspots, somebody else soon would have. It is much more difficult to believe that if Michelangelo had not been born, somebody else would have provided us with an aesthetic experience like the one we have on confronting the statue of Moses. Similarly, it is difficult to think that if Beethoven had not been born, the uniqueness of his ninth symphony would have been captured by some other composer.

The same argument has been repeated time and time again, in reference not to creativity but to history in general. Is history made by a few men such as Julius Caesar, Charlemagne, Napoleon, Washington, Lincoln, Bismarck, Lenin, Hitler, Churchill, and so on, or were these people made by their times? The statement that had Cleopatra's nose been crooked, the whole subsequent history of the Western world would have been different—is it really true?

In specific reference to creativity, I agree with White that a genius is a person in whose psyche* a significant synthesis of cultural elements has occurred. But White, in a cavalier manner, bypasses the study of the capacity of the individual who makes this "significant synthesis." He recognizes that cultural patterns receive their "fulfillment in the lives and work of a few persons." Yet he does not attempt to explain the nature of this synthesis. Actually, *the significant synthesis is the creative process itself*. It is so significant and unpredictable as to appear magic. Even when a culture is propitious, the significant synthesis occurs in a very small percentage of its people.

* I substitute the word "psyche" for the word "organism" used by White.

The works of Kroeber and others have convinced me that individual potentiality * for genius is much more frequent than the occurrence of genius. Nevertheless we should not forget that this potentiality exists. It is because the potentiality for creativity is deemed to be much more frequent than its occurrence that educators are very much interested in discovering ways of activating this potentiality. Moreover, I have become convinced from the above-mentioned studies that some cultures have promoted creativity much more than others. I propose to call these cultures and/or societies *creativogenic*. The creativogenic culture and the potentially creative person are the two necessary components of creativity. They exist in a special rapport that we shall study in the rest of this chapter.

The Psychological Versus the Superorganic Origins of Personality and Culture

IN ORDER to study the problem of the individual-psychological versus the sociocultural origin of creativity, we must reopen the whole field of the origin of both personality and culture. Are personality and culture psychological or social in origin? This is an immense topic, to which I cannot possibly do justice in this book. Rather, I shall draw from a paper of mine published in the *American Anthropologist* (1956a), in which I discussed this problem and advanced a hypothesis to which I still adhere.

In 1949 Fromm, writing as a psychoanalyst who was also interested in social issues, distinguished three main approaches that have been pursued in the study of the origins of personality and culture: (1) the naive, orthodox Freudian approach, (2) the modified Freudian approach, and (3) the socio-psychological approach. According to the orthodox Freudian approach, everything found in a culture has to be explained in relation to the biological characteristics of man or, more specifically, in relation to the libido theory. Cultural patterns are consequences of libidinal trends; for instance, capitalism must be explained as a result of anal eroticism. The modified Freudian approach, best represented by Kardiner (1939, 1945), attributes great impor-

---

* I would prefer to use the word "possibility" rather than the word "potentiality," for reasons elaborated later. Here I use the word "potentiality" for clarity's sake.

tance to the methods of child training and their impact on the development of personality. Although Fromm recognized that this method is more acceptable than the first, he stressed the fact that it, too, closely follows the "main orthodox Freudian approach." In fact it does not study child training in its totality—that is, in the total interpersonal relation between parents and children, with interchanges of love, affection, and other feelings—but instead merely studies the impact of parental influence on elementary physiological functions or on what Freud called the erogenous zones. (For instance, toilet training is considered of paramount importance for the understanding of culture.) Third, the "socio-psychological" approach sees the development of personality, or at least of "the social character," as a result of exposure of the individual to a certain type of structured society. The social character will make people "want to act as they have to act" (Fromm 1949).

These different approaches reflect two different schools of thought in the fields of psychiatry and anthropology. The Freudian approaches see personality and culture mostly as a result of the instinctual needs of man. Culture, through personality, is the product of man, is psychological in origin, and has the purpose of being the means of satisfying his needs. The other approach is almost the opposite: man is to a large extent the product of the environment, that is, of the culture to which he belongs. This second school of thought is represented in psychiatry and psychoanalysis chiefly by Fromm and Sullivan. Sullivan sees the individual as the result of the interpersonal forces to which he is subjected, especially the interpersonal contacts that he had with his parents during childhood. Parents are carriers of culture. Psychopathological conditions are seen as the result of disturbed relationships with the parents or with parent-substitutes. John Dewey and George Mead have indirectly contributed to these conceptions. A similar school of thought is followed in anthropology by those who adhere to the superorganic theory of culture, such as White (1949a) and to a certain extent Kroeber (1948), whose studies we have taken into consideration in the previous section; and, in sociology, by Durkheim, with the concept of collective consciousness (1950).

Perhaps a combination of the two approaches is possible. Let us forget for a while the problem of the origin of culture and concentrate on the contacts between the individual and culture (considered here, for the sake of simplification, as a separate entity). The individual may be roughly seen as having two contacts with culture. For one, he has certain biological equipment with which he tries to understand the environment and satisfy his needs; without the possession of this equipment he could not make the first contact with culture. Such contact is purely psychological. The individual offers or exposes his biological potentialities to culture. Whereas in studying this first contact, academic psychologists have concentrated on the learning abilities of the human being, orthodox psychoanalysts have instead focused their interest on motivation—that is, on the need to satisfy needs or instincts, and particularly the need to preserve oneself and obtain sexual gratification. But it is obvious that all these facets have to be included in the first contact. We may state that the biological equipment for the first contact consists chiefly of a combination of Freud's instincts and Kant's a priori forms of mind.

The second contact between the individual and culture is represented by the acquisition, on the part of the individual, of things already present in culture. This acquisition is mediated by interpersonal relationships and, as George Mead, Dewey, Fromm, and Sullivan emphasize, it constitutes a great part of the individual. Without what he obtains from culture, man would not be much different from other animals. This process may be represented by Figure 13-1: I represents the individual, and the dark core stands for his biological part; C represents culture; a indicates the functions that permit a contact between I and C (that is, chiefly, the instincts and the a priori forms of mind); and b represents what the individual obtains from culture. The last-named is like a stream that will go to constitute the outer, dotted part of I—that is, the part that will transform man from a biological to a sociobiological animal. Whereas, in the origin of personality and of its disorders, some academic psychological schools of thought and the orthodox psychoanalytic school attribute more importance to the dark core of I and to a, the cultural psychoanalytic school (represented by Fromm and Sullivan) and the behavioristic psychological school attribute more importance to b and to the dotted part of I.

My contention is that the phenomenon in its totality consists of a circular process that is represented in the diagram. The diagram may also be used as a graphic representation of an interpretation of culture. Culture is seen as a combination of facts that derive from the basic psychological equipment of man (represented in the diagram as the

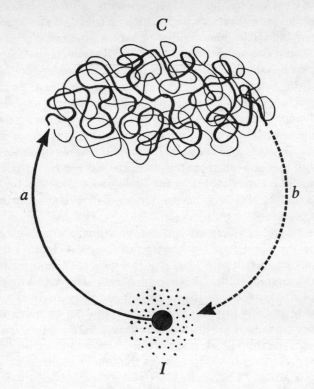

C

a

b

I

Figure 13-1

heavy lines of the network in *C*), and of nonpsychological facts (geographical and historical variables, represented in the diagram as the thin lines of the network). Although it could not originate without *a*, culture undergoes a tremendous expansion and intermediary life of its own. It may be compared to mathematics, which could not originate without the basic laws of thought, but which expands tremendously from generation to generation, to such an extent that no single man, even a mathematician, can master the whole of it. Mathematics nevertheless influences the life of every individual in our present culture. It has become an inherent part of our vision of the world, of the concept we have of ourselves, of our way of living. Mathematics thus starts as a part of *a* but becomes a part of the dotted part of *I*.

The same thing could be repeated about culture in general, of which mathematics is only a small part. Culture begins and ends psychologically. It begins psychologically, inasmuch as it needs the fundamental neurological equipment of man. It ends psychologically, inasmuch as it operates as a great formative and psychodynamic force on the individual. It has, however, a life and growth of its own.

The diagram is, of course, extremely simplified. For instance, *b* includes all interpersonal relations as well as some biological functions already used in *a*. Furthermore, the diagram (like every graphic symbol) gives no more than a static representation of a phenomenon that is in perennial change. It seems to emphasize the forces leading to a certain equilibrium, rather than the unceasing unrest that always threatens this equilibrium.

The diagram shows that the individual and culture are parts of a very dynamic circular process. They are coexistent and mutually dependent. No part could live without the other. Man cannot live without culture; culture cannot exist without man. There are many phenomena in nature where a similar mutual dependency is found: for instance, in cases of symbiosis and parasitism which show that a certain species cannot live without another. Many readers may object to this interpretation of culture because of what seems an obvious fact: that man must have existed before culture. But man without culture would be limited to the dark core of *I*. He would be entirely a biological entity, not a sociobiological entity as we know him. To become a sociobiological entity, he needs a symbiosis with culture.

Examples of symbiosis and parasitism may again help us to understand the beginning of this circular process. We know that at certain periods in history, for some undetermined reasons, mutations occur in certain species, on account of which they can reproduce only in a condition of parasitism or symbiosis with a second species. If this second species were nonexistent or unavailable, the first species would perish. In the same way we may think that at a certain period in history a mutation occurred in some primates, on account of which a high symbolism with consequent a priori Kantian forms of mind became a potentiality. This potentiality became a reality on account of the presence of similar living beings. In fact, it is only the response of other beings which changes potential high symbolism into actual high symbolism (Arieti 1955, 1967, 1974). Rudimentary high symbolism permitted the organization of the others into a rudimental cultural society. The rudimental society sent cultural feedbacks to men, so that they could perpetuate their mutation. Without the feedbacks from the community the mutation would not be maintained; or it would remain at a rudimentary stage, so that the species would not become hominized but would remain at a stage not much different from that of apes or from that of feral men who have occasionally been described (Leuba 1954). Moreover, this particular circular process not only perpetuated the species that underwent the mutation, as in the mentioned biological examples, but it also brought about a progressive growth on both sides, leading to the simultaneous and possibly endless enrichment of man and culture.

The Rapport between the Creativogenic Culture and the Creative-To-Be Person

THE RELATION between C and I, represented in Figure 13-1, seems to indicate a feedback mechanism. A feedback mechanism is one that maintains a particular status, like the homeostasis of the organism. It seems to have a purpose: to monitor some parts of the cycle so as to prevent changes or aberrations. Thus it is often called a servomechanism. For instance, when some parts of a refrigerator, through a thermostat, "inform" the system that the temperature has gone above or below a desired level, other parts of the system put mechanisms into motion that reestablish the wanted temperature.

Actually the I–C rapport can be better seen as an open system, as described by Von Bertalanffy (1955), even if it retains some characteristics of a feedback mechanism. Were adaptation to the environment on the part of the individual and society's maintenance of the status quo with absolute conservativism and traditionalism, the exclusively desirable aims of the relation, then we could, with a stretch of the imagination, see this relation solely as a feedback, self-regulating mechanism. But no living organism is closed; it needs exchanges with the environment to maintain a steady state, and no society or culture is immutable. Both the individual (I) and culture (C) are open systems, the individual open to culture and culture to the individual. The concept of feedback mechanisms is still applicable to this relation, just as many feedback mechanisms apply to the physiology of the biological mechanism, but within the seemingly rigid structure of a feedback

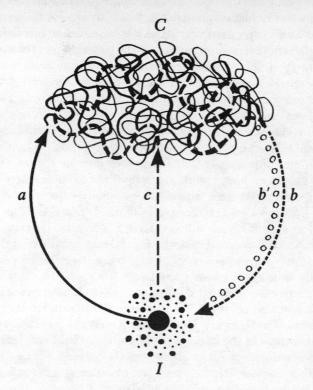

Figure 13-2

mechanism we can still discern the openness and openendedness of the individual human being and of culture. Creativity adds almost constantly to the open society and culture. And creativity is an addition to the open individual.

Figure 13-2, representing the relation between the creative person and the creativogenic culture, shows some variations from Figure 13-2. In addition to the usual relation with culture, I (who in this case is an individual candidate for creativity) receives b', or particular ways offered to him by C. These particular ways do not make I great but give him the possibility of becoming great if I has unusual characteristics that permit him to be stimulated by b' in specific ways. As said, b' represents a set of characteristics of C, a combination of elements that—by being particularly accentuated, or by being together—makes C creativogenic and offers the elements and the climate for the innovation (represented in the middle of the upper part of Figure 13-2 as intermittent line of black square dots). But b' would not be perceived or accepted by I if that particular I did not have, inside himself, certain special characteristics (represented by the larger dots in the lower part of Figure 13-2). These spots are parts of I ready to receive b' and to form thereby a magic synthesis—to produce an innovation that will again be offered to Culture, through c. And c, which only a few men possess, goes back to C to become one of the millions of threads of which C is composed. It will strongly affect a part of culture—for example, music—and, in small, almost imperceptible ways, the whole culture (intermittent line of black square dots in Figure 13-2). Although people endowed with c are few, the accumulation of them through centuries brings about an enormous expansion of C. Although I (in this case the creative individual) and C (in this case the creativogenic culture) are still involved in a circular relation, I is also an open system, receiving material from the external world through b and b'. And C is an open system too, receiving from all people and especially from those endowed with c.

There is no doubt that culture must provide a certain set of characteristics, at a given time and space, in order to provide b' to individual persons. To this extent authors like Kroeber, Gray, and White are correct in stressing the importance of culture. However, let us repeat that culture does not make great men. It only offers, to those who meet other conditions, the *possibility* of *becoming* great. Some men must have a special set of characteristics to be able to use b' and achieve a new synthesis. This set of characteristics is valid only for a particular b' and not for others. Thus we cannot even call these men with this special set "potentially creative." They have only an unpredictable possibility for creativity that, in order to become a potentiality, must fit in with other unpredictable possibilities. Thus what these men possess cannot be compared to the potentiality of an acorn to become an oak. The creative outcome is not as definite as an oak, but something made unpredictable by the openness of the system. We shall discuss in Chapter 14 the sets of characteristics a creativogenic society is likely to have. The kinds of sets the creative-to-be person is likely to have we shall study in Chapters 15 and 16.

The meeting of a creativogenic culture with a potentially creative person is an improbable event. The event becomes less improbable, the more creativogenic the culture is and the more ready the individual is for a particular type of creativity. Biology certainly plays a role, as we shall discuss in future chapters, but culture operates in two ways: by offering the necessary material to I, and by facilitating the occurrence in I of those characteristics that make him more susceptible to b's stimulation.

Can all these phenomena be understood in a framework of pure determinism—that is, as an inevitable outcome of previous conditions? This hardly seems the case when human motivation and will are involved. But general system theory can again help us to understand the problem, with the concept of *macrodeterminacy* (Sutherland 1973). A system may be treated as deterministic at higher levels or at the level of the whole itself; for instance, the whole culture. However, the lower-order components of the system may not follow determinacy. For instance, we may predict that a certain culture with given characteristics is likely to be or become creativogenic, but it will not be possible to determine who the creative people will be.

Chapter 14

The Creativogenic Society

Nine Positive Social Factors

THE PRECEDING CHAPTER has enabled us to reach two important conclusions. First, some societies and cultures have enhanced and some others inhibited creativity. Second, although the creative process is an intrapsychic phenomenon, it is part of an open system. The magic synthesis does not occur without input from the external world, and it is greatly facilitated by a proper climate or milieu.

Were we thus able to individualize the promoting as well as the inhibiting sociocultural factors, we would possibly be in a position to suggest those changes that are more likely to foster creativity. I say "possibly," but not "certainly." In fact, the possibility exists that society may not be able to produce promoting factors or to prevent negative ones at will. It could also be that society and culture, in their capacity to foster or hinder creativity, act as a whole and not by virtue of individual characteristics. Were this the case, it would be impossible to effect desirable changes voluntarily. However, this hypothesis seems unlikely. I want to make clear that I do not deny that society and culture may have a total or gestaltic influence upon the individual. However, I believe that this total influence is only one of the many types of influence by which society and culture affect the individual. Thus the *total* character of society and culture has only a partial influence. Moreover, the introduction of a single new factor—such as movies, television, the automobile—may sometimes change the character of the total culture. With the full awareness that changing individual factors (or learning to individualize them) does not necessarily bring about the capacity to obtain desirable results, we will pursue our study here in a pioneer spirit, with the hope and expectation that our successors will do more accurate and effective work.

A society based on fair and just laws, providing the best possible psychological and economic conditions for all citizens, seems to be a good milieu for creativity. It is a plausible assumption that a "good," "healthy," or "sane" society promotes creativity, as the study of Gray (1961) has indicated. One may fairly assume that if a society sponsors the "four freedoms"—freedom from fear and want, freedom of speech and worship—as Franklin D. Roosevelt advocated, more people will strive toward creativity than in a society deprived of these freedoms. It is difficult to believe that if people are in dire danger, or hungry, or sick, or in a state of slavery, they are likely to write symphonies or poems.

On the other hand, the qualities that we have mentioned are desirable for any society, not just for a creative society. We can postulate that in order to provide a climate propitious to creativity, society must have more specific characteristics. In what follows I shall describe and discuss nine factors that are socio-cultural in nature and presumably creativogenic. In several instances these factors overlap and can only artificially be separated. In other instances they are antithetical and unlikely to coexist. Only the first one seems essential; all the others have but a facilitating influence, in varying degree.

The first factor is the *availability of cultural (and certain physical) means*. An elite, at least, must exist to preserve these cultural means. It is easy to understand why no musician like Beethoven could flourish in a place such as Africa in the eighteenth century, where there was no possibility of studying music adequately. Even in England a Beethoven would have had only the smallest likelihood of becoming a great composer. England, so great in literature, philosophy, and science, did not have enough cultural patrimony for the development of music when Beethoven lived. Similarly, no Michelangelo would have risen to greatness in Alaska, Rumania, or Madagascar. The availability of means also extends to physical means, such as access to scientific equipment or to material such as marble, iron, wood, paint, and so on for artistic work.

Thus one may reasonably conclude that political leaders who wish to further creativity must promote the existence and growth of cultural media. Some legislators and politicians who are ready to provide assistance to the indigent or to recommend utilitarian works such as roads and highways are often deaf to cultural needs, however. Obviously that which ensures survival comes first; but cultural media should not be considered a luxury or entertainment—as "bread and circuses," as some Roman emperors thought. Instead such media are indispensible for the growth of civilization.

The second characteristic of a creativogenic culture—difficult to distinguish from the first, at times—is *openness to cultural stimuli*. In other words, the cultural stimuli and milieus must not only be present, they must also be requested, desired, made easily available. Openness on the part of the population generally turns into real receptivity. A creativogenic culture must be concerned with more than such positive goals as safety, security, and the preservation of the physical environment. It must not focus exclusively or excessively on only one aspect of human life, whether that be religion, militarism, comfort, sensuousness, or something else. For instance, a society like the one prevailing in Europe in the Middle Ages—especially in that part of the Middle Ages called the Dark Ages—was not characterized by openness to various cultural stimuli. Cultural media were available only to a few people, generally the clergy, and they concerned themselves only with the salvation of the soul. Geniuses were rare then, and those that appeared made contributions almost exclusively to theological philosophy (Thomas Aquinas) or to the practice of religious life (Francis of Assisi).

The third creativogenic characteristic is *stress on becoming, not just on being*. A culture that puts emphasis *only* on immediate gratification, sensuousness, comfort, and immediate pleasure does not promote creativity. The contrast between *being* and *becoming* that some cultural trends emphasize, with the understanding that only being counts because tomorrow is to be distrusted, is unwarranted and harmful. At a human level, *becoming* is part of *being*. Mature man is always becoming because he is constantly affected by a universe of changing symbols. Today he is somewhat different from the way he was yesterday, and tomorrow he will be different from the way he is today. He listens, reads, learns, feels; he observes daily events that are personal or collective, private or public, scientific or experiential, practical or theoretical, rational or irrational, moral or immoral. The creative man is conscious of the fact that creativity is something that grows, has duration, and requires the future as well as the present. Becoming does not mean losing, or failing to acquire a self-identity. It also does not mean that the creative person must give up sensuousness or immediate gratification or the beauty of the moment. But if the beauty of the fleeting moment is to predispose a person to creativity, it must be perceived as a recurring if not a universal beauty. In experiencing it, the creative person has become what he now is; being and becoming must be experienced together. A society that promotes nothing but being will lead to decadence and not to growth.

The fourth characteristic of a creativogenic culture is *free access to cultural media for all citizens, without discrimination*. It is well known that throughout history, cultural media have been made available only to a limited group of people. The privileged class at times was the aristocracy, at times the clergy, at times the wealthy bourgeoisie, at times the religious or ethnic majority, and, almost always, predominantly the male sex. The groups discriminated against were often allowed to be influenced by the cultural media, or to obtain a smattering awareness of them, but they were seldom permitted to advance beyond a simple education or encouraged to proceed toward creativity.

If we scan any list of geniuses, we are immediately struck by the fact that men outnumber women by far. Must we conclude that women are inferior to men in the field of creativity? Many people believe so, and have believed so for many centuries; and they are allegedly supported by statistics. But statisticians know that numbers cannot be accepted at face value. They have to be interpreted. There is in fact no biological basis for this alleged inferiority of women in the field of creativity. Men and women differ anatomically and physiologically in some of their organs, endocrine glands, muscles, and bones; but these differences cannot serve to explain different performances so far as creativity is concerned. The only part of the organism that could physiologically explain the difference would be the central nervous system. But no researcher has thus far detected any differences in the central nervous systems of the two sexes that do so. The average adult human brain weighs about 1,400 grams, or approximately 2 percent of the total body weight. Inasmuch as women generally weigh less than men, their brains may also weigh less, but the variation is insignificant. When the ratio of brain weight to body weight is studied, it was found that generally women have a proportionately larger brain than men. What would be significant would be a difference in the number of neurons, but to my knowledge nobody has determined that women have a smaller number of neurons in their brains or a smaller number of neuronal ramifications. Estimates indicate that there are approximately 15 billion neurons in the cortex of both sexes. And the cortex, of course, is the essential organ for creativity. An anatomist or pathologist examining a brain removed from the body would not be able to say whether the brain was extracted from a male or a female. All neuroanatomical works, purporting to prove "the imperfections" of the female brain, have been superficial and not trustworthy (Stephanie Shields, 1975).

Since the time when primordial men left their arboreal haunts and became hunters, women were relegated to the functions of motherhood and household because they were physically weaker and less suited to hunting. The institution of the patriarchal society perpetuated this role. Subsequently, the socio-cultural environment was so devised as not to elicit in women a motivation to be creative. Some psychoanalysts (for instance, Ferenczi) have suggested that the motivation "to create" children has been a form of sublimation for women that has detracted them from other forms of creativity. Giving birth to children and raising them is certainly a demanding and in many respects creative job. However, we must not overlook the fact that this type of "sublimation" is what society has usually expected. In many eras and in some countries, even today, a woman who is not willing "to sublimate" in this way is considered peculiar or ready to abdicate her femininity. Virginia Woolf, a very creative woman, describes the position of women in England and elsewhere very well in her book *A Room of One's Own* (1929). On account of this position, women did not have the opportunity to emerge in any cultural field—as Woolf describes in the hypothetical case of an imaginary sister of William Shakespeare. The sister has the same initial abilities as her famous brother, but has no chance whatsoever of actualizing them in the England of her time. Even had she been able to go to school, the opportunity to write a play or have it performed or published would not have been there, just because she was a woman.

Even eminent people who have studied this problem have not

been devoid of prejudices about women. Cattell made early statistical studies of men of science in the United States (1903, 1906, 1910a, 1910b, 1926). In an article published in 1910 (1910b), he remarked that women engaged in scientific work in America neither increased in number nor improved their standing from 1903 to 1910. But from this he concluded that "There does not appear to be any social prejudice against women engaged in scientific work, and it is difficult to avoid the conclusions that there is an innate sexual disqualification." In a cavalier fashion, after only a superficial examination of the problem, he assumed that there was no prejudice and that therefore the disqualification must be *innate!* He accepted the possibility, however, that lack of encouragement played a role.

Cora Sutton Castle (1913) pursued the method developed by Cattell and made a list of 868 eminent women, through twenty-six centuries and from forty-two countries, who had achieved eminence as sovereigns, politicians, mothers, and mistresses. England, France, and Germany, in descending order, had the largest number of eminent women, but in degree of merit the French women ranked higher than those of any other nationality. American women ranked below average. Castle also made the following statement: these eminent women showed a marked tendency to acquire prominence in the field that was the same as or closely related to that of their fathers. On the whole, eminent women had not made particularly successful wives, since 11.6 percent of the 781 recorded unions ended in separation or divorce. This percentage seemed large at the time of the study; Castle may also have considered the percentage great in relation to the prevailing points of view about separation and divorce over the several centuries that she studied. She did not seem able to decide whether women are *innately inferior*, or whether the lack of opportunity accounted for their small showing among prominent persons during this long time period. And yet the author herself remarked that 63.1 percent of all the eminent women on her list lived in the very last two centuries covered by the inquiry, and 36.9 percent in the previous 24 centuries. This tremendous disparity should have demonstrated to her that the environment did have a great deal to do with the statistics.

Even when women have shown definite talent for several creative fields, they have been discouraged from pursuing their inclinations and encouraged to aim only at marriage, motherhood, and housekeeping. Throughout most of known history, women have been restricted to a few occupations. In many countries they have remained legally under the control of their fathers, husbands, or older brothers. If they did not get married, their condition was even worse. They were channeled toward subsidiary or less prominent positions. In the last two centuries—especially in the last fifty and even more so in the last twenty years—the situation has improved, but it still leaves much to be desired. Too many women (as compared to men) are still directed toward secretarial positions if they are lucky, and toward servile positions if they are not so lucky.

In conclusion, the striking disparity in the creativity displayed by men and women should convince everybody, not of the alleged inferiority of women, but of the extent and degree to which women have been mistreated by society. It is fair to assume that, given equal status and opportunities, they would have contributed as much as men.

In many instances discrimination against women is disguised in forms that do not appear discriminatory at all. As a matter of fact, some of these ways seem to fit into the framework of a liberal education. Torrance (1962) has illustrated how an overemphasis or misplaced emphasis on sex roles can affect children. He found that girls are reluctant to work with science toys and often declare that these toys are not suitable for them, whereas boys demonstrate twice as many ideas as girls in experiments with these materials. Torrance demonstrated, however, that this situation can be modified significantly by changing teaching conditions. Thus it is obvious that environmental pressures are already at work at early ages to stultify girls' motivations toward advancing in certain fields.

What we have said about women could be repeated about other groups of people: for instance, about minorities that had no access to cultural enlightenment. For instance, Jews who lived in Eastern Europe had no possibility for many centuries of pursuing a scientific career and consequently could not contribute to science; most of their contributions consisted of Biblical and Talmudic studies. And the severe oppression and later discrimination to which black people have been subjected in the United States and elsewhere is responsible for their lack of contributions in many fields. As Elkins (1968) has recently reported, in every southern state of the United States except Maryland and Kentucky, before the Civil War, it was forbidden to teach slaves reading and writing because education might promote insurrection and rebellion. In North Carolina it was a crime to distribute books to them, including the Bible. How could we expect people excluded by law from learning to read and write to produce geniuses?

It is true that free Africans in Africa have not contributed much to science and literature, but this lack of contribution can again be attributed to general socio-cultural conditions. When Tacitus, in writing about the Germans in 90–95 A.D., remarked about their lack of contributions, he could not have predicted that future generations of the same Germans could give to the world such people as Leibniz, Kant, Goethe, and Bach.

In conclusion, we cannot avoid experiencing a sense of utter dismay when we think of the waste of so much talent among women, oppressed minorities, and people kept from having access to cultural enrichment by the undeveloped state of their society. Who could predict how much more advanced civilization would be today were all the denizens of the earth given the possibility of participating in the growth of culture?

Cases may be pointed out where an unfair, restrictive, punitive, or oppressive society was in fact a stimulus to creativity. Individual instances are too numerous to be mentioned here, but one may think of Boethius, the great Roman statesman and philosopher, who wrote his famous *De Consolatione Philosophiae* during his imprisonment. Pellico also wrote in prison and prison was known all too well by Dostoevsky and Solzhenitsyn. Exile was imposed on such great people as Cicero, Ovid, Dante, and Marx—and again, among our contemporaries, Solzhenitsyn. If we examined all these cases accurately, we might say that the oppression they underwent was limited and did not have the intensity exhibited during the slavery of the blacks in the United States, or the persecution of the Jews by the Nazis. Even though Boethius was eventually executed in 524 A.D., he was mainly subjected to a Gothic rule that—thanks to the good offices of Boethius himself—was relatively nonmalevolent. Boethius, at least, was permitted to read, write, and meditate while he was in prison. Dante, condemned to death unless he left Florence, found benefactors in various parts of Italy. Marx could find refuge in England.

Black people in Louisiana developed the field of jazz music after their emancipation as a result of the Civil War. Similarly, after the removal of discriminatory anti-Semitic laws in many parts of Europe, Jews emerged as a cultural force in the second part of the nineteenth century. We can perhaps conclude that *freedom, or even retention of mod-*

erate discrimination, after severe oppression or absolute exclusion, is an incentive to creativity. This is the fifth creativogenic factor on our list. If such is the case, a great deal may be expected from women and black people in the next few decades.

It is easy to understand how a moderate discrimination, not so severe as to seriously injure the human spirit, may in many cases stimulate people even more than absolute freedom. A desire to challenge the difficulties, to fight for the abolition of whatever discrimination has remained, and to obtain what was previously denied can all be powerful motivations. Needless to say, I do *not* recommend this fifth way of promoting creativity, but I record it here as an explanation of what has happened in many instances.

A sixth important factor is *exposure to different and even contrasting cultural stimuli.* In most cultures, both the valuable and the not-so-valuable features tend to remain stable. Once they are well ingrained, they tend to become static. The fact that they have passed the test of time gives them respectability and predisposes people to retain them. However, when new stimuli are acquired from different cultures, the endowed person increases the possibility of creative syntheses never before conceived. One of the reasons why ancient Greece acquire her cultural prominence was her openness to different cultures and receptivity to some of their elements. As a matter of fact, some historians trace the beginning of Greek decline to a law made by the great Pericles which forbade foreigners to live in Athens.

Among other examples, Sicily and England have benefited from foreign invasions, with consequent exposure to different cultures; and the high achievements attained by Swiss citizens may be partially ascribed to the meeting and cross-fertilization of three different cultures: French, German, and Italian. The psychiatrist Ruesch (1957) has pointed out that, in proportion to her population, Switzerland has a much larger number of Nobel Prize winners than the United States.

The Italian Renaissance emerged as a combination of the rediscovered classic Greco-Roman culture and the medieval Christian culture in an environment of relative freedom and prosperity. The previous "age of faith" had eclipsed the classical world of antiquity, which, because it was pagan, was considered alien to the aim of saving the soul and therefore to be completely eliminated from study and consideration. In the thirteenth century, Christianity was by no means abolished but Christian medieval culture did disintegrate.

Christianity retained an important but not an all-inclusive role, permitting a new look at the classic Greco-Roman world.

Hellenism was not only artistically but also politically reborn in Italy. As a matter of fact, from the eleventh century on, Italian cities had obtained self-government with few or no ties to imperial and ecclesiastic authorities. The Italian "comuni" modeled their constitution on the Greek city-state. The preoccupation with reproducing reality, as the Greeks of the classic period had done, led to the invention of oil painting. However, as we mentioned in Chapter 9, the Italian Renaissance can by no means be considered a resuscitation of an extinct Hellenism. Hellenism and Christianity, which had fought each other for a millennium, could finally meet and merge. Christianity, the winner and no longer afraid of the pagan world, could accept and assimilate the greatness of the ancients. Exposure to the vital aspects of both cultures made possible the appearance of a Dante, a Petrarch, a Giotto. The contrasting elements of the two previous cultures permitted a synthesis on which the subsequent growth of Western culture was based.

Another example of the fruitful fusion of different elements occurs at the beginning of American democracy. The ideas and principles that brought forth the American revolution emerged from a combination of English philosophy, values, and traditions with the new adventurous, enterprising, and individualistic spirit of the American colonists.

The United States of America is in a privileged position today by virtue of its many cultural minorities living in what is basically an Anglo-Saxon culture. In general, if a mingling of all the minorities occurs, rather than an assimilation of these minorities into the predominant culture, then favorable conditions for creativity will arise. This leads to the seventh creativogenic factor: *tolerance for and interest in diverging views*. We refer here not only to views coming from different cultures, but to all kinds of divergences. A creative product often disturbs people because of its unfamiliarity. People feel more comfortable with what they know. The familiar ways do not demand altering old habits and acquiring new ones, do not bring about surprises that may be unpleasant. It is parsimonious to stick to the old.

Tolerance must be followed by an attitude of benevolent and inquisitive interest in whatever is new. Something newly created has a greater probability of being properly recognized if people are inclined to believe that they will obtain more from innovation than from perpetuation of the old ways. Furthermore, unless society—or at least an elite within it—acquires a tolerance for what was unacceptable before, the new has only a limited possibility of being recognized or of developing and expanding thereafter. If sufficient Christians of the thirteenth century had not developed a tolerance for the Hellenic age, no Renaissance would have emerged. If a French elite had not acquired a tolerance for unrealistic representation, modern art would not have developed. If scientists like Galileo had not relinquished intolerance for the experimental empirical method, modern science would not have developed. If the Church, after Galileo, had not acquired a tolerance for the new findings of science, even if they contrasted with a literal interpretation of the Bible, scientific creativity would have been hindered. Had Darwin lived at the time of Galileo, he would hardly have allowed himself to reach the conclusions he did, even had he obtained the necessary evidence.

Tolerance must exist at many levels. Society as a whole must be inclined to give careful consideration to different ideas, beliefs, customs, styles of life—to whatever appears original and divergent. The uncommon may not yet be creative, but if it becomes harmoniously blended with the common, it may produce new magic syntheses. Schools and institutions must permit independence of mind, dissent from society's norms, and unusualness in the broadest possible ways, including some sexual habits. Fears of losing their place in the establishment or the academic citadel should not induce teachers to resent pupils who advance unconventional ideas or are eager for new experimentations.

The eighth creativogenic factor is the *interaction of significant persons*. Significant persons do influence each other through their products and not necessarily by direct personal contact. Pythagoras and Euclid influenced thousands of mathematicians throughout Western history. Homer had a strong impact on Virgil, and Virgil on Dante. But this influence through the creative product is not what we are considering in this section. Nor are we considering the encounter of a particular teacher like Cimabue with a particular pupil like Giotto. Although these encounters are of crucial importance and bring about bursts of creativity, their influence is better studied on an individual basis. What we are considering here are groups of individuals who, by the accident of living in the same time and place, or by having the possibility of working in concert, determine an extraordinary effect. Such a possibility occurs more frequently in relation to social and historical events, but it is occasionally also found in science. In art it occurs relatively frequently, in film making.

The example that comes to mind first in reference to science is the release of atomic energy in a chain reaction. Manley (1960) called it "a triumph of experiment, deduction and theory to which many scientists, engineers and technicians contributed." However, since many facts about this development were never revealed, it is difficult to evaluate whether the individual contributions of such people as Fermi, Urey, Pegram or others, played the essential and indispensable role.

In the case of socio-politico-historical creativity, group interaction is easily accepted. For instance, many historians agree that if a small group of people consisting of Benjamin Franklin, George Washington, John Adams, Thomas Jefferson, John Jay, Alexander Hamilton, and James Madison had not lived and emerged at the same time, the American Revolution and the writing of the American constitution could not have taken place (see Morris 1973). (Some authors add a few more persons—Samuel Adams, James Wilson, and Thomas Paine—to this group of founding fathers.) It is difficult to think of comparable leadership in any other country. The importance of the contrasting socio-cultural elements in the America of that time has already been discussed; however, the astounding effect of the encounter of these men, emerging from a total population of less than three million, was also necessary. What if these people had not appeared and influenced one another? They determined the destiny of the United States during their time and have continued to do so since then. They were important leaders not only during the Revolutionary War but also in the development of the federal and national governments. Even the other great revolution of the same century, the French Revolution, did not have leaders of comparable caliber. The groundwork for the French Revolution, however, was prepared by a group of remarkable philosophers, such as Rousseau, Voltaire, and Diderot.

The unity of Italy after many centuries of servitude or of being divided into small states is also an important example of socio-political creativity. It is generally attributed (in addition to the preparatory work of an elite) to the simultaneous appearance of three great men: Mazzini, an inspiring idealist; Garibaldi, a military man; and Cavour, the able minister of foreign affairs. The presence of a fourth man was also necessary, not because of his brilliance or creativity, but because of the position he happened to hold at that particular time. I am referring to Victor Emanuel II, who was king of the little kingdom of Piedmont and Sardinia, and who offered a constitution and monarchy under which the whole of Italy could be accepted as a legitimate political unit.

The promotion of incentives and awards is the ninth and last factor that we shall consider. The greatest award to creativity is creativity itself; nothing could please the creative person more than the act itself of doing, or having accomplished, his creative work. Nevertheless, external incentives and awards strengthen the motivation, and they have a well-known reinforcing effect. In ancient Greece, the prizes given to athletes and playwrights served to promote athletics and the theater. Indeed, throughout history—from the crown of laurel given to such poets as Petrarch, to the conferring of Nobel Prizes in our own time—the institution of prizes has promoted creativity. Torrance (1963, 1964, 1969) has repeatedly and very appropriately quoted Plato's famous statement that "What is honored in a country will be cultivated there."

As we have already discussed, the fact that creative people have emerged in hostile environments does not disprove the fact that, statistically speaking, a society that honors and enhances creativity is more likely to bring it about. Financial security seems to have been of help to such people as Goethe, Darwin, Byron, and Croce, although we also know of poverty-stricken creative people like Rembrandt, Balzac, Rousseau, Dostoevsky, and many, many others.

Let us now give a final overview to the nine socio-cultural creativogenic factors that we have considered:

1. Availability of cultural means.
2. Openness to cultural stimuli.
3. Stress on becoming and not just on being.
4. Free access to cultural media for all citizens, without discrimination.
5. Freedom, or even the retention of moderate discrimination, after severe oppression or absolute exclusion.
6. Exposure to different and even contrasting cultural stimuli.
7. Tolerance for diverging views.
8. Interaction of significant persons.
9. Promotion of incentives and awards.

Probably only the first one is absolutely necessary. The other eight, although important, are not such factors that a tremendous effort on the part of the creative person could not overcome or remedy their absence. But although important, these nine factors are not sufficient to bring about creativity. They constitute only the *input* for the open system of individual creativity described in Chapter 13. What are essential are the intrapsychic elements of the creative person.

Another often-debated question is whether a so-called "happy" society can provide a good climate for creativity. Indeed it does seem that if people are contented in their milieu, they tend to be conservative and unenthusiastic about innovations. The answer to the question really hinges on the definition of happiness. A society that is really happy does not want to put limitations on any advancement of the human spirit. On the other hand, it is probably true that some forms of creativity—for instance, in religion, social reforms, and politics—are facilitated by mass discontent. The necessities of war may also promote inventiveness. For instance, the need to defeat Hitler facilitated the development of nuclear science. Finally, we must consider that beneficial cultural changes are also often determined by adverse historical events. The Romans, for instance, imposed their civilization by force on the nations they conquered.

The Phenomenon of Creativity among Jews in Modern Times

IS IT POSSIBLE to ascertain whether the nine factors that we have described in the previous section are really creativogenic? The answer is no. However, we can search for groups of people living in our era, or in the not too distant past, who have been creative far beyond what would have been expected from their numbers, and see whether they were in fact exposed to the nine factors that we have outlined. It is obvious that any conclusion is only presumptive or tentative, however.

One group that lends itself relatively easily to examination is that of the Jewish people from the middle of the nineteenth century to our time. Jews have been persecuted for many centuries in Europe. The persecution has ranged from the massacre of whole communities to pogroms and discriminations of various kinds. Only at the time of the

French Revolution was concern for the plight of the Jews expressed by the responsible elements of society. Mirabeau (1749–1791) wrote, "There is only one thing to be lamented, that so highly gifted a nation should so long have been kept in a state wherein it was impossible for its powers to develop, and every farsighted man must rejoice in the acquisition of useful fellow-citizens from among the Jews." However, it was Napoleon Bonaparte, after his return from victory at Austerlitz (1806) who paid great consideration to the emancipation of the Jews. He wrote, "I desire to take every means to ensure that the rights which were restored to the Jewish people be not illusory." He added that he hoped to find a Jerusalem for them in France. Napoleon's innovations were slowly implemented after his fall. Their spirit remained, however; and with the revolution of 1848, which began in France and expanded to Prussia, Austria, and Italy, a wave of liberation developed that soon conferred rights to Jews equal to those of other citizens. Since then an outstanding development of creativity took place on the part of Jews or of people of Jewish origin. Of the four people who have revolutionized the socio-cultural world since then, two (Freud and Einstein) were Jews, and one (Marx) was the son of Jewish parents converted to Christianity. (Darwin was the fourth man.)

It may be illuminating to examine briefly the contributions of Jews in fields in which they had made only minimal contributions before the emancipation: music and fine arts. Whereas before the emancipation the only Jew who had distinguished himself in music was the Italian Salomone Rossi (1565–1628), after the emancipation such people emerged as Giacomo Meyerbeer (1791–1864), Felix Mendelssohn (1809–1847), Jacques Offenbach (1819–1880), Gustav Mahler (1860–1911), Arnold Schoenberg (1874–1951), Ernest Bloch (1880–1959), and George Gershwin (1898–1937). And in modern art such names emerged as those of Camille Pissarro (1830–1903), Isidor Kaufmann (1853–1921), Jehudo Epstein (1870–1945), Amedeo Modigliani (1884–1920), Chaim Soutine (1893–1943), and Marc Chagall (1887–   ).

Jews who have emerged in the field of science are too numerous to be mentioned here. Lewis S. Feuer (1963) speaks of an actual scientific revolution among the Jews after the emancipation. He wrote, "The Italian Jewish community . . . was one of the smallest in Europe; at the time of *risorgimento*, in the nineteenth century, it consisted of only forty thousand persons. But with the advent of freedom, there was no country of Europe where the Jewish contribution was proportionately so great. To science it gave Levi Civita, creator of tensor calculus; Peano, pioneer in the foundations of mathematics; Vito Volterra, analyst of hysteresis; and Federico Enriques, philosopher of science."

Indeed, it would be too long and be out of place to try to enumerate the Jewish contributions to all fields of culture during this modern period. However, it may be interesting to examine the proportion of Jews, or people of Jewish descent, who have been awarded Nobel Prizes since 1899. The following tables and graphs clearly disclose the Jewish percentage of Nobel laureates from 1901 to 1970.* Nobel winners after 1970 are not included. The rate of Jewish winners is compared to that of the general world and to that of four representative nations: Argentina, France, Germany, and Italy. (The population of the Jewish minority was subtracted from the populations of these nations.) Table 14-1 shows the number of Nobel Prize winners per unit population (one million people) for each time period. The last column indicates the average of the seven periods for each ethnic group. Tables 14-1 and 14-2 illustrate graphically the incidence of five ethnic groups of Nobel Prize winners. Table 14-2 shows the ratio of each national group's prize-winning quotient to that of the remaining population (Jewish population of that particular nation being excluded). The last column gives the ratios of the averages from Table 14-1, not the average of the ratios shown in Table 14-2.

These statistics show that in the seventy-year period from 1901 to 1970, the ratio of Argentine winners to winners from the rest of the world is 1.3; that of the Italian, 1.6; of the German, 4.4; of the French, 6.3. But the ratio of the Jewish winners is 28 times greater than that of the rest of the world population.

Graph 14-1 shows how the percentage of Jews, although always greater than that of the world population, Argentinian, Italian, German, and French people, undergoes a sharp decline during the period of Nazi persecution. All the graphs are self-explanatory. It is interesting to note that Jews exceed in all categories with the exception of the Peace Prize, where they are surpassed by the French and the Argentinians. If we examine the five fields in which prizes are assigned, we

* Mr. Marcel Meth prepared the statistical work necessary for this research. His contribution is greatly appreciated.

Table 14–1
Nobel Prize Winners Per Million *

	1901–1910	1911–1920	1921–1930	1931–1940	1941–1950	1951–1960	1961–1970	Average over Seventy Years
Jewish Winners	0.68	0.35	0.46	0.13	0.57	0.83	1.42	0.64
Non-Jewish Winners	0.034	0.020	0.024	0.022	0.018	0.023	0.019	0.023
French Non-Jewish Winners	0.26	0.19	0.16	0.12	0.024	0.12	0.042	0.13
German Non-Jewish Winners	0.19	0.097	0.12	0.085	0.041	0.044	0.080	0.093
Italian Non-Jewish Winners	0.13	0.00	0.025	0.023	0.00	0.042	0.039	0.037
Argentinian Non-Jewish Winners	0.00	0.00	0.00	0.084	0.070	0.00	0.046	0.029

* These figures are rounded off.

notice that the greatest Jewish contributions are in the fields of medicine and physics. Their contribution to chemistry and literature, although superior to that of other groups examined, is less outstanding.*

* The nationality of a winner, in the tables, was considered to be the one the winner had at the time the prize was awarded. The population was considered in groups of ten years, taking the average population for one year during each period. These means were obtained by averaging the extremes (first and last years) of each period. Because of the small degree of variance in birth and death rates, this procedure should be of significant accuracy. Sources of information: *Encyclopaedia Judaica* (1971, Vol. 13, pp. 890–891, 894, 895); *The World Almanac and Encyclopedia* (1921, p. 441; 1941, p. 510); *The World Almanac and Book of Facts* (1951, p. 433); *Statistical Abstract of the United States* (1901, p. 363; 1911, p. 911; 1922, pp. 689–690; 1931, pp. 584–585; 1941, pp. 850–851; 1952, p. 923; 1962, p. 911); *American Jewish Yearbook* (1901–1902, p. 159; 1911–1912, p. 269; 1922–1923, pp. 300–302; 1927–1928, p. 232; 1931–1932, pp. 282–283; 1934–1935, pp. 377–378; 1937, p. 560; 1940, p. 584; 1950, pp. 247–248; 1960, pp. 351–353; 1961, p. 382; 1970, pp. 538–53); Matras (1973); *Information Please Almanac* (1951, 1975); Department of Economic and Social Affairs. *Growth of the World* (1969 n. 44, p. 14), [Marcel Meth]

Table 14–2
Ratio of Nationality to World Winners

	1901–1910	1911–1920	1921–1930	1931–1940	1941–1950	1951–1960	1961–1970	Average over Seventy Years
Jewish Winners Non-Jewish Winners	20	18	19	5.7	32	36	75	28
(Non-Jewish) French Winners (Non-Jewish, Non-French) World Winners	9.3	11	7.4	6.0	1.4	5.3	2.3	6.3
(Non-Jewish) German Winners (Non-Jewish, Non-German) World Winners	6.9	5.6	5.4	4.3	2.4	1.7	4.1	4.4
(Non-Jewish) Italian Winners (Non-Jewish, Non-Italian) World Winners	4.1	0.0	1.0	1.1	0.0	1.8	2.1	1.6
(Non-Jewish) Argentinian Winners (Non-Jewish, Non-Argentinian) World Winners	0.0	0.0	0.0	3.8	4.0	0.0	2.4	1.3

How are these statistics to be evaluated? According to Feuer (1963), the best-known theory that has been advanced to account for the high contribution to science is probably the one set forth by Veblen (1934). According to Veblen, the Jew is an alienated intellectual. He has abandoned his "thearchic culture" without finding a "secure place in the scheme of gentile conventions into which he is thrown." The Jew's alienation makes him a skeptic, a dispassionate inquirer, a complete follower of the scientific method. According to Veblen, to preserve the high level of his contribution the Jew must be preserved in his state of alienation.

Feuer rejects Veblen's interpretation and sees it as a projection of

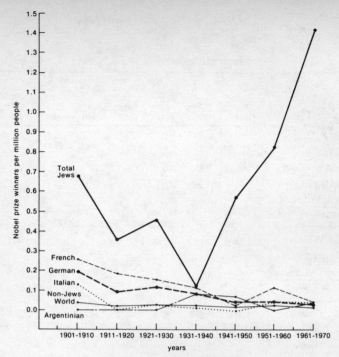

Graph 14-1a

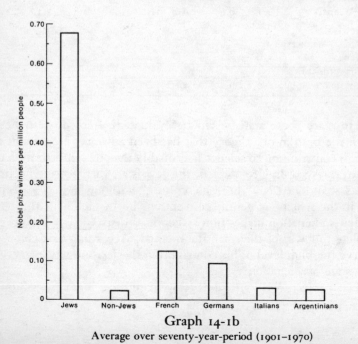

Graph 14-1b

Average over seventy-year-period (1901–1970)

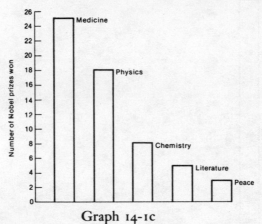

Graph 14-1c

Number of Nobel Prizes won by Jews by categories over seventy-year-period
(1901-1970)

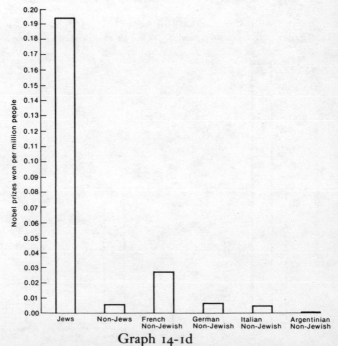

Graph 14-1d

Average over seventy-year-period of Nobel Prizes for physics (1901-1970)

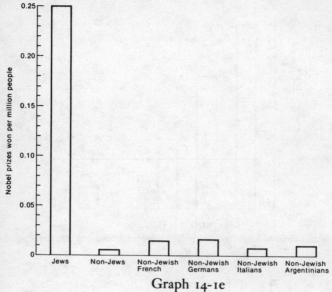

Graph 14-1e

Average over seventy-year-period of Nobel Prizes for medicine (1901–1970)

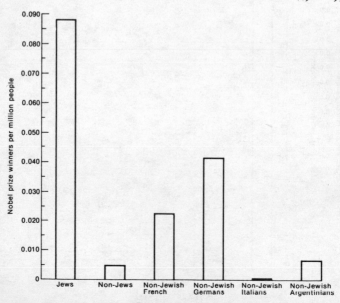

Graph 14-1f

Average over seventy-year-period of Nobel Prizes for chemistry (1901–1970)

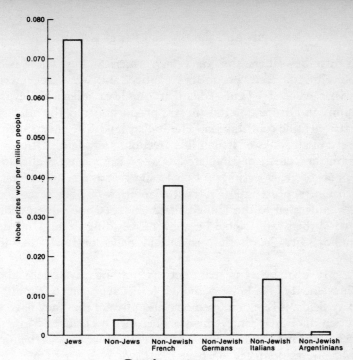

Graph 14-1g

Average over seventy-year-period of Nobel Prizes for literature (1901–1970)

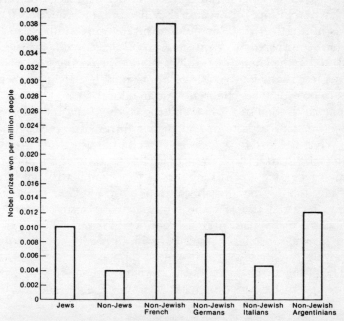

Graph 14-1c

Average over seventy-year-period of Nobel Prizes for peace (1901–1970)

his own life's labors, the Norwegian-American boy who was never at home in American "pecuniary" culture, and who felt "interned" in American society. Feuer adds that "the least 'alienated' Jewish community in Europe, the Italian, was proportionately the most vigorous in its scientific contribution. The Italian Jewish scientists mixed most freely in all walks of Italian life; freedom and identification with the dominant secularism stimulated its work, not a sense of alienation." In support of Feuer's criticism I could add that as a result of Fascist persecution, approximately 1,500 Italian Jews of both sexes and of all ages emigrated to the United States in 1939 and subsequent years. Two of them won Nobel Prizes while residing in the United States: Emilio Segre (in physics, 1959) and Salvador Luria (in medicine, 1969).

My own belief is that there is nothing mysterious about the achievement of the Jews. Although Jews have achieved prominence in many fields, it is only in medicine and physics that they have reached the zenith of their achievements. There are no Dantes, Shakespeares, Bachs, or Michelangelos among the Jews. If we look at the nine creativogenic factors listed on page [324], we realize that most of them were available to the Jews. Taking them in turn:

The Jews have not excelled when, either because of persecution (as in Eastern Europe) or because they lived in underdeveloped countries (as in North Africa), no cultural means were available to them. Jews have prospered in Western Europe (except during the Nazi period) and in the United States, where their belonging, to a relatively large degree, to the bourgeoisie or upper middle class gave them the means to provide their children with an education.

The cultivation of reading and the study of the Bible fostered a love for literacy, education, and higher forms of knowledge in the Jews. When the love for education is well established, it is relatively easy to make the transition from an exclusive study of religious books to studies including other disciplines as well. Familiarity with the abstract ideation of the Jewish religion (abstract God, rejection of imagery, focus on ethics) made Jews particularly suited for the abstractions of mathematical and scientific thinking. There was thus among Jews an openness to cultural stimuli hardly equalled by any other group.

The prophetic character of the Jewish religion—the emphasis on the ethical transformation of man, on the one side, and the uncertainty as to what tomorrow will bring—led Jews to emphasize *becoming* and not just *being*.

When we consider the fourth factor—free access to cultural media for all citizens without discrimination—we recall having already observed that Jews could excel only when no discrimination existed against them and they consequently had free access to cultural media. Also in modern times, Jews did not show prejudice against women who pursued careers. Among the famous Jewish women of modern times we could mention Rosa Luxemburg (1871–1919), an economist and revolutionary well known for her theory of imperialism; and Emmy Noether (1882–1935), daughter and sister of other eminent mathematicians, who became, according to Bell (1937), the "leading woman mathematician of our time, the most creative abstract algebraist in the world." She also initiated advances in noncommutative algebra. Finally we must mention Golda Meir (1898–   ), who is one of the few women to achieve premiership in our century.

Factors 5, 6, and 7 certainly apply to the Jewish people. From what we have already mentioned, it is easy to assume that "freedom or even retention of moderate discrimination after severe oppression or absolute exclusion" describes the conditions in which Jews found themselves after the emancipation. After centuries of oppression, they had a strong desire to emerge and to compensate for the past deprivation. Wherever anti-Semitism was not exerted to an incapacitating degree, Jews were motivated to fight it and to neutralize its adverse effects. Sensitized as they were to society's unfairness, they were always in favor of social innovations and reforms. Also, factor 6, "exposure to different and even contrasting cultural stimuli," applies particularly to Jews. The meeting of the old Hebrew culture with the rest of Western civilization provided such a contrast. Even in assimilated Jews, old habits of thought (such as a preference for abstract thinking) continued to prevail. Tolerance for diverging views, whether they come from the majority or other minorities, has always been a prevailing attitude among Jews. In the Old Testament, Jews are always reminded that they were a persecuted minority in the land of Egypt and that they should practice no discrimination whatsoever against the stranger, the outsider, the guest, the neighbor. Having been a minority for such a large part of their history, they have come to appreciate very highly the value of tolerance.

Interactions of significant persons have probably occurred more frequently among the Jews because of their many international connections. Factor 9 has also affected Jews, not in the sense that incentives and awards were reserved to them alone, but in the sense that they have honored scholarship and innovation very highly. They have again confirmed Plato's statement that what is honored is going to be cultivated.

In conclusion, the evidence reported in this chapter does not prove that the Jews are biologically superior to non-Jews. Their great achievements since the middle of the nineteenth century can be attributed to a large extent to socio-cultural factors prevailing in Jewish milieus. The study of these socio-cultural factors is useful because, if we exclude factor 5 for obvious reasons and promote the other eight, we may find that they can benefit Jews and non-Jews alike, and as a matter of fact the whole of mankind.

PART FIVE

The Individual and the

Cultivation of

Creativity

Chapter 15
The Creative Person

MANY AUTHORS have tried to define the personality of the creative individual, or at least to differentiate the individual characteristics that make a person creative. The topic is intriguing and promising. Were we able to reach some conclusions, we would be in a better position (1) to promote the special characteristics, and (2) to recognize people who already have such characteristics, so that we could encourage them toward creative pursuits.

Two major approaches can be recognized in the study of the creative personality. One is holistic; that is, it is the study of the personality of the creative person in its totality, or at least its major divisions. The second approach is the study of the specific ingredients of such a personality.

The Total Personality

MASLOW is representative of the first approach (1959a, 1972). According to him, creative people are self-actualizing persons, not dissimilar to those who undergo what he called "peak experiences." These are profound and invasive moments of life that change the person and his appreciation of the world, perhaps through aesthetic, loving, insightful, orgasmic, and mystical experiences.

The Individual and the Cultivation of Creativity

In a paper delivered in 1968 shortly before his death and published posthumously (1972), Maslow stated that the personality characteristics listed by Torrance (1962) as conducive to creativity correlate by and large with those Maslow described in self-actualizing people. Maslow believed that the determinants of creativeness are literally in the thousands; it is futile to trace them back in an attempt to develop an easy road to creativity. He believed that people who search for these easy routes give the impression of "looking for some secret button to push, like switching a light on and off."

Maslow thought that the creative person is a particular or special kind of human being who has to be considered holistically and not atomistically. There is no prescription for the pursuit of creativeness, just as there is no easy prescription for fighting prejudices. These pursuits have to be cultivated indirectly. He quoted his colleague, R. Jones (1960), who ran a group therapy course with high school seniors and found at the end of the year that racial and ethnic prejudice had gone down, in spite of the fact that throughout the course he had not even mentioned those words. Prejudice is neither created nor combated by direct approach but in a roundabout fashion, by preparing a general climate against it. The same can be said of creativity.

Maslow's approach elicits a sympathetic response in us. We feel he is right when he says that there is no special button for creativity and that the creative person has to be interpreted holistically. The trouble is that this approach does not lend itself to educational pursuits and does not offer even general directions. It generally ends up with tautological statements such as that "the creative person must have a creative personality" or that "in order to promote creativity, we must prepare a climate for creativity."

Some authors have felt it advisable to stress again the difference between talent and genius or the highest degree of creativity. Talent is seen as an inborn characteristic that has to be cultivated in order to bring about (in some cases) genius or great creativity. In his book *Genius and Creative Intelligence* (1931), Nathaniel Hirsh discussed, among many other aspects of the problem, the difference between talent and genius. He wrote (pp. 288–289): "Geniuses themselves . . . know that they are not of the same breed as talented persons and are cognizant of greater differences in relation to the talented than to any other group, including the peasant and the prince, the insane and the imbecile. By inherent nature they are antagonistic: the genius creates, the man of talent improves; the genius intuits, the man of talent analyzes and explores; the genius aspires, his life goal is creativity; the talented are animated by ambition and their life goal is power; the genius is ever a stranger in a strange land, a momentary sojourner in a strange interlude; the talented are those for whom the earth is a paradise and social adjustment a natural and frictionless vocation. But the genius also has talent, and the development of his talent enables him to objectify his creativity and render it permanent. Genius with but little talent is like a great intellect with poor linguistic abilities; talent without genius is like a brilliant tongue attached to a feeble head."

Hirsh quoted the philosopher Schopenhauer, who wrote, ". . . talent is an excellence which lies rather in the greater versatility and acuteness of discursive than of intuitive knowledge. He who is endowed with talent thinks more quickly and more correctly than others; but the genius beholds another world from them all, although only because he has a more profound perception of the world which lies before them also, in that it presents in his mind more objectively and consequently in greater purity and distinctness." Hirsh seems to approve of the concept of genius to which Schopenhauer, himself a genius, adhered. In *The World As Will and Idea* (Vol. III, on Genius), Schopenhauer wrote that the fundamental characteristic of genius is to see the particular in the universal. I believe that implied in Schopenhauer's statement is the qualification "when such insight is not apparent." One such case would be that of Newton, as reported in Chapter 11, who saw the falling apple as a particular of the universal "body subjected to gravity."

Hirsh also wrote (pp. 291–292), "Another characteristic of genius, according to Schopenhauer, proceeding from their unique kind of knowing is objectivity of the mind of the genius. This is natural, since their thinking is separated from the bodily inclination and subjective desires. The works of genius are produced by an inner or 'instinctive necessity'; genius never proceeds from intention or choice, nor from utility nor gain. For the genius, his works are an *end*, sufficient and necessary in themselves; for others a *means*."

Lange-Eichbaum (1932), too, marked a distinction between talent and genius. Whereas talent is an inborn endowment, "genius is the consummation of sociological, religious, and psychological factors." According to Lange-Eichbaum there is no need to breed talent, as talent is much more common than people assume. It is more advisable "to promote the development of extant talent . . . than to undertake the doubtful experiment of breeding talent for a remote future."

Creativity and Intelligence

MANY RESEARCHERS have investigated whether there is a correlation between intelligence and creativity. There is as yet no unanimous consent on the matter. The prevailing opinion is that highly intelligent persons are not necessarily creative. Although creative people are intelligent persons, an exceptionally high I.Q. is not a prerequisite for creativity. On the contrary, it may inhibit the inner resources of the individual because his self-criticism becomes too rigid or he learns too quickly what the cultural environment has to offer. We must add that a great ability to deduce according to the laws of logic and mathematics makes for disciplined thinkers but not necessarily for creative people.

Getzel and Jackson (1962) made a careful study of creativity (giftedness) and intelligence in children and concluded that they could identify two groups of students, one exhibiting high intelligence but not concomitantly high creativity as its salient characteristic, the other high creativity but not concomitantly high intelligence. Getzel and Jackson compared the scholastic achievements of one group of pupils, who ranked in the upper 20 percent on traditional measures of intelligence (I.Q. tests) but not in the upper 20 percent on tests of creativity, with another group in which they put students who ranked in the upper 20 percent on creativity but not on I.Q. In spite of a difference of 23 I.Q. points between the two groups, there was no measurable difference in achievement.

Torrance (1962, 1964) replicated Getzel and Jackson's studies: six of eight replications yielded results almost identical to those they had obtained. Even in the two exceptions, a significant relationship was detected between measures of creativity and measures of achievement. Moreover, considerable overachievement among the highly creative was evident.

Low correlations between intelligence and creativity have also been reported by other authors (Hammer 1961; Flescher 1963; Cir-

cirelli 1965). Cline, Richards, and Abe (1962) reported that a combination of intelligence and creativity brings about much more academic achievement than either alone. Wade (1968) concluded, as a result of her study of more than 105 tenth-grade students, that although there is a certain correlation between intelligence and creativity, "there is also some reason to suspect that creativity is fostered by a particular type of environment which has little effect on intelligence. The correlation between intelligence and creativity can easily be attributed to the common factors involved; the remaining variance appears to depend on the psychological safety and freedom (to use Rogers's concepts) in which the child is encouraged to present himself as an independent individual."

Anastasi and Schaefer (1971) are not so sure that creativity and intelligence are distinct and independent entities. As a result of their study of creativity among high school students in the New York metropolitan area, as well as data collected in the literature, they found a great correlation. They concluded by proposing "that the term 'creativity,' like the term 'intelligence,' be recognized as referring to a loosely defined, broad, and many-faceted concept. Both terms will undoubtedly survive as independent concepts because they provide convenient shortcuts in designating complex behavior domains of considerable practical importance. But neither corresponds to a precisely defined or distinct entity. Each comprises a multiplicity of identifiable traits, organized in a pattern of relationships that cuts across the two domains."

Correlations between intelligence and creativity were also determined by the study of the life history of great men. Some, such as Darwin, Einstein, and Churchill, did not do well in school. On the other hand, Cox (1926), collecting information on the childhood attainments of three hundred historical geniuses, demonstrated that they were far above average. Darwin's childhood I.Q. was about 150, and Goethe, Pascal, and Macauley had I.Q.'s of above 180. As reported by Johnson (1972), "We know that John Stuart Mill was reading at age three, so we can divide mental age by chronological age and get an I.Q. estimate of 200 for young John. A mental age of about fourteen is necessary for algebra and he learned algebra at eight, so another I.Q. estimate would be 175. In Mill's case there are several such facts that permit estimates, the average of which is 190 for his childhood and 170 for his youth." Relying partly on the works of Cox

(1926), Johnson reports that Goethe, who wrote poetry in Latin when he was eight, was scored 185 for his childhood and 200 for his youth. Pascal scored 180, Voltaire 175, Mozart 155. In general, great philosophers averaged 170, poets, novelists, and dramatists 160, and scientists 155.

Needless to say, these data are based on anecdotal information or on very biased biographies or autobiographies. There seems to be a certain correlation between intelligence and creativity; however, there also seems to be a considerable amount of divergence. There is no doubt that many very intelligent people do not distinguish themselves for creativity, while many creative people do not seem to have an exceptionally high I.Q. In my own psychoanalytic and psychiatric practice I have come in contact, not with geniuses, but with creative people who have emerged to a considerably high degree in literature, entertainment, and science, and especially in the business world. Although I could not draw up accurate statistics, I believe I may say that only in 45 to 50 percent of my cases was an outstanding creative life correlated to a very high I.Q. None of these creative people, however, had an estimated I.Q. inferior to 120. It is possible that in at least some cases the I.Q. would have been higher had these persons not undergone personality difficulties at the time of testing.

The Specific Personality Characteristics of the Creative Individual

AS ALREADY MENTIONED, a very large number of authors have tried in various ways to detect and describe unusual characteristics in the personality of the creative individual. To what extent these characteristics are specific, necessary, or sufficient to promote creativity remains to be established. It also remains to be determined whether these characteristics really correspond to existent psychological entities, or whether they are merely verbal expressions of subjective evaluations. Some adjectives or terms—for example, *divergent*—condense into one word meanings that in other classifications are divided into many categories. Some of these descriptions or designations follow common sense or common parlance and are easily understood, however. We shall review here the most common lists, or what seem to me to be the most important classifications, of the characteristics of the creative individual.

According to Nathaniel Hirsh (1931, pp. 321–331) the genius stands out because of six special personality traits: he is (1) bashful, (2) oversensitive, (3) sincere, and (4) melancholy; and he (5) requires solitude and (6) values friendship, which he considers a "sacred relation."

Torrance (1962) surveyed a large number of studies and compiled a list of eighty-four characteristics that aimed at differentiating highly creative persons from less creative ones. He listed them in alphabetic order, from "*a*ccepts disorder" to "*w*ithdrawn." Most of the characteristics seem desirable for any human being; for example, a highly creative person is described as altruistic, energetic, industrious, persistent, self-assertive, and versatile. But some entries on the list refer to diverging traits; for example, the person is attracted to the mysterious, defies conventions, is independent in judgment and thinking, has oddities of habit, is radical. Others at first impression seem negative: the person is discontented, disturbs organization, is a fault-finder, makes mistakes, is stubborn and temperamental, and so on.

Torrance is in agreement with Smillie (1959) in objecting to an overemphasis on traditional academic values, and in thinking that the limited conceptualizations of intelligence represented by the Stanford-Binet and the Wechsler tests do not disclose the unique and creative qualities of those who do not fit the patterns measured by the tests. He also supports McNeil (1960) in believing that creativity requires unconventional thinking and in considering creativity and conformity antithetical. We must differentiate between the talented conformists "who can be trained to become the brilliant enhancers, embroiderers, and manipulators of the ideas of others, and the equally talented nonconformists who may make imaginative breakthroughs to new knowledge" (Torrance 1962, p. 20). Torrance stresses that creativity requires both sensitivity and independence. In Western culture sensitivity is a feminine virtue, while independence is masculine. Thus Torrance believes that we may expect the creative boy to appear more effeminate than his peers, and the creative girl more masculine than other girls.

In a clear article, Mary Henle (1962) describes the conditions for creative thinking. The first requisite is *receptivity*. According to Henle, "We cannot get creative ideas by searching for them; but if we are not receptive to them, they will not come. Creative ideas are not, in other words, under our voluntary control; yet they require a certain attitude on our part." Henle adds that the original idea comes to thinkers "like a foreign guest," as Goethe said. Receptiveness "involves detaching oneself from one's ongoing concerns and without particular expectations, heeding the ideas that come." Receptivity to ideas also demands that they be actively welcomed. A second condition of creative thinking, according to Henle, is *immersion* in one's subject matter. This immersion not only gives us the materials with which to think, it also acquaints us with the difficulties of the problem. Other requirements are the *ability to see the right questions, to use errors,* and *to have detached devotion.* In explaining "detached devotion," Henle very aptly writes that creative work seems to demand both passionate interest and a certain degree of detachment.

Guilford, to whose work we have already given consideration in Chapter 2, stressed the cognitive characteristics of the creative person. He found that *a generalized sensitivity to problems* is a prerequisite to creativity (1950). This factor was later identified as an evaluative ability: a judgment that things are not all right and that goals have not been achieved (Guilford 1957a). The person is attuned to the realization of what needs to be done.

A second factor found by Guilford is *fluency of thinking,* or fertility of ideas. Actually, according to works that Guilford did with collaborators (Wilson, Guilford et al. 1954), there are four separate fluency factors. The first three have to do with words: (1) word fluency, or the ability to produce words, each containing a specified letter or combination of letters; (2) associational fluency, or the ability to produce as many synonyms as the testee can find for a given word in a limited time; and (3) expressional fluency, or the ability to juxtapose words to meet the requirements of sentence structure. The fourth, and most important, is ideational fluency, the ability to produce ideas to fulfill certain requirements in a limited time: to offer solutions to problems.

Another important factor for creativity is *flexibility,* or the ability to abandon old ways of thinking and initiate different directions. Flexibility may be *spontaneous,* when it is a disposition to advance a large variety of ideas without inertia being exhibited by thought processes; flexibility is *adaptive,* when it is aimed at the solution of a specific problem.

Other factors are *originality*, or the ability to produce uncommon responses and unconventional associations; and *redefinition*, or the ability to reorganize what we know or see in new ways. Later Guilford and some associates (Berger, Guilford, and Christensen 1957) added a new factor, *elaboration*, or the capacity to use two or more abilities for the construction of a more complex object. Guilford also proposed a theoretical model of the intellect that, in the words of Torrance (1963), provided workers in this area with something analogous to Mendeleev's periodic table of the elements: the three categories, "materials, operations, and products," were represented in a three-dimensional diagram. How much will come from this classification is for future researchers to determine. The reader is referred to the original works (Guilford 1957a, 1959).

Taylor is another author who has explored creativity in many ways. In a review article (1964) he distinguishes three groups of factors that have a great deal to do with creativity: namely, intellectual, motivational, and personality factors. Among the intellectual factors he includes memory, cognition, evaluation, convergent production, and divergent production. Among the motivational factors he includes drive, dedication to work, resourcefulness, striving for general principles, desire to bring order out of disorder, and desire for discovery. Among the personality factors he includes independence, self-sufficiency, tolerance of ambiguity, femininity of interests, and professional self-confidence.

Frank Barron is outstanding, among the authors who have worked on creativity, for his repeated efforts to understand and to cultivate this human faculty. It is impossible to review here all of his contributions to the study of the personality of the creative person. Among the works that appeal particularly to me are the ones on "The Disposition Toward Originality" (Barron 1963a) and "The Needs for Order and for Disorder as Motives in Creative Activity" (Barron 1963b). Barron believes that originality is almost habitual with persons who have new insights—but at this point we must stress that Barron does not consider just any type of originality, as discussed in Chapter 1; he takes into consideration only uncommon but correct solutions to special tests that he has devised. Thus originality, for Barron, is equivalent to producing unusual adaptive responses. In other words, the concept of originality for him is very close to that of creativity itself.

Barron's subjects, who were Ph.D. candidates in the sciences, showed a marked preference for complex and asymmetrical line drawings as opposed to simple and symmetrical drawings. Five hypotheses suggested by his previous work were confirmed: (1) that original persons prefer complexity and some degree of apparent imbalance in phenomena; (2) that original persons are more complex psychodynamically and have greater personal scope; (3) that original persons are more independent in their judgments; (4) that original persons are more self-assertive and dominant; and (5) that original persons reject suppression as a mechanism for the control of impulse. Barron also makes pertinent comments on these findings. In discussing the confirmed hypothesis 5, he states that although suppression is a common way of achieving unity, this method works only in the short run and not when the person faces increasing complexity. Originality "flourishes where suppression is at a minimum and where some measure of disintegration is tolerable in the interests of a final higher level of integration." And dominance, referred to in hypothesis 4, means a "need for personal mastery, not merely over other persons, but over all experience."

For the purpose of evaluating the need for order and disorder in creative people, Barron showed different drawings to doctoral candidates in several departments of the faculty of science at the University of California. The drawings varied from very simple geometrical forms such as straight lines, circles, squares, and triangles, to very disarranged configurations that were almost childish scrawls. Barron was able to establish a correlation between "originality" and a preference for disordered, irregular, or even chaotic figures. He added that the same kind of preference was shown by artists, even among active painters. He concluded that creative individuals have an attraction for phenomenal fields that do not reproduce geometrical order but that require new perceptual schemata to become intelligible, harmonious, and capable of arousing the aesthetic sentiment.

Barron's findings seem to confirm my own structural analysis of the creative process, described in Part Three of this book. The "need for disorder" is the acceptance of primary process and immature forms. The "need for order," for the purpose of removing the disorder, is the need to use the secondary process. The tertiary process, or the matching of the secondary and primary processes, will bring about new schemata or a new order.

Barron clearly states that the human mind discerns repetition and thus classifies. But the creative intellect is that which is ready "to abandon classifications known from the past and to acknowledge in its strongest form the proposition that life . . . is pregnant with the unheard-of possibilities and may be the vehicle for transformations without precedent." In Part Three we have given detailed confirmation to these statements of Barron. Barron also suggests that the creative individual who prefers irregularities and apparent disorder and trusts himself in searching for a new order has learned these attitudes from the difficult interpersonal relations he had early in life.

Barron concludes with a general framework of hypotheses. He finds twelve basic characteristics in creative people: (1) they are more observant; (2) they express only part-truths; (3) in addition to seeing things as others do, they see things as others do not; (4) they are independent in their cognitive faculties, which they value very much; (5) they are motivated by their talent and values; (6) they are more capable of holding many ideas at once and comparing more ideas, hence making a richer synthesis; (7) they have more sexual drive and are more vigorous from a physical point of view, and more sensitive; (8) they have more complex lives and see a more complex universe; (9) they become more aware of unconscious motives and fantasy life; (10) they have strong egos that permit them to regress and to return to normality; (11) they allow the distinction between subject and object to disappear for certain periods of time, as in love and mysticism; and (12) the objective freedom of their organism is at a maximum, and their creativity is a function of objective freedom.

I believe we could accept eleven of Barron's twelve characteristics. I am somewhat reluctant to accept number 7, since many creative people have not in fact been physically more vigorous than others.

The Personality of the Scientist

MANY AUTHORS have studied the particular type of personality found in special fields of creativity, especially science. Anne Roe is among the most eminent, if not actually *the* most eminent, of those authors who have attempted to determine the personality characteristics of people who excelled in specific fields. In her works on artists (1946a, 1946b), Roe determined that no criteria could be found that could truly be considered indicative of the ability to be a successful painter. The results of the Rorschach tests administered to these artists disclosed extreme heterogeneity; no single personality pattern common to all members could be differentiated.

Roe also studied 23 eminent male biologists (Roe 1951). "An outstanding feature in the history of all of these men is the persistence and intensity of their devotion to their work." The men came from a family environment lacking in close affective bonds. They were shy and started to date girls relatively late. Most of them did not have any special interest in social contacts. Roe found that these men were persistent, stubborn and rather conventional, and that they disliked the imaginary aspects of life. She postulated that some of these traits might have been caused by the fact that the men had already achieved prominence.

In another important study (1953), Roe compared what she called social scientists (that is, psychologists and anthropologists) to biologists and physical scientists. All the subjects examined were people who had achieved prominence in their own field. She found that overprotection was a common trait in the interrelation of the social scientists with their own parents. The physicists and biologists had fewer interpersonal interactions, were shy and reserved, and dated later in life. The social scientists showed more family and personal difficulties. Roe found that the families of scientists placed a great value on learning and played a role in influencing the development of a "research" attitude. Biologists and experimental physicists depended more on visual imagery in their thinking; theoretical physicists and social scientists tended to depend more on verbal and similar symbols. Rorschach and TAT testing provided no clues as to the eventual success of these eminent scientists. Only such habits and traits as long hours spent working and a preference for their own work could have been adequate predictive factors.

In her book *The Making of a Scientist* (1952), Roe summarized much of her previous efforts. She concluded that there are no differential characteristics between scientists and non-scientists, or between people who chose various fields of science. However, some life patterns emerge when we study the history of these people. Most of them came from families where the fathers were professional and where intellectual values received great esteem. When a father was not present, there was a teacher who stimulated a research attitude. Another outstanding feature was the need for independence and autonomy. This probably derived from insecurities in the environment, the loss of a parent, or overprotection.

Bernice T. Eiduson made an accurate report of her study on forty living research scientists (1962). She reached the following conclusion: "The ultimate picture of any man does not derive from rating all the factors about him evenly, and then adding up the ratings. In fact, just the contrary is true. Some data appear very relevant to his over-all functioning; others less so. In the case of the scientist, the varying degree of emphasis is extremely significant in understanding him, for some of the factors in his psychological makeup have become dominant and have overshadowed others which seemed less important."

Eiduson found that these scientists had been singled out already as gifted children. There was little intimacy between the scientist and his family. The positive ties were apparently related to achievement. When ill, they found pleasure in indulging in daydreaming, fantasizing, solving problems and puzzles, reading, and learning. In half the cases the father was absent or at home so infrequently that the child scarcely knew him.

Eiduson could isolate only a few common denominators in personality, all of which focused around work: "great emotional investment in intellectual things, a sufficient degree of narcissism necessary to think that what they were doing was good and could only be done by them; an emotional emptying of themselves into people and things connected with work; a sensitivity to stimuli. Even when fears and anxieties were analyzed, these were found to be bound in conflicts around work." The scientists she studied were strikingly similar to each other in only one way: their cognitive and perceptual styles. They were all oriented to the new, the unfamiliar, or to reorganizing the old material in new ways, and they accepted the anxiety required for such reorganization.

Eiduson recognizes, in the cognitive style of the subjects she studied, the fact that they grew up as intellectual rebels. She believes that it was a lack of emotional support in the family "that made them turn more to themselves than to others, and which made them appreciate the intellectual rather than the primarily emotional sources of gratifications." Among the last remarks made in Eiduson's book is that her study showed no one factor in background or experience that was *the* raison d'etre for wanting to go into scientific work.

Among the early books on the subject which are still influential today is the one by Rossman (1931), to which we have already referred in Chapter 2. Rossman sent a questionnaire to 710 inventors who had obtained patents, and asked what the characteristics of a successful inventor are. Perseverance was the characteristic mentioned most frequently, with 503 answers. Second came imagination, with 207; knowledge and memory came third, with 183; business ability fourth, with 162; originality fifth, with 151; common sense sixth, with 134; analytic ability seventh, with 113; and self-confidence eighth, with 96 answers. It is surprising that imagination, although scoring high, had less than half the points that perseverance received and that originality scored somewhat less than knowledge and memory. Self-confidence, too, made a poor score. It is to be remembered, however, that the group of people studied consisted of subjects interested in practical inventions or improvements of pre-existing patents—not, in general, people given to great discoveries or to the building of theoretical systems.

Multiple Creativity and the Renaissance Man

A CONSIDERABLE NUMBER of creative people have achieved great prominence in several fields. These persons are often called Renaissance men because it was during the Renaissance in Italy that a number of them emerged. These people make us consider whether creativity is related to specific content or is a general faculty of the mind. For instance, could a person musically as endowed as Johann Sebastian Bach have become, in the proper milieu, an artist like Rembrandt or a poet like Shakespeare? Openness to various fields seems to exist in most creative men. As a matter of fact, one of the origins of their creativity lies in applying notions and principles of one field to another field, especially in scientific pursuits. On the other hand, it is unlikely that a person will achieve a high degree of excellence in disparate fields, perhaps even impossible in view of the many factors necessary to determine genius in even a single field. It is easy to establish that people endowed with multiple creativity did their creative work in fields which were closely related. If they worked in several unrelated fields, they left the mark of greatness in only one of them. For instance, Marie Curie, together with her husband Pierre, did outstanding work on radiation, for which they shared the Nobel Prize in physics in 1903. In 1911 she received the Nobel Prize in chemistry for discovering radium and polonium. The relation between the fields is obvious.

But let us take a few examples of Renaissance men who lived in the Renaissance or afterwards. Michelangelo, who achieved greatness in sculpture, painting, and architecture, also wrote poetry. Although especially great as a sculptor, he was also a great painter and architect. Thus he excelled in related fields of art, but not in poetry. Probably his poems would be ignored today if they had not been written by Michelangelo the artist.

The most frequently mentioned example is that of Leonardo da Vinci, a person uniquely well-versed in art, science, and literature. Although it is true that Leonardo had an unusual knowledge and understanding of many sciences and technologies and that he was far ahead of most of his contemporaries in those fields, his life as a scientist is more one of frustration than of accomplishment. He developed a project for diverting the course of the Arno river and rendering it navigable from its mouth to Florence, but this undertaking failed. Projects which also failed were the building of airplanes and submarines. Although he was hired as military engineer by Ludovico Sforza of Milan, and by Francis I, king of France, he did not go much further than designing bridges and mortars. A multiple staircase built around a common core so that people could go up and down at the same time without being aware of each other was devised by Leonardo but actually executed after his death. These achievements and interests, although revealing the extraordinary grasp of his mind, did not make him great. Leonardo remains one of the greatest painters of all times, the genius who left "Mona Lisa" and "The Last Supper" to posterity.

Another well-known man who lived in the Renaissance is Leon Battista Alberti. His accomplishments in architecture include such masterpieces as the church of Saint Francis in Rimini, the facade of the church Santa Maria Novella, and the palace Rucellai in Florence. Alberti wrote a ten-volume treatise on architecture and was skilled as a musician, painter, poet, philosopher, and Latinist. He also wrote a treatise on domestic life which might not please at all present day feminists. After Leonardo, Alberti is probably the person who comes closest to the ideal of the Renaissance man. The fact remains, however, that he reached greatness only in architecture.

Long after the Renaissance Wolfgang Goethe made attempts to refute Newton's theory of light, made important botanical studies, especially on leaves, and discovered the intermaxillary bone in man. He remains known, however, as a poet and dramatist, and famous principally as the author of *Faust*.

In our time one of the persons closest to the ideal of Renaissance man is Jean-Paul Sartre, well known as a philosopher, dramatist, novelist, and as an active member of the Resistance in Paris during the Second World War. It is possible to recognize in all his accomplishments, however, a common source: his existential philosophy.

Sickness and Creativity

THE IDEA that a positive correlation exists between genius (or at least intellectual eminence) and mental illness is an old one that recurs from time to time. A well-known Italian psychiatrist, Cesare Lombroso, who strongly believed that such a correlation existed, gained a large consensus among the psychiatric profession in many countries. Lombroso wrote that his work was but an outcome and conclusion of that of previous psychiatrists (Morel, Moreau, and Jacoby). In 1864 Lombroso wrote an essay entitled "Genius and Insanity," which was translated into English in 1891 and was followed by many other writings on the same subject.* The sixth edition of his book *L'Uomo di Genio* (1894) can be considered his most complete statement on the subject. Lombroso tried to prove that many geniuses had neurological diseases, neuroses, or full-fledged psychoses. According to him, Julius Caesar, Paul of Tarsus, Mohammed, Petrarch, Molière, Napoleon, Handel, Flaubert, Dostoevsky, and other geniuses suffered from epilepsy. Lombroso also reported that Ampère, Comte, Tasso, Newton,

* For a scholarly review of Lombroso's life and work, see Mora (1964).

Rousseau, and Schopenhauer had attacks of insanity. Mental illness was particularly frequent among great musicians: Mozart, Schumann, Beethoven, Donizetti, Pergolesi, Handel, Dussek, Hoffmann, and Gluck. (In the category of "attacks of insanity," Lombroso included such psychiatric conditions as delusional and hallucinatory syndromes, depressions, and manic states.)

There is no doubt that Lombroso reported several cases of creative men who, according to indisputable evidence, *did* have attacks of psychosis. But in many other cases that he reported, it was difficult to tell whether the artists had suffered from real psychoses or from what other authors would call "peculiarities" of character and temperament. Although Lombroso's writings are interesting, they are limited in scope, as they deal chiefly with the negative qualities of great men. He did not deal with the positive qualities or with the processes that transform psychopathology into creative activity. In his last writings Lombroso expressed the opinion that the quality of being a genius is associated with epilepsy. The peculiarities of these geniuses, including the disposition to be creative, would be explained as epileptic equivalents. He felt that being a genius may be the expression of a "degenerative psychosis."

For several decades Lombroso's works enjoyed a great popularity not just in Western Europe but also in America and in Russia. Eventually their lack of scientific basis, absence of clear-cut definitions of genius and insanity, and inability to prove the veracity of anecdotal reports made even Lombroso's own pupils skeptical about his work. Lombroso's contributions, however, will retain historical importance, for they represent one of the first and most prolonged attempts to find connections between psychopathology and creativity.

Furthermore, even a cursory perusal of his major work (1894) will disclose material of great interest that is susceptible to being interpreted in different ways. Lombroso's attempts to show that insane people "almost reached" brilliant ideas and discoveries, and that geniuses gave clear-cut examples of insanity, in fact point again to the prominence of primary-process mechanisms in these two groups of people. (Of course, Lombroso could not understand the strange similarities among these people in terms of such a thing as primary process.) One of the many worthy subjects covered in Lombroso's long work is that of people called *mattoidi* in Italian. These are people who are almost but not totally *matti* (crazy), and who disclose unusual propensities in literature, art, science. Among the literary *mattoidi* he mentions Hecart, a French author who wrote that "it is a habit of crazy people to be interested in futility." Hecart wrote a biography of the insane people of the town of Valenciennes and a strange book entitled *Anagrammana; poème en VII chant*, published in Valenciennes in 1821, but according to the author allegedly published in Anagrammatopolis, in the fourteenth year of the anagrammatic era. Lombroso gives the following excerpt as an example of the plays on words, and especially anagrams, that abound in this poem.

> *Lecteur, il* sied *que je vous* dise
> *Que le* sbire *fera la* brise,
> *Que le* dupeur *est sans* pudeur
> *Qu'on peut* maculeur *sans* clameur
>
> *Le* nomade *a mis la* madonne
> *A la* paterne *de* Petronne
> *Quand le grand* Dacier *était* diacre
> *Le* caffier *cultive du* fiacre.

The last of 1,200 similarly anagrammatic lines is the following:

> *Moi, je vais* poser *mon* repos.

Many writers have pursued Lombroso's work and have modified some of his conclusions. A. C. Jacobson (1926) concluded that although creative individuals may be of insane temperament, their insanity traits hinder creativity. Thus these creative people with insane temperaments produce their best work in the healthiest periods of their life. The mixing of ethnic stock, according to Jacobson, brings forth new ideas but also serious conflicts. It thus favors both creativity and insanity. He concluded that although eugenics would wipe out degenerations and insanities, it would also eliminate genius.

Lange-Eichbaum (1932) mentioned a large group of geniuses who became psychotic, but only after they had completed their great work. In this group he included, among others, Baudelaire, Copernicus, Donizetti, Faraday, Kant, Linnaeus, Newton, and Stendhal. Other creative people did their work in the midst of psychosis. With some—for instance, Monet, Maupassant, and Rousseau—their psychosis and their work remained distinct. With others—for instance,

Holderlin and Van Gogh—the psychosis affected the content and the form of the creative work. Lange-Eichbaum included the majority of geniuses in another large group: the psychopaths. Among them are Beethoven, Byron, Heine, Michelangelo, and Schopenhauer. We must remember that this German author did not use the word "psychopath" as it is used in American psychiatry. He did not necessarily mean a "sociopath" or a person who manifests antisocial behavior, but rather an eccentric or queer personality either near the border of mental disorder or suffering from a real but not full-fledged psychotic disorder.

In his study of British genius, Havelock Ellis (1904) collected 1,030 names from the *Dictionary of National Biography* and found that only forty-four of them (that is, 4.2 percent) were demonstrably psychotic. He concluded: "The association between genius and insanity is not, I believe, without significance, but in the face of the fact that its occurrence is only demonstrated in less than five per cent of cases, we must put out of court any theory as to genius being a form of insanity."

Roth (1969) has convincingly demonstrated that the poet Heine suffered from porphyria. On the other hand, in a not totally convincing book, Pickering (1974) describes the "creative malady" of Charles Darwin, Florence Nightingale, Mary Baker Eddy, Sigmund Freud, Marcel Proust, and Elizabeth Browning. While he was waiting for the *Beagle* to sail for the famous expedition, Darwin started to have palpitations, pain about the heart, and breathlessness. According to Pickering, Darwin suffered from a psychoneurosis. Florence Nightingale, too, suffered from a psychoneurosis, although it could be that for a certain period of time she was a morphine addict. Pickering believes that Mary Baker Eddy was suffering from hysteria, due to her unresolved conflict between her actual personality and the one she wanted to project to the world. Pickering relies on Jones's biography of Freud to conclude that the founder of psychoanalysis was suffering from anxiety-hysteria. Marcel Proust suffered from asthma, but was also eccentric and neurotic. Pickering concludes that Proust's illness represented his escape from his grief and guilt caused by his mother's death. He escaped into a partly real and partly imaginary world that to some extent had existed prior to his mother's death. Elizabeth Barrett was a morphine addict by the time Robert Browning entered her life, and she remained so until her death.

I found this book of Pickering's not at all illuminating concerning the creative process of these six great Victorians. The book, however, is informative about their illnesses and the petty aspects of their lives.

Conclusion

IN THE CONCLUDING SECTION of an excellent article on creative persons, Taylor and Holland (1964) state (p. 41): "If we look at predictors by class rather than by specific scales or inventories, we get a crude ordering. The biographical items and past achievements are our most efficient predictors. Self-ratings and direct expressions of goals and aspirations are next. Originality and personality inventories run a very poor third. Aptitude and intelligence measures rank fourth (except where restriction-of-range corrections are really applicable), followed finally by parental attitudes."

If we scan the contributions of the authors whom we have selected for review in this chapter, and if we continue to peruse the extremely rich literature on the subject that we have not quoted, we must regretfully state that we have not come up with clear-cut ideas. Global approaches, like that of Maslow, give us generalities only. Approaches that attempt to differentiate specific psychological characteristics sometimes contradict one another and at other times place unequal importance on the various traits. In most instances the characteristics individualized by the authors are *desirable* traits that would be welcome not only in creative persons but in everybody; it is not necessary to be creative in order to benefit from sincerity, receptivity to new ideas, generalized sensitivity, fluency of thinking, flexibility, independence of judgment, and so on.

Some characteristics, however, recur too frequently to be due only to chance or to the particular predilections of the researchers. Intelligence *is* required. However, it is not to be confused with creativity, and it does not have to reach extreme scores on I.Q. tests. Deviant thinking is prominent. Spontaneity is also important, but so are diligence and perseverance. Straight thinking is important, but mental illness has not been a deterrent in outstanding cases. As a matter of fact, I may add that the great innovators in the study and treatment of mental illness have not been immune to psychiatric disorders themselves. If Sigmund Freud only had a psychoneurosis (Jones 1953), Carl Jung (as he himself makes the reader understand) had something more serious, and Harry Stack Sullivan had several schizophrenic episodes.

Some of the traits described as useful and desirable may actually be detrimental if not accompanied by other traits. For instance, intelligence, which we have mentioned several times as important for life and creativity, may actually handicap creativity if not accompanied by originality and if used for a too-strict self-criticism and inhibition. On the other hand, originality may lead us astray if not corrected by self-criticism. Divergent thinking may even bring us to psychosis, if it is not matched by logical processes. Perseverance may lead to scholarship but not to creativity, if the person's interests are narrowly restricted—as unfortunately happens in much academic work. A profound knowledge of a certain field makes one more aware of the areas of the field in which new, creative ideas are needed. And yet if the person has spent too much energy and time working in that restricted field, he may not have a grasp of the various disciplines necessary for the cross-fertilization and transposing of concepts that are so important in creative work. Rather than a single trait, then, it is a special combination of several traits—in a special family environment, in some socio-historical situations, occurring at a given time and place—that produces the synthesis we call creativity.

Chapter 16

The Cultivation of Creativity in the Individual Person

Introductory Remarks

THE SCIENCE of promoting creativity in the individual person is in its initial stages. I think that we must be candid on this matter and admit that all of us, the authors concerned with this problem, have so far only been able to come up with rudimentary and tentative notions. There is still a great discrepancy between what we know about the creative process and our ability to use this knowledge for the purpose of promoting creativity. Our modesty in admitting our results, however, should not eclipse our pride in participating in a pioneer work, with the hope that new advances soon will become apparent.

In this chapter I shall review the contributions of some of the major workers in this field. Then I shall present my own observations and recommendations, drawn from my psychoanalytic-psychotherapeutic experiences with a relatively large number of creative people. To be sure, the notions derived from the studies of many authors, including myself, have to be confirmed or disproved by much more evidence than is available now. Statistical data are difficult to find because standards are lacking.

We must also recognize that on the whole, American culture has not enhanced creativity on an individual basis. The psychiatrist Ruesch, writing in 1957, pointed out that Switzerland had a much larger number of Nobel Prize winners than the United States in proportion to her population. Ruesch was justified in expressing surprise. Many are the thinkers who have become displeased with American attitudes toward creativity. In 1964 the historian Arnold Toynbee wrote an article entitled "Is America Neglecting Her Creative Minority?" He stated that "To give a fair chance to potential creativity is a matter of life and death for any society. This is all-important, because the outstanding creative ability of a fairly small percentage of the population is mankind's ultimate capital asset . . ." He adds that "if . . . society sets itself to neutralize outstanding ability, it will have failed in its duty to its members, and it will bring upon itself a retribution for which it will have only itself to blame."

Personally, I share Ruesch's surprise—especially when, reviewing the nine socio-cultural creativogenic factors discussed in Chapter 14, I conclude that most of these factors are present in American society. Why then has America not lived up to these theoretical expectations?

American culture, perhaps following the attitude toward work and the acquisitive spirit of the early pioneers, has placed greater value on doing than on creating, especially when what is created is artistic or theoretical. America is predominantly a nation of doers; and as doers Americans are generally very efficient, both in technology and productivity.

The nine socio-cultural factors mentioned in Chapter 14 can be channeled more toward productivity in general than toward that particular form of productivity which is creativity. Furthermore, the socio-cultural factors need to be complemented by other factors operating on a more personal level, or at least they must not be neutralized by adverse factors acting on that level. By now it is time that we in America reexamine our methods of fostering creativity, just as we reexamined our teaching methods after Sputnik. Indeed, people such as Frank Barron, Morris Stein, Calvin Taylor, E. Paul Torrance, and many others, animated by pioneering zeal and fervor, have already attempted to remedy the situation.

Although creativity may occur at any age of life, as we shall discuss later in this chapter, it seems logical to assume (although it is by no means certain) that an inclination toward creativity must be fostered in childhood and/or adolescence. This assumption is based on autobiographical writings of creative people, on histories collected from the psychotherapeutic treatment of creative people, and especially on our knowledge that it is in childhood and adolescence that the major trends of our psychological life are formed.

At first we would be inclined to think that the best environment for enhancing creativity in the individual is the home itself. We know that such has been the case for a considerable number of great men—for example the great Renaissance sculptor Giovanni Pisano (1250–1320), son of the first great Italian sculptor Niccola Pisano (1225–1284); John Stuart Mill (1806–1873), son of John Mill (1773–1836); Johann Strauss "the younger" (1825–1899), son of Johann Strauss "the elder" (1804–1849); Anna Freud (1895–   ), daughter of Sigmund Freud (1856–1939); and several others. Statistically, however, these cases are not sufficient to permit conclusions.

As a matter of fact, clinical observations disclose that most parents, although believing that they help their children in fostering creativity, actually do not do so. On closer examination we realize that they do not practice what they believe; they have good intentions, but they give wrong directions. Many parents show inhibiting anxieties, such as worrying whether their children appear unusual, introverted, peculiar. They are more concerned with external success and popularity than with inner growth and creativity; between practicality and creativity, many parents choose practicality. In a society where economic competition is so important, most parents first of all want to make sure that their children, once grown up, will be self-supporting. In some cases the particular situation of the family (some children much older than others, some children living with grandparents instead of with their parents, and so on) has made that type of family especially suitable, in specific ways, for enhancing creativity. But again, these are sporadic cases. It seems that if we want to promote creativity on a larger scale, it is more promising to do so through the educational system during childhood, adolescence, and youth.

Creativity and the Educational System

TORRANCE is the major author to concern himself with the problem of creativity in relation to our system of grammar and high school education. He has collected valuable data about the creative potentialities of the youngster and about the factors in the scholastic system that hinder creativity; and he has made valuable suggestions about promoting whatever creative tendencies the young student happens to have (Torrance 1962, 1963, 1964, 1965, 1969; Torrance and Myers 1972).

Torrance has shown that creative abilities develop rapidly from kindergarten through the third grade, with boys tending to excel over girls. A sharp decrement occurs between the third and fourth grades, during which period boys trail girls. Gains occur in the fifth and sixth grades, and again drop in the seventh. The eighth, ninth, tenth, and eleventh grades are characterized by growth. Some children give up their creativity at about their fourth-grade level, and never reacquire it.

There are reasons for the severe decreases in the fourth and seventh grades. Torrance has listed the common educational hindrances to creative thinking: "premature attempts to eliminate fantasy; restrictions on manipulativeness and curiosity; overemphasis or misplaced emphasis on sex roles; overemphasis on prevention, fear and timidity; misplaced emphasis on certain verbal skills; emphasis on destructive criticism; and coercive pressures from peers" (1963).

According to Torrance, the teacher-pupil relationship must be bent toward creativity; it should not be based on a "stimulus-response situation but on a living relationship, a coexperiencing." Children who dare to imagine, who do not obsequiously follow the beaten path, unfortunately constitute a problem to teachers who feel safer in following the prescribed recommendations. Torrance also describes other characteristics in the American scholastic system that are adverse to creativity. One of them is the tendency to equate divergence with abnormality. Although this idea had been largely discredited shortly after the time of Lombroso (see Chapter 15), the belief has persisted in some conservative milieus that a different outlook or a deviance of any sort means abnormality and illness.

Another cultural trait, detrimental to creativity, that affects the child even in grammar school is the orientation on success rather than on achievement for its own sake. Still another is peer-orientation, which exerts much more pressure to conform than does adult-orientation. I might add that Torrance probably means that peer-orientation tends to lead to what Riesman et al. (1950) called an "other-directed personality," with the emphasis on immediate action and short-term goals. Although adult-orientation, too, may exert pressure to conform, such orientation leads more to what Riesman called an inner-directed personality. This type of personality is more conducive to reflection and distant goals; and unless overwhelmed by strong feelings of guilt and obsessive needs to comply and conform, it is more favorable to creativity.

Finally, Torrance lists the work–play dichotomy as adverse to a climate for creativity. Work and play should not be considered antithetical. School work may be joyful, too, and play may be very constructive and instructive.

Torrance sets forth five principles that teachers should follow to reward creative thinking: (1) treat unusual questions with respect; (2) treat unusual ideas with respect; (3) show children that their ideas have value; (4) provide opportunities for self-initiated learning and give credit for it; and (5) provide periods of nonevaluated practice or learning. This last principle requires some explanation. External evaluation may constitute a threat and creates a need for defensiveness. Children need periods during which they are not evaluated. Free ideation is thus not inhibited. Torrance postulated that the declines in creative thinking ability that occur at about ages five, nine, thirteen, and seventeen in the United States derive from cultural discontinuities and consequent personality disturbances. By cultural discontinuity he meant the new demands and changes in habits that a particular culture produces at certain ages. Using Sullivan's (1953) classification of different ages, Torrance concluded that the decline at about age five coincides with the end of childhood and the beginning of the juvenile stage. During this period the child must learn to compromise, to accommodate to social requests, and to accept authorities outside of his own home. The second decline occurs at the onset of the preadolescent stage, with its needs for consensual validation, for peer approval and identification, and for conformity. The third decline takes place at the onset of adolescence, with its sex problems, its need for acceptance by the opposite sex, and many further social demands for conformity.

Torrance also devised special tests that point out the child's conflict between the need to diverge and the pressure to conform. For instance, children are asked to make up stories using ten suggested topics or a similar topic of their own. One suggested topic was "The Lion That Won't Roar." A very revealing example is the story of Lippy, "A Lion that Won't Roar."

> Lippy Lion, a friend of mine, has a little problem. He won't roar! He used to roar, but now he won't. His name used to be Roarer, too. I'll tell you why.
> When Roarer was about your age, he would always roar and scare people. Now this made his mother and father worry. Everybody was always complaining. So they decided they should talk to Roarer.
> They went to his bedroom. . . . But when they started talking he roared and scared them downstairs. So finally they went to a magician. They talked things over until he had an idea. Then the three went home together.
> The magician said his words and said, "He'll never want to roar again."
> The next morning he went to scare his mother by roaring, but all that came out was a little squeak. He tried again but only a squeak came out. But he pled and pled to get his roar back, so the magician made it so he could roar. But Roarer didn't believe him. So now that he can roar he won't.
> Soon they had to name him Lippy.*

It is evident that the child who wrote the story identified with Lippy, the lion. Everybody is scared of Lippy's divergent quality, his roaring. Finally Lippy is taken to a magician. Who this magician symbolizes is not too hard to imagine. He may be a teacher, a counselor, a psychologist, a therapist, a doctor. Lippy is inhibited twice, or in two different ways. The first time occurs when he receives the injunction by the magician not to roar. The second inhibition occurs when, although the magician has rescinded the injunction, Lippy cannot roar. By then the inhibition has been introjected, has become part of Lippy's superego or personality, so that the poor lion cannot roar. It is amazing to discover, from this and other stories reported by Torrance, how much insight children have into their problems in con-

---

* Reproduced with permission of author and of publisher. Copyright © 1962, Prentice-Hall, Inc.

nection with divergence and creativity. However, it is fair to assume that this insight is unconscious or only partially unconscious. Probably the child who was able to reveal his problem creatively in the story of Lippy would not have been able to explain with a more direct statement how pressured and inhibited he felt.

It is impossible to adequately summarize Torrance's many contributions. He must be considered the apostle for the acceptance and encouragement of diverging thinking, in an educational system in which it is seldom tolerated.

Promoting Creativity in Young Adults

MANY AUTHORS have tackled the problem of creativity in young adult life. It is too early to evaluate results. It seems, however, that in many cases the procedures used for the individual or for groups, even if not capable of eliciting great creativity or new crops of geniuses, have at least been able to expand the functions of the individuals concerned. They seem to have become capable of feeling more, experiencing more, thinking in more directions, and daring more.

On the other hand, whether some specific group techniques obtained even these results is still a debatable question. We must keep in mind that what at times seems an expansion of the personality actually hides an underlying thinness; a willingness to share with others sometimes hides a reluctance to get in touch with the inner self. Moreover, multiple stimulations may lead to excessive preoccupation with external life without concern for inner growth. Thus each individual case, each institution or school that offers methods for the promotion of creativity has to be studied and evaluated on a separate basis. These group methods are effective if they also promote perseverance, firmness, and commitment to the new patterns of growth that appear in the individual.

An additional consideration has to be made when we read some books and articles that claim to enhance creativity in adults with easy methods. Some of these methods do not really promote creativity or really try to enlarge whatever talent a person may have in art, science, literature, or other fields of creative endeavor. The methods I refer to here give suggestions as to how to market one's ideas and activities, to make them salable and popular, predominantly for monetary gain. Of course there is nothing wrong in obtaining financial reward for one's accomplishments; but if popularity and financial reward are the only preoccupations, or the predominant ones, they may become a straightjacket for any striving toward any type of true personal growth.

Alex F. Osborn typifies the pragmatic approach. More than a theoretical thinker, he has been defined as an "applied thinker." In his book *Applied Imagination* he constructively condenses what he drew from his career as an educator, writer, financier, advertiser, artist, and leader in philanthropies and social movements. His book, first published in 1953 and adopted by M.I.T., had an enormous success and went through numerous reprints. Osborn believes that creativity will never be a science. Much of it will always remain a mystery. But certainly it is an applied, teachable, and learnable art. By means of his book he wants to help the individual understand and apply "his own innate creativity to all aspects of his personal and vocational life."

One of Osborn's leading points is what he called the *brainstorming principle:* instead of trying to think both critically and imaginatively at the same time, we should use our critical mind at one time and our creative mind at another. He devised the brainstorming technique in 1939. A group holds sessions together and advances new ideas. Four basic rules are to be respected: (1) criticism is ruled out; (2) free-wheeling is welcomed—"the wilder the idea, the better"; (3) quantity is desired—the greater the number of ideas, the greater the likelihood of good results; and (4) combination and improvement are sought. Participants should suggest how ideas from other members of the group could be improved. The brainstorm session should be animated by a spirit of self-encouragement and a rejection of perfectionism. Osborn suggests that the ideal number of participants is between five and ten. The group has a leader who explains the rules, sees to it that they are not violated, and makes sure that ideas are not criticized and that the group does not break down into subgroups.

Osborn lists the factors that cramp creativity: sticking to previous habits, self-discouragement, timidity, and urbanization (since urban life tends to remove imaginative strength in all except "the few who work in the arts and in the creative phases of business and science"). A decline in creative incentive can also result from a loss of belief in the idea that hard work pays. On the other hand, certain habits such as traveling, playing games, solving puzzles, pursuing hobbies, reading, and writing promote creative powers. Although imagination is essential for creativity, not all imagination is useful. Osborn calls daydreaming "the most common use of non-creative imagination." He also calls "worry" or "anxious fear" noncreative form of imagination.

There is no doubt that Osborn has done a great deal to arouse people from complacent, stagnant positions into activity. This is a great accomplishment in itself. Whether he has really enhanced Creativity with a capital C, rather than just the practical contingencies of business life (or, at most, their technological applications) remains to be determined. Reading his book, one feels that the reader is assumed to be more concerned with increasing his profits than with searching for new syntheses. To give an example, on page 82 he mentions that one of his groups held seven brainstorm sessions within a single month. One meeting turned up 45 suggestions for a home-appliance client, another resulted in 56 ideas for a money-raising campaign, and another one offered 124 ideas on how to sell more blankets. Thus a down-to-earth attitude, difficult to reconcile with the aura of creativity, hovers over Osborn's book. Although some people such as Shakespeare, Leonardo da Vinci, and Einstein are mentioned, nothing of the majesty of their work is taken into close examination. Nevertheless the book doubtless has many practical, useful suggestions. When I read it, I recognized that I had adopted (and had seen other people successfully adopt) many of the author's recommendations, not in the process of creativity, but in *managerial capacities*. I have been a member of several committees (to outline plans of societies, to organize programs for meetings, to advertise lectures, and so on), and I felt that when my colleagues and I applied Osborn's four rules—avoiding criticism for a certain period of time, free-wheeling, having a large quantity of ideas, and searching for combinations of some of them—good results were indeed obtained.

Osborn also takes some stands with which a psychiatrist cannot be in agreement. Daydreaming, for instance, as we shall see in detail later in this chapter, cannot be considered "the most common use of noncreative imagination." Also, it is not true that worry and "anxious fear" are noncreative forms of imagination. I have seen many creative people ridden by anxiety, and the biographies of many great people also testify to this. Obviously if the anxiety is overwhelming or destructive to a great degree, the person cannot focus on any constructive activity. However, worry, anxious fear, discontent, and anxiety in general may be useful as promoters of creative work, which may in turn dispel these feelings, make them more acceptable, or channel them into new directions.

Many researchers have pursued the directions suggested by Osborn. Parnes (1962) suggests that brainstorming is part of a total process. While the storm goes on, ideas should be advanced without evaluation, or in accordance with the principle of deferred judgment. Other authors (for instance, Taylor, Berry, and Block 1957) express doubt about the claims made for these group techniques.

Altering the Body's Chemistry

THIS SECTION will be rather brief, because it deals with a method that the author, a psychiatrist, cannot recommend. The use of alcohol as a supposed promoter of creativity has been known since ancient times. The marvelous wine of France has been celebrated by many creative people of that country. The exultations of Rabelais (1494?–1553) about the effect of the wonderful fluid are well known. And the words of Baudelaire (1821–1867) are no less enthusiastic. He wrote:

> *Il faut être toujours ivre. Tout est là: c'est l'unique question. Pour ne pas sentir l'horrible fardeau du Temps qui brise vos épaules et vous penche vers la terre, il faut vous enivrer sans trêve.*

> *We must always be drunk. That's all, the only question. In order not to feel the horrible burden of Time which breaks your shoulders and bends you toward the soil, you must become drunk without rest.*

Many writers such as Gautier, Poe, Baudelaire, and Rimbaud found inspiration in the effect of alcohol; but whether it was alcohol per se that stimulated their creativity is questionable. In other words, the effect of alcohol became something to write about, an object of inspiration, or a content of artistic work, rather than something that actually changed the neurophysiology of the brain in a way favorable to creativity. Edgar Allan Poe (1809–1849) had an attack of delirium tremens (alcoholic psychosis) in June 1848, about three months before his death.

Ann Roe is one of the first authors to study alcoholic consumption systematically in relation to creativity, particularly among painters (1946c). She divided painters into moderate, social, and excessive drinkers. The excessive drinkers indulged in alcohol in order to reduce their anxiety to a level that permitted them to paint. Nash (1962) feels that alcohol may help creativity, inasmuch as it facilitates the flow of ideas and makes it easier to transgress "the boundaries of previously fixed belief." My own observations with alcoholic patients lead me to the following tentative conclusions: (1) the use of alcohol does not promote the use of primary-process mechanisms, in contrast to the use of marijuana, LSD, and mescaline; (2) the use of alcohol in small quantities may remove excessive anxiety and inhibitions and may be useful in that capacity, but not as a promoter of innovative ideas; and (3) the use of alcohol may be useful as a life experience for those writers who want to portray the life of the alcoholic or extol the beauty of inebriation.

It is well known that some creative people have used opium and opium derivatives. The drug was used in antiquity in Asia Minor, Greece, and Rome, but it became practically unknown in Europe until Paracelsus (1493–1541) reestablished its use, in the form of laudanum, for the removal or amelioration of pain and coughing and as a sedative. De Quincey (1785–1859) and Coleridge (1772–1834) are among the writers who used opium. De Quincey refers to opium in the following way: "O just, subtle, and mighty opium! . . . eloquent opium! That with thy potent rhetoric . . ." (Cooke 1974). But it is more than doubtful that opium consumers actually increase their creativity thereby. It *is* certain that with the use of this drug they are able to remove anxiety, pain, and some inhibitions. There is no uncontroversial proof that opium facilitates the use of the primary process.

Since ancient times people have also devised several different methods of changing the chemistry of the body for the purpose of enhancing creativity. Huxley has described them in *The Doors of Perception* (1963). One of them—increasing the carbon dioxide of the body with various modalities—has a long history; it may be effected simply by holding one's breath. Lack of oxygen in the brain has the same effect. The mountain ascents made by religious leaders or mystics seem to have enhanced their revelatory experiences. My own experience in visiting Macchu Picchu in Peru made me aware of the disastrous effect that such altitudes had on me and on many other tourists. Not only were we not creative at all, we suffered from several signs of physical and psychological dysfunction. Of course, people today reach such high altitudes quickly, by plane, before the body has time to adjust to the lack of oxygen by producing more red corpuscles. In the past such elevations were reached more slowly; so it is possible that the symbolic values given to the heights of the mountain and to the solitude found there were the source of mystical inspiration rather than the rarefied air. I am also doubtful that other methods, such as fasting and self-flagellation, could be conducive to creativity —except for the purpose of describing the experiences as such, or the meanings attributed to them.

As for the use of marijuana, hashish, mescaline, and LSD, my experiences with many patients lead me to the following conclusions:

1. Intake of these substances definitely enhances the use of primary-process mechanisms. Especially in imagery and in the use of language, we observe phenomena that also appear in schizophrenia and in the creative process.

2. The use of the secondary process is impaired during the use of these substances, so that the harmonious matching of the primary and secondary processes *cannot* take place. Thus it is more than dubious that creative work could be performed by people while they are under the influence of these drugs.

3. In a large minority of users of mescaline and LSD, in particular, I have seen such results as brain damage, the precipitation of temporary or chronic psychoses, attempted self-mutilating and suicidal actions, and even attempted or actual murder. Thus under no circumstances could this practice be recommended, even if the presumed creative work could be accomplished. The problem remains whether small doses of these substances are not harmful and are therefore acceptable. In many instances it is impossible to predict whether even smallest doses will adversely affect an individual, since people show great variations in their responses to drugs. Small doses of marijuana seem harmless for a great majority of people.

The enhancement of creativity in drug users, after the effect of the drug has faded, is difficult to evaluate. Krippner (1969) studied 91 artists who had had one or more psychedelic experiences. In this group of 91 "were an award-winning film maker, a Guggenheim Fellow in poetry, and a recipient of Ford, Fulbright, and Rockefeller study grants in painting." I myself have treated several creative people, especially in the entertainment field, who had used mescaline and LSD, but (1) they had shown their creative abilities long before they had started to use these drugs; (2) the use of these drugs was very limited; (3) they did not create during the effect of the drugs; and (4) their creative activity subsequent to the use of drugs seemed not to have been affected at all by the use of these drugs. It is true that a considerable number of persons have described stupendous psychedelic experiences during which they had mystical episodes, such as being in contact with God, or being able to transcend "the particular" and reach "the universal." However, none of these people whom I have examined or treated were able to use these experiences for creative purposes. As a result of their clinical experiences, many psychiatrists have disclaimed that psychedelic experiences with LSD enhance creativity (Balis 1974; Freedman 1968; Frosch, Robbins and Stern 1967; Mamlet 1967; Zegans, Pollard and Brown 1967).

In a beautiful article Anna Balakian (1974) describes the attitude of the great surrealist André Breton in relation to drugs. Breton felt that his surrealist colleagues who indulged in "artificial aberration of the psychosensory mechanism" were "unsuitable subjects for surrealist exploration of the human psyche." Breton felt that the human being was endowed with a psychosensory mechanism of utmost flexibility. Modern civilization had reduced this mechanism to a uniform, rigid, conformistic, boring performance. For the expansion of consciousness and enrichment of sensory experience no artificial stimulant is necessary, but only the acquisition of a surrealistic attitude. Balakian ends her excellent article with the words "Surrealism is, in fact, intoxication . . ."

Simple Attitudes and Conditions for Fostering Creativity

AS A THERAPIST and educator I have recommended the adoption of simple attitudes for the fostering of creativity in the individual (Arieti 1966, 1975). Although these recommendations are particularly suitable for the adolescent and the young adult, they are also applicable to any subsequent age. The reader will soon realize that I do not resort to toxic procedures, the setting of strange milieus, or the performance of difficult tasks, but to the acquisition of simple attitudes, habits, and conditions.

The first condition to be considered is *aloneness*. Aloneness may be viewed as a partial sensory deprivation; to a much smaller degree, it tends to reproduce what experimentally-induced sensory deprivation brings about. A solitary individual is not constantly and directly exposed to the conventional stimulations and is less in danger of being overcome by the clichés of society. It is more possible for him to listen to his inner self, to come in contact with his inner basic resources and with some manifestations of the primary process. Thus, although aloneness *can* turn into painful loneliness, it does not do so when the person who is alone is in the company of, in contact with, himself. A new inner horizon opens up—for exploring, for providing different types of awareness and meaning, for unexpected kinds of inspiration. In addition to being alone, many creative persons want to be removed from excessive stimuli and distractions of any sort, and especially from noise. Aloneness, of course, should not be confused with a protracted or painful loneliness imposed by others or by one's psychological difficulties. Nor should it be confused with withdrawal from others, persistent shyness, or constant solitude. It should only mean being able to remain alone periodically for a few hours. Unfortunately, being alone is not advocated in our modern styles of educating adolescents. On the contrary, gregariousness and popularity are held in high esteem. The emphasis today is on "togetherness," on group activity, and on what Riesman and co-authors (1950) call "other-directedness." Calling a person an introvert has become a derogatory remark.

Aloneness, as we have characterized it, should be recommended not only as a preparation for a life of creativity, but also, when creative work is in process, as a state of being. At the present time the emphasis is on teamwork, especially in scientific research. It is highly doubtful whether an original idea can come from a team, although teamwork is often useful for expanding and applying an original idea once it arises and, more than anything else, for developing the technology by which an original idea is applied for practical purposes.

In some fields of creativity teamwork is almost unthinkable, although it is occasionally resorted to in second-rate work. One cannot even theoretically imagine such classics as *The Divine Comedy*, Michelangelo's statue of Moses, Shakespeare's *Macbeth*, or Beethoven's Ninth Symphony being created by more than one person. In science, too, great discoveries and inventions have been made by single individuals. When more than one individual has made the same discovery or invention, the innovating ideas were arrived at independently (for instance, Newton and Leibniz in the case of the calculus, and Wallace and Darwin with respect to evolution). There are some exceptions to the preference for aloneness felt by creative persons, however. A relatively large number of painters, or people working in several types of visual art, prefer to work in the company or presence of other people. A patient of mine, a nationally well-known creator of a comic strip, could not be inspired and produce unless other people were close to him. Some painters also need the proximity of other people while they are working, perhaps because they have been trained to work with models or in studios or classrooms shared by colleagues.

The second condition that seems to promote creativity is in direct opposition to the present spirit of American culture: *inactivity*. By inactivity, of course, we do not mean withdrawal or excessive loafing, but taking time off to do "nothing," so far as a critical observer can see. If a person must always fix his attention on external work, he limits the possibility of developing his inner resources. Here again, American upbringing pursues the opposite approach: high school and college students are encouraged to work during summer vacations. Any kind of manual labor is considered valuable in building the character of the future adult citizen. As a general rule, it is commendable to encourage youngsters to work. It promotes a sense of responsibility and of good citizenship. However, people with creative tendencies should, whenever possible, be given relatively long stretches of time for thinking and feeling about other things when they do not have to attend to school work. And what we have just said about youngsters could, with some modifications, also be said about adults who have already shown creative tendencies. Too much in the way of routine stifles mental activity and creativity. Moreover, even a creative career that has already started should be allowed to proceed at its own pace, which may be very slow, irregular, and intermittent.

The third creativity-promoting condition is *daydreaming*, a form of mental activity frowned upon by people who are immersed in the practicality of life and who want immediate action. The reader remembers that even Osborn called daydreaming "the most common use of noncreative imagination." Daydreaming is often discouraged as unrealistic or, at least, as tending to enlarge the gap between the individual's ambitions and his capacities. Often it is discouraged because it is thought to promote a vicarious fantasy life that slows up the implementing of realistic and approved-of behavior. Although it is true that excessive daydreaming may have these characteristics, it is equally true that daydreaming is a source of fantasy life that may open up unforeseeable new realms of growth and discovery for the individual. It is in daydreams that the individual permits himself to stray from the usual paths and go on little excursions into irrational worlds. Daydreaming affords human beings relief from the everyday conventions of society.

Singer (1966), one of the major researchers in the field of daydreaming, wrote that "one might anticipate that persons engaging in frequent daydreaming would be characterized by a considerable exploratory tendency, at least at the ideational level, and perhaps by creativity in their storytelling abilities." Singer (1961) and his associates (Singer and Schonbar 1961; Singer and McCraven 1961) found evidence in both children and adults of frequent general daydreaming among those people whose written or dictated stories were rated by judges as the most original and creative.

Daydreaming may not be useful if it remains solely autobiographical—that is, involved only with the person himself, projected into the past or the future. As we shall see shortly, however, a considerable amount of autobiographical thinking is useful nevertheless. Daydreaming is also useful as a promoter of other mental activities. Similar to aloneness, it promotes inwardness and introspection.

As a rule, the youngster who daydreams proceeds (either spontaneously or under friendly suggestion from an educator) toward the fourth creativity-promoting condition, *free thinking*. Free thinking is different from "free association" as it is practiced in classic Freudian psychoanalysis. In the psychoanalytic situation, free association is not as free as it seems. The patient knows that he is supposed to think about himself, or to reveal data pertinent to himself; thus he consciously or unconsciously screens out material that has nothing to do with himself. For instance, it is rather unlikely that he would talk about mathematical problems or classifications of marine species unless they are related to some facets of his life. For the same reason, free thinking is different from daydreaming, which deals predominantly with the individual himself. In free thinking, the person must allow his mind to wander in any direction without restraints or organization. Eventually any type of thinking becomes more or less organized of course; but in a state of abandon, or freedom from inhibition, the individual will realize that in the free-thinking state, similarities (that is, analogies) between perceptions, apperceptions, concepts, or even systems and abstractions tend to occur repeatedly.

The free thinker must not discard these occurrences. Rather, he must be in *a state of readiness for catching similarities*. This is the fifth creativity-promoting condition. In my work on wit (1950a), I began to illustrate the value of similarity or analogy in creativity—a value that I have amply demonstrated in many subsequent works (1964, 1966, 1967), including the present one. Another author, Gordon (1961), referred to the same process as *synectics*, or the "joining together of different and apparently irrelevant elements." Gordon distinguishes four types of analogy: personal, direct, and symbolic analogy, and fantasy. In personal analogy the individual imagines himself to be the material with which he works. For example, Kekule identified himself in a dream with a snake swallowing its tail, and saw an analogy to the benzene molecule as a ring rather than a chain of carbon atoms. Direct analogy is that used by creative people like Bell, who compared the human ear to a machine (which became the telephone). Symbolic analogy is usually a visual image; and fantasy is an image that does not need to comply with the known physical laws of the world.

The synectics method started as a group method. But it is obvious from what has been said in this book and in my previous writings on the subject that the occurrence of analogy—that is, the recognition of similarities—is one of the main processes of individual creativity. From my studies of schizophrenia I could deduce that this process is an archaic one, relying on mechanisms of the primary process (the id and the archaic ego). Thus the person who wants to enhance his creative processes must allow himself to indulge in the practice of catching similarities. Similarities, however, are often disguised as superficial or accidental resemblances, and as a matter of fact they are in fact probably so in 99 percent of the cases. Even if the statistical odds against catching a productive similarity are overwhelming, the individual should not drop the habit of registering all such similarities.

This leads me to discuss another requirement for the creative person which is even more difficult to accept: *gullibility*, the sixth condition for promoting creativity. Osborn spoke of ruling out criticism during group brainstorming sessions. Gullibility also includes ruling out criticism and suspending judgment for a certain period of time, but it goes beyond that stage; it also goes beyond accepting similarities as accidental or due to mere coincidence. It includes a primitive, pristine regard for similarities that are differentiated from the manifold of the universe in the context of a hypothesis—however seemingly absurd and rudimentally conceived—that the similarity has a meaning. In addition, gullibility means a willingness to explore everything: to be open, innocent, and naive before rejecting anything. It means accepting (at least temporarily or until proved wrong) that there are certain underlying orderly arrangements in everything beyond and within us. More than the inventing of new things, creativity often implies the discovery of these underlying orderly arrangements.

The alleged discovery of underlying arrangements may also, of course, be part of paranoiac-paranoid ideation; and the acceptance of a similarity as a significant fact may be part of schizophrenic thinking in general. However, the creative person does not accept such insights (or seeming insights) indiscriminately. He is gullible only to the extent of not discarding them a priori as nonsense. In fact, he goes a step further: he becomes more attuned to what seem to him to be truths. However, his final acceptance or rejection of an insight must depend on his secondary-process mechanisms.

Even though at a certain point the creative person must transcend autobiographical preoccupations, some important issues or psychological leitmotives tend to recur during the attempts at daydreaming and free thinking. As a matter of fact, the *remembrance and inner replaying of past traumatic conflicts* is the seventh and very important condition for promoting creativity. It is generally assumed that once a person has overcome psychological conflicts or the effects of an early trauma, he should try to forget them. (Forgetting, in these cases, may require a voluntary act of mental suppression.) The assumption, however, is not justified.

Some creative people recognize that this belief is not right, while falling into another error themselves. They believe that the neurotic conflict is a prerequisite for creativity. At times they are reluctant to undergo psychotherapy or psychoanalytic therapy because they are afraid that if they lost their conflicts, they would also lose the motivation and need to create. But we must remember that conflicts *always* exist in the psyche of man. It is our job, then, to distinguish between nontraumatic conflicts and traumatic or neurotic conflicts.

Those conflicts are traumatic or neurotic that limit the functions of the psyche or transform them into abnormal processes. (Nontraumatic conflicts need not concern us here.) The creative person's traumatic or neurotic conflicts should of course be resolved. But they should not be ignored after their solution. If these conflicts are not dealt with, they will continue to be too deeply felt and too personal. The creative person will not be able to transcend his own subjective involvement, and his work will lack universal significance or general resonance. The resolved (or almost-resolved) conflict, on the other hand, can be viewed by the creative person both with a sense of familiarity and as if from a distance, thus becoming more easily transformed into a work of art or a scientific theory or discovery. Roth (1976) considers conflict "one of the two great motivating forces for original work, the other being the desire for self-expression immanent in all of us." Arlow and Brenner write (1964): "The successful resolution of conflicts may result in the formation of permanent ego structures or functions which are stable in nature, which are under the control of the ego, and whose mode of activity no longer reflects the impulsive nature of the original drive component. Sublimations, character traits, and various ego interests are examples of the products of this type of resolution of psychic conflicts."

We have already discussed conflict as motivation in Chapter 2. For the sake of exposition, however, we want to stress again that conflict and its resolution are important not just as motivation for creativity but also as matter related to the content of the creative works. We shall also repeat once more that what is most important is not the past or present conflict, but the ability to transform it into creative work.

Alertness and *discipline* are the ninth and tenth conditions necessary to creativity. Although they are also necessary prerequisites for productivity in general, they take on a particular aspect in creativity. Alertness and discipline are often the conditions enabling the creative person to recognize—whether suddenly, gradually, or after prolonged preparation and incubation—that some particular similarity that he had not dismissed as insignificant, accidental, capricious, fallacious, or inconsequential, is in fact grounded on a phenomenon or system of which there was no previous sufficient awareness.

Many would-be creative persons, especially in the artistic fields, like to believe that only such qualities as imagination, inspiration, intuition, and talent are important. They are reluctant to submit themselves to the rigor of learning techniques and practicing discipline and logical thinking, on the pretext that all these things would stultify their creativity. They ignore the fact that even such people as Giotto, Leonardo, Freud, and Einstein had teachers. A humorous remark which by now has become commonplace, but in which there is a great deal of metaphorical truth, is that creativity is 10 percent inspiration and 90 percent perspiration.

The personal traits and attitudes we have mentioned can and should be encouraged in our educational systems as well as in our daily lives. These characteristics, so briefly sketched (as well as others to be discovered in future studies), facilitate new combinations of primary and secondary processes that lead to the tertiary process.

Nena and George O'Neill, in their useful and pleasant book *Shifting Gears* (1974), review the conditions for creativity which I have discussed in my previous writings. They conclude (p. 238): "Thus we see that while most of the conditions for creativity require a suspension of control, an openness to the inner areas of the self, the last and most important is using our will to put what we have discovered into action—just as in the shifting gears it is not enough to focus and center and make the decision. Without the commitment to action, our creativity may never emerge."

Again and again we see the dichotomy of the creative process, even in the conditions that I have just recommended. Whereas some of these conditions require suspension of control, and openness to the almost automatic effusions of the primary sources, others require the greatest discipline, acuteness, control, checking, and discussion. And all of them must occur in a general atmosphere of devotion, dedication, and commitment.

Creativity in the Middle Years and in Advanced Age

ALTHOUGH we have paid great consideration to adolescents and young adults in their initiation into a life of creativity, we must remember that creativity is recommended for all ages.

The Individual and the Cultivation of Creativity

At a certain time in the life of many individuals, generally toward the middle years but at times as early as the middle twenties, a sense of discouragement prevails. The individual feels he will never be able to create. He must give up. Often, on closer examination, we recognize that persons of this type have been handicapped by a grandiose image of themselves, as first described by Karen Horney (1945, 1950). Early in life they conceived a grandiose self that would live up to great ambitions and expectations. The person would become a great writer, a famous painter, a celebrated composer, dancer, or scientist, and so on. With the passage of time the person realizes that he will not accomplish these great deeds; he then considers himself a failure, and lives the rest of his days in a state of renunciation.

It would be inappropriate in this book to discuss all the psychological and psychiatric implications and ramifications of these complexes (see Horney 1945, 1950; Arieti 1967, Chapter 14). But as far as creativity is concerned, we must (especially through psychotherapy) help the individual to see that he distorts his own self-image inasmuch as he sees only two possibilities: grandeur or failure. Only in extremely rare instances does a creative career bring about fame with the first attempt. The first works of creative men are not generally first-class accomplishments; even an average work should not be interpreted as indicating defeat or failure. An attitude of humility, of willingness to make even the smallest contributions and to accept a life of commitment and dedication, must be part of the potentially creative person's way of life.

I have found that many people can start to be creative, even late in life, if they are able to give up grandiose expectations (at least for the first works). Many patients of mine, especially mothers who had raised several children, felt gaps opening in their lives or found themselves in a state of disorientation when their children went off to college or at least came to require less attention. When such mothers are potentially creative, they feel frustrated when they confront a home that has become "an empty nest." They would like very much to be productive, but are afraid that their long absence from such activity has stultified whatever abilities they once had. Well, it is never too late! Needless to say, my statistics are limited; but while it would be too much to expect another Madame Curie, Virginia Woolf, or Emily Dickinson from the individuals who have come to my attention, I have noticed tremendous progress and considerable results in a large number of them.

The Cultivation of Creativity in the Individual Person

Neugarten and Datan (1974) conclude an excellent article on "The Middle Years" with the following sentence: "Whether perceived as losses or gains, the life events of middle age may produce new stresses for the individual, but they also bring occasions to demonstrate an enriched sense of self and new capacities for coping with complexity." I would like to add that they may demonstrate the fulfillment of a renewed aspiration toward that special complexity which is creativity.

Another problem concerns the span of creativity itself. Can creative people continue to be so throughout life, or is the creative vein depleted at an early age? Cases can be chosen to demonstrate either one view or the other. And related to this question is that of the relative longevity of creative people: Do they live a longer or shorter life than average men? Jaques (1970) studied the death rate among creative artists and "got the impression that the age of thirty-seven seemed to figure rather prominently in the death of individuals of this category." He took a random sample of some 310 painters, composers, poets, writers, and sculptors of undisputed greatness and found that the death rate showed a sudden jump between thirty-five and thirty-nine, at which period it was much above the normal death rate. The group collected by Jaques included Raphael, Mozart, Rimbaud, Purcell, and Baudelaire. Jaques found a big drop below the normal death rate between the ages of forty and forty-four, followed by a return to a normal death rate in the late forties.

Jaques sees a middle-age crisis in those creative people who survive that period of life. The crisis may express itself in three different ways: (1) creativity may come to an end because of death or because the vein is depleted; (2) the creative capacity may begin for the first time at that age; or (3) a decisive change in the quality and content of creativeness may take place. According to Jaques, the creativity of the twenties and early thirties tends to be "a hot-from-the-fire" creativity. It is spontaneous, intense, or precipitative, like the works of Mozart, Keats, Shelley, and Rimbaud. The creativity of the late thirties and thereafter, is what Jaques calls "sculpted creativity." The inspiration may be just as intense and the unconscious work as active as before, but there is much intermediary processing between the initial and the final stages.

Jaques quotes Riviere (1958), who, in one of her writings, described Freud's exhorting her in connection with some psychoanalytic ideas: ". . . write it, write it, put it down in black and white . . . get it out, produce it, make something of it—*outside you*, that is; give it an existence independently of you . . ."

I myself, in many years of teaching young psychiatrists, psychologists, and workers in related areas, have encouraged them to win out over their own hesitations and to write, without expecting the first work to be a masterpiece to be preserved for posterity. I have noticed that unexpressed competition with the great innovators in the field often inhibits young professionals. Equally strong in its inhibiting effect is the already-mentioned unconscious need to live in accordance with a grandiose image, without going through the intermediary steps and vicissitudes. I found that if a young professional has not started to externalize some of his ideas in writing by the age of thirty-five, his chance of doing so later is sharply decreased.

Productivity does not follow a constant pace in creative men. Periods of great creativity alternate with periods devoted to scholarship, observation, or even mere meditation. At times a cycle seems to repeat itself. Jones (1953) has described a cycle of seven years in Freud's creativity. Michelangelo was very active until the age of forty. He did his Pietà at the age of twenty-five, David at twenty-nine, the Sistine Chapel at thirty-seven, and completed Moses by forty. From forty to fifty-five he accomplished practically nothing, but from the age of fifty-five to the rest of his life he continued to produce masterpieces. Then there is the different and well-known case of the composer Rossini, who by the age of thirty-nine had already written all his operas, including the famous Barber of Seville. From the age of thirty-nine to the age of his death, at seventy-four, he wrote very little music and none of great significance.

Manniche and Falk (1957) studied the age of Nobel Prize winners in the fields of medicine, physics, and chemistry from 1901 to 1950. They found that for the period 1901–1925 the mean age at the time of receiving the Nobel award was 51.1 for medicine, 47.8 for physics, and 50.4 for chemistry. For the period 1925–1950 the mean age was 56.9 for medicine, 44.6 for physics, and 51.1 for chemistry. The authors collected evidence that the work for which these scientists were awarded was done, on the average, approximately ten years before they received the award.

Jaques (1970) is impressed by great men who had already accomplished their greatest work at a young age: for instance, Racine, who at the age of thirty-eight had already written Phèdre; Goya, who emerged as a great painter between the ages of thirty-five and thirty-eight; and Ben Jonson, who by the age of forty-three had written all his great plays. On the other hand, Butler, a psychiatrist well known for his studies in psychiatry of old age, has stressed, in a very erudite article (1967), how many great men have enjoyed a very long life and have been productive until the end. His article is a mine of information that must be read by anyone interested in the topic. He mentioned the following as illustrations of persistent creativity in later life: Sophocles, Michelangelo, Titian, Tintoretto, Cervantes, Hals, Voltaire, Goethe, Tennyson, Humboldt, Franck, Hugo, Verdi, Tolstoy, Shaw, and Freud. (Other names, such as Haydn's, come to mind, and many more could be added. Some famous examples lived in our own time: Winston Churchill, Bertrand Russell, Pablo Picasso.) Titian painted the famous battle of Lepanto at the age of ninety-eight and lived to be 100. Verdi composed *Falstaff* at the age of eighty and died at the age of eighty-eight. Tolstoy, who died at the age of eighty-two, wrote *Resurrection* ten years before his death.

Lehmann (1953) wrote that "with some dramatic exceptions, our greatest creative thinkers have been rather long-lived." Butler advances the hypothesis that longevity and creativity are associated. In the quoted article he presents a long list of great men, from Augustine to Freud, who have written autobiographical memoirs. The list is imposing, and it suggests that writing one's memoirs has a therapeutic and possibly life-prolonging aspect.

One conclusion seems easy to draw from the various sources of information that we have collected. Creativity can occur at any age, even the most advanced, and seems to have a salutary effect on the creative person. We may also hypothetically state that memory impairment does not seem to be prominent in creative people who reach a very advanced age; or if it exists, it is easily compensated for by other factors such as a broader vision of life and easy associative powers.

PART SIX

Creativity in the

Larger Contexts of

Neurology, Biology,

General System Theory,

and the Spirit of Man

Chapter 17

The Neurology of Creativity and Biological Creativity

The Cerebral Cortex

ANY ATTEMPT toward a neurological or neurophysiological interpretation of creativity can be made only in the most pioneering and tentative way. What we know for certain is commonplace and does not need to be repeated, namely, that a human brain is necessary for creativity. Why only a human brain and not that of any other animal species? Is it because of its larger size, or because of the number of specific cells, or neurons, of which it is constituted? Certainly the size of the brain and the number of neurons are essential prerequisites. Let us remember, however, that the brain of our nearest primate relative, the chimpanzee, has approximately 80 percent as many neurons as our brains do. Yet while the chimpanzee is by far superior to nonprimate species and much more similar to us than to them, he has very little imagination, no language, and no real creativity. Can a 20 percent difference in neurons explain the abysmal difference between the psychological life of a chimpanzee and that of a man? Apparently yes. But this conclusion necessitates collateral inferences. When a certain number of neurons is reached in the cerebral cortex, a new dimension, a new outlook, a new level of life emerges that is not predictable, not grounded in what existed before.

According to some recent calculations, the human cortex has fifteen billion neurons (Noback and Demarest 1972, 1975), and consequently that of the chimpanzee has twelve billion. If this is so, then the addition of three billion neurons is responsible for a new quality of life that was not foreseeable from the physiology and behavior of animals with less endowed cortexes. Of course, it is not possible even to venture a guess as to how many more neurons would be necessary for another leap similar in significance to that which has occurred from chimpanzee to man. Would a billion more neurons determine only a moderate improvement? Would three billion more neurons, developed in the cortex of an animal species living in this planet or in a different solar system, endow that species with capacities whose scope and understanding we cannot even conceive? If we refrain from such speculations and simply examine the cerebral cortex of the human being as it is now, we can certainly conclude that it is the most complicated entity in the universe known to us.

The complexity of human life and the complexity of creativity, in particular, mirror the cortical complexity. This complexity reveals itself in its astronomical magnitude if we consider that each neuron has prolongations and ramifications (the axon and dendrites) with which it makes connections with other cells. It has been calculated that an average cortical cell receives about 2,000 contacts from the ramifications of other cells. Thus this incredibly complicated network can make patterns of neurons whose numbers reach unimaginable proportions; the most complicated computer is appallingly simple in comparison. The mathematics involved in such patterns is in its infancy, although important pioneer studies have already been made (Burns 1968; Smith and Smith 1965; Smith and Burns 1960).

The nervous impulse is transmitted from neuron to neuron. The interconnection between neurons, the synapse, may be activated for a tenth of a second. The interval between a synaptic activation of a neuron and the activation of another synapse on the part of this neuron may take place in a millisecond (Eccles 1973). We thus have a firmament of connections, and a multitude of impulses spreading in all directions in a very rapid time. Some neurons form wavefronts (or grouping discharges) at the same time or in consecutive order, and the peripheries of these wavefronts subliminally activate other neurons and determine the emergence of new wavefronts.

Perceptions and interpretations of the world are carried out through patterns of neurons. The neurons can be compared to musical notes, except that they are more complicated and enormously more numerous. But just as the same notes, in different combinations, produce different melodies, so neurons in different combinations produce different images and thoughts. Perceptions, memories, and higher mental processes are mediated by spatiotemporal patterns of neuronal activations. In each pattern, neurons are connected by selective synaptic changes. A repetition of an experience reactivates the pattern of the original experience. These patterns are called *engrams*. In the cerebral cortex immense numbers of patterns of specific neuronal connections are ready for replay (Eccles 1973). However, these engrams are not static structures. To some extent they change. Eccles, relying on the work of other authors in addition to his own, concludes that in contrast to the commonly accepted view of the brain as a static structure, at the microlevel it is a structurally plastic entity, inasmuch as at any given time some synapses are mature, others are developing, and others are regressing.

In an earlier article (1958) Eccles wrote that a neuron operates on a power level of about one thousand millionth of a watt. (Thus the whole brain operates on about ten watts.) Eccles wrote that the substance that transmits the stimulus at some synapses is liberated in quanta of a few thousand molecules only. Thus on the long extremity (or axon side) of the neuron, vesicles containing the transmitting substance "are so tiny that, in accordance with the Heisenberg uncertainty principle, there is a relatively large uncertainty as to their location over a period as brief as a millisecond" (Eccles 1958).

The writings of Burns are also very important (1968). He defines a nerve net as "a population of similar neurons which are functionally interconnected so that, when fully excitable, activity among some of them always spreads to invade the remainder." In his remarkable and erudite book he writes not only of the stability of cortical neurons but also of their uncertain responses. As a matter of fact, he gives his book the very significant title, *The Uncertain Nervous System*.

Although we have not entered at all deeply into the immense complexity of the anatomy and physiology of the cerebral cortex, we are now in position to enunciate two principles:

1. With the development of a large number of neurons in the course of evolution, the possibility emerges for high mental activities, including creativity. All these high activities can be included in "the symbolic process."

2. The velocity of the processes, the size of the molecules involved at the synapses, and the unpredictability of the synaptic responses or of the routes taken by the nervous impulse, are compatible with creativity's elements of newness and unpredictability. In other words, the structure of the cortical apparatus is consistent with a margin of indeterminacy concerning mental processes in general and creativity in particular. Not everything about a high mental function can be predicted from what we know about the cerebral cortex, nor can everything be predicted from the experiences of the external world that bring about the formation of specific engrams. That is, the indeterminacy principle of Heisenberg, or something similar, may to some extent be applicable to the cerebral cortex as well. The concept of strict causality has to be abandoned, to be replaced by the law of probability.

If we look at the history of civilization, we can certainly state that unpredictability is one of its prominent characteristics. Nobody could have predicted the development of science, literature, and art as they unfolded throughout history, or as they unfold in the life of a single individual.

However, it would be an error to say that *nothing* can be predicted, or, neurologically speaking, that we know nothing about the neurons that will be part of a given engram. As a matter of fact, the opposite is true. We know, for instance, that certain parts of the brain have special roles in some mental activities, including creativity. Before discussing the localization of functions, however, let us remember that the nervous system probably acts as a whole, in addition to these specific functions. Again Burns writes, "It would not be surprising if statistical methods ultimately demonstrate some small, but measurable, influence of any active group of neurons upon all other parts of the nervous system, however remote." Nevertheless, he reminds us that large communities of central neurons behave in a relatively autonomous fashion.

The Creative Cortical Areas

THE CORTEX is divided into two main parts: the phylogenetically older allocortex, which consists of about 10 percent of the entire cortex and is in turn divided into the archipallium and paleocortex; and the neopallium, which forms the bulk of the cerebral cortex. The neopallium (or neocortex) is essential for creativity.

Many areas of the cortex have specific functions. The specificity is not absolute; some areas are much more involved than others, however, and have a definite role in some functions. These are the primary sensory areas in the postcentral gyrus, usually designated (after Brodmann) as areas 1, 2, 3; the primary visual area, 17; the primary auditory area, 41; the primary motor area, 4; the premotor areas, 6 and 8; and the language areas, 39, 44, and 45. Textbooks of neuroanatomy and neurophysiology describe how these areas are necessary for visual, auditory, tactile, pain, temperature, and other perceptions of the external world; for voluntary action; for speaking; and for the understanding of written and spoken language. These areas are thus basic for the common life of man. Penfield (1966) characterized the parts of the cortex that we have just mentioned as "committed"; that is, they are committed to very definite functions. And Penfield stressed again that whereas most of the cortex of other animals is "committed to sensory or motor functions," the greatest part of man's cortex is "uncommitted." To be more exact, its function is undetermined, at least at birth.

I have divided this "uncommitted" cortex into two areas that I have designated as the TOP area (for reasons soon indicated) and the prefrontal or PF area (Arieti 1955, 1956b, 1975), and I have tried to show that these areas, too, become very committed. However, what the result of this commitment will be cannot be determined. The percentage of predictability and probability is relatively high when we consider the lowest of the high functions, such as solutions of some basic problems. However, the higher the function and the more neurons involved, the higher is the indeterminacy.

The TOP and PF areas, or association areas, are occasionally also called "silent" areas because their function is still mysterious or silent. Actually they are the areas where the greatest number of associations and syntheses arise from inputs coming from all the other parts of the brain. It is in these areas that the highest mental processes occur, such as symbolic activities, anticipations of the future, and abstractions of any kind. In both hemispheres the TOP area includes parts of the *t*emporal, *o*ccipital, and *p*arietal lobes, from the first letters of which it derives its name. Specifically it consists of a large part of the temporal lobe (Brodmann's areas 20, 21, and 37) and a small part of the parietal and occipital lobes (consisting of the most central parts of Brodmann's areas 7, 19, 39, and 40), as seen in Figure 17-1. From a physiological point of view the TOP area may be considered as the center of functionality of a much larger area including all of the parietal and occipital and most of the temporal lobes. These three lobes form the part of the brain that receives stimuli from the external world and processes them into progressively higher constructs. All of the stimuli coming from other parts of the cortex are synthesized and elaborated into the highest mental constructs in the TOP area. Of course, we must not consider this area as isolated or as functioning by itself. First of all, it is associated with the corresponding area of the opposite hemisphere by means of fibers that pass through the corpus callosum. It has important connections with the frontal lobes, without which it could not function at all, and it is also connected with much lower structures through the archipallium.

We should not think that only the TOP area is required for the highest mental processes. The neuronal networks (or engrams) that mediate the highest mental processes extend to many other areas. However, as I have discussed in detail elsewhere (Arieti 1955, 1956b, 1974), the TOP area is needed for the highest processes of abstraction. Perceptions, images, primitive symbols, verbal symbols, and others, are elaborated here into the highest conceptualizations, hypotheses, ideals, ethics, aesthetics, scientific pursuits, and syntheses.

The TOP area could not function without the concerted activity of the PF (prefrontal) area, which consists of Brodmann's areas 9 through 12. The PF area has four major functions. The first is to maintain a steadfastness of purpose against distracting impulses from the environment (Malmo 1942); in other words, the function of focal attention. The importance of focal attention as a prerequisite for higher mental processes has been illustrated by Schachtel (1954). As Schachtel wrote, each act of focal attention consists not just of one sustained approach to the object to which it is directed, but of several renewed approaches. Focal attention requires the ability to suppress

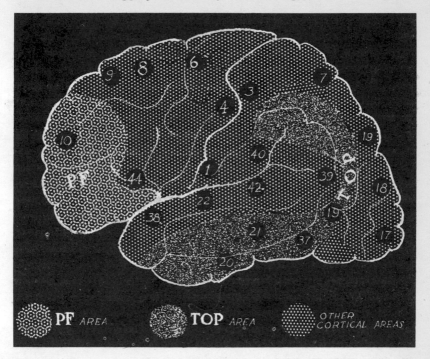

Figure 17-1

secondary stimuli and to delay the response to them. It is obvious that the high elaboration of stimuli mentioned in connection with the TOP areas could not take place if this function of the PF areas did not permit it.

A second function of the PF areas is to anticipate the future (Freeman and Watts 1942), a third function is to permit planned or seriatim functions. By seriatim functions is meant the organization or synthesis of skilled acts or thoughts into an orderly series (Morgan 1943). Seriatim functions imply the ability (1) to anticipate a goal, and (2) to organize and synthesize acts or thoughts in a given temporal sequence for the purpose of reaching the anticipated goal (Brickner 1936). Finally, the fourth function of the PF areas is to make choices and to initiate the transformation of the mental choice into a motor action.

There seems to be no doubt that the TOP and PF areas elaborate the psychological material coming from other areas of the central nervous system and are responsible for higher thinking and for the planning of complicated actions. No matter how undetermined their function is at birth, and no matter how "silent" their work seems to be, these areas soon become the greatest participants in human life.

In previous works (Arieti 1955, 1956b, 1974) I have demonstrated that in these two areas, as well as in some connections of these two areas with the archipallium, are mediated those abnormal psychological functions that occur in schizophrenia. I may now add that in these very same TOP and PF areas occur those psychological processes that are necessary for any creative work.*

The association of schizophrenia and creativity with the cerebral cortex is neither strange nor paradoxical or coincidental. In schizophrenia the highest functions (mediated in the TOP and PF areas) are disturbed. In creativity the functions of these areas unfold in unusually positive ways. Although the same areas are involved in the two conditions, it seems logical to assume that the manner of functioning is different. Unfortunately we do not know, *at a neurophysiological level*, how the networks of these two areas function abnormally in schizophrenia as a consequence of psychological or organic factors. It is even more difficult to determine how differently these two networks function in the creative person relative to the average individual. Both in the schizophrenic and in the creative person we know much more about the psychological processes than about the concomitant neurophysiological mechanisms. Obviously when it comes to creativity, unusual networks of neurons are formed.

Recently some workers have tried to demonstrate that the brain works in two different modes, the active and the receptive (Deikman 1971). Interesting works by Sperry (1961, 1967) have given new impetus to the old belief of Wigan (1844) that a man with two cerebral hemispheres must have two minds. According to Bogen (1969), propositional thought is typically lateralized in the left hemisphere, and appositional thought in the right. Having collected suggestions and hypotheses from various authors, Bogen comes to the belief that the left hemisphere tends, in its functions, to be atomistic, analytic, symbolic, abstract, digital, secondary-process, and so on. The right hemi-

---

* Penfield (1966) called the "uncommitted" cortex interpretative. Certainly interpretation is one of its major functions, but it is not the only one unless we consider every high mental function as having *only* an interpretative aspect.

sphere tends to be global, synthetic, perceptual, concrete, analogic, primary-process, and so on. If these observations are correct, it would seem that both hemispheres—the right predominantly as the organ of the primary and the left of the secondary process—are necessary for creativity. The hypotheses are indeed intriguing, but in my opinion the neurological evidence is by no means conclusive.

Engrams and Complex Functional Systems

AN EXPERIENCE leaves a trace, called an engram, in some neurons. The engram is the enduring basis that accounts not only for the memory of that experience but also for the later reactivation of the experience in the form of recall, or as a constituent of new psychological experiences. The unfolding of the human psyche may ultimately be considered as a formation and transformation of engrams (and groupings of engrams) throughout life.

Engrams and groupings of engrams make the concept of localizations of functions in the cerebral cortex a relative one. The great Russian neuropsychologist Luria (1966, 1973) writes that mental functions are complex functional systems that cannot be localized in narrow areas. These systems consist of working zones of the nervous system, which function concertedly or toward a common aim. External stimuli act as essential elements in the establishment of functional connections between individual parts of the brain. These functional systems become "new functional organs" (Leontiev 1959). Luria quotes Vygotsky (1960), who called this process the principle of "extracortical organization of complex mental functions." Luria also stressed that these functional systems are never static but always changing.

By enlarging the concept of the engram to that of a complex functional system, Luria further clarifies the particular structure (and ongoing structuring) of the psyche. The growth or development of the psyche is different from the development of the organism. The embryo, and later the developing organism, follow pathways already established. In other words, all the "information" that the embryo needs (and almost all the information that the developing somatic organism needs) is already coded into the structures of their genes. The psyche, however, largely makes up its own patterns of development. Indeed, psychological life is the history of the formation of these engrams, or functional systems, and of their interrelations. These systems are the result of the combined participation of biological factors (the general genetic structure and the specific neurological genetic structure) and environmental factors (the general process of socialization occurring in every man, and the specific sociocultural environment).

In the psyche of each individual, genetic programming plays only a partial role. A great deal of the psyche's content has not been programmed genetically. Whatever derives from the sociocultural environment is immense, and it probably goes on accumulating every day of our life. If we consider the problem mathematically, however, it seems that we do not have to worry that the psyche has too much to absorb. If we calculate that billions of neurons are involved and that their combinations (and the combinations of their ramifications) are infinite, we do not have to despair about the immensity of the input. Of course, the input has to be offered with periods of rest, avoiding refractory phases and unhealthy conflicts. Once the engrams and the functional systems are formed, the mental activity of an individual and his behavior become predictable and determinable to a considerable extent. As a matter of fact, not only the establishment of conditioned reflexes but any form of learning, including the building of concepts and of functional systems, is an economic device used by the human being to cope with the immensity of the universe and of one's experiences.

The retracing of beaten paths in our cerebral neurons, in our thoughts and emotions, and in our actions permits the human being a certain relaxation, tranquillity, and peace of mind, with sufficient energy left over for the myriads of things he wishes to attend to. The development of the psyche can also be viewed as a way to decrease the indeterminacy of the once-"uncommitted" cortex.

Returning to the matter of creativity: functional systems develop in the life of each individual, and it will be difficult to determine in which ways the average person differs from the creative person in the formation and use of these systems. (To my knowledge, Luria does not advance hypotheses about the creative process in his writings.) If our knowledge of the neuropsychology of the usual high mental functions is limited, that of the neuropsychology of the creative process is almost nonexistent. We can only speculate on the possibility of certain characteristics and mechanisms. Among the hypotheses that we can advance is the following one: the TOP and PF cortex of the creative person is probably likely to revisit the determined or "committed" cortex many more times, or to send back impulses to it. We have seen in Part Three how important the visual, auditory, and verbal perceptions and images are for most forms of creativity. Although an intelligent but uncreative person also uses neuronal networks of the TOP and PF areas very often, the mind of the creative person, in the act of doing creative work, participates consciously or unconsciously in a dialogue between these two areas and the rest of the cortex.

A second assumption is that in the TOP and PF areas there are different levels of integration (or different functional systems and subsystems). Some systems, presumably those connected more closely with genetic factors, are predominantly archaic or use a primary-process type of organization. Again, then, the mind of the creative person participates in a dialogue between the archaic systems and the secondary-process systems.

Another hypothetical point has to be made. Pavlov described (not in the creative person but in the healthy average organism) *an optimal level of cortical tone* that is required for organized, goal-directed mental activity. During this optimal level of cortical tone, the law of strength prevails. That is, every strong (or biologically significant) stimulus evokes a strong response, while every weak stimulus evokes a weak response (Luria, 1973). In a state which is not the optimal level, the law of strength is violated. Weak stimuli may evoke responses equally strong as do strong stimuli (the "equalizing phase"), or may evoke stronger responses than do stronger stimuli (the "paradoxical phase"). They may even continue to evoke a response, whereas strong stimuli cease to do so altogether (the "ultraparadoxical phase,"). These phasic states (that is, states in which there is no optimal level of cortical tone) remind us of what happens in dreams. As a matter of fact, we know how a usually weak stimulus—for instance, the appearance of a cat—may affect us as strongly in a dream as the appearance of a tiger. Indifference to strong stimuli and persistence of the effect of usually weak stimuli are also common in dreams. In the creative person, too, a weak stimulus, such as a characteristic of an object, may become a strong one when used as a metaphor. A weak stimulus such as a falling apple may evoke the concept of the force of gravity.

In 1949, Moruzzi and Magoun demonstrated that the structures that maintain and regulate the cortical tone do not lie in the cortex itself, but in the subcortex and brain stem. These structures form a nerve net called the *reticular formation*. The reticular formation controls the state of awakeness, alertness, and activation by environmental and organismic stimuli. At the same time that it activates some parts, it inhibits others. It could very well be that neurological structures that are usually inhibited in the average person, maintain a readiness for activation in the creative person.

The medial zones of the cerebral hemispheres—those areas called the paleocortex, archipallium, cingular gyrus, and Papez's hippocampal circle—have a great deal to do with the determination of an emotional tone and therefore must be important, too, in any creative process; but how, it is hard to say. Probably they are ready to respond strongly to connections that generally do not elicit such responses.

How new functional systems (or new functions of established functional systems) develop is impossible to say. If similarity also plays a role in the neurophysiology of the cortex, it could be that two engrams become connected when they have a part in common. Let us say that the two engrams which, in my mind, represent Brahms and Mozart, have in common those neurons (or parts of neurons) that represent the concept "great composers." It could be that it is the common part of an engram that reactivates the second engram or sends the impulse to the total. But in the creative process, two or more engrams are not only associated or reactivated together; the rest of the psyche bears witness that, underlying the association, there is a new phenomenon, which in its turn will be represented by a new engram. The apple and the moon not only have the common quality of being attracted by the earth; they are part of the class of gravitational bodies, a new engram appearing for the first time in the mind of Newton. In these cases of creativity the old meanings, by being interconnected and interpreted, form a new meaningfulness.

There is one final, important consideration. Although the creative process evolves in the infinite meanders of the TOP and PF areas, it must ultimately return to the committed or determined cortex. The ultimate commitment is in fact to assume a representation; and for this representation the motor areas, the visual and auditory areas, and the language centers are needed. The creative person cannot put his creative product into writing, or on a canvas, or on a piece of marble, or in mathematical formulas without the functions of these areas. The impulse thus returns to the primary sources after the most complicated and unpredictable gestation—a gestation in no way comparable to that of an embryo.

Creativity and Neuropathology

IS THE WHOLE BRAIN necessary for creativity? Could a person with great lesions of the brain be creative? The matter is debatable. Luria, Tsvetkova, and Futer (1965) reported the case of a famous composer who, after a hemorrhage in the left temporal region, was unable to distinguish the sounds of speech or to understand words spoken to him, and yet continued "to compose brilliant musical works." Bonvicini (1926) reported the case of the painter Daniel Urrabieta (known under the name Vierge) who, after cerebral apoplexy resulting in right hemiplegia, severe motor aphasia, and alexia, but no semantic aphasia, started to paint using the left hand and achieved such success that he became a famous illustrator in the most important French periodicals. Alajouanine, too (1948), reported three patients who retained artistic creativity after they developed aphasia. Zaimov, Kitov, and Kolev (1969) reported the case of a Bulgarian painter who developed hemiplegia and aphasia as a result of cerebral apoplexy. This painter, famous before his illness, continued to paint afterwards with great success. As with Vierge, he used the left hand instead of the right; his painting also changed tonality, as light colors came to be used more frequently; and the compositions became less stylized. At the time of the report, sixteen years after the cerebral accident, the painter continued to work with great success and his paintings were highly appreciated. (Other writers follow Head [1926] in stating that aphasic patients show definite flaws in their drawings.)

It is difficult to explain these cases of severely brain injured people who could continue their creative work, since most people with such lesions are severely incapacitated. Those who retained their ability probably were not affected seriously in some functional systems of the TOP and PF areas. We must also recognize that the above-mentioned injured people who retained creative ability did not achieve heights in their fields comparable to those of a Mozart or a Rembrandt. What was spectacular in their cases was the fact that they could be creative at all, in spite of the seriousness of their lesions.

The study of creativity in people in whom some sensorial input was defective or totally absent is also very rewarding. Lowenfeld (1959) reported how painting and sculpture were possible in weak-sighted and even blind individuals. Other authors have demonstrated how creativity and poetry in particular could be cultivated in deaf children (Buck and Kramer 1972, 1973, 1974; Kramer and Buck, in press.)

Buck and Kramer follow Furth (1966) in believing that reduced ability in the deaf can be explained by a deprivation in linguistic training. They have demonstrated that an accepting, respecting environment "can give rise to conditions which provide a bridge to the high level of intellectual and creative potential which many deaf children possess." The authors have collected unusually beautiful poems, written by deaf children, which show that even the deaf can obtain a sense of rhythm from nonauditory functions of the body. Some of these poems have a definite respect for meter, as well as assonances, alliterations, and metaphors.

Another important problem, which tangentially concerns creativity, is what has been referred to by the anthropologist Ashley Montagu (1972) as "sociogenic brain damage." Valentine and Valentine (1975) have recently given strong support to Montagu's concept, although differing on some collateral views. Montagu writes, "Social malnourishment, both structurally and functionally, can be just as brain/mind-damaging as physical malnourishment. Such sociogenic malnourishment affects the brains of millions of human beings not only in the United States but all over the world. It is a form of brain damage which has received far too little attention. Yet it constitutes an epidemic problem of major proportions . . ." Montagu describes how malnutrition caused by poverty and ghetto living may cause damage to the brain. However, his main point is that psychological impoverishment, stemming from environments that do not stimulate people sufficiently, produces a social deprivation syndrome characterized by short attention span, learning difficulties, low test scores, and poor scholastic achievements. Some of the children so affected may be diagnosed as suffering from pituitary dwarfism or mental retardation, yet when rescued from the damaging environment they may achieve normal development (Reinhardt and Brash 1969).

It is obvious that creativity is unlikely to occur in an environment that causes sociogenic brain damage, except in those privileged groups that can escape the damaging influences. However, it is gratifying to know that the condition can be remedied. If we correlate Montagu's findings with those reported in Chapter 14, we can even hope of changing an environment that causes "sociogenic brain damage" into a creativogenic one.

Biological Creativity

THE CONCEPT of the tertiary process attempts to explain the innovating power of creativity. A new combination of what already existed is not a rearrangement of the old. A new combination may engender the emergence of a new entity, with unforeseeable characteristics, just as a special combination of two gases, hydrogen and oxygen, brings about that apparently unrelated liquid which is water. Only *creation*, not creativity, can be considered as emerging *ex nihilo* (from nothingness). But creation is a theological concept, not a scientific one. Human creativity has no other resort but the use of what is available. However, the range of what is available is enlarged by the resumed use of primary-process and archaic secondary-process mechanisms.

Although we cannot study creation scientifically, we can attempt to study what was not created by man. Biological evolution, in its innumerable creative aspects, comes closer to our understanding: at this stage in our knowledge we can recognize, in the long course of evolution, developmental processes similar to those found in human creativity. Obviously it is not evolution that follows man, but man who follows evolution—or who follows something related to evolution in his civilization. And both biological evolution and civilization may follow norms applicable to various systems, as general system theory teaches.

Biological creativity is evident in many examples offered by the phylogeny of the central nervous system. When new nervous structures emerge as a result of series of mutations and take over some functions from lower structures, these lower structures—which, at a psychological level, correspond to our obsolete, archaic, or primary-process mechanisms—are not eliminated. Instead they are readjusted and reintegrated to form a functional subsystem with the higher structure. For instance, the evolution of movement culminates with the appearance of the motor cortex in mammals. When the motor cortex takes over the government of voluntary movements, the basal ganglia that were also present in lower species do not fall into disuse. In their new integration with the cortex, they modify and increase the flexibility of postural movements and add automatic movements. They also organize the coordination of the movements of the flexors and extensors of the limbs.

To take another example, the archipallium, which is very important in lower mammals for the elaboration of olfactory perceptions, to a large extent loses this specific function in higher mammals, which depend less on the sense of smell. But as Papez's studies have indicated (1937), the archipallium does not discontinue functioning in higher mammals. In a process of biological creativity, it becomes reintegrated with neopallial areas and comes to play an important role in the experiencing of emotions.

Neurology could provide many similar examples. However, we do not need to confine our examples to this science, which is closely related to psychology. The appearance of new species in biological evolution can be explained in similar ways, provided we also take environmental changes into account.

Mutations are inaccuracies in the hereditary constitution: they are alterations that may involve the addition of a new chromosome, the loss of a chromosome, or some change within a chromosome. When mutations occur, new gamuts of spontaneity unfold, and good results may develop from some of them. As we have already mentioned in Chapter 1, "spontaneity" means a certain range of organismic possibilities offered by the intrinsic qualities of the organism. However, at a given level of evolution, these possibilities do not tend to remain spontaneous but to follow the so-called law of effect. In other words, when a spontaneous activity becomes connected with an environmental situation and the effect is good from the point of view of survival or of improved function, it tends to remain fixated and eventually to become an automatic or even an innate function.

The molecular groupings that constitute the mutated organism have a different margin of instability. The bonds between the atoms form arrangements that are likely to have a number of new possibilities. Most of these mutations, which can be compared to our psycho-pathological or primary-process forms, are harmful from the point of view of survival. They do not permit adaptation. But an extremely small number of mutations *are* favorable, if they happen to occur when improbable environmental situations have also developed which enhance their survival and enable them to compete successfully with other, nonmutant forms.

For example, the common tapeworm belongs to the family of cestodes, organisms that appeared on earth long before man. At one point in the history of the species, it happened that some cestodes underwent a mutation. A new instability endangered the survival of these mutated groups, which could survive only in such an improbable environment as the intestine of mammals, and some only in the intestine of man. But if some of these mutated cestodes did land by chance in human intestines, the effect would be good—for the cestodes, not for man—and the species would survive as the tapeworm. The mutation of some cestodes was not preestablished, and the presence of men who came in contact with these cestodes was also casual. But this improbable encounter of two factors produced a system, *created* a pattern of development necessary for the survival of the tapeworm as a new species. A new steady state, *similar* to other steady states in open systems, came to be. A steady state is a state in which energies are constantly used to maintain the relationship of the parts and keep them from decay (Bertalanffy 1955, 1967, 1968). As we have mentioned in Chapter 13, the "openness" of the open system refers to special relations with the environment which permit the survival of the system and its dynamics. Had man not existed then, that particular strain of mutant cestodes would have perished. But man happened to exist, and the mutant cestode emerged in an act of biological creativity—much to our discomfort. (Biological creativity, in contrast to human creativity, does not have to be desirable from a human point of view.)

Mutations provide the raw material of evolution: blind variations. Special environmental situations act like secondary-process mechanisms and transform pathological forms into something new, more complicated, and capable of survival. That which at first was an accident or a random occurrence becomes integrated into a more organized pattern. In other words, a selective retention followed a blind variation. The blindness, or absolute lack of selectivity, of the mutation was met by an unusually appropriate environmental condition. This condition *appears* to our first understanding as selected and purposeful.

Phylogenetic creativity has two assets at its disposal. One is infinite time, so that even the most improbable mutations and the most improbable combinations with favorable environmental conditions eventually do occur. The second is the survival and genetic reproduction of the favorable combinations. With these two assets, evolutionary creativity pushes toward order, integration, and complexity.

Man does not have infinite time at his disposal. But with his cognitive mechanisms, his cumulative experience transmitted from previous generations, and—most of all—his conscious purpose and goal-directedness, he is able to immeasurably reduce the time required for creativity. For example, some instruments devised by men, such as optical and photographic equipment, computers of various types, and so on, are the equivalents of organs of the body that took billions of years to evolve merely through chance mutations and favorable environmental situations. Man's primary process has replaced nature's blind variations, and the secondary process has replaced the proper environment. In a very interesting article Campbell (1960) has shown how blind variation and selective retention operate both in biological evolution and in human creativity.

The main difference between human and biological creativity is to be found in the subjective state of search and attainment that man experiences. Similar subjective states occur in many other psychological processes, which I have described in *The Intrapsychic Self*. In the realm of creativity, the subjective experience reaches a culminating point in the inspiration of the artist, in the revelation of the religious person, in the "Eureka" experience of the scientist. This subjectivity is part of the whole mysterious phenomenon of private experience, which transcends any scientific understanding of man (Stent 1975). Throughout the chapters of Part Three it was acknowledged that we reached an impasse when we tried to explain why a given object, whether natural or created by man, evokes a specific private response. In spite of our dissatisfaction, we have not yet succeeded in overcoming the Cartesian dichotomy of mind and matter.

Chapter 18

Some General Issues and Conclusions

Randomness and Order, Discovery and Rediscovery

IN BOTH HUMAN and biological creativity, we are confronted with new aspects of reality that cannot be explained or predicted in terms of preexisting conditions. Is it possible to explain, in terms of logical and ineluctable steps, how biological evolution derived the virus, the amoeba, and finally man from the randomness of inorganic atoms? Are the elements of a product of creativity really unrelated, or do they only seem unrelated?

In human creativity, too, the elements often seem disconnected, like the example of the Venus de Milo and the ugly lady mentioned in Chapter 7, or Newton's apple and the moon. The creative person is able to transform the sea of irrelevancy in which he finds himself into a vision of order and beauty, or he sees how a tiny fragment of seeming cosmic futility collides and coincides with a piece of obviousness. He is provided with the capacity to transform randomness and disparity into organized structure.

Whether what appears new to us is really new or not, constitutes a problem that has been debated for a long time. Many great thinkers, following Socrates and Plato, have sustained the idea that any discovery is actually a rediscovery. It may be a rediscovery of the preexistent truth in a platonic world of ideas, or of the noumena of Kant. The truth that is discovered and seems new was actually either hidden in our mind, our unconscious, or in a part of the universe that is unknown to us. Any form of creativity would thus be the transformation of a piece of transcendence into a piece of immanence. This concept has lost ground in the last few centuries, especially with the empirico-positivistic approach and the development of science. And yet in science it is easy to accept that discoveries are in fact rediscoveries of something inherent in nature. When Newton discovered the force of gravity, it was accepted that such a force always existed; it was not invented by him. Certainly a play by Shakespeare or a symphony by Beethoven was in the realm of possibility; it evokes emotions and ideas that were latently in us. However, the precise effect and the plan of development of these works could not have been foreseen.

At any rate, whether that which comes to immanent existence is or is not the unfolding of a transcendental previous state is a philosophical or religious problem that lies beyond the scope of our inquiry. My opinion is that in the realm of physical reality, creativity can consist both of a rediscovery of what already existed in hidden form, and of the emergence of something new. In both cases it does deal with the new. In scientific cases—for example, that of Newton—the thing that was completely new and not just a rediscovery was the way in which he "rediscovered" the force of gravity, a way that could not have been predicted. In science, creativity often consists of the ability to extract a formerly obscure or apparently inessential aspect from all the relevant data. Again, the means by which this extraction can take place are in many cases unusual and improbable.

If we interpret creativity merely as a discovery of what was implied, we must exclude the concept of infinity. Infinity transcends the number of finite and predictable things. As we have seen in Chapter 17, the cerebral cortex presents infinite possibilities and an indeterminate number of neuronal patterns. We also know that the human mind, too, can conceive infinite systems of symbolism, as in mathematics. Even if the universe is finite, it may include infinite systems.

Structures and General Systems

IF WE ACCEPT the concept of infinity and indeterminacy, must we give up the idea of finding structures and rules that govern the creative process? The present book has demonstrated that this is not so. Within the realm of indeterminacy and probability, structures and systems and patterns emerge. We have seen that many authors have attempted to differentiate these patterns. Some, like those mentioned in Chapter 2, have also described general models that do not include specific elements. Some patterns, recognizable in certain areas, have been extended by various authors to other fields, with uncertain validity. In a number of cases, adventitious characteristics (such as ambiguity) have been mistaken for essential ones.

Rothenberg (1971) believes that creativity is based on what he calls *Janusian thinking*. Janusian thinking (from Janus, the god with two faces) is "the capacity to conceive and utilize two or more opposite or contradictory ideas, concepts, or images simultaneously." Rothenberg received strong inspiration from Eugene O'Neill's play *The Iceman Cometh*. According to Rothenberg, the central iceman symbol in the play has at least three contradictory connotations: (1) the iceman is death; (2) the iceman is Christ, since the play can be seen as a modern parable of the Last Supper; and (3) the iceman is a sexually potent adulterer.

Rothenberg is correct in stating that two or more opposite or contradictory ideas or images are used in some creative processes. His ideas fit the Hegelian theory of thesis and antithesis, which lead to a synthesis. We, too, have seen such occurrences in examples given earlier, especially in Chapters 7 and 8. In many other cases, however, the ideas are merely different and unrelated. Moreover, Rothenberg does not enter into the problem of how the different ideas are coordinated.

In Part Three of this book I have tried to describe the patterns of creativity or the structures of creativity in various fields. These structures and patterns do not derive from direct experience; they are related to deep structures, inaccessible to direct observation. But these deep structures can be inferred indirectly from examination of the overt surface structures. Psychoanalysis and psychostructuralism follow this method.

The deep structures that explain schizophrenic thinking and

primitive human thinking (Arieti 1948, 1955), or that underlie our linguistic patterns (Chomsky 1957), become involved with higher and logical structures. A condition of fantastic improbability—the unpredictable agreement between different levels of structures—brings about the desirable new creation. If the randomness of the external experiences and the indeterminacy of neuronal circuits eventually turn out to produce a creative product, it is on account of these deep structures organized within the framework of our neurological apparatus.

Why are structures formed? Why do repetitive patterns occur? We cannot any longer accept a naive behaviorism that dismisses these problems. On the other hand, we must admit that we do not know the answers, in spite of many philosophical attempts to find them.

For Croce (1909), intuition is the undifferentiated unity of the perception of the real and of the simple image of the possible. He unifies perception and imagery (based on the real or on the possible) under the term *intuition*. The unsettled state of the meaning of intuition allows Croce to put together two extremely complicated phenomena. Perception is a mysterious phenomenon, inasmuch as it transforms a physical event (the stimulus) into a subjective experience. It permits a conversion from matter to psyche. But more than that: the psyche mirrors the matter. In imagery we have a related phenomenon even when the stimulus is absent. The image is a mirror of another mirror (perception). But as we have seen in Chapter 3, although the image is not a faithful mirror, it is a creative mirror.

Deep structures occur in a background of knowledge which Kant called a priori, because it occurs before experience. This a priori knowledge includes the concepts of space, time, and causality. In Chapter 6 I described three basic modes of operation, which can also be considered a priori categories.

How can these a priori concepts happen to fit the world and permit life? In *The Intrapsychic Self* (Arieti 1967, Chapter 11) I described how these categories are only a priori so far as the individual is concerned. However, they are a posteriori if we consider evolution as a whole. Evolution had to "learn" them from the external environment and transmit them from generation to generation. All these structures, whether they are concepts of time and space, or the three modes of operation described in Chapter 6, happen to fit the world because the hereditary depositories of our mental functions were selected for their evolutionary fitness.* Whatever mutation or mental structure did not fit was dropped from genetic transmission.

If these categories, systems, structures, and so on were incorporated into our nervous system, they preexisted in the external world. General system theory collects them and applies them to any system: psychological, social, biological, or physical. As an example, I would like to take the statement of the great comparative psychologist Heinz Werner (1957b), who stated that in psychological development "there is a progression from a state of relative undifferentiatedness to one of increasing differentiation and hierarchical integration." These words and concepts sound strangely similar to those of Herbert Spencer, who, speaking not about psychological development but about the universe, saw it as moving from "an indefinite, incoherent homogeneity to a definite, coherent heterogeneity, passing through a series of integrations and differentiations" (*First Principles*, 4th edition). Can't we add that every time a creative product is completed, a new, coherent heterogeneity (after passing through a series of integrations and differentiations) is added to the many already existing, so that the world as a whole becomes more heterogeneous?

To return to the creative process: it may be worthwhile to stress that although it has a structure, it is an open system, both as an intrapsychic phenomenon and as the outcome of environmental factors. In any closed system the principle of equifinality rules: the final state is unequivocally determined by the initial conditions (Bertalanffy 1955). In the creative process, as well as in any open system, the initial conditions do not determine the final outcome. In Chapter 13 we have seen that although the relations between society and the individual can in some respects be visualized as a feedback mechanism, they are better interpreted according to the characteristics of an open system.

The creative product can also be reexamined in view of the three modes of operation described in Chapter 6. There is, first of all, the simple and precreative mode of contiguity with which we experience the world. Whatever is experienced together tends to be reexperienced together if it produces *one* effect in the organism. The world is thus segmented into the usual unities. But when we approach the creative stage, the most important characteristic common to the pri-

---

* They fit, however, only what Capek (1957) called a mesocosm, a world of middle dimensions. They do not necessarily fit a microcosm (a world of subatomic dimensions) or the macrocosm (the universe at large.) See also Arieti (1967, Chapter 11).

mary, secondary, and tertiary processes resides in what I have called the second mode of operation, or the ability to differentiate similarities from manifold experience (Chapters 5 and 6). Similarity indicates that there is some kind of recurrence and, therefore, regularity in the universe. It is from these segments of regularity that the human mind plunges into the understanding of the cosmos and into the making of its own inner reality. In psychopathology, normality, and creativity, the ability to register similarity is the common guiding principle—a tremulous little light with which to search and attain, with which to break the secret of the universal night and make a piece of understanding a piece of ourselves.

It is on the varying responses to similarity that the ultimate rise or fall of man depends. We can represent these variations by resorting to the imagery of an expression. For the primary process, all that glitters is gold. It is the labor of the secondary process to discover that not *all* that glitters is gold. The tertiary process will do at least one of two things: Either it will create a new class of glittering objects, or, by bestowing the glittering on other substances, it will beautify them artistically, as gold can do. We may prolong the metaphor a little longer. The primitive in us would like us to respond joyfully to everything that glitters as if it were gold. But our mature self tells us, "Don't be a fool. Stick to reality. Not everything that glitters is gold." And the fortunate ones among us who have the key to creativity will collect and distinguish the glittering substances and form glittering classes or confer the glittering look to other objects.

No matter the importance of similarity and the other characteristics described in the various chapters of this book, they are not enough in themselves to produce a creative product. The creative person must first recognize that they are *partes pro toto*. Using the third mode of operation, he sees in them a totality, a unity, a way to bring about the magic synthesis. The creative or tertiary process generates unities never experienced before, and segments the world in new ways. The new addition or segmentation may be of as little significance as a new ornament, or as far-reaching in its effect as the advent of monotheism, the Copernican revolution, the theory of relativity.

Author's Assessment of His Work

WHEN an author's presentation is about to come to a close, he as a rule reassesses his work. He must be careful lest his dedication make him err either toward too much complacency or overly harsh self-criticism. In a field like the study of creativity, no preparation is adequate or commensurate with the arduous task, which is open to so many disparate inquiries. Nevertheless, an author must ask himself whether or not his preparation (in this particular case, that of a psychiatrist, psychoanalyst, with training in neurology and psychology and non-professional interests in various fields) is appropriate. In the present case he must also compare his findings with those of psychiatrists and psychoanalysts who follow different schools of thought. Although some of these issues have been examined in Chapters 1 and 2, it may be useful to reconsider them briefly now, as the reader has become acquainted with the ground that has been explored and the methodology that has been adopted.

Frankly, I think that the concept of the tertiary process, as a matching of the primary and secondary processes, and the examination of the modalities by which this matching takes place, brings us closer to viewing the underlying structure of creativity. The investigations within various fields reported in Part Three have, in my opinion, provided new ways of understanding and appreciating the creative product. The impact of Freud, with his concept of the primary process and of the symbolic activity of the mind, is felt throughout this book. Moreover, a psychoanalytic frame of reference has evoked in this work, too, special modes and attitudes. I have attempted not to be overly concerned with the manifest aspect of psychological phenomena, but to delve into depth psychology, attempt to retrace the intricate ramifications of symbolism, and observe how the primitive is transformed and, to use a current expression, recycled, into higher activities. On the other hand, the limits of the influence of Freud and of the classic psychoanalytic school in the present work must also be defined.

I have not referred to Freud's structural theory, or division of the psyche into id, ego, and superego, because I have found it more fruitful and pertinent to use instead Freud's concept of the primary process, to which I have connected some aspects of the id as well as the archaic ego. In my own frame of reference the participation of the secondary process pertains to the ego, while the unconscious motivation concerns some aspects of the id and superego. I have not made use of recent developments of the Freudian school because I could not attune my research to them. In Chapter 2 I have already referred to Kris's brilliant but partial interpretation of creativity as "regression in the service of the ego." Hartmann's (1955) theory of sublimation states that libidinal and aggressive energy is neutralized, that is, changed from the instinctual to a noninstinctual mode, but does not disclose how the noninstinctual mode becomes creative. Erikson's formulation of epigenesis of the ego (1953) is a major contribution that had profound repercussions in modern psychiatry and psychoanalysis. It prepares the ground for the study of creativity by taking into consideration the onset of initiative and industry in the child, but does not study creativity itself.

Clinical psychiatry has greatly helped my research. The study and treatment of schizophrenic patients in particular has offered me the possibility of examining some mental processes, almost as if they were made available by laboratory experiments. I was able to retrace many of these processes as they occur in the tertiary process, too.

The study of the interrelation between creativity and the sociocultural environment, as reported in Part Four, has, in my opinion, led to promising results. On the other hand, I feel that the report given in Part Five of many authors' works, including my own, on the personality of the creative individual is a collection of important material, but has not led to new and much needed insights. The creative person remains the keeper of the secret of what makes his personality creative—a secret that he cannot reveal to himself or to others. What is no longer a secret is how his creative process unfolds, reaches conclusion, and what conditions facilitate its occurrence. In Part Five some initial suggestions also were given for promoting creativity, but much work remains to be done in this area. The pioneer application to creativity of neurological knowledge and of general system theory, as described in Part Six, promises rewarding developments.

This rapid review discloses how closely we have looked at some parts of the vast panorama and how superficially we were compelled to glimpse at others. The field of inquiry is immense and the obstacles enormous. The disentangling of some of the components of the magic synthesis requires sharp analyses and major syntheses. The researcher patiently paves his way; not even he can say whether or not he has seen some magic sparks. Final assessment rests with those who come to know his work.

Concluding Remarks: Man and Creativity

ALTHOUGH CREATIVITY is by no means the only way in which the human being can grow, it is one of the most important. The growth occurs not only in the creative person but in all those who are affected by the innovation.

It would be an easy task in these final remarks to support creativity again by reminding the reader of the need for it in our present society. What comes to mind first is the need for scientific discoveries and inventions to solve the problems originating from increased population; shortage of food, land, and water; air pollution; decreased supplies of energy; increased rates of certain diseases; crime; and so on. But what also comes to mind is that science alone, dissociated from other forms of creativity, cannot solve all the dimensions of human misery and discomfort, and may even increase the potential dangers to life on earth. Innovations in the fields of ethics, politics, sociology, and religion, however, may answer questions to the perennial quest for peace, trust between people, and mutual help. One also recognizes that art, literature, and music are essential to achieve a spiritual level of life in which discord and hate are less likely to occur.

Gigantic as these practical results of creativity are, they constitute only its effects and possibly its motivation; but it is in the essence of man that the root of creativity resides. This essence may be explained in terms of a complicated neurology susceptible of infinite combinations. It may be interpreted, in Vico's terms, as the function of a finite center that tends toward infinity. Man alone is aware of his finitude and of the infinite, and of his need to cope with both. When he tries to decrease the unknown with his creativity, he remains surrounded by transcendence, mystery, and God's creation. He runs and runs toward an ultimate goal, which always escapes.

Is this another version of the myth of Sisyphus? Is man doomed forever to roll heavy stones to the summits of mountains, stones that always roll down again and have to be carried uphill once more? The answer is no. Contrary to Sisyphus, the creative man does not start from the foot of the mountain again, but from where other people have left off. It is true that the infinite cannot be conquered, and therefore even when he reaches the peak of a mountain with his heavy burden, he will discover that there are other and higher mountains to climb. But another human being will take over the task. Creative man is Sisyphus in reverse, and has to climb and climb and climb *ad infinitum*. The infinity is not in time only, but within the goal itself.

The metaphor of the vertical climbing is easily understood in the field of science, where there is a more or less linear sequence: for instance, no Euclid is possible without a Pythagoras, no Galileo without a Euclid, no Einstein without a Galileo. But in some fields such as literature and art, no linear development is discernible. For instance, a Shakespeare does not presuppose a Dante. The growth here seems more additive than normative. But creative people in the fields of art and literature accrue collateral vistas to the experience of being human. Thus even if the metaphor is literally—that is, geometrically—inexact, these artists and literary men continue the ascent.

Sisyphus-in-reverse is not at all like the greedy king of Corinth of the old myth. Whatever he gets, he gives to others; whatever he gives to others, he retains. Although he will not reach the peak of the ultimate mountain, the horizons that open before his eyes are vaster and vaster. And he rejoices in his heart, knowing that his labor has not been in vain, since those horizons will be shared by millions of brothers and sisters, not just today, but as long as people will live on earth.

Thus, what remained unfinished as a cognitive ascent finds an end as an act of social love.

Bibliography

Ach, N., 1935, "Analyse des Willens." *Handbuch der Biologischen Arbeitsmethoden*, Abt. VII. Berlin: Urban und Schwartzenberg.

Adler, A., 1944, "Disintegration and Restoration of Optic Recognition in Visual Agnosia." *Archives of Neurology and Psychiatry*, 51: 243–259.

———, 1950, "Course and Outcome of Visual Agnosia." *Journal of Nervous and Mental Disease*, 111: 41–51.

Agosti, S., 1972, *Il Testo Poetico. Teoria e pratiche d'analisi*. Milan: Rizzoli.

Alajouanine, T., 1948, "Aphasia and Artistic Realization." *Brain*, 71: 229–241.

Anastasi, A., and Schaefer, C. E., 1971, "Note on the Concepts of Creativity and Intelligence." *Journal of Creative Behavior*, 5: 113–116.

Arieti, S., 1948, "Special Logic of Schizophrenic and Other Types of Autistic Thought." *Psychiatry*, 11: 325–338.

———, 1950a, "New Views on the Psychology and Psychopathology of Wit and of the Comic." *Psychiatry*, 13: 43–62.

———, 1950b, "Primitive Intellectual Mechanisms in Psychopathological Conditions: Study of the Archaic Ego." *American Journal of Psychotherapy*, 4: 4.

———, 1952, "Anti-psychoanalytic Cultural Forces in the Development of Western Civilization." *American Journal of Psychotherapy*, 6: 63–78.

———, 1955, *Interpretation of Schizophrenia*. New York: Brunner.

———, 1956a, "Some Basic Problems Common to Anthropology and Modern Psychiatry." *American Anthropologist*, 58: 26–30.

———, 1956b, "The Possibility of Psychosomatic Involvement of the Central Nervous System in Schizophrenia." *Journal of Nervous and Mental Disease*, 123: 324–333.

———, 1961, "The Loss of Reality." *Psychoanalysis and the Psychoanalytic Review*, 48: 3–24.

———, 1962, "The Microgeny of Thought and Perception." *Archives of General Psychiatry*, 6: 454–468.

———, 1964, "The Rise of Creativity: From Primary to Tertiary Process." *Contemporary Psychoanalysis*, 1: 51–68.

———, 1965, "Contributions to Cognition from Psychoanalytic Theory." In Masserman, J. (ed.), *Science and Psychoanalysis*, Vol. 8, pp. 16–37. New York: Grune and Stratton.

Bibliography

————, 1966, "Creativity and Its Cultivation: Relation to Psychopathology and Mental Health." In Arieti, S. (ed.), *American Handbook of Psychiatry*, Vol. 3, pp. 722–74. New York: Basic Books.

————, 1967, *The Intrapsychic Self: Feeling, Cognition and Creativity in Health and Mental Illness*. New York: Basic Books.

————, 1968, "The Meeting of the Inner and the External World: In Schizophrenia, Everyday Life and Creativity." *American Journal of Psychoanalysis*, 29: 115–130.

————, 1972, *The Will To Be Human*. New York: Quadrangle.

————, 1974, *Interpretation of Schizophrenia*, 2d ed., New York: Basic Books.

————, 1975, "Creativity and Its Cultivation: Relation to Psychopathology and Mental Health." In Arieti, S. (ed.), *American Handbook of Psychiatry*, 2d ed. Vol. 6, pp. 230–250. New York: Basic Books.

Arieti, S., and Bemporad, J., 1974, "Rare, Unclassifiable and Collective Psychiatric Syndromes." In Arieti, S. (ed.), *American Handbook of Psychiatry*, 2d ed. Vol. 3, pp. 710–722. New York: Basic Books.

Arlow, J. A., and Brenner, C., 1964, *Psychoanalytic Concepts and the Structural Theory*. New York: International Universities Press.

Arnheim, R., 1954, *Art and Visual Perception: A Psychology of the Creative Eye*. Berkeley: University of California Press.

————, 1969, *Visual Thinking*. Berkeley: University of California Press.

Bachelard, G., 1960, *The Poetics of Reverie*. Boston: Beacon. (Paperback, 1971.)

————, 1971, *On Poetic Imagination and Reverie*. Indianapolis: Bobbs-Merrill.

Balakian, A., 1970, *Surrealism: The Road to the Absolute*. New York: Dutton.

————, 1974, "Breton and Drugs." In *Intoxication and Literature*. New Haven: Yale French Studies.

Baldwin, J. M., 1929, Quoted by Piaget, 1929.

Balis, G. U., 1974, "The Use of Psychomimetic and Related Conscious-Altering Drugs." In Arieti, S. (ed.), *American Handbook of Psychiatry*, 2d ed. Vol. 3, pp. 404–446. New York: Basic Books.

Barron, F., 1963a, "The Disposition Toward Originality." In Taylor, C. W., and Barron, F. (eds.), *Scientific Creativity: Its Recognition and Development*, pp. 139–152. New York: Wiley.

————, 1963b, "The Needs for Order and for Disorder as Motives in Creative Activity." In Taylor, C. W., and Barron, F. (eds.), *Scientific Creativity: Its Recognition and Development*, pp. 153–160. New York: Wiley.

Baudelaire, C., 1961, *Oeuvres Complètes*. Paris: Pleiade.

Bell, C., 1913, *Art*. New York: Putnam.

Bell, E. T., 1937, *Men of Mathematics*. Quoted by Feuer, 1963.

Bemporad, J., 1974, "Psychiatry and Religion." In Arieti, S. (ed.), *American Handbook of Psychiatry*, 2d ed. Vol. 1, pp. 1000–1008. New York: Basic Books.

Berger, R. M., Guilford, J. P., and Christensen, P. R., 1957, "A Factor-analytic Study of Planning Abilities." *Psychological Monographs*, 71: 6.

Bergson, H., 1912, *An Introduction to Metaphysics*. New York: Putnam.

Bertalanffy, L. von, 1955, "General System Theory." *Main Currents in Modern Thought*, 11: 75–83.

————, 1967, *Robots, Men and Minds*. New York: Braziller.

———, 1968, "The Model of Open System." In Bertalanffy, L. von, *General System Theory*, pp. 139–154. New York: Braziller.

Bieber, I., 1974, "Sadism and Masochism: Phenomenology and Psychodynamics." In Arieti, S. (ed.), *American Handbook of Psychiatry*, 2d ed. Vol. 3, pp. 316–333. New York: Basic Books.

Binet, A., 1903, *Étude Experimentale de l'Intelligence*. Paris: Schleicher.

———, 1911, "Qu'est-ce qu'une emotion, qu'est-ce qu'un acte intellectuel?" *Année Psychologique*, 1: 47.

Bishop, M., 1963, *Petrarch and His World*. Bloomington: Indiana University Press.

Boase, A. M., 1967, *The Poetry of France*. Vol. III, *1800–1900*. London: Methuen.

Bobon, J., and Maccagnani, G., 1962, "Contributo Allo Studio della Comunicazione non-verbale in psicopatologia." *Riviste sperimentale di Fremiatria*, 86: 1097–1173.

Bogen, J. E., 1969, "The Other Side of the Brain: An Appositional Mind." *Bulletin Los Angeles Neurological Societies*, 34: 135–162.

Bonvicini, G., 1926, "Die Aphasie der Malers Vierge." *Wien. med. Wschr.* 76: 88–91.

Boulding, K., 1956, "General Systems Theory—the Skeleton of Science." *Management Science*, 2: 197–208.

Breton, A., 1932, *Les Vases Communicantes*. Paris: Cahiers Libre.

———, 1952, *La Clé des Champs*. Paris: Sagittaire.

Breton, A., and Eluard, P., 1930, *L'Immaculée Conception*. Paris: Editions Surrealists.

Breuer, J., and Freud, S., 1895, *Studies on Hysteria*. In Strachey, J. (ed.), *Standard Ed.*, Vol. 2, Hogarth, London, 1955.

Brickner, R. M., 1936, *The Intellectual Functions of the Frontal Lobes: A Study Based upon Observation of a Man Following Partial Bilateral Frontal Lobectomy*. New York: Macmillan.

Brill, A. A. (ed.), 1938, *The Basic Writings of Sigmund Freud*, New York: Modern Library.

Bruner, J. S., Goodnow, J. J., and Austin, G. A., 1956, *A Study of Thinking*. New York: Wiley.

Buck, L. A., and Kramer, A., 1972, "Intellectual and Creative Potential in Deaf Children." Presented at Poetry Therapy Day. Cumberland Hospital, Brooklyn, N.Y..

———, 1973, "Opening New Worlds to the Deaf and to the Disturbed." In Leedy, J. J. (ed.), *Poetry the Healer*. Philadelphia: Lippincott.

———, 1974, "The Cultivation of Poetry in the Deaf." Presented at Second World Poetry Therapy Conference, Cumberland Hospital, Brooklyn, N.Y.

Bugelski, R., 1956, *The Psychology of Learning*. New York: Holt.

Bullough, E., 1957, *Aesthetics: Lectures and Essays*. Stanford, Calif.: Stanford University Press.

Burns, B. D., 1968, *The Uncertain Nervous System*. London: Edward Arnold.

Butler, R. N., 1967, "The Destiny of Creativity in Later Life: Studies of Creative People and the Creative Process." In Levin, S., and Kahana, R. J. (eds.), *Psychodynamic Studies on Aging*. New York: International Universities.

Bychowsky, G., 1943, "Physiology of Schizophrenic Thinking." *Journal of Nervous and Mental Disease*, 98: 368–386.

Campbell, D. T., 1960, "Blind Variation and Selective Retention in Creative Thought as in Other Knowledge Processes." *Psychological Review*, 67: 380–400.

Bibliography

Capek, M., 1957, "The Development of Reichenbach's Epistemology." *Review of Metaphysics*, 9: 42.

Cassirer, E., 1946, *Language and Myth*. New York: Harper & Row.

———, 1953, 1955, 1957, *The Philosophy of Symbolic Forms*. Vols. 1, 2, 3. New Haven: Yale University Press.

Castle, C. S., 1913, "A Statistical Study of Eminent Women." In Columbia University, *Contributions to Philosophy and Psychology*. Vol. 22, No. 1. New York: Science Press.

Cattell, J. McK., 1903, "A Statistical Study of Eminent Men." *Popular Science Monthly*, 52: 359–377.

———, 1906, "A Statistical Study of American Men of Science: The Selection of a Group of One Thousand Scientific Men." *Science*, New Series, 24: 658–665.

———, 1910a, "A Further Statistical Study of American Men of Science I." *Science*, New Series, 32: 633–648.

———, 1910b, "A Further Statistical Study of American Men of Science II." *Science*, New Series, 32: 672–688.

———, 1926, "The Scientific Men of the World." *Scientific Monthly*, 23: 468–471.

Ciardi, J., 1959, *How Does a Poem Mean?* Boston: Houghton Mifflin.

Cicirelli, V. G., 1965, "Form of the Relationship between Creativity, IQ, and Academic Achievement." *Journal of Educational Psychology*, 56: 303–308.

Chomsky, N., 1957, *Syntax Structures*. The Hague: Mouton.

Clark, K., 1956, *The Nude*. Princeton: Princeton University Press.

Clark, R. W., 1971, *Einstein: The Life and Times*. New York: World.

Cline, V., Richards, J. M., and Abe, C., 1962, "Validity for a Battery of Creativity Tests in a High School Sample." *Educational and Psychological Measurement*, 22: 781–784.

Condillac, E., 1746, *Essae sur l'origine des connaissances humaines*. Paris.

Contini, G., 1951, "Preliminari sulla lingua del Petrarca." In *Paragone*, 16: 3–26. Quoted by Agosti, 1972.

Cooke, M. G., 1974, "De Quincey, Coleridge, and the Formal Uses of Intoxication." In *Intoxication and Literature*, New Haven: Yale French Studies.

Cox, C. M., 1926, *The Early Mental Traits of Three Hundred Geniuses*. Stanford: Stanford University Press.

Croce, B., 1929, *Aesthetics*. London: Macmillan and Co., Ltd.

Dali, S., 1930, *La Femme Visible*. Paris: Editions surrealistes.

———, 1935, *Concept of the Irrational*. New York: Julian Levy.

———, 1942, *The Secret Life of Salvador Dali*. New York: Dial Press.

Danzel, T. W., 1924, *Kultur und Religionen des Primitiven Menschen*. Stuttgart.

Darwin, C., 1872, *The Expression of the Emotions in Man and Animals*. London: Murray. Quoted by Keith-Spiegel, 1972.

Deikman, A. J., 1971, "Bimodal Consciousness." *Archives of General Psychiatry*, 25: 481–489.

De Martino, E., 1948, *Il Mondo Magico*. Turin: Quoted by Tullio-Altan (1960).

Dentler, R. A., and Mackler, B., 1964, "Originality: Some Social and Personal Determinants." *Behavioral Science*, 9: 1–7.

Dreistadt, R., 1974, "The Psychology of Creativity: How Einstein Discovered the Theory of Relativity." *Psychology*, 11: 15–25.

Bibliography

Drew, E., 1959, *Poetry: A Modern Guide to its Understanding and Enjoyment*. New York: Dell Publishing Co.

Ducasse, J., 1929, *The Philosophy of Art*. New York: Dial.

Durkheim, E., 1950, *The Role of Sociological Method*. Glencoe, Ill.: Free Press.

Eccles, J. C., 1958, "The Physiology of Imagination." *Scientific American*, 199: 135–146.

———, 1973, *The Understanding of the Brain*. New York: McGraw-Hill.

Eiduson, B. T., 1962, *Scientists: Their Psychological World*. New York: Basic Books.

Einstein, A., 1952, "Letter to Jacques Hadamard." Reported in Ghiselin (ed.), 1952.

Ehrenzweig, A., 1957, *The Psychoanalysis of Artistic Vision and Hearing*. New York: Julian Press.

———, 1967, *The Hidden Order of Art: A Study in the Psychology of Artistic Imagination*. Berkeley: University of California Press.

Elkins, S. M., 1968, *Slavery: A Problem in American Institutional and Intellectual Life*. Chicago: University of Chicago Press.

Ellis, H., 1904, *A Study of British Genius*. London: Hurst and Blackett.

Encyclopaedia Judaica, 1971, Article on Nobel Prizes. Vol. 12, p. 1202. Jerusalem: Encyclopaedia Judaica.

Erikson, E. H., 1953, "Growth and Crises of the Healthy Personality." In Kluckhohln, C., Murray, H. A., and Schneider, O. M., *Personality*. New York: Knopf.

———, 1968, *Identity Youth and Crisis*. New York: Norton.

Fechner, G. T., 1876, *Vorschule der Aesthetik*. Leipzig: Breitkopf und Härtel.

Ferrari, S., and Oliverio, A., 1973, *Il Significato del Disegno Infantile*. Turin: Boringhieri.

Ferrio, C., 1948, *La Psiche e i Nervi*. Turin: Utet.

Feuer, L. S., 1963, *The Scientific Intellectual*. New York: Basic Books.

Fisher, C., 1954, "Dream and Perception: The Role of Preconscious and Primary Modes of Perception in Dream Formation." *Journal of the American Psychoanalytic Association*, 2: 380–445.

Fisher, C., and Paul, I. H., 1959, "The Effect of Subliminal Visual Stimulation on Images and Dreams: A Validation Study." *Journal of the American Psychoanalytic Association*, 7: 35–83.

Flescher, I., 1963, "Anxiety and Achievement of Intellectually Gifted and Creatively Gifted Children." *Journal of Psychology*, 56: 251–268.

Foss, M., 1949, *Symbol and Metaphor in Human Experience*. Princeton: Princeton University Press.

Frank, P., 1957, *Philosophy of Science*. Englewood Cliffs, N.J.: Prentice-Hall.

Frazer, J. G., 1922, *The Golden Bough*. New York: Macmillan.

Freedman, D. X., 1968, "On the Use and Abuse of LSD." *Archives of General Psychiatry*, 18:330–347.

Freeman, W., and Watts, J. W., 1942, *Psychosurgery*. Springfield, Ill.: Charles C. Thomas.

Freud, S., 1901, *The Interpretation of Dreams*. New York: Basic Books, 1960.

———, 1908, "Character and Anal Eroticism." *Collected Papers*, Vol. 2, p. 48. New York: Basic Books, 1959.

———, 1916, *Wit and Its Relation to the Unconscious*. New York: Moffat, Yard. Also in

Brill, A. A. (ed.), *The Basic Writings of Sigmund Freud*. New York: Modern Library, 1938.

———, 1925, "Negation." *Collected Papers*, Vol. 5, p. 181. New York: Basic Books, 1959.

———, 1928, *The Future of an Illusion*. New York: Liveright, 1949.

Fromm, E., 1949, "Psychoanalytic Characterology and Its Application to the Understanding of Culture." In Sargent, S. S., and Smith, M. W. (eds.), *Culture and Personality*, New York: Wenner-Gren Foundation for Anthropological Research.

Frosch, W. A., Robbins, E., and Stern, M., 1967, "Motivation for Self-Administration of LSD." *Psychiatric Quarterly*, 41: 56–61.

Froeschels, E., 1948, *Philosophy in Wit*. New York: Philosophical Library.

Furth, H. G., 1966, *Thinking without Language. Psychological Implications of Deafness*. New York: Free Press.

Galton, F., 1870, *Hereditary Genius*. New York: Appleton.

Gesell, A., 1940, *The First Five Years of Life*. New York: Harper and Row.

Getzel, J. W., and Jackson, P. W., 1962, *Creativity and Intelligence*. New York: Wiley.

Ghiselin, B., 1952, *The Creative Process*. Berkeley: University of California Press.

Ghiselin, M. T., 1973, "Darwin and Evolutionary Psychology." *Science*, 179: 964–968.

Gill, M. M., and Brennan, M., 1959, *Hypnosis and Related States*. New York: International Universities.

Goldstein, J. H., and McGhee, P. E. (eds.), 1972, *The Psychology of Humor*. New York: Academic Press.

Goldstein, K., and Gelb, A., 1920, *Psychologische Analyse hirnpathologischer Fälle*, Vol. 1. Leipzig: T. A. Barth.

Gordon, H. L., 1949, *The Maggid of Caro*. New York: Pardes.

Gordon, W. J. J., 1961, *Synectics: The Development of Creative Capacity*. New York: Harper and Row.

Gouldner, A. W., 1970, *The Coming Crisis of Western Civilization*. New York: Basic Books.

Gray, C. E., 1958, "The Epicyclical Evolution of Graeco-Roman Civilization." *American Anthropologist*, 60: 13–31.

———, 1961, "An Epicyclical Model for Western Civilization." *American Anthropologist*, 63: 1014–1037.

———, 1966, "A Measurement of Creativity in Western Civilization." *American Anthropologist*, 68: 1384–1417.

Greenacre, P., 1957, "The Childhood of the Artist." *Psychoanalytic Study of the Child*, 12: 47–72. New York: International Universities.

Gregory, J. C., 1924, *The Nature of Laughter*. London: Routledge and Kegan Paul.

Guilford, J. P., 1950, "Creativity." *American Psychologist*, 5: 444–454.

———, 1957a, "A Revised Structure of Intellect." *Rep. Psychol. Lat.*, 19: Los Angeles: University of Southern California.

———, 1957b, "Creative Ability in the Arts." *Psychological Review*, 64: 110–118.

———, 1959, "Traits of Creativity." In Anderson, H. H. (ed.), *Creativity and Its Cultivation*, pp. 142–161. New York: Harper and Row.

Hadamard, J., 1945, *The Psychology of Invention in the Mathematical Field*. Princeton: Princeton University Press.

Hammer, E. F., 1961, *Creativity*. New York: Random House.

Bibliography

Hartmann, H., 1955, "Notes on the Theory of Sublimation." *The Psychoanalytic Study of the Child*, 10: 9–29.

———, 1964, *Essays on Ego Psychology*. New York: International University Press.

Head, H., 1926, *Aphasia and Kindred Disorders of Speech*. Cambridge: Cambridge University Press.

Hebb, D. O., 1949, *The Organization of Behavior*. New York: Wiley.

Hecker, J. F. C., 1832, *Die Tanzwuth: eine Volkskrankheit im Mittelalter*. Berlin.

Helmholtz, H. von, 1896, *Vortrage und Reden*, 5th auff. Brammschweig: Vieweg und John.

Henle, M., 1962, "The Birth and Death of Ideas." In Gruber, H. E., Terrell, G., and Wertheimer, M. (eds.), *Contemporary Approaches to Creative Thinking*. New York: Atherton Press.

Hirsh, N. D. M., 1931, *Genius and Creative Intelligence*. Cambridge: Sci-Art Publishers.

Horney, K., 1945, *Our Inner Conflicts*. New York: Norton.

———, 1950, *Neurosis and Human Growth*. New York: Norton.

Horowitz, M. J., 1970, *Image Formation and Cognition*. New York: Appleton-Century-Crofts.

Huguet, E., 1904, *Les Métaphores et les Comparaisons dans l'Ouevre de Victor Hugo*. Quoted by Konrad, 1958.

Huizinga, J., 1924, *The Waning of the Middle Ages*. (Reprinted, Garden City, N.Y.: Doubleday, Anchor Books, 1956.)

Hull, C. L., 1920, "Quantitative Aspects of the Evolution of Concepts." *Psychological Monographs*, 123.

Huxley, A., 1963, *The Doors of Perception*. New York: Harper and Row.

Jackson, J. H., 1932, *Selected Writings*. London: Haddon and Stoughton. Reprinted by Basic Books, N.Y., 1958.

Jacobson, A. C., 1926, *Genius: Some Reevaluations*. New York: Greenberg.

Jaensch, E. R., 1930, *Eidetic Imagery and Typological Methods of Investigation*. London: Kegan, Paul.

James, H., 1908, *The Spoils of Poynton*. New York: Scribner.

James, W., 1880, "Great Men, Great Thoughts and the Environment." *Atlantic Monthly*, 46: 441–459.

———, 1902, *The Varieties of Religious Experience*. Reprinted, New York: Modern Library, 1929.

———, 1911, *Some Problems of Philosophy*. New York: Longmans, Green.

Jaques, E., 1970, *Work, Creativity and Social Justice*. London: Heinemann.

Johnson, D. M., 1972, *Systematic Introduction to the Psychology of Thinking*. New York: Harper and Row.

Jones, E., 1953, *The Life and Work of Sigmund Freud*. New York: Basic Books.

Jones, R., 1960, *An Application of Psychoanalysis to Education*. Springfield, Ill.: Charles C. Thomas.

Jung, C. G., 1933, *Modern Man in Search of a Soul*. London: Routledge and Kegan Paul.

———, 1959, "The Archetypes and the Collective Unconscious." *Collected Works*, New York: Pantheon.

Kandinsky, W., 1947, *Concerning the Spiritual in Art*. New York: Wittenborn.

Bibliography

Kaplan, B., 1960, "Radical Metaphor, Aesthetic and the Origin of Language." *Review of Existential Psychology and Psychiatry*, 2: 75–84.

Kardiner, A., 1939, *The Individual and His Society*. New York: Columbia University Press.

———, 1945, *The Psychological Frontiers of Society*. New York: Columbia University Press.

Kaufmann, Y., 1960, *The Religion of Israel*. Chicago: University of Chicago Press.

Keith-Spiegel, P., 1972, "Early Conceptions of Humor: Varieties and Issues." In Goldstein, and McGhee (eds.), *The Psychology of Humor*, pp. 3–39. New York: Academic Press.

Koestler, A., 1949, *Insight and Outlook*. New York: Macmillan.

———, 1964, *The Act of Creation*. New York: Macmillan.

Konrad, H., 1958, *Étude sur la Métaphore*. Paris: Vrin.

Kramer, A., and Buck, L. A., (in press) "Creativeness in Deaf Children."

Kretschmer, E., 1934, *A Text-Book of Medical Psychology*. London: Oxford University Press.

Krippner, S., 1969, "The Psychedelic State, the Hypnotic Trance, and the Creative Act." In C. T. Tart (ed.), *Altered States of Consciousness*, New York: Wiley. Quoted by Stein, 1974.

Kris, E., 1950, "On Preconscious Mental Processes." *Psychoanalytic Quarterly*, 19: 542. Reprinted in Kris, 1952.

———, 1952, *Psychoanalytic Explorations in Art*. New York: International Universities.

Kroeber, A., 1944, *Configurations of Culture Growth*. Berkeley and Los Angeles: University of California Press.

Kubie, L. S., 1958, *Neurotic Distortion of the Creative Process*. Lawrence: University of Kansas Press.

Kühn, H., 1923, *Die Kunst der Primitiven*. Munich.

Lange-Eichbaum, W., 1932, *The Problem of Genius*, translated by E. and C. Paul. New York: Macmillan.

Langer, S. K., 1953, *Feeling and Form*. New York: Scribners.

Langevin, R., and Day, H. I., 1972, "Physiological Correlates of Humor." In Goldstein, J. H., and McGhee, P. E. (eds.), *The Psychology of Humor*. Pp. 129–142, New York: Academic Press.

Lash, K., 1948, "A Theory of the Comic as Insight." *Journal of Philosophy*, 45: 113–121.

Laski, M., 1961, *Ecstasy: A Study of Some Secular and Religious Experiences*. London: Cresset Press.

Lasswell, H., 1959, "The social setting of creativity." In Anderson, H. (ed.), *Creativity and Its Cultivation*, pp. 203–221, New York: Harpers.

Laszlo, E., 1972, *The Systems View of the World*. New York: Braziller.

Leedy, J. J. (ed.), 1969, *Poetry Therapy*. Philadelphia: Lippincott.

———, 1973, *Poetry the Healer*. Philadelphia: Lippincott.

Lehmann, H. C., 1953, *Age and Achievement*. Princeton: Princeton University Press. Quoted by Butler, 1967.

Leontiev, A. N., 1959, "Problems in Mental Development." *Izd. Akad. Pedagog. Nauk RSFSR* (in Russian). Quoted by Luria, 1973.

Bibliography

Leuba, C., 1954, *The Natural Man*. Garden City, N.Y.: Doubleday.

Levin, M., 1936, "On the Causation of Mental Symptoms. *Journal of Mental Science*, 82: 1–27.

Lévy-Bruhl, L., 1910, *Les Fonctions Mentales dans les Sociétés Inférieures*. Paris: Alcan.

———, 1922, *La Mentalité Primitive*. Paris: Alcan.

Lombroso, C., 1891, *The Man of Genius*. London: Walter Scott.

———, 1894, *L'Uomo di Genio in Rapporto Alla Psichiatria, Alla Storia Ed All'Estetica*, 6th ed. Turin: Fratelli Bocca.

Lowenfeld, V., 1951, *Creative and Mental Growth*. New York: Macmillan.

———, 1959, *The Nature of Creative Activity*. London: Routledge and Kegan Paul.

Luria, A. R., 1966, *Higher Cortical Functions in Man*. New York: Basic Books.

———, 1973, *The Working Brain: An Introduction to Neuropsychology*. New York: Basic Books.

Luria, A. R., Tsvetkova, L. A., and Futer, J. C., 1965, "Aphasia in a Composer." *Journal of Neurological Science*, 2.

Malmo, R. B., 1942, "Interference Factors in Delayed Response in Monkeys after Removal of Frontal Lobes." *Journal of Neurophysiology*, 5: 295.

Maltzman, I., 1960, "On the Training of Originality." *Psychological Review*, 67: 229–242.

Mamlet, L. N., 1967, " 'Consciousness-Limiting' Side Effects of 'Consciousness-Expanding' Drugs." *American Journal of Orthopsychiatry*, 3: 296–297.

Manley, J. H., 1960, "Atomic Energy." In *Encyclopaedia Britannica*, Vol. 2, pp. 647–652. Chicago: Benton.

Manniche, E., and Falk, G., 1957, "Age and the Nobel Prize." *Behavioral Science*, 2: 301–307.

Marbe, K., 1901, *Experimentell-psychologische Untersuchungen über das Urteil*. Leipzig: Quoted by Humphrey, G., *Thinking: An Introduction to Experimental Psychology*. London: Methuen, 1951.

Marmontel, J. F., 1787, *Elements de littérature*. Paris.

Martineau, W. H., 1972, "A Model of the Social Functions of Humor." In Goldstein, J. H., and McGhee, P. E. (eds.), *The Psychology of Humor*, pp. 101–125, New York: Academic Press.

Maslow, A. H., 1948, "Cognition of the Individual and of the Generic." *Psychological Review*, 55: 22–40. Reprinted in Maslow, A. H., 1954.

———, 1954, *Motivation and Personality*. New York: Harper and Brothers.

———, 1959a, "Creativity in Self-Actualizing People." In Anderson, H. H. (ed.), 1959, *Creativity and Its Cultivation*. New York: Harper and Brothers.

———, 1959b, "Cognition of Being in the Peak Experiences." *Journal of Genetic Psychology*, 94: 43–66.

———, 1961, "Peak Experiences as Acute Identity Experiences." *American Journal of Psychoanalysis*, 21: 254–260.

———, 1972, "A Holistic Approach to Creativity." In Taylor, C. W., *Climate for Creativity*, pp. 287–293, New York: Pergamon Press.

Matussek, P., 1974, *Kreativität als Chance*. München: Piper.

McGhee, P. E., 1972, "On the Cognitive Origins of Incongruity Humor: Fantasy Assimilation versus Reality Assimilation." In Goldstein, J. H., and McGhee, P. E.

(eds.), *The Psychology of Humor*, pp. 61–80, New York: Academic Press.

McNeil, E. B., 1960, "The Paradox of Education for the Gifted." *Improving College and University Teaching*, 8: 111–115.

Menon, V. K., 1931, *A Theory of Laughter*. London: Allen and Unwin. Quoted by Keith-Spiegel, 1972.

Mondrian, P., 1914, "Plastic Art and Pure Plastic Art." Reprinted in Herbert, R. L. (ed.), *Modern Artists on Art*, Englewood Cliffs, N.J.: Prentice-Hall, 1964.

Money-Kyrle, R., 1958, "Psycho-Analysis and Philosophy." In Sutherland, J. D. (ed.), *Psychoanalysis and Contemporary Thought*, London: Hogarth Press.

Montagu, A., 1972, "Sociogenic Brain Damage." *American Anthropologist*, 74: 1045–1061.

Mora, G., 1964, "One Hundred Years from Lombroso's First Essay 'Genius and Insanity.' " *The American Journal of Psychiatry*, 121: 562–571.

Morgan, C. T., 1943, *Physiological Psychology*. New York and London: McGraw-Hill.

Morris, R. B., 1973, *Seven Who Shaped Our Destiny: The Founding Fathers as Revolutionaries*.

Moruzzi, G., and Magoun, H. W., 1949, "Brain stem reticular formation and activation of the E.E.G." *Electroenceph. Clin. Neurophysiol.*, 1: 455–473.

Munro, T., 1956, *Toward Science in Aesthetics: Selected Essays*. New York: The Liberal Arts Press.

Muratori, L. A., 1774, *Della forza della fantasia umana*. Naples: Sangiacomo.

Nash, H., 1962, *Alcohol and Caffeine*. Sprinffield, Ill.: Charles C. Thomas.

Neugarten, B. L., and Datan, N., 1974, "The Middle Years." In Arieti, S. (ed.), *American Handbook of Psychiatry*, 2d ed. Vol. 1, pp. 592–608. New York: Basic Books.

Nietzsche, F., 1872, *The Birth of Tragedy*. Garden City, N.Y.: Doubleday Anchor Books.

———, 1927, *Ecce Homo*. New York: Random House.

Noback, C. R., and Demarest, R. J., 1972, *The Nervous System: Introduction and Review*. New York: McGraw-Hill.

———, 1975, *The Human Nervous System. Basic Principles of Neurobiology*. New York: McGraw-Hill.

O'Neill, N., and O'Neill, G., 1974, *Shifting Gears: Finding Security in a Changing World*. New York: M. Evans.

Osborn, A. F., 1953, *Applied Imagination*. New York: Scribner's.

Otto, R., 1923, *The Idea of the Holy*. Reprinted, London: Oxford University Press, 1957.

Papez, J. W., 1937, "A Proposed Mechanism of Emotion." *Archives of Neurology and Psychiatry*, 38: 725–743.

Parnes, S. J., 1962, "Do You Really Understand Brainstorming?" In S. J. Parnes and H. F. Harding (eds.), *A Sourcebook for Creative Thinking*, New York: Scribner.

Patrick, C., 1935, "Creative Thought in Poets." *Archives of Psychology*, 26: 1–74.

———, 1937, "Creative Thought in Artists." *Journal of Psychology*, 4: 35–73.

———, 1938, "Scientific Thought." *Journal of Psychology*, 5: 55–83.

Patrick, R., 1972, *Egyptian Mythology*. London: Octopus Books.

Bibliography

Penfield, W., 1966, "Speech, Perception and the Uncommitted Cortex." In Eccles, J. C. (ed.), *Brain and Conscious Experience*, pp. 217–237, New York: Springer-Verlag.

Philipson, M., 1963, *Outline of Jungian Aesthetics*. Evanston: Northwestern University Press.

Piaget, J., 1929, *The Child's Conception of the World*. New York: Harcourt, Brace.

———, 1952, *The Origins of Intelligence in Children*. New York: International Universities.

Pickering, G., 1974, *Creative Malady*. New York: Oxford University Press.

Pietropinto, A., 1973, "Exploring the Unconscious through Nonsense Poetry." In Leedy, J. J., 1973.

Poincaré, H., 1913, "Mathematical Creation." In *The Foundation of Science*, Lancaster: The Science Press, 1946.

Pötzl, O., 1917, "Experimentell erregte Traumbilder in ihren Beziehungen zum indirekten Sehen." *Zeitschrift für Neurol. und Psychiat.*, 37: 278–349.

Preuss, K. T., 1914, *Die Geistige Kultur der Naturvölker*. Leipzig: Teubner.

Pritchard, R. M., Heron, W., and Hebb, D. O., 1960, "Visual Perception Approached by the Method of Stabilized Images." *Canadian Journal of Psychology*, 14: 67–77.

Quasimodo, S., 1960, *Il poeta e il politico e altri saggi*. Milan: Schwarz.

Ragghianti, C. L., 1968, *Great Museums of the World: National Museum of Tokyo*. Feltham, England: Hamlyn Publishing Firm.

Raphael, M., 1947, *Prehistoric Pottery and Civilization in Egypt*, Bollingen Series VIII. New York: Pantheon.

Read, H., 1955, *Icon and Idea*. Cambridge: Harvard University Press.

———, 1964, *The Meaning of Art*. London: Faber and Faber.

Reichenbach, H., 1938, *Experience and Prediction*. Chicago: University of Chicago Press.

———, 1951, *The Rise of Scientific Philosophy*. Berkeley: University of California Press.

Reik, T., 1946, *Ritual: Psychoanalytic Studies*. New York: Farrar, Straus.

Reinhardt, J. B., and Brash, A. L., 1969. "Psychosocial Dwarfism: Environmentally Induced Recovery." *Psychosomatic Medicine* 31: 165–172.

Riesen, A. H., 1947, "The Development of Visual Perception in Man and Chimpanzee." *Science*, 106: 107–108.

Riesman, D., with Glazer, N., and Denney, R., 1950, *The Lonely Crowd*. New Haven: Yale University Press.

Riviere, J., 1958, "A Character Trait of Freud's." In Sutherland, J. D., *Psychoanalysis and Contemporary Thought*, London: Hogarth.

Roe, A., 1946a, "The personality of artists." *Educ. Psychol. Measmt.* 6: 401–408.

———, 1946b, "Painting and Personality." *Rorschach Research Exchange*, 10: 86–100.

———, 1946c, "Alcohol and Creative Work." *Quarterly Journal of Studies of Alcohol*, 6: 401–408.

———, 1951, "A Psychological Study of Eminent Biologists." *Psychological Monographs*, 65: No. 14.

———, 1952, *The Making of a Scientist*. New York: Dodd, Mead.

———, 1953, "A Psychological Study of Eminent Psychologists and Anthropologists, and a Comparison with Biological and Physical Scientists." *Psychological Monograph*, 67: 2.

Rossman, J., 1931, *The Psychology of the Inventor*. Washington: Inventors Publishing.

Roth, N., 1969, "The Porphyria of Heinrich Heine." *Comprehensive Psychiatry*, 10: 90–106.

———, 1976, "Free Association and Creativity." *Journal of the American Academy of Psychoanalysis*, 4: in press.

Rothenberg, A., 1971, "The Process of Janusian Thinking in Creativity." *Archives of General Psychiatry*, 24: 195–205.

Ruesch, J., 1957, "The Trouble with Psychiatric Research." *Archives of Neurology and Psychiatry*, 77: 93–107.

Russell, B., 1919, *Introduction to Mathematical Philosophy*.

———, 1945, *History of Western Philosophy*. New York: Simon and Schuster.

Saisselin, R. G., 1970, *The Rule of Reason and the Ruses of the Heart*. Cleveland: Press of Case Western Reserve University.

Schachtel, E. G., 1954, "The Development of Focal Attention and the Emergence of Reality." *Psychiatry*, 17: 309.

———, 1959, *Metamorphosis*. New York: Basic Books.

Scheler, M., 1928, *Man's Place in Nature*. (Reprinted, Boston: Beacon Press, 1961.)

Schleirmacher, F., 1958, *On Religion*. London: Routledge and Kegan Paul. (Reprinted, New York: Harper and Brothers.)

Sechehaye, M. A., 1951, *Symbolic Realization*. New York: International Universities.

Segy, L., 1967, "Geometric Art and Aspects of Reality: A Phenomenological Approach." *Centennial Review*, 11: 419–455.

Shields, Stephanie A., 1975, "Functionalism, Darwinism, and the Psychology of Women: A Study in Social Myth." *American Psychologist* 30: 739–754.

Silverberg, W. V., 1952, *Childhood Experience and Personal Destiny*. New York: Springer.

Singer, J. L., 1961, "Imagination and Writing Ability in Young Children." *Journal of Personality*, 29: 396–413.

———, 1966, *Daydreaming*. New York: Random House.

Singer, J. L., and McCraven, V., 1961, "Some Characteristics of Adult Daydreaming." *Journal of Psychology*, 51: 151–164.

Singer, J. L., and Schonbar, R., 1961, "Correlates of Daydreaming: A Dimension of Self-awareness." *Journal of Consulting Psychology*, 25: 1–6.

Singleton, C. S., 1954, *Commedia: Elements of Structure*. Cambridge: Harvard University Press.

Skinner, B. F., 1971, *Beyond Freedom and Dignity*. New York: Knopf.

Slonimsky, H., 1956, "The Philosophy Implicit in the Midrash." *Hebrew Union College Annual*, 26: 235–290.

———, 1965, "Prayer." *Jewish Teacher* 1: 51. Reprinted in Slonimsky, H., *Essays*. Chicago: Quadrangle Books, 1967.

Smillic, D., 1959, *Tests and Definitions of Intelligence*. Quoted by Torrance, E. P., 1962.

Smith, D. R., and Smith, G. K., 1965, "A Statistical Analysis of the Continual Activity of Single Cortical Neurons in the Cat Unanaesthetized Isolated Forebrain." *Biophysical Journal*, 5: 47–74.

Bibliography

Smith, G. K., and Burns, B. D., 1960, "A Biological Interval Analyser." *Nature*, 187: 512–513.

Soby, J. T., 1946, *Salvador Dali*. New York: Museum of Modern Art, distributed by Simon and Schuster.

Sorokin, P. A., 1951, *Social Philosophies of an Age of Crisis*. Boston: Beacon Press.

Spencer, H., 1860, "The Physiology of Laughter." *Macmillan's Magazine*, 1: 395–402. Quoted by Keith-Spiegel, 1972.

———, 1873, *The Study of Sociology*. New York: Quoted by White, 1949.

Sperber, H., 1955, "Expressive Aspects of Political Language." In Werner, H. (ed.), *On Expressive Language*, Worcester: Clark University Press.

Sperry, R. W., 1961, "Cerebral organization and behavior." *Science*, 133: 1749–1757.

———, 1967, "Split-brain Approach to Learning Problems." In Quarton, G. C., Melnechuck, T., and Schmitt, F. O. (eds.), *The Neurosciences: A Study Program*. New York: Rockefeller University Press.

Spitz, R. A. (in collaboration with W. Godfrey Cobliner), 1965, *The First Year of Life*. New York: International Universities Press.

Stace, W. T., 1960, *The Teachings of the Mystics*. New York: Mentor Books.

Stein, M. I., 1967, "Creativity and Culture." In Mooney, R. L., and Razik, T. A. (eds.), *Explorations in Creativity*, New York: Harper.

———, 1974, *Stimulating Creativity*, Vol. 1: *Individual Procedures*. New York: Academic Press.

Stent, G. S., 1975, "Limits to the Scientific Understanding of Man." *Science*, 187: 1052–1057.

Storr, A., 1972, *The Dynamics of Creation*. New York: Atheneum.

Suls, J. M., 1972, "A Two-stage Model for the Appreciation of Jokes and Cartoons: An Information-processing Analysis." In Goldstein and McGhee (eds.), *The Psychology of Humor*, pp. 81–100. New York: Academic Press.

Sutherland, J. W., 1973, *A General Systems Philosophy for the Social and Behavioral Sciences*. New York: Braziller.

Taylor, C. W., 1964, "Some Knowns, Needs, and Leads." In Taylor, C. W. (ed.), *Creativity: Progress and Potential*, New York: McGraw-Hill.

Taylor, C. W., Berry, P. C., and Block, C. H., 1957, "Does Group Participation When Using Brainstorming Facilitate or Inhibit Creative Thinking?" *ONR Technical Memorandum*. Psychology Department, Yale University.

Taylor, C. W., and Holland, J., 1964, "Predictors of Creative Performance." In Taylor, C. W. (ed.), *Creativity: Progress and Potential*, New York: McGraw-Hill.

Tillich, P., 1957, *Dynamics of Faith*. New York: Harper.

Tinbergen, N., 1951, *The Study of Instinct*. Clarendon: Oxford University Press.

Tolstoy, L. N., 1898, *What Is Art?* (Reprinted, Oxford: Oxford University Press, 1955.)

Torrance, E. P., 1962, *Guiding Creative Talent*. Englewood Cliffs, N.J.: Prentice-Hall.

———, 1963, *Education and the Creative Potential*. Minneapolis: University of Minnesota Press.

———, 1964, "Education and Creativity." In Taylor, C. W. (ed.), *Creativity: Progress and Potential*, New York: McGraw-Hill.

Bibliography

————, 1965, *Rewarding Creative Behavior*. Englewood Cliffs, N.J.: Prentice-Hall.

————, 1969, "What Is Honored: Comparative Studies of Creative Achievement and Motivation." *Journal of Creative Behavior*, 3: 149–154.

Torrance, E. P., and Myers, R. E., 1972, *Creative Learning and Teaching*. New York: Dodd, Mead.

Toynbee, A., 1964, "Is America Neglecting her Creative Minority?" In C. W. Taylor (ed.), *Widening Horizons in Creativity*, pp. 3–9. New York: Wiley.

Tullio-Altan, C., 1960, *Lo spirito religioso del mondo primitivo*. Milan: Saggiatore.

Tylor, E. B., 1874, *Primitive Culture*. London:

Usener, H., 1896, *Götternamen: Versuch einer Lehre von der religiösen Begriffsbildung*. Bonn: Quoted by Cassirer, 1946.

Valentine, C. A., and Valentine B., 1975, "Brain Damage and the Intellectual Defense of Inequality." *Current Anthropology*, 16: 117–150.

Veblen, T., 1934, *Essays on Our Changing Order*. Quoted by Feuer, 1963.

Verworn, M., 1914, *Ideoplastische Kunst*. Jena.

Vico, G., 1725, *Principi di una Scienza Nuova*. Naples. (Third Revised Edition, 1749).

Vinacke, W. E., 1952, *The Psychology of Thinking*. New York: McGraw-Hill.

Von Domarus, E., 1944, "The Specific Laws of Logic in Schizophrenia." In Kasanin, J. S. (ed.), *Language and Thought in Schizophrenia: Collected Papers*, pp. 104–114. Berkeley: University of California Press.

Von Senden, M., 1960, *Space and Sight. The Perception of Space and Shape in Congenitally Blind Patients Before and After Operation*. London: Methuen.

Vygotsky, L. S., 1960, "Development of the Higher Mental Functions." *Izd. Akad. Pedagog. Nauk. RSFSR*. Quoted by Luria, 1973.

————, 1962, *Thought and Language*. Cambridge, Mass.: M.I.T. Press.

Wade, S., 1968, "Differences between Intelligence and Creativity. Some Speculation on the Role of Environment." *The Journal of Creative Behavior*, 2: 97–102.

Walkup, L. E., 1967, "Creativity in Science through Visualization." *Journal of Creative Behavior*, 1: 283–290.

Wallas, G., 1926, *The Art of Thought*. New York: Harcourt, Brace.

Weissman, P., 1967, "Theoretical Considerations of Ego Regression and Ego Functions in Creativity." *Psychoanalytic Quarterly*, 36: 37–50.

————, 1968, "Psychological Concomitants of Ego Functioning in Creativity." *International Journal of Psycho-Analysis*, 49: 464–469.

Werblowsky, R. J. Z., 1962, *Joseph Karo: Lawyer and Mystic*. Oxford: Oxford University Press.

Werner, H., 1956, "Microgenesis and Aphasia." *Journal of Abnormal Soc. Psychol.*, 52: 347–353.

————, 1957a, *Comparative Psychology of Mental Development*. New York: International Universities.

————, 1957b, "The Concept of Development from a Comparative and Organismic Point of View." In Harris, D. B. (ed.), *The Concept of Development: An Issue in the Study of Human Behavior*, Minneapolis: University of Minnesota Press.

Werner, H., and Kaplan, B., 1963, *Symbol Formation: An Organismic-Developmental Approach to Language and the Expression of Thought*. New York: Wiley.

Wertheimer, M., 1945, *Productive Thinking*. New York: Harper.

Bibliography

Wheelwright, P., 1954, *The Burning Fountain. A Study in the Language of Symbolism.* Bloomington: Indiana University Press.

———, 1962, *Metaphor and Reality.* Bloomington: Indiana University Press.

White, L. A., 1949a, *The Science of Culture.* New York: Farrar, Straus.

———, 1949b, "Genius: Its Causes and Incidence." In White, L. A., *The Science of Culture. A Study of Man and Civilization*, pp. 190–232. New York: Farrar, Straus.

Wigan, A. L., 1844, *The Duality of the Mind.* London: Longman. Quoted by Bogen, 1969.

Wilson, R. C., Guilford, J. P., Christensen, P. R., and Lewis, D. J., 1954 "A Factoranalytical Study of Creative Thinking Abilities." *Psychometrika* 19: 297–311.

Wimsatt, W. K., Jr., 1954, *The Verbal Icon. Studies in the Meaning of Poetry.* New York: Noonday Press.

Woolf, V., 1929, *A Room of One's Own.* New York: Harcourt, Brace.

Zaimov, K., Kitov, D., and Kolev, N., 1969, "Aphasie chez un peintre." *Encephale*, pp. 377–417.

Zegans, L. S., Pollard, J. C., and Brown, D., 1967, "The Effects of LSD-25 on Creativity and Tolerance to Regression." *Archives of General Psychiatry*, 16: 740–749.

Zielsen, E., 1926, "Die Entstehung des Geniesbegriffes, ein Beitrag zur Ideengeschichte der Antike und des Frühkapitalismus." Tübingen: Mohr. Quoted by Nahm, M. C., *The Artist as Creator.* Baltimore: Johns Hopkins Press, 1956.

Name Index

Abe, C., 343
Ach, N., 54
Adler, Alexandra, 44
Adler, Alfred, 300
Agosti, S., 160, 168-169
Alajouanine, T., 399
Alberti, Leon Battista, 353-354
Alighieri, S. *See* Dante
Anastasi, A., 343
Antonioni, M., 301
Aquinas. *See* Thomas Aquinas
Archimedes, 279-280
Arcimboldi, Giuseppe, 229
Arieti, Silvano, 4, 8, 12, 34, 41, 45, 46,
53, 54, 67n, 69, 72, 73, 75, 85, 93, 94,
98, 101, 114n, 115, 117, 120, 126, 162,
174, 196, 221-223, 229, 236, 237, 243,
251, 253n, 254, 264, 265, 278, 289, 303,
307, 372, 376, 380, 391, 392, 394, 404,
408, 409n
Aristotle, 67, 87, 136, 150, 176, 187
Arlow, J. A., 378
Arnheim, Rudolph, 194, 220-221

Bachelard, Gaston, 49
Balakian, Anna, 83, 143, 228, 372
Baldwin, J. M., 51
Balis, G. U., 372
Barrett, Elizabeth, 357
Barron, Frank, 347-349
Baudelaire, C., 369
Baumgarten, Alexander G., 172

Beatrice, *see* Portinari, Beatrice
Beethoven, Ludwig von, 240, 260
Bell, Clive, 136
Bellini, Vincenzo, 300
Bell, E. T., 335
Bemporad, Jack, 248, 253n
Berger, R. M., 347
Bergson, Henri, 61, 91-92
Berry, P. C., 369
Bertalanffy, L. von, 94, 288-290, 308,
403, 409
Bieber, I., 126
Binet, A., 54
Bishop, M., 32n
Bismarck, O. E., 302
Blake, William, 136-142, 149-150, 175-
176, 272
Block, C. H., 369
Boase, A. M., 143
Bobon, 214n
Boethius, Anicius Manlius Severinus,
319
Boito, Arrigo, 301
Bogen, J. E., 394
Bonaparte, N. *See* Napoleon
Bonvicini, G., 399
Boulding, K., 290
Brash, A. L., 400
Brennan, M., 253
Brenner, C., 378
Breton, André, 83, 143, 226, 228, 372
Breuer, J., 221
Brickner, R. M., 393
Brill, A. A., 104

Name Index

Subject Index

A priori categories, Kantian, 304, 307, 408

Aboriginal societies: paleologic thinking in, 71-73; *See also* Primitive peoples

Abraham, myths about, 247

Abstract art, 232, 234, 248; *See also* Modern art

Abstraction (abstract concept), 138, 139, 392; endocepts and, 55-56; Judaism and, 247, 248, 334; in neolithic art, 199; in philosophy, 283-288; primitive peoples and, 182-183; religion and, 249; *See also* Concepts

Absurdity, 228, 231

Act of Creation, The (Koestler), 17

Adolescence, 30

Adualism, 245; artistic, 177, 179-180; in poetry, 154-156; in schizophrenia, 51, 156

Advertising, 202

Aesthetic distance, 177-179

Aesthetic pleasure, 172-180, 235; in vitalistic art, 202

Aesthetic process, 135-187

Aesthetic synthesis or unities, 180-187

Africans, 319

Alcohol, 369-370

Alertness, discipline and, 378-379

Allegory, 33, 147, 148, 184*n*

Allocortex, 391

Aloneness, 373-374

Ambiguity, in jokes, 103, 129

Amorphous cognition, 53-65

Analogies, 376; *See also* Similarity

Ananke (necessity), 246

Animals, 38, 41-42, 265

Anti-intellectualism, 91-92

Anti-Semitism, 319, 335; in jokes, 120, 125, 126

Aphasia, 399

Aphrodite of Knidos, 218

Apollonian force, 205

Applied Imagination, The (Osborn), 367

Archaic modes, 257-258

Archaic terms, 159

Archetypes, 26, 27

Archipallium, 402

Aristotelian logic, 4; paleologic thinking and, 67, 69, 73-75, 78; *See also* Secondary process

Aristotelian philosophy, 249

Ars Poetica (Horace), 188

Art (visual art): idealism in, 217-221; modern, 221-234, 326; *See also* Drawings; Painting; Sculpture; *and specific topics*

"Art, L'" (Gautier), 190-191

Art and Visual Perception (Arnheim), 220

"As if" phenomenon, 154-156, 277

Associations: "clang," 79-80; free, *see* Free association; of ideas, *pars pro toto* mode of operation, 97-98; invariable, 278-279; paleologic, *see* Paleologic thinking; *See also* Identification; Similarity

Assonances, 81, 160, 167

Assyrian paintings, 200

Subject Index